THE STORY OF
THE COPE

The Templecrone Co-Operative Society
Dungloe, Co Donegal

PATRICK BONER

Templecrone Press

the **cope**

ISBN 978-0-955417-71-9

First published in 2009
The Templecrone Press
Templecrone Co-operative Society
Main Street, Dungloe
Co. Donegal, Republic of Ireland
Tel. no.: +353 74 9521022

Typeset in Bitstrem Arrus BT.

Typesetting, Layout and Printing:
Browne Printers Ltd. Letterkenny, Co. Donegal, Ireland
Tel. +353 74 9121387

CONTENTS

*This book
is dedicated
to Packie Bonner (1918-2007)
and to Carrie*

Introduction

by Pat Dunleavy
Chairman of the Cope Committee

It is with great pleasure that I welcome, on behalf of the Cope, this book celebrating its history. It vividly illustrates in pictures, stories and personal memories the extraordinary tale of how a small group of people, led by an inspirational leader, fought against considerable odds to create an extremely successful business which brought huge social and economic benefits to the people of West Donegal.

There is a saying that "from tiny acorns, mighty oaks do grow". The growth of the Templecrone Agricultural Co-operative Society, from its humble beginnings in the rocky hills of Cleendra to the thriving business it is today, is evidence of the truth of this saying.

The Cope's first year's turnover in 1906 was £381. Today the annual turnover is in excess of €17m – a staggering increase, even allowing for the change in the real value of money over the past century. In 1906, the Cope provided no 'employment' or 'wages' as such. Today we employ 140 people and, for the past hundred years, we have consistently provided good local employment, thus enabling many people to remain at home who would otherwise have had to emigrate.

Pat Dunleavy, Cope Committee Chairman, and Mark Sharkey, Cope Managing Director, in the new Supermarket, Dungloe, on the 26th July 2008. The Cope unveiled a statue to Paddy the Cope in the new Cope Street and held a special Fun Day to commemorate the event (Cope photo, by Brian Sweeney).

The Cope Committee: (standing) Tony Cannon, Dom Bonner, Pat Bonner, Jimmy Durnin, Eugene Doherty, Kevin Bonner, Pat Dunleavy; (seated) Denis Ward, Marguerite McGee, Johnnie Doherty, Connie Devenney, Breda Langan-Sweeney, Hugh McGee.

The Cope's employees were and are the backbone of the organisation and are our principal resource. Their hard work and diligence have contributed greatly to our success. Their valuable contribution to the Rosses' community and economy is something of which we in the Cope can be rightly proud.

A hundred years ago, our floor space was a small one-roomed stone building up a hillside nearly four miles from Dungloe. It measured 13ft by 12ft. Today, we have completed our most ambitious expansion ever. We have built a new 'state of the art' Builders' Providers in Sheskinarone and a new supermarket in Annagry. We have updated our stores in Kincasslagh and Lettermacaward and modernised all our other departments in Dungloe. Last summer our flagship new supermarket reopened in Dungloe. In total our retail space now comprises 70,000 square feet and 130,000 square feet in total when car parks and yards are included.

However, this tangible commercial reality, while vitally important to our future, is not the only yardstick by which we should measure our success. The Cope's core values are twofold. We provide excellent value for money as well as top class service and choice and, importantly, we provide opportunities for local employment, especially for young people.

The Cope has always had to reinvent itself with the changing times. Today, we know we aren't the only show in town so we have to be the best at what we do. Our recent expansion and developments have required us to invest in the region of €8m. This investment positions us very well for the upturn which will surely follow as the world economy recovers from its biggest downturn in seventy years. Our ambition is that the Cope should provide its customers with all their needs, just as Paddy and Sally saw in the Pumpherston Co-op in Scotland over a hundred years ago. Local shopping is now as competitive and economical as shopping elsewhere and will increase in importance in the future.

In order to be successful an organisation needs to be continually innovative. It needs to grow and change to meet challenges. Immobility is not an option in our modern very competitive world. Paddy the Cope keenly understood this. He was always attuned to the need for change and new developments. He started new ventures when the opportunity arose and made difficult decisions to close loss-making ones when necessary. One story in this book which encapsulates Paddy's modernising attitude is the story told of Seamus MacManus who, writing in 1930, was amazed to find that Paddy, in the then remote West Donegal, was using a Dictaphone and found it "a very helpful device, saving a lot of paperwork". Paddy was always ahead of his time. He was an example to us all – fearless, innovative and energetic.

The picture of our founder that emerges from his autobiography 'My Story', which we have recently republished, is both inspirational and energising. His heart was with his people and he was assiduous in pursuing the good of the community. He continually imagined new ways with which to improve the social and economic well being of his institution and of the people. His legacy is the thriving business you see today and the affirmation of the concept of co-operation.

I would like to say a special thanks to Patrick Boner the author of this book. His research was thorough and extensive. The result is this remarkable volume, which has a wealth of information on the Cope and on local history in general not previously published.

Finally, please enjoy reading this book. The story it tells and the changes to our lives it recounts, through many hundreds of photographs and stories, is indeed a remarkable one.

Bain sult as an leabhar tábhachtach seo.

Pat Dunleavy
Cope Chairman
July 2009

Foreword

Pat the Cope Gallagher
TD South West Donegal and MEP North West Region

Pat the Cope Gallagher, grandson of Paddy the Cope, has been a Fianna Fail TD in Donegal since 1981 and has held with distinction a range of posts at Ministerial level. In the June 2009 European elections Pat won election as a MEP for the North West region (Photograph courtesy Pat the Cope Gallagher).

It is with the greatest of pleasure that I welcome this book celebrating a hundred years of the Cope, the name I proudly bear. The founder, my grandfather Paddy the Cope, was an extraordinary man - a man perhaps who would have triumphed in any age but the fact that he did so from such humble beginnings is an inspiration to us all. This book, filled with many wonderful stories and photographs, is a tribute not just to him but to all of the Cope people who have worked tirelessly to build a lasting enterprise and a monument to community and cooperation.

My memories of Paddy are still very fresh. We grew up with him, living with him in the in the Cope House where the new supermarket is today; I was 18 when he passed on in 1966. We used to call him 'Daddy Trout' as he was always bringing in fish he had caught. As he stepped back in later years from the day to day running of the Cope, fishing was a great pastime for him.

I remember a very friendly man, someone with whom it was easy to get along with. I often wish we had kept a diary of all the people who came to visit him in the house from President de Valera, politicians, journalists, and many, many visitors from other countries, all come to see the man who performed such miracles in such difficult circumstances.

What comes through in his book 'My Story' is a deep sense of family and community. Whether he is in Scotland working, in London or America with his hand knit samples, his heart and mind are always in the Rosses – thinking about

Paddy the Cope in the 1960s surrounded by some of his grandchildren – at the back is Mary (Logue), Pat (future TD, Minister and MEP) and Mary Jo; seated next to Paddy are Nancy and Jim. The picture was taken in the Cope House on the Main Street Dungloe where Paddy lived until he passed on in 1966. The story goes that Paddy was not that keen to have his photo taken – his arms were being held down as he was keen to get to a football match (Gallagher Family Collection).

how he could help his people, how he could bring employment to the area to save people having to work away like he had to himself.

He was a man who did what he wanted to, what he thought was right, up to the very end of his life. I remember one time when he was past 90 and suffering from a bad cold. My mother said to him that he shouldn't be going out and certainly not to Dublin (he still used to travel to Dublin on his own then). Paddy said "Mary, you are right; I will go back to bed". Instead, he went to his room, got dressed and packed a suitcase which he proceeded to throw out the bathroom window at the back. He crept out of the house, picked up the case and got a lift with the Cope lorry and headed to Dublin. No-one realised he was gone until later in the day!

He was a very ingenious man, always looking for ways to improve things – he was terribly hard on waste and always saved what he could to use it again. I'm sure he would have embraced the Green movement – one of his and the Cope's early successes was using the Dungloe River and old Mill Race to bring electricity to Dungloe in 1923, fully 33 years before the ESB came. Wherever I go I take delight in telling his and the Cope's story, which is known in many places across the world. I was even presented with an Icelandic translation of Paddy the Cope's autobiography when I visited Iceland with a parliamentary delegation in 1983.

One of the very pleasant surprises in this book is the rediscovery of writings and stories that Sally, Paddy's wife, my grandmother, set down in secret in the 1940s. These are a wonderful addition to Paddy's own story and have a special meaning to me and my family as she wrote these for all of us, her grandchildren. I hope that these can receive the wider audience they clearly deserve. In praising Paddy, Sally often hasn't received the credit due to her – I'm glad to see this being rectified. I myself was born nine days after she had gone. I had always thought of her as an unassuming woman, who quietly supported Paddy through everything. Her stories, their vigour and humour are a revelation.

Is iomaí leabhar a chur sé a ainm leo, agus ba ghnáth le Paddy scríobh os cionn teideal an leabhair "Tá súil agam go mbainfidh tú sult as MÓ SCÉAL". Tá súil agamsa fosta go mbainfidh tusa sult as an leabhar seo, agus go mbeidh tú ag guí gach rath ar An Chope agus ar mhuintir An Chope ar feadh céad bliain eile.

Beatha agus sláinte.

Pat the Cope Gallagher,
TD and MEP

July 2009

Sally the Cope with her son Jim in c1920. The rediscovery in 2006 of Sally's stories, written to her grandchildren, about how the Cope was founded, and her role in it, has led to a re-evaluation of her influence and importance in the Cope story. (Cope Family Archive)

Acknowledgements

This book, celebrating the story of the Cope, is a companion to Paddy the Cope's recently republished autobiography 'My Story'.[1] To get a real sense of the astonishing story of the Cope and of just what it was like to live in much harder times, Paddy's own story is indispensable. It is highly recommended to both young and old as highly entertaining reading and as a marvellous, living social history.

Editing a book like this requires a lot of help from many people: hunting out photographs, remembering stories, help in identifying places, people, boats, buildings etc. Many people, especially the Cope family members, have been absolutely wonderful. Everyone asked has given their time and memories and photographs. The spirit of co-operation that kindled the Cope revolution is still alive and kicking and there is clearly enduring warmth for the Cope and for the memory of Paddy the Cope himself of course.

The Gallagher family on both sides, Packie the Cope and Jim the Cope, Paddy and Sally's two sons, have provided many photographs, stories and memories. A big thank you to Sally, Annie, Pat the Cope, Paddy (Jim) the Cope and Cha, Mary Jo and Jim – and to all the other family members who I know have been looking for and passing on photos. And a special thank you to Packie's son, the late Jim the Cope, Paddy the Cope's grandson. His collecting foresight, interest in the history of the Rosses and his Cope connections created an archive which was very useful.

I have drawn heavily on previously written pieces, particularly my late uncle Packie Bonner's essays in 1981, done for the 75th Cope anniversary. These I have simply cut and pasted – they read as well now as then. Full credit has been given for these and other works quoted.

Thanks are also due to Hugh McGee for his own personal photos and memories and for keeping and enriching the Cope Archive – a nucleus of photos, articles and memories which are at the heart of this book. Brian Sweeney has taken it on himself to be the official Cope photographer today. He has done an excellent job in recording the Cope today. The Cope Board has given great backing to the project - and they have been very patient.

Special thanks also to (in no particular order): IAWS, now ARZYTA (Tom Tynan); Marie (Brennan) Glackin; Delia (Cannon) O'Donnell; Rose (Johnny) Boner; Jimmy Sharkey; James Mickey and Anne (Browne) Gallagher; Michael Dawson – whose expertise and patience has brought many a damaged photo back to life; Donald Devenney, Maghery; Donald Martin, Killybegs; James

---

1 'My Story', Paddy the Cope, Patrick Gallagher's Autobiography; Templecrone Press, 2006.

Plunkett Smith, Killybegs; Eugene Doherty; Breda (Ward) Smith; Frank Sweeney; Seán Boner; Denis Tynan of Glenties for his marvellous photographs; Annette (Oglesby) Gallagher and Annie McGarvey, Kincasslagh; Francis Ferry Boyle; Pat Dunleavy; Peter Paul Ward, Clougherdiller; Connie Devenney; Ian Christie; Thelma Schoonmaker; Marianne Bower; Aideen Gillane; Mícheál O Dhomnaill; Gerry Brennan; Packie Walsh; Eoin McGarvey; Dom Bonner; Seamus Rodgers; Denis Ward; Patrick Kyles; Joseph Kyles; James Glackin and Gracie Glackin, Maghery; Kevin Bonner; Breda Langan; Ian Whittaker; Peggy April (Ivy Rose Vintage Reproductions); Fr Michael McCullagh; Patrick Ward (Panda); Jamesie Byrne; Vincent (Vincie John) O'Donnell; Richard H. Huelin; Liz Pallot of The Pallot Steam Museum; Flemings Motors of Boherbue, Mallow, Co Cork; Michael James Pat Gallagher, Cleendra; Nancy James Pat (Gallagher) McCready, Cleendra; Connie Ellen John Boyle, Meenmore; Brian Manus O'Donnell; Mary McCole, Cathal McCole; Breid O'Donnell (McCole); Joseph Hegarty, Stranorlar; Kate Ferry, Neily Ferry, Crickamore; Mary Bonner, Kimmage, Dublin; Danny McGee, Bathgate; Breid Gallagher, Mill Road; Margaret Rose Bonner; John Price Williams (for his encyclopaedic knowledge of motor cars); Maria Bonner, Carrie Bonner, Igor Kruk and many more – if I've not put your name down, please accept my apologies.

The professional local and national archives have been magnificent in helping, providing advice and use of their photographs: The National Photographic Archive, Dublin (Sandra McDermott); The Derry Harbour Museum (Bernadette Walsh); Limerick City Museum (Larry Walsh for the 'Sally the Cope' archive); University College Dublin Archives (Lisa Collins); Donegal Library, Letterkenny; Donegal County Archives, Lifford (Ciara Joyce); The Trustees of the National Library of Scotland (Eoin Shalloo); Bord Fáilte; The Irish Press (Joan Hyland); ESB (Brendan Delany and Pat Yeates); The Geological Survey of Ireland (Sarah Gately and Vincent Gallagher); The Derry Journal and Donegal Democrat (Letterkenny Library, Archives and Research Section); ICOS, Plunkett House Merrion Square Dublin 2 (Ciara Pelly); West Lothian Council Libraries (Sybil Cavanagh); The National Archives, Bishop Street, Dublin; The RHS Picture Library (Lucy Waitt); The Irish Architectural Archive (Anne Martha Rowan), Merrion Square, Dublin; the Horace Plunkett Foundation (Elodie Malhomme, Mike Perry).

The IAOS correspondence with the Templecrone Cope (carefully lodged in the National Archive in Bishop Street) is a wonderful source of information on the day to day workings of the Cope from 1905 until the 1950s. It adds colour to what we know from Paddy the Cope's account and fleshes out details that were lost in the two great Cope fires of 1945 and 1951.

Thanks are due of course to Paddy and Sally for their respective stories, which are both wonderful sources and social history in their own right. Sally's freshly discovered stories, written for her grandchildren, numbering some 130 or more pages all told, were discovered in Limerick City Museum. They are a wonderful new perspective on the 'Copeman' (one of Paddy's nicknames) and the foundation of the Cope itself. They have provided an opportunity to reassess how important Sally herself was in the Cope story. Paddy the Cope recalled in his 90th year:

> "...I was born in a wee one-roomed house in the Rosses. My father was poor. There were nine of us and we had one cow. I had only two years at school. I went to Scotland, and there I learned about co-operative societies. When I came back, my wife, Sally, got the idea of starting a co-operative society at home..."[2]

Sally's stories deserve republishing in full in their own right; something Paddy himself hoped would happen and said so on a number of occasions. Late in life, he had thoughts of combining his and Sally's stories into one but he was well into his nineties by then and the task was beyond him.

And in case, there is a second or follow on edition of this book, please look out for photographs – never throw them away, write carefully (and softly) on the back who is who and if there is a story, write it down. Ideally, have the photographs scanned – it is much easier to do these days. Make a diary of reminiscences, anecdotes – you will be amazed how interesting people, younger people included, will find them. Don't worry if the photo is in a bad state of repair, it is remarkable what can be done with photo restoration software these days.

Many, many photographs must have been lost in the big Cope fires[3] but I am convinced that more is out there in official archives and also family photo albums or in boxes, suitcases, etc. There are, I am sure, photographs of the interior of the knitting factory; of the other Cope boats; of the Mill interior; and the electricity operation – and the old Burtonport Cope, the Cooperage...

Lastly, some of the common quotes I've heard:

"No-one had cameras in those days."

"You have me tortured looking for pictures."

"We used to have a suitcase full of photos but they were all thrown out." (That is a painful thing to hear!)

And very painful, heard just this year (2009):

"I go through the photos and if I don't know the people I put them in the fire"[4]

---

2   *Irish Times 2nd April 1960.*

3   *Chapter 6, The Bakery.*

4   *It would be impolite to mention any names – but I am sure the people being quoted will recognise their words!.*

THE HARBOUR, BURTONPORT VR 8113

Burtonport in c1905, photographed for the Valentine Series and reproduced as a contemporary postcard. On the left is Campbell's Hotel; the long three storey building is O'Donnell's Hotel, built in 1903, to cater for travellers on the recently opened Burtonport station on the Londonderry & Lough Swilly Railway (Valentine, no. VR 8113, National Photographic Archive).

There is a lot of information in here – dates, names, facts. There will be things I have got wrong, if so they are *my* mistakes not the people who provided the information. I've tried to use the local style of naming wherever I can. For example, Paddy the Cope was born Patrick Gallagher but called Paddy Pat Bán, pronounced Bawn, after his father Pat Bán (Gallagher). However, it can be a complicated business and not easy for someone who didn't grow up round here.

I hope you enjoy the book. It was fun to edit and great to meet so many fine people in the process.

Patrick Boner

'Foirnis'
Lackbeg
Burtonport 2009

Please send any comments, corrections, further information (particularly photographs) to: cnaimhsi@gmail.com

A note on currencies

A mixture of pound sterling (£) and dollar ($) currencies are used throughout this book. Making sense of the 1906 value of money in a euro-world a hundred years later is very difficult. For example, when the nine year old Paddy Gallagher went to the Lagan in 1880, he earned £3 for six months' work. This does not mean that he worked for only €3.50 or two cents a day in modern money. £3 wasn't great money but it was enough then to help his parents plug the gap between survival and destitution.

The Cope began in 1906 with 14 half crowns, £1.75 or about €2 at today's exchange rates. The modern day equivalent would be c€600 or even €700, depending on what basis of comparison is used. The initial half crown was a down payment of one eighth on a £1 payment for the share in the Society – so €700 would become more like €5,000, a more serious amount of money, certainly not trivial. Paddy's £3 would become nearer to €1,000, still not great for six months' work today but getting to be a little more respectable – and it went further then of course.

Younger people who have never live with the 'old money' may well find the mention of pennies, half crowns etc hard to follow. Compared to decimal currency, where everything is divisible by ten, the 'old money' was very complicated – seeing the various coins listed below, it makes one wonder how we used to manage.

A pound was subdivided into ten monetary units:

A farthing – a quarter of a penny – 960 of these to a £1
A ha'penny - a half of a penny – 480 of these to a £1
There were 240 pennies in a pound
3d bit – a thruppeny bit - three pennies
6d – sixpence - six pennies
Shilling – twelve pence, twenty of these to a pound
Florin – two shillings, ten of these to a pound
Half Crown – eight of these to a pound
Crown – five shillings – four to a pound
Ten shilling note – half of £1

Exchange Rates:

In the early period, £1 was equivalent to roughly $4.70 – many people rounded this up to $5. Later as the £ sterling depreciated, this declined to $4 – hence the terms Crown (five shillings = a quarter of a pound = a Dollar) and Dollar being used interchangeably. [Editor: I remember this myself when growing up in the 1950s and 1960s – a half crown would be called half a dollar]

	1 £	1 sh.	1 d.
20 Mark 45 Pfennig	1 M. 2 Pf.	8½ Pf.
24 Kronen 2 Heller	1 Kr. 20 H.	10 H.
25 Francs 22 Centimes	1 fr. 26 cts.	10½ cts.
18 Kroner 16 Öre	91 Öre	7½ Öre
12 Gulden/Florins 11 Cents	60½ cts.	5 cts.
9 Rubel / Roubles 46 Kop.	47¼ Kp.	4 Kop.
4 Dollars ($) 86⅔ Cents	24⅓ cts.	2 cts.

Großbritannien.   Great Britain.
Grande-Bretagne.   Gran Bretaña.

*1 Pound Sterling (£) = 20 Shillings
 1 Shilling (sh.) = 12 Pence
 1 Penny (d.) = 4 Farthings.
(* Pfund, Livre, Libra.)

Ireland and Great Britain shared a common currency in 1906. The Free State used British coins until 1928, some six years after independence. The new, very attractive coinage was developed by a committee chaired by WB Yeats – the values, farthings, halfpennies, pennies etc mirrored exactly the British coins in use). In this contemporary German postcard, the range of coins in use in 1906 is shown. Coins from the Victorian era (1837-1901) – and earlier – would have been in circulation with ones from the Edward VII (1902-1910) period. Some exchange rates are given – the dollar was then trading at £1 = $4 and 87 cents. The pound was made up of 240 old pennies, or 960 farthings, a nightmare for reckoning – it is all a lot simpler since decimalisation (Contemporary postcard c1906, PB Collection).

The £ sterling declined still further post World War Two to $2.80 as a bankrupt British Empire struggled to adjust to a new world order with the United States as the emerging economic superpower. In 1967, the pound was further devalued to $2.40 and in the 1980s, parity £1 = $1 was almost reached. From 1923, the punt, the Irish pound, has shadowed sterling – usually slightly under parity for most of the period. Of late, sterling has fallen significantly against the euro, bringing the pound sterling significantly below the old sterling-punt exchange rate.

Purchasing power:

A motion moved by Senator Luke Duffy, Secretary of the Labour Party, to a debate on the level of pensions in the Seanad Éireann in July 1946 helps explain the relative buying power of money in 1908 and 1946. It also gives a sense of what you could buy with the old money when the Cope started. Some of the values are hard to take in: three herrings for a penny (half a cent!) and milk at a penny a pint.

"...When the old age pension was first provided, in 1908, the rate was 5/- per week. It was not a very generous pension, but it was a considerable improvement on the amount provided at that time by the poor law authorities and it did bear some relationship to the cost of living. As a matter of fact, I offer the suggestion that the 5/- a week granted to the old age pensioner in 1908, when the old age pensioner was permitted to have a private income from other sources of £21 a year—8/- a week making a total income of 13/- a week—was equivalent in terms of purchasing power to £2 per week to-day. The maximum pension which a person who is practically destitute can get at this moment is 16/-a week. That is to say, if a person has a private income of more than 6/- a week, the old age pension is cut by 1/-for every 1/- that the recipient's income exceeds 6/-. In other words, we have set a target of 16/- a week and given notice to all and sundry that if you are going to be the recipient of compensation, assistance, or whatever you may like to call it, from public funds, you must not have an income of more than 16/- a week, as compared with the 13/- permitted in 1908 which, in my opinion, was then the equivalent of 40/- a week to-day.

Let me quote a few figures to emphasise this point. In the first place, there is a firm figure available for 1904. That is the year in which the British authorities prepared the figures which subsequently became the basis for the cost-of-living index figure of which we hear so much in every discussion nowadays. The figure ascertained by the British authorities as the minimum sum required to maintain a working class family in 1904 was 22/6d. From that calculation they assumed that for every adult person the minimum figure would be - I am not quite sure that it is for food only - 4/6d. I do know that in 1908 the weekly cost of providing provisions and necessaries for an able-bodied man in a union workhouse was 3/3d. The cost of providing clothing, of course in the union workhouse, was 9d, making the total cost of maintenance in a poor law institution 4/- per week. Therefore the old age pension at 5/- represented a payment 25 per cent in excess of the cost of maintaining an old person in a poor law institution. Does our old age pension provide a figure 25 per cent in excess of the cost of maintaining a person to-day in a poor law institution? The answer is definitely "No" as I shall show in a moment or two.

Let us inquire further as to whether or not the 5/- a week did correspond more closely to the needs of an old person than the 10/- we provide to-day. For one thing, there is evidence that the price of a pair of gent's boots in 1908 was 6/6. The nearest thing provided to-day in the shape of men's boots, although very much inferior in quality, I am informed would cost 27/6 or 30/-. The 4 lb loaf, which to-day is costing 1/-, cost 5d in 1908. Potatoes then cost 5d a stone, and milk 1d per pint. Butter was 8d per lb and the humble herring was at the rate of three a 1d.

An early Christmas card, dating from c1910 and showing a view of the Main Street with the Northern Bank on the right. The Cope's founder, Paddy the Cope, was born on Christmas Day 1870 (Mícheál O Dhomnaill Collection)

If we may go more intimately into this question of human needs it may be permissible to recall that the price of the "pint" was 2d. The price of an ounce of tobacco, which is now 1/3d, was 2½d in 1908. So that the price of tobacco has multiplied six times, the price of the "pint" has multiplied four times, potatoes are four or five times more expensive, bread is two and a half times and milk three and a half times dearer. I think I am safe in asserting that while there was considerable criticism of the inadequacy of the 5/- pension in 1908—and I think with some justification if we consider the old age pensioner as a social being with human rights—that 5/- went very much nearer to meeting the needs of an old person in 1908 than 10/- does to-day…"[1]

The pension referred to was 5/- a week for 1908, roughly 30c a week without allowing for inflation. The State Pension today is roughly between €150 and €230 a week (as at Jan 2009) which is a multiple of between 500 to 766 of the 1908 figure.

---

1   From the excellent Historical Debates website for the Seanad 17th July 1946: http://historical-debates. oireachtas.ie/S/0032/S.0032.194607170006.html.

Chapter 1

Cleendra

...an unlikely beginning

The Templecrone Co-Operative Agricultural Society, incorporated on January 16th 1906, began life in the small, rocky townland of Cleendra, four miles outside Dungloe in the Rosses, West Donegal. That it came into being at all is a small miracle; that it survived and flourished to become the largest business in Donegal – and the third largest co-operative in Ireland in 1917 by turnover - is one of the most extraordinary success stories of the last century.

The roots of its success lay in the big social changes of its time, in the pattern of migratory work which took people away to Scotland but, most importantly of all, in the courage of a small group of people - and their inspirational leader, Patrick Gallagher, known in the local way as Paddy Pat Bawn, but who came to be known as Paddy the Cope or 'the Copeman'.

100 YEARS AGO

It is very hard, almost impossible, to put oneself into the mind of someone a hundred years ago. Most of us today take for granted a standard of living that would have been beyond the wildest dreams of most people in 1906. In West Donegal, and indeed the rest of Ireland, the previous years had been very difficult; the deep scar of *An Gorta Mór*, the Great Hunger of 1845-50, was still fresh in the memory. Everyday life was certainly not easy before the Famine; afterwards, there was a sense of inevitability about leaving Ireland as a matter of survival. Decades of emigration had reduced the population of Donegal from 296,448 in 1841 to 173,722 in 1901, a staggering 41.4% reduction (the population in 2006 was 147,241, still less than half of the 1841 figure even after recent population growth)[1]. The real decline may have been even higher when casualties from the Famine and underlying pre-Famine growth rates are factored in.

Templecrone Population 1841-1901

Against the national and county declines of 40%, the recorded population of Templecrone recovered and actually increased by 15% in the period 1841 to 1901 from 9,849 to 11,382[2]. It is possible that these numbers do not fully

---

1   *CSO – Central Statistics Office Ireland – www.cso.ie.*

2   *Census of Ireland – Province of Ulster, County of Donegal HMSO, from 1841-1911. James Tuke writing in the Irish Times on 15th May 1889 had also noticed similar counter-intuitive population increases (1841-81), picking out individual townlands for particularly significant increases: Annagarry (sic) 334 to 636 and Cloughlass 18 to 85. Templecrone population – (1851: 9,592, 1861: 10,331, 1871: 10,853, 1881: 11,525, 1891: 10,719).*

THE COUNTRY I'M LEAVING BEHIND.

To be had at the Poet's Box, 190 Overgate, Dundee.

My barque leaves the harbour to-morrow,
  Across the wide ocean to go,
Bnt, Kitty, my burden of sorrow
  Is more than I'd wish you to know.
There's a dreary dark cloud hanging o'er me,
  And a mighty big cloud on my mind,
And I think of the prospects before me,
  And the country I'm leaving behind.

CHORUS.

Then farewell to the green hills of Erin,
  And the darling so faithful and kind ;
Where'er I may be I'll still think of thee,
  And the country I'm leaving behind.

Now, Kitty, leave over your crying,
  And don't be uneasy for me ;
It's my fortune I'd be after trying
  On the sunny shores over the sea.
Each moment that passes shall find thee
  Still reigning supreme in my mind ;
And the image of Kitty shall bind me
  To the country I'm leaving behind.

Though the land be abounding in treasure,
  And fair maids of every degree,
My eyes may behold them with pleasure,
  But my heart will be longing for thee,
Let stormy clouds gather above me,
  And friendship prove stale or unkind,
I'll know there is one heart will love me
  In the country I'm leaving behind.

In Paddy's 'My Story', he recalls his father Pat Bawn, at an airneál, singing a song he calls 'My Barque Leaves The Harbour Tonight'. The occasion was an emigration 'wake' for Paddy's sister Mary who was going to America.

The words are the first line of an emigration song 'The Country I'm Leaving Behind'. Seasonal workers most likely brought the song back from Scotland. It is also claimed as a song in Nova Scotia and Newfoundland (Published in the 1880s, words S. Henry, music Marie McConnell; image courtesy of the Trustees of The National Library of Scotland)

"...We all went to the airneál. As soon as we went in, my father sang, 'My Barque leaves the Harbour tomorrow'. My mother put her head in her lap. I am sure she was crying while he was singing. That was the real break of the family. Annie, Maggie, Sarah, Bridget, and Madgie followed. James and Hannah remained at home. Maggie joined the Sisters of Charity and became a nun in Pittsburgh. My other six sisters got married. Sarah and Hannah are in Dungloe, Annie in Dublin, Mary, Bridget and Madgie in America. James is in the old home in Cleendra and two of his boys are working in the Cope..." (Paddy the Cope, 'My Story', 1939)

The airneál played an important part in the life of the Cleendra community, as it did for the people of Donegal and the rest of Ireland where it is sometimes called ceiliing. People would gather at someone's house of an evening, often a different house each time, and tell old stories, sing songs, learn new dance steps, get the news and generally enjoy each other's company. In the Donegal dialect, it is often said as 'going gairneál', i.e. going ag airneál.

Remembered by Anthony Boner (Manny Anne) and Kevin Bonner.

represent what was really happening, what with under-declaration (there is evidence of systematic exclusion of sub-tenants and their families), miscounting, seasonal migration, emigration to America etc. There are also changes due to the fishing development later in the period (1890s), the coming of the railway (Burtonport Station opened in 1903 but construction began well ahead of this in the 1890s), coastguard stations (e.g. Burtonport 1895) etc. However it is a quite unexpected statistic, totally against the national and county trends, and deserving of further evaluation. It is possible that the 'survival model' operating in the Rosses, working away in Scotland and the Lagan, emigration to the USA, with money being sent back and a mixed fishing and farming economy, was more successful than had been previously thought. Whatever the real story – and there are of course undeniable instances of hardship and tragedy – it seems to demonstrate that a hardy, resilient people were able to survive and if not thrive, then manage with hard work and ingenuity to cope in very difficult times.

Emigration to America was a fact of life. A poignant moment in Paddy's 'My Story' is when money was sent from America to pay for the passage of his sister Mary (he goes on to say that five of his sisters followed Mary). The tears and sorrow which attended her 'wake' are captured vividly in Paddy's book.[3] The emigration 'wake' which preceded every departure was an emotional event. The long journey by ship across the Atlantic was costly and could be hazardous. Both the people staying, and those going, were acutely aware it could be the last time they would ever see each other. Part of Paddy's motivation, as the Cope developed, was to find employment for as many local people as he could to minimise the need for seasonal or permanent migration.

For those that stayed, life was grinding, hard work. Every piece of land that could be worked was tilled – by men, women and children - or in use for pasture, for grazing. Much of this land was 'made' by hand from poor bog land and application of seaweed and hard work. As returning emigrants have often commented over the years, one of the most obvious changes since those days is just how little cultivation now goes on, how many 'gardens' are now grown wild with 'whin bushes' and briars. Hard work on the land was still not enough to keep families from starving or falling into debt. Children, boys, as young as nine or ten would be sent to Letterkenny or Strabane to the Hiring Fairs where they would go on to work hard and long on the Lagan, that triangle of good land covering East Donegal, Derry and Tyrone. Paddy, who went away at nine himself, called this a 'slavery' and he was not far wrong.

In 1879, the year before Paddy headed for Strabane, the potato crop failed and famine followed, the so called An Gorta Beag (the small famine). Unlike the earlier famine of the 1840s, the death toll was relatively light but there was most certainly hunger, fear and sheer panic at the prospect of what might happen.

---

3   'My Story' Paddy the Cope.

Necessity compelled seasonal workers from Templecrone, both men and women, to leave Donegal for work in the Lagan or in Scotland for long stretches of the year (often from March to as late as November). They brought back much needed hard currency, a vital supplement to what could be sweated from the poor lands of the Rosses. This Caledonian Bank £1 note is a now scarce (and very valuable) survival from those times. The Caledonian Bank was founded in 1838 and was absorbed by the Bank of Scotland in 1908. Its (Scots) Gaelic motto, seen around the edges - Tir nam Beann, nan Gleann, s'an Gaisgeach - translates as 'Land of Mountains, Glens and Heroes'. (Private Collection in The Rosses)

James H Tuke, writing in 1880 about the Gweedore Parish (but applying as much to the Rosses), captures just how parlous the financial position could get:

> "…In addition to the failure of the potato crop, the men, who go en masse to Scotland for the harvest, had returned last year without any earnings, and some had even to borrow money both for going and returning. On the average, two men or boys from each family go in this way. In ordinary years, a sum of about £8,000, averaging £8 for each family, is the result of this movement. This pays both the rent and the debt at the store for the previous year's supplies, which it is, unfortunately, the custom to owe. In ordinary years the younger boys and girls also go to other parts of Ulster, "The Laggan," (as it is called), on hire for the summer months, and the wages they bring back amount

The Story of the Cope

This is a Nineteenth century advertising card for Sweeney's Atlantic House in Foyle St Londonderry. 'Supper, bed and breakfast, Tariff 2s 6d'. While waiting for the sailing, passengers for emigration to America or for seasonal work in Scotland would stay in such places the night before the voyage to Glasgow - if they could afford it. The four-masted sailing ship on Mr Sweeney's advert is a barque, a sailing ship with at least three and typically four masts (PB collection).

to nearly £8,000. Last year both resources failed. Thus this parish alone, containing about 6,000 persons, was poorer by £16,000 than in ordinary years..."[4]

When they were old enough, in Paddy's case he was 16, young men and women would leave Donegal on the 'Derry Boat', heading for Scotland where they would find work for a season or longer, 'tattie hoking' (picking potatoes) or thinning turnips. If they were lucky or that bit older, getting better paid work like Paddy in the mines and tunnels. Money earned was sent home to help pay for the family's basic living costs; groceries were bought locally 'on tick' from merchants in Dungloe and accounts had to be settled later in the year.

THE BEGINNING

In response to the Land League and Home Rule movements, there had been a tide of change sweeping Ireland. The Land Acts aimed to transfer land back to tenants and, from the late 1880s, the Co-operative movement, founded by Sir Horace Plunkett sought to empower local farmers by providing capital, help

---

4 'Irish Distress and Its Remedies: The Land Question: A visit to Donegal and Connaught in the Spring of 1880', James H Tuke 1880.

in organising and offering professional advice. Cynics labelled government sponsored activities like these (and also, in the 1890s onwards, those of the Congested District Board) 'killing Home Rule with kindness'.

Templecrone was not exactly fertile soil for an agricultural co-operative – it was more rock and bog than the lush farmland found in the Lagan. Further to the south, thriving co-operative creameries were established in the great farming counties. Creameries were by far the most successful cooperatives, much favoured by the organisers who were able to achieve remarkable results time after time. For West Donegal, such a business model was not tenable; some other explanation is necessary to explain the success of the cooperative ideal in Templecrone. The key to their extraordinary achievement was to be found in the vision, grit and determination of one individual, Paddy the Cope, the small community of hill farmers in Cleendra initially but, ultimately, all of the people of Templecrone Parish.

So what was it about Paddy Pat Bawn in 1906 that sparked a revolution? Well, to start with, he was a well-liked and respected man in his community, someone whose opinion mattered, and someone with what we would call today 'leadership skills'. Hard-working since the age of nine in 1880, when he walked the 36 miles to Ballybofey, on his way to the Strabane hiring fair, he had been back and forth to Scotland since 1887, almost 20 years before the start of the Cope. He had always returned home – his rocky home and his people were hugely important to him; this pours out of almost every page of his autobiography 'My Story'.

SCOTLAND

It is apparent from Paddy's own accounts and those of his wife Sally that he had been very successful in Scotland. He'd earned very good wages for the time and had a number of men working for him, anything from 5-7 men or more at a time, in the oil shale and coal mines. He would have been someone whose opinion was worth listening to: he'd worked away, returned, made money and had ideas developed in Scotland about how things could be improved back home.

Paddy and Sally's later experiences in Scotland were pivotal. They married on Sunday night 8th May 1898, took the mail car to Fintown and from there the train to Derry. The next day they took the 'Derry Boat' to the Broomielaw, Glasgow. Paddy was 27, Sally 21, born on 17th March 1877. She was known as Sally Madgie[5] and was also a Gallagher, a different branch of the clan, from the Fair Hill, Dungloe. Sally's own stories, totalling more than 130 pages and written in the mid 1940s for her grandchildren, tell us about the journey:

---

5   Sally's actual first name, which she never seems to have used, was Sarah. In the 1911 Census, the household is listed as follows: Pat Gallagher, Head, J.P. and Shopkeeper, aged 39; Sarah Gallagher, aged 34, wife; and Patrick, aged 8, a scholar. The census also states they had been married 13 years and had two children, with one still living. Both Pat and Sarah can speak Irish and English and can both read and write, the Census states.

The shale oil industry boomed in Scotland in the late 19th century and many men from Donegal went over to work in the mines. Paddy worked at the Holmes Oil Co Ltd in Uphall; in 1896 it had 126 underground and 15 surface workers. This is a photograph of the nearby and very similar Broxburn Oil works in c1910 – Broxburn and Uphall are a mile apart. In 1896, there were two Broxburn mines, one with 163 underground and 25 surface workers, the other with 463 and 49). Paddy had a gang of men under him and made great money for the time which helped him and Sally buy a farm and set up home when they returned to Cleendra. Paddy worked in a number of mines on his many trips to Scotland from c1886/7, including a two year stint in the Denny Place coal pit in Stirling, about 30 miles from Glasgow (Photo courtesy Peter Caldwell from his excellent local history book of photographs 'Old Broxburn and Uphall', Stenlake Publishing)

"…Paddy went up to the Chapel and said, "Sally, Father Gallagher agrees to marry us at eight o'clock on Sunday night."

About eight o'clock, Maggie and I went up to the Chapel.

No sign of Paddy. I got uneasy. We were only a few minutes but I thought it was hours, when in comes Paddy and his cousin Eddie Boyle, and it was not long before Father Gallagher came in.

When he married us, we went into the Sacristy to sign the Register.

PADDY: How much have I to give you, Father?

FR. GALLAGHER: The usual is 25/-. (He touched Paddy's Gold Cross) But a gentleman like you, I'll leave it to yourself.

PADDY: I have very little money, and Sally and I are going to Scotland in the morning.

FR. GALLAGHER: Going to Scotland! God bless you. I wish you the height of luck. Wait here for five minutes till I come back.
(When he came back, he reached two five pound notes to Paddy)
"Take that and if you ever have a tenner to spare, send it to me."

PADDY: No thank you, Father, I have enough, it is far too kind of you. He gave the two five pound notes back to Father Gallagher and he gave us an extra blessing.

That was 8 May 1898.

As arranged, we parted. Paddy went home, came into town about 12 o'clock carrying all his clothes. Walked eight miles the night of his marriage. Paddy went into Johnny Boyle's yard and slept in a good bed with Paddy Manus over the horses.

Madgie [Sally's sister] had me up early next morning; she had my clothes packed nicely. I went over to the kitchen bed, woke up my father and mother. I caught my father's hand and said, "Good-bye, I am going to Scotland. I got married last night to Paddy Pat Bán, of Cleendra." Father said: "May God and His Holy Mother bless you." I then caught my mother's hand. She cried, but she did not say a word.

As arranged, Madgie remained in the house. I took my parcel with me over to the Corner House. Carberry, the Mail Car Driver, was at the corner and so was Paddy. It was eight o'clock in the morning. It was a side-car. I got up on one side, Paddy on the other. As Carberry was getting up on the dicky, my father came running up the street, nothing on him but his trousers and shirt. When he came to me, he got up on the step, kissed me and gave me a handful of silver. He then went to the other side and shook hands with Paddy. He said, "Paddy, my boy, be good to my Sally."

Then Carberry gave the horse the whip for Fintown - 14 miles from Dungloe. We then got the train for Derry. I had my breakfast at home. Paddy had not tasted a bite when we reached Derry. We went into an eating-house and had our breakfast.

We then went up to Mullholland's. Paddy said I would have to get a coat and hat, as I could not wear the shawl in Scotland. If I did the Scotch would think I was a fisherwoman.

We got the coat and hat and Paddy said, "When we come home again you will always wear the shawl."

Paddy and Sally left for Scotland in May 1898 – they took the mailcar to Fintown via Doochary where they caught the County Donegal Railways train to Derry. This photograph (taken by the old Northern Bank) appeared in the 1946 edition of Paddy's 'My Story'. There has been much debate locally as to whether it is an original photograph or one staged much later (c1945) for inclusion in Paddy's book. Behind the mailcar, there are several buildings which did not exist in 1898; in particular, Charlie Boyle's house by the Bayview bar, which juts out into the street. This was not built until c1930 – making the photograph a staged one (Paddy the Cope's 'My Story').

This contemporary (1908) cigarette card shows the Dunfanaghy mail car, stopped at Daniel Ferry's 'Half Way House' Dunlewey (Gweedore); it was the same type as that taken by Paddy and Sally to Fintown where they caught the train to Derry. The train from Burtonport, or Dungloe Road, to Derry was still five years away in 1898. The price of the mail car from Dungloe to Fintown at this time was two shillings per person and left about 3.45pm; a private 'Day-car' was 2/6d, half a crown, and left Dungloe at 9 am each day – the newlywed Gallaghers would have taken the latter (Gallaher's Irish View Scenery no. 133, PB Collection).

Well, we then went to the Ship's ticket office. He got two tickets for Glasgow, 4/- each. Down in the Steerage there were seats along the side and at the wide end. It was a V-shaped place. The seats were all occupied. Three or four boys got up and offered me their seats. I sat down. Paddy went up to the deck to get the bundle and case. Oh! The cattle began to roar. I thought they must have been crying after the beating they got. When Paddy came back I got up. I was going to thank the boy whose seat I had occupied, when the ship gave a heave. I staggered, Paddy caught hold of me, and two of the boys got up and caught me. One said, "Sit down you and your friend. Take our seats."

The "Rose" steadied a bit. I said, "Thank you boys, but I cannot remain here. Paddy I'll be sick in a minute." He caught my arm and we went on deck; two of the boys came after us with our parcels. One of them said, "If you don't mind we will keep them below for you as they might get wet here." Paddy said, "Will you take the case and this thing (my hat) down below? You are very good." Off they went.

We sat on the hatch. Paddy put the parcel that my jacket was in to my back. Strange, when we went out to the deep the ship only gave wee lurches. It was a splendid night. Paddy had some biscuits in his pockets, but we did not get hungry. We landed at the Broomielaw in the morning at 9 o'clock, got ashore and went to Queen Street, and inquired for a train to Uphall and were told that we could get one at 2.30 p.m. Paddy left his bundle and my case at the station and we went into an eating-house and had a good breakfast which cost one and three pence each Paddy gave three pence to the attendant and said, "My wife wants to change her clothes, could she use a room for a few minutes?" That was the first time he called me his wife and it gave me a grand thrill. The attendant said, "Yes Sir, come along with me, Madam." I went with her and took off my shawl and put on the jacket and hat, and then came back to where Paddy was. Paddy got up and said, "We will go for, a walk." Out we went. I said, Paddy do you not like me with the new jacket and hat." He said, "Sally, I would like you, (and always will) if you had only a bag about you, but with God's help we will never see that day. But, Sally, you just looked as nice with the shawl on, when we go back home you will wear your shawl again." I said, "I will, Paddy, I don't feel half as comfortable in this rig. Must I always wear a hat and jacket in Scotland? "Paddy said, "Only when you go out. The Scotch women never wear shawls, except the women who sell fish at the street corners…"[6]

The following account gives some idea of what it was like travelling on the Derry Boat:

"The Derry-Glasgow passenger service, some 139 miles in distance, started in the early 1820s as an extension to a tourist service from

---

6   *Sally the Cope Gallagher Personal Archives – Limerick City Museum.*

375-10   **LONDONDERRY. THE QUAYS AND BAY.**   RAPID PHOTO. E C

The newlyweds, now Mr and Mrs Gallagher (no change of surname was necessary, Sally was also Gallagher), set off for Glasgow from 'The Quays' in Derry in 1898. This contemporary postcard is from a photo dating from circa 1900. At this time there was a daily – afternoon – sailing from Derry to Glasgow on ships of the Glasgow, Dublin & Londonderry Steamship Company, which became, from 1906, the Laird Line. (Postcard by Rapid Photo, PB Collection).

Derry at the turn of the Nineteenth century was a very busy port. In this fine Lawrence Collection photograph, ships can be seen waiting by the quay and the Guildhall clock is visible towards the back. The railway track was extended along the quayside, allowing goods to be loaded straight onto ships or, if being imported, taken off the ship and conveniently to trains at the city station for onward distribution (National Photographic Archive, L_ROY_2563)

EMBARKING AT THE BROOMIELAW. 50

Broomielaw, Glasgow in the 1890s was a very busy port, noisy and dirty from the steamships and the
cattle and other freight they carried. At this time, there was still a mix between sail and steam including
paddle steamers. It was well used to the comings and goings of seasonal workers from Donegal – Paddy
and Sally arrived here in May 1898 and took the train from Queen Street station to Uphall, West Lothian,
where they lodged in the 'Randy Rows'. In this image, the paddle steamers in the foreground were setting

off with holidaymakers for Scottish resorts on the coast or the islands – it was called 'gaun doon the watter' (going down the water). In the background can be seen the passenger steamships which went from here to Derry, Belfast, Liverpool and Dublin (Vintage George Washington Wilson photograph, no 5066, c1880s, image courtesy www.past-to-present.com)

Sally's account of her and Paddy's courtship and journey to Scotland tells of their travelling in 1898 from Derry to Glasgow on a ship of the Glasgow Dublin & Londonderry Steam Packet Company. This photograph, with passengers crammed by the rails, is of the *SS Olive* launched in 1893, which may well have been the ship they travelled on. Sally states it was the SS Rose, which did not launch until 1902; she or Paddy may of course have travelled on this ship later. SS Olive was the largest ship in the fleet at her launch (length 260', breadth 33', draught 17') and had accommodation for 100 saloon and 1,000 steerage passengers with fan ventilation to the main and 'tween decks, which were fitted for transporting cattle (Photograph and information from the excellent 'Clydebuilt' website www.clydesite.co.uk and from 'Clyde and Other Coastal Steamers, Duckworth and Langmuir, T Stephenson & Sons 1939, 1977 edition)

The *SS Rose*, shown here at Broomielaw, Glasgow, the ship Sally the Cope refers to in her story, was launched in June 1902. Paddy will have travelled on it himself (probably on his return from Scotland for good in c1902 when Sally was expecting their first child Annie) - like many of their contemporaries off to or returning from the gutting or 'tattie hoking'. The *Rose* could carry 140 first class and 6-700 steerage passengers and had a speed of 15½ knots. She was 251 ft long with a breadth of 36 ft and beam of 15 ft (Photograph and information source as for the *SS Olive* above).

LANDING STAGE AT BROOMIELAW

This first of two postcards from Broomielaw was issued for the 1901 Glasgow Exhibition. Postcards were a *huge* global craze in the period between 1894 (when pictures were first allowed on the front of postcards in Britain) and 1914. They were sent across the world and collected by many people; their survival provides both a social and historical record of the time. They were cheap - postage was half price (a halfpenny) – and equivalent to the mobile phone 'text messages' of their day, often being sent in the morning with a message about meeting in the evening (Official Glasgow Exhibition postcard; PB Collection).

Glasgow to the Giant's Causeway (the first ship was the wooden paddle steamer 'Britannia', 93' in length). From the 1860s, it became a regular sailing, leaving every afternoon at its peak in the 1890s and first decade of the 20th century, in both directions. At times intense overcrowding occurred. In the mid-1830s, when the steerage fare had been reduced to 1 shilling, one of the Scottish newspapers reported: 'Every boat that arrives at the Broomielaw from Derry is literally crowded with hundreds of poor creatures who are huddled together with horned cattle, pigs, sheep and lambs'. Conditions on board were certainly deplorable. Furthermore, when passengers reached their destination they were sometimes refused permission to land unless they could produce visible means of support or a ticket for America. Those turned back had to face again the cold and misery of another night spent on the exposed deck on the Irish Sea. The inhuman conditions on board many of the steamers, especially those which plied from Dublin or Drogheda, led to a government inquiry in 1849 and to a reluctant recognition that perhaps steerage passengers were entitled to the same treatment as cattle…"[7]

---

7   'Irish Passenger Steamship Services: Volume 1 North of Ireland' by DB McNeill (David & Charles, Newton Abbot, 1969).

This picture postcard is again of the Broomielaw and dates from 1900; at this stage, messages were only allowed on the front space, only the address was permitted on the back (this rule was relaxed in 1902). It's not hard to imagine Sally sending her friends and relatives a quick postcard on landing and then later, picture postcards of Uphall and Broxburn where they were staying – none would seem to have survived (Contemporary postcard by the period's premier publishers, Raphael Tuck; PB Collection)

Passenger fares when Paddy and Sally crossed to Glasgow were four shillings steerage and 12s 6d for saloon class. The fare for a cow was one shilling.

Unlike Paddy's previous journeys, when (as he recounts) he saved little and spent much of his hard earned money 'socialising' (as we would euphemistically call it today), he was now a married man, with a wife who helped him by managing the money side of things. Sally had got beyond the 'third book' in school - that was as far as Paddy had reached before he was hired in the Lagan. It is clear from her account that she looked after the finances in Scotland. She was the one dealing with the Pumpherstown Co-operative, paying in the money, keeping a record of their savings, keeping lodgers etc. When they came back for good, they had substantial savings behind them.

Sally recalls how the idea took root in Scotland:

> "...Paddy often talked about Mrs. Gillespie of Nedire, with whom he had lodged, and said that she did all her dealings in the Co-operative Store. The local shopkeeper called every day looking for orders; I always gave him an order for any goods I wanted. The first Saturday that Paddy

The Story of the Cope

The Buchan Arms, Broxburn c1890 was also known as the Shamrock Bar on account of the number of Irishmen who would frequent it. Paddy would meet his friends here after mass in Broxburn Church. The innkeeper in 1894 photo was Thomas Doyle and it was also called Doyle's for a while. In Paddy's time in Broxburn, it is said that Jack Mulhern from Dungloe was manager there (Photograph courtesy of Peter Caldwell).

came in with his pay, I said, "Paddy you are always talking about the Co-operative store, what you think about our dealing in the store?" Paddy said, "Well, Sally, whatever you say." I replied, "Paddy, I think we should try it, although neither Mrs. O'Donnell nor Mrs. McCahill is dealing in the store, they say the local shopkeeper is very obliging and that he gives them all the credit they want, but Paddy, if we can, we will never look for credit. My mother said that the people at home, who dealt on credit, were slaves, and that they would do any work which the shopkeeper wanted them to do. My mother would sell the last hen she had in the house before she would ask a penny's worth of credit.

Paddy then said, "Well Sally, I know what credit is; it kept my poor father's head under the grindstone for many years. I'll go to Pumpherston Store now and see if they will take us in as members."

Off he went. He came back with a share book; he handed me the book. I don't remember the number, he said, "To become a member the share was five pounds, but that the manager, Mr. Pratt, was a very nice man and said I could become a member by paying one pound down and the other four as early as possible."

In four weeks, we had the five pound share fully paid. The first week Paddy was working for himself we had one pound nineteen shillings. He handed me the whole lot. I gave him half-crown for the pocket money. From that day to this, October 1947, thanks be to God, I never had to ask for the loan of one penny or anything else.

In about ten weeks we got a house in Uphall village – a room and a kitchen. There were two beds in the room and one in the kitchen. We went into Edinburgh one Saturday and got our photographs taken. We bought some furniture and bed clothes in a second-hand shop. As soon as the boys heard we got a house, they came rushing to Paddy and me, wanting to lodge with us. Paddy would not let me take in more than four, so the first Saturday night we were in the house, we took in the lodgers. We had to carry all the water upstairs, from the street. There were no sculleries. Our house was packed every night but I rarely made tea for them.

Many a night they woke us out of our sleep. Four of the men that were working for Paddy lodged with us. I charged them 12/- per week. We became members of the Co-operative Store and the 48/- was more than I wanted to feed them every Monday morning. I went to the Pumpherstown Co-operative Store, lodged the money on deposit. We got 5% interest and at the end of each quarter we got a dividend of 3/- [15%] on every pound's worth of goods we purchased from the Store. I never lifted one penny of the dividend. I left it all on deposit in the Co-operative Store.

All the lodgers that were working in the daytime had to be up at 5 o'clock in the morning. All had to be at their work at 6 a.m. In those days, your Grandfather never missed a shift and when the day's wages were only 4/6d for labourers, your Grandfather would hand me at least six pounds every weekend. He kept enough to take all the boys to Terrace's. He used to have from five to seven men working for him, and if anyone praised him he would say that he was just lucky that he was in a soft place, that the 'scheal" was easy to get but those who knew him would say he was one of the most Nacky workers, that he never had a miss-fire, never missed a shot; always went off.

Every Monday morning I went to Pumpherston Co-op. and lodged on deposit at least six pounds. We got 5% interest on our money and 2/- dividend every quarter on the goods we bought from the society. We bought all our goods from them..."[8]

---

8   *Sally the Cope Gallagher Personal Archives – Limerick City Museum.*

Paddy and Sally stayed in the 'Randy Rows' (Stankards Row) in Uphall, in a house identical to this; such houses were called a 'butt and ben' (i.e. one room and one kitchen): "...Both the room and kitchen had two recesses with beds, a curtain being drawn across the front. Small as these houses were. Many families took in lodgers..." Paddy and Sally took in four lodgers, men who worked with Paddy in Holmes Mine (Photograph and quotation courtesy of Peter Caldwell's book, op. cit.)

A modern photo of Broxburn Roman Catholic Church (SS John Cantius and Nicholas, completed 1881) where Paddy and his friends would go to mass. The church, which covered both Uphall and Broxburn, was built in response to the large numbers of Irish Catholics who came to the area in the latter half of the 19th century to work in the shale oil mines (From the Church website: www.broxburncatholicchurch.co.uk/)

It was their experience in Scotland, in particular at the Pumpherston Co-Operative Society that gave Paddy and Sally the idea to try to start a local co-operative in Cleendra. Sally was very much a part of the idea; it was her managing of their money in Scotland and understanding how the co-operative system worked (e.g. dividends paid against purchases) coupled with Paddy's drive and determination which laid the basis for the emergence and development of the Templecrone Co-Operative Society eight years later in 1906 (Photograph from a c1910 postcard courtesy of Danny McGee, Bathgate from West Lothian Council Libraries).

The Story of the Cope

The Scottish Co-operative movement and the Pumpherston store in particular, were highly developed and were to provide Sally initially and then Paddy with a model for what was to come later:

> "...The Pumpherston Store contained bakery, fleshing, shoemaking and dressmaking departments. The original building soon proved too small and was extended in 1891 and again in 1900 to include grocery, ironmongery and drapery. Added later were departments selling coats, suits and shoes, and butchermeat; and an office and meeting-room..."[9]

Sally's record has them in Scotland till late 1901, when she became pregnant for the first time (her baby Annie was to live only to the age of 3): "...When we were three and a half years in Scotland, to our delight there was a baby expected..." Sally returned home so that their baby could be born in Ireland and she could have the support of her family; the tradition was to go home to the mother's house to have a baby. Paddy followed soon after that, arriving in either late 1901 or the early part of early 1902, after Annie was born.[10]

BACK IN CLEENDRA

The first key event in the development of the Cope story is when George Russell (AE), organiser for the IAOS (Irish Agricultural Organisation Society) came to Dungloe in 1903 to set up an Agricultural Bank. These banks were designed to make loans available to small farmers who could not raise capital in any other way. It was entirely due to AE, who gently twisted the local traders' arms, that Paddy was elected onto the committee at all. Paddy's experiences with the Bank were not satisfactory – when he tried to use it to buy agricultural supplies, like high quality manure at lower prices, he was over-ruled. Local traders and middle men did not want farmers buying direct and cutting them out of this valuable business. It was as a member of the bank committee that he first became aware of the IAWS (Irish Agricultural Wholesale Society) and their far higher quality products and their much lower prices.

Getting hold of good quality manure at reasonable prices was very important, particularly in poor soil areas like the Rosses, as the following commentary from 1890 illustrates:

> "...The mode of husbandry which is practised is very primitive, being all spade labour. The people have no farmyard manure, and use seaweed or "black wrack" instead; but they also follow the pernicious practice of

---

9   Pumpherston, Story of a Shale Oil Village, Luath Press, 2002, Note: Pumpherston has a number of contemporary spellings including Pumperstown and Pumperston as used by Sally the Cope.

10 In the 1946 edition of 'My Story', Paddy dates Sally's pregnancy and their return to Cleendra to 1898. This does not align with Sally's record, which is likely to be more accurate. The 1939 edition makes no reference to dates).

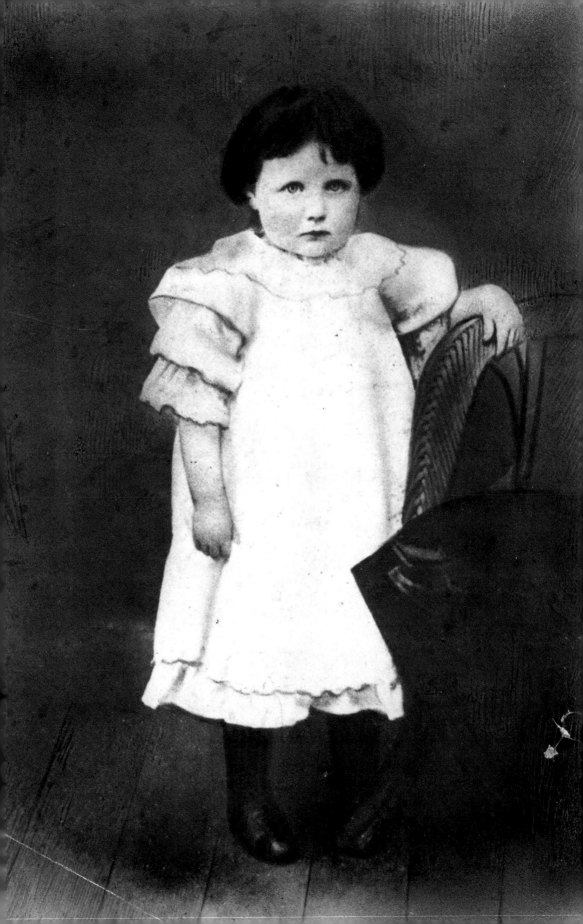

Sally returned from Scotland in 1901 to have her first baby, Annie; Paddy had stayed on in Scotland and then came back (for good), arriving after she was born. Sally's sister Madgie wrote to Paddy: "...The child is going to be christened this evening, and is to be called Annie for your mother..." Paddy's mother was called Nancy and Annie is the English for Nancy, Sally tells us. One of the most poignant passages in Sally the Cope's stories tells of the early death at the age of three of their beloved daughter:

"...Next day, he was ploughing. When I gave him his dinner, I went out to feed the hens, When I came back in wee Annie was not in the kitchen. I went out to look for her, I could not see her. I began to call "Annie". I heard Paddy shouting "She is here". I Looked over and saw her sitting in front of him on the plough. The life nearly left me. I ran over to the field. I said "God bless me Paddy, give me the child. If she falls she will be killed." He said, "No fear of her falling, I have her tied" He had his muffler round her and himself. I said, "I'll take Annie to the house for fear anything might happen." Annie began to cry "Mamie don't take me away from my father." I left her. About an hour after he came in with her. Every day after, while ploughing in the field, he would have Annie sitting in front of him on the plough.

One day wee Annie got sick. I was watching for Paddy to come home. When he came in I had wee Annie in my arms, I was crying. He said "Sally dear what is wrong with you." I said "Paddy, wee Annie is very sick." He took her from me, sat on the stone, had her on his knees, said "Annie what is wrong with you?" She looked at him, moved her lips a little but did not speak. He began to cry. He said "Sally take Annie. I will go in for Dr. Gardiner." I said "Wait to you get your tea first." He said "No tea for me till the doctor sees our darling." Off he went. He and the doctor were back in about half an hour. I had Annie lying in the kitchen bed. The doctor examined her, asked for a spoon, opened her mouth, put the blade of the spoon in her mouth, looked in, took out the spoon, shook his head, said she had croope. Annie died the second day. She wanted a month of being three years. It was the biggest funeral that ever was in the Rosses up to that time. The day she was buried Paddy went out. He did not tell me where he was going. He frightened me. He did not come in till after twelve o'clock. I asked him where was he? He said "I went to the spink and prayed to God to send Annie back to us." But he didn't. Oh that was sad parting with wee Annie..."

burning the land in order to make it produce a crop. They collect a quantity of turf and make a big fire, and when it is red hot place bits of burning turf, or "coals" as they call them, at intervals all over the field, putting two pieces together. They then place a small quantity of dry surface earth round and over the coals, gradually increasing it till they have a good heap. This burns into a white ash, and when they think they have enough to cover the field they place the ashes in a heap and let it stand. When it is cool they mix it with the surrounding earth, leave it for a day or two, and then spread it all over the field. They then make their drills or ridges, covering in the burnt stuff, add a little artificial manure, and put in their potatoes. The system of burning leads to late planting, as they have to wait till the ground is fairly dry. Their only rotation of crops is potatoes and oats, oats and potatoes, and they say the land is "so old there is no heart in it". The burning naturally exhausts the land, and though by law the landlord can recover a penalty when it is done, practically he cannot interfere.

The seaweed produces a good crop, and is worth £4 a ton. It is best when used along with artificial manure, a practice which is increasing, but when used by itself the potatoes are soft and watery and therefore more likely to be affected by disease. If it has to be carted any distance, they dry and stack it like hay, in order to make it light. They spread the seaweed, whether fresh or dry, on the land, leave it uncovered for a time, and then set their potatoes in it. The men put the crops into the ground, but, as they are away at harvest time, it is left to the women and children to save them, with the aid of any men who are too old to go away to work..."[11]

Naively perhaps, Paddy and the Cleendra farmers thought all they had to do was place an order directly to the IAWS but they met with a refusal saying that they, the IAWS, only dealt with co-operative societies not individuals. They tried the Ulster Manure Company who also refused to supply them, directing them to one of their traders in Dungloe.[12] At this point, Paddy began to get desperate. His judgement and reputation were on the line so he decided he needed to try something a little different. He was able to persuade, with a charm and guile he recounts entertainingly in 'My Story', a creamery manager in Donegal Town to place the first order of manures for him through the IAWS; the first delivery came in through Burtonport and was shipped across the bay to Maghery:

"...We agreed, when I collected the money, to get the manures into Burtonport for this reason. Quite a lot of the people who gave an order were in debt and were afraid that if the shopkeepers saw them coming through the town with the manures, that they would immediately

---

11   *The Times, 13th October 1890: Congested Districts of Ireland II: The Rosses. Anthony Manny Anne (Boner) remembers 'burning the land' like this with turf coals as late as the 1930s; he also recalls cutting wrack off Milltown with his brother Packie in his father Manny Anne's boat in the 1930s and 1940s.*

12   *'My Story' Paddy the Cope 1939.*

process them. The station was north of Dungloe, and Cleendra was south-west, but we could boat the manures from Burtonport and the town shop-keepers would not see us.

The day the manures arrived was a big day. The price was seven shillings and five pence a bag and the shopkeepers charged twelve shillings and sixpence. When I paid the freight at the station, it was twenty-five shillings less than we calculated. I told the men we had twenty-three shillings left and we spent it on tea and bread. We cleared all the manures. It was a bit of a sensation in the whole parish, and in the next parish, the lower Rosses…"[13]

This was a successful operation but it was clearly a one off, never to be repeated 'guerrilla' action. Doing it on a regular basis required them to become a registered co-operative society.

After much badgering, recorded in surviving letters, Paddy managed to persuade the IAOS to send an organiser to Cleendra. Setting a date for the first meeting with the organiser, Mr Thomas Shaw, proved difficult. Paddy wrote to the IAOS on 6th Nov 1905 (in Sally's hand):

"…we decided yesterday not to fix a date yet as fortunately there are plenty of herring just now along our Shore and the people here is engaged in the fishing. They go out always on Sunday evenings and that is the most suitable day for holding a meeting…"[14]

The story of the first meetings, the half crown subscriptions, and the resistance to their revolution from local traders is captured wonderfully in Paddy's book and Sally's stories.

"…When Paddy came home he made me write a letter to AE telling him that the organiser only came to Dungloe, saw the merchants and returned to Dublin. Please send another. That he would be met at the station. Not to stop in Dungloe. Paddy signed the letter, he always signed them. A week afterwards Paddy met Mr Shaw at Dungloe Road Station. He took him up to our house. We had a good feed for him in the room and the floor covered with nice clean bags. We had good turf and we kept on a roaring fire while he was in the house. It was arranged that the meeting would be in our house. Dan Sweeney, the then Roshine schoolmaster, although he lived in Dungloe beside the shopkeepers, sent one of the scholars with a note to Paddy to say he would give the school for the meeting. So the meeting was held in the school…"[15]

---

13 *My Story: Paddy the Cope, Patrick Gallagher 1939, 1942, 1949, 1979, 2006.*

14 *IAOS records: 1088/871/1-8, National Archives, Bishop St Dublin.*

15 *Sally the Cope Gallagher Personal Archives – Limerick City Museum.*

In 1905 before becoming a cooperative, Paddy organised the farmers of Cleendra to join together to order some manures. Their very first shipment of 'basic slag' (artificial manure) was delivered to Burtonport by rail and shipped across Dungloe Bay to Maghery in many small boats, much like the white one in the foreground. It was all done secretly to avoid the Dungloe traders getting to hear. It is almost certain that word would have got back anyway as both John and James Sweeney, sons of John Sweeney in Dungloe, had shops in the Port, as did other traders. This is a contemporary photograph of 'Burtonport Quay' with, left to right, the Harbour Bar, Campbell's Hotel and O'Donnell's Hotel, built by Jimmy Frank O'Donnell, harbourmaster. The Post Office at this time was in O'Donnell's, just to the left of the main entrance (Lawrence Collection L_ROY_9436, National Photographic Archive).

BURTONPORT QUAY. Co DONEGAL. 9436 W.L.

Patrick Gallagher
Cleendra Dungloe
Co Donegal
Dear Sirs   6th October 05
I beg to ask your Society to send a lecturer to Cleendra to start a Co operative Society for Groceries seed and manures and to make sale of Faron produce the small Farmers hear is very willing to join I hope your Society will kindly send me a book of rules for Same I will make all the arangements You tell me for the Lecturer ... Your Respectfully Secretary P Gallagher
I.A.O.S.

Secretary.
Is this work for Shaw or Mr Adams? A latter is now in the Donegal district and will undertake it at less expense. Of course I shall explain to Mr. Gallagher that we cant organise groceries &c.
Auther.
(1) Better explain to Mr G. that we dont organise Stores
(2) Pass on to Mr Adams to deal with when in district

Paddy was very persistent with the Irish Agricultural Organisation Society (IAOS), writing to them on at least three occasions (one can imagine how he would have made use of the telephone or email if they had been available in Cleendra then!). In this first letter, from 6th October 1905, he requests that a lecturer be sent to Cleendra and also a rule book for setting up a society to sell 'groceries, seeds and manures' and 'to make sale of farm produce' (IAOS Records, National Archives, Bishop Street Dublin).

This IAOS internal note was written the day after Paddy's letter was dated and debates whether Mr Shaw or Adams should be sent – the latter was already in Donegal so it would cost less (in the event it was Shaw who came to Cleendra). RA - Robert Anderson (Secretary of the IAOS from 1895-1921) writes the lower message to the Assistant Secretary and is at pains to stress that they "...don't organise groceries..." – this was to become a very big issue for the IAOS as they helped the Templecrone Cope develop, eventually leading to withdrawal of government support and funding for the IAOS after lobbying by commercial interests (IAOS records, National Archives).

Paddy said to the IAOS organiser, Thomas Shaw:

> "...I would like a Society the same as they have in Scotland, where we could get everything we wanted. 'I am sorry,' said Mr. Shaw, 'we cannot organize a Society for that purpose; we can only organize a Society for agricultural purposes.'
> 'What purpose is that for?' I asked.
> 'Dealing in seed, manures and agricultural implements, also eggs and butter,' he said.
> 'Can you deal in spades and shovels?' I said.
> 'Yes, you can, that comes under agricultural work.'
> 'All right, Mr. Shaw,' said I, 'that is what we want, we want nothing else.'
> That was the first deliberate lie I told in my life..."[16]

---

16 *My Story: Paddy the Cope, Patrick Gallagher (1939, 1942, 1949, 1979, 2006).*

The IAOS replied promptly to Paddy (9th October) and Paddy in this second letter of 11th October 1905 keeps the pressure on, asking that an organiser be sent for a meeting on the 15th. Concerned (with some justification it has to be said) that the organiser might not be able to find Cleendra, Paddy offers to meet him in Dungloe (IAOS records, National Archives)

Paddy, tenacious man that he was, fired off another letter on 12th December 1905. The IAOS's Thomas Shaw had not been able to attend their meeting but Paddy wanted to press on. Shaw did eventually make it to Cleendra, as both Paddy and Sally recall in their stories. Used as he was to cooperatives being set up in lush creamery country, he was somewhat taken aback at how unpromising the countryside was for starting a cooperative. Aware he had alarmed the IAOS officials with talk of 'groceries' he said that all they really wanted was to be able to order fertiliser – 'Basic Slag immediately and we want to get it on the best terms' ('basic slag' is a limestone/phosphate fertiliser so this was a legitimate agricultural activity for the IAOS to help with). He finishes by requesting information on how to set up a Society (IAOS records, National Archives).

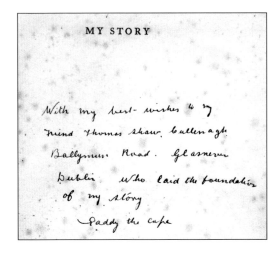

MY STORY

With my best wishes to my friend Thomas Shaw. Ballenagh Ballymun Road. Glasnevin Dublin. who laid the foundation of my story

Paddy the Cope

Paddy wrote this warm, personal message to IAOS organiser Thomas Shaw in a copy of his book when it was published some 34 years later (1939). Mr Shaw was the IAOS man who travelled to Cleendra in 1905 to advise Paddy and his friends how to start a Co-operative Society (Inscribed in a 1939 Jonathan Cape copy of 'My Story' by Paddy the Cope; from Cope Chairman Pat Dunleavy's collection).

Sally the Cope writing in her memoirs in the 1940s, recalls the meeting when the first members joined what was to be the Templecrone Society:

> "...Mr. Shaw: "If you decide to start an agricultural Society, you must appoint a Secretary.
>
> Paddy: "I propose John O'Donnell". Denis Hunter seconded it.
>
> Mr. Shaw: "Now all that wish to become members, come forward and give us your names."
>
> Well children dear, the first that rushed up was Paddy's aunt, Maggie Gallagher. She is now in Elizabeth in America. Ninety-three years of age she is. No.1 Rodger Doogan. 2 Dooney O'Donnell. 3 Paddy Gallagher. 4 John O'Donnell. 5 Frank Huston. 6 John Boyle. 7 Mick Huston. 8 Sheila O'Donnell. 9 Neil O'Donnell 10 John O'Donnell. 11 Denis Mc Fadden. 12 John Gillespie. 13 in all.
>
> Paddy, John O'Donnell and Mr. Shaw came up to the house after the meeting
>
> While I was making the tea Shaw said "I am sorry I cannot have a Co-operative Society here, you have 13 men and women willing to become members. You would need a hundred or two. This is the most wretched part in Ireland, nothing but bog and river; I don't know how anyone can live in it."
>
> I had a good young duck for the tea; I said "Sit over now the tea is ready." They sat over. Paddy went to the dresser, came back with a bottle of whiskey, drew the cork, poured out 3 glasses. Then in comes Paddy's

father. He said "I want to meet the nice gentleman you have here from Dublin." Paddy introduced them. Pat sat at the fire. Paddy put whiskey in the cup for his father. We had only the three glasses. Paddy lifted his own, said "We must take an appetiser before we start, lift your glasses." Shaw lifted his. John said "I don't touch it." Paddy, Shaw and Pat drank theirs. Pat said "Dambut it is good." I am sure the Society will be good too,"

Shaw said "Mr. Gallagher there will be no Society." Pat said "Why do you say that?" Shaw: "There are only thirteen people willing to join." Pat said "Good enough, that is plenty when Paddy is in it. Anything he ever put his hands to he made a success." When they finished the tea Paddy filled up the glasses again. When they drank it Paddy said: "Mr. Shaw I hope and pray you will register the Society. I am as sure as I drank that wee lock of whiskey we will make a success. See my father there he was not at the meeting and I am sure he will become a member." Pat got up, reached Shaw a pound, "If that is not enough I'll give you twenty." Shaw said "I can't take any money. If you wish give it to Mr. O'Donnell." Pat hands the pound to John O'Donnell. Pat said "Another wee drop of that good whiskey." Paddy did.

When they drank it I went and laid a hand on each of Mr. Shaw's shoulders. I said "Mr. Shaw we have seven or eight hundred pounds in West Calder Co-operative Society. Paddy will you agree to bring it over and give it to John O'Donnell?" Paddy said he would. I said "Wait a minute." I went to the chest, handed Mr. Shaw our deposit book, in it was seven hundred and ninety three pounds fourteen and three pence. I put my hands again on his shoulders. I said "I appeal to you Mr. Shaw to register our Society." He looked at me for a long time, then stood up, caught my hands, said "Who could refuse you? I'll register it should I be dismissed." I looked at Paddy. Oh children, if you saw the lovely smile he had on.

Paddy sent word to the members to come to our house the next night. Paddy told then that what he wanted them for was to decide what name they would call the Society. Frank said "What the hell name would we call it but Cleendra." Paddy said "I am as sure as I'm here that in a short time we will have members from every town in this parish and lower parish too. I propose we call it the name of the parish "Templecrone" that will suit the two parishes. This parish is upper Templecrone and the lower Rosses parish is Lower Templecrone and St. Crone was a great saint, she will keep us right." it was agreed to call it "Templecrone Co-operative Agricultural Society…"[17]

He succeeded in registering The Templecrone Co-Operative Society on 16th January 1906. Paddy himself was never a share owner, neither then nor later. It is a remarkable fact that he was content to be the guiding light and effectively a Cope employee rather than a shareholder.

---

17 *Sally the Cope Gallagher Personal Archives – Limerick City Museum.*

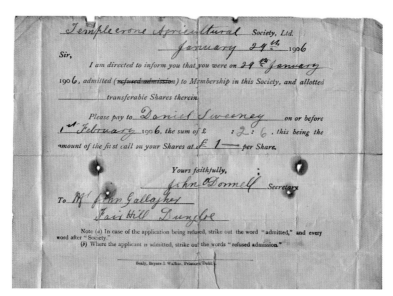

Irish Agricultural Organisation Society, Ltd.,

Offices—22 Lincoln Place,

Dublin.

Encs.

TELEGRAPHIC ADDRESS:
"ORGANISE, DUBLIN."
TELEPHONE No. 1090.

A.514/06.

ALL COMMUNICATIONS
TO BE ADDRESSED TO
"THE SECRETARY."

20th Jan. 1906.

Re Templecrone Co-op. Agrl. Soc. Ltd.

Dear Sir,

I beg to inform you that your Society was registered on the 16th inst.

The Industrial & Provident Societies Act, 1893, provides that every registered Society must keep a sufficient number of copies of its rules on hand, so as to supply a copy to every member on payment of the price fixed by its Committee (4d. per copy is suggested), and also in order to supply a copy to any other person on demand, and on payment of 1/-.

Arrangements have been made with MESSRS. SEALY, BRYERS AND WALKER, MIDDLE ABBEY STREET, DUBLIN, to print Societies' rules at the rate of 3½d. per copy, or £1 10s. 0d. per hundred copies which is the smallest number any Society ought to order at the commencement. Kindly let them know whether you will require a larger number of copies, and give them the address to which they are to be sent when printed.

Yours faithfully,

Mr. John O'Donnell,

Clanderry,

Dungloe, Co Donegal.

Secretary.

The Templecrone Co-Operative Agricultural Society Ltd was formally registered on 16th January 1906. By this stage, momentum was building, subscriptions had reached £10 from the initial 14 half crowns (£1.75) and the Cope had started to try and source supplies. Registration was only a start though; it would be a struggle all the way as resistance from the local traders stiffened (IAOS records, National Archives)

This is a very early, January 29th 1906, Cope £1 share certificate belonging to John Gallagher, from the Fair Hill. John was a brother of Sally the Cope Gallagher, Paddy's wife. The share had a 2/6d deposit, full payment was £1. The Cope's first Secretary was John O'Donnell; Daniel Sweeney, the local Roshine schoolmaster who provided the school for the early Cope meetings, was the first Treasurer and took over as Secretary in 1909 (Breid Gallagher, Mill Road).

Thomas Shaw later reported back to Robert Anderson, IAOS Secretary:

> "...I attended a meeting of farmers of the Dungloe district of Co. Donegal on 9th January 1906 at Roshine National School. The meeting was largely attended and all present are very anxious to have a Society established. Mr P. Gallagher was in the chair and in introducing me explained the circumstances leading up to my visit to the district. The people in that remote part of the country have never heard of the Co-operative Movement with the exception of an Agricultural Bank which was established in Dungloe by Mr Russell in 1903.
>
> There are three manure agents in Dungloe: Messrs JT Boyle, JT Sweeney and Jas Sweeney and the farmers were simply at the mercy of these men. No guarantee as to analysis was given by these dealers in respect of the manure sold to them nor was any brand on the bags to indicate the nature of the contents. The most peculiar thing about the manure trade done by these agents was that no matter what was asked for, the price was the same viz. 8/- per bag for Cash or 10/- for credit. As cash payments were practically unknown here – not being the custom – the prices charged for the manures was 10/- to 12/- per bag according to the length of credit given. Thus I found, on the best authority, that in addition to the <u>profit</u> made by these local dealers on the manures, they charged the poor people with interest of 100% per annum (!) and in some cases much more. The farmers according to Mr Gallagher's statement, had not even the courage to ask what they would have to pay, but merely took what they got at the merchant's price, and without the slightest knowledge of what they were getting.
>
> The first inkling Mr Gallagher got of the way in which he and his neighbours were fleeced was through some leaflets from the IAOS and a manure price list from the IAWS which were sent down by Mr Russell to the Agricultural Bank. Mr Gallagher is a member of the Bank Committee and got hold of the leaflets and list which he took home and carefully studied with the result that he at once called a meeting of his fellow farmers and showed them the Co-operative prices as compared to the extortionate prices they were paying. It was then decided to apply to the IAOS to send down an organiser to establish a society with the result that I was instructed to carry out this work.
>
> The greatest enthusiasm prevailed at the meeting at which I got the necessary signatures for the registration and enough to attend the first business meeting on 24th inst..."[18]

The pricing and quality of the 'gombeen' manure was a scandal and not just in Templecrone:

---

18   *IAOS records: 1088/871/1-8, National Archives, Bishop St Dublin.*

Paddy the Cope, aged 41, is standing in the doorway of the Cleendra shop in 1912 in a photo was taken by Harold Barbour, Chairman of the IAWS (Irish Agricultural Wholesale Society). Barbour was a great supporter of the Cope, was an early shareholder and often travelled to Dungloe for the Templecrone Co-op's AGM. In 1912, he also travelled around Ireland visiting other co-operatives, leaving a valuable photographic archive. Cleendra was no longer being used as a shop (its glass windows are already broken) – the Cope business in Dungloe was expanding fast and branches had been set up in nearby Maghery and also in Lettermacaward (Harold Barbour Photograph Collection, University College Dublin Archives (UCDA P168)

The Story of the Cope

"...speaking of the quality of some of the artificial manures on the market, one of the delegates to an annual meeting of the Irish Agricultural Organisation Society said that if a man were to take a bag of sand and put a herring with it and call it an artificial manure, he would be doing nothing more extraordinary than many of the traders were in the habit of doing...!"[19]

How did the Cope get its name? Sally the Cope's memoir tells the story:

"...The reason they called it the Cope was that John Gillespie, when speaking stuttered, and one day he was in a public house in Dungloe and was asked, "What name had they on the foreign Society that they had in Cleendra?" John said "Tep-Tep-Co-Co- Cope." So it is called Cope from that day to this day..."[20]

So it was then that in 1906, Paddy the Cope (then aged 35) and the farming families of Cleendra set up in a small 12 x 13 foot stone building on the rocky slopes of Cleendra. It was certainly not all plain sailing: persuading suppliers to take their orders was difficult. They were more used to dealing through local merchants; no-one was keen to help upstart farmers whose aim was to cut out the middleman.

An American writer, Marie Harrison, visited Dungloe ten years later and recorded:

"...The success of the sale of agricultural necessities led to the opening of a general store, which began to supply tea, sugar, meal and flour. That was a day of revelation to the women. It was worthwhile to tramp along the hill-sides to reach 'the funny little store' where they could buy their foodstuffs cheaper than in the village shops. The price of flour tumbled abruptly from twelve shillings to nine shillings a bag..."[21]

Encouraged by this initial venture, the Cope began to expand, slowly at first but by expanding from their own nearby townlands to right across Templecrone, they soon began to grow very rapidly. Very early on, they hit upon what we would call today a successful business model whereby they would buy in eggs – at better rates than the local merchants - and sell them on in bulk. With the money generated for the people selling eggs and for the Cope, they would then sell back directly to people groceries – tea and sugar etc – which became the start of the famous 'Tea Vans', initially by horse and cart and eventually, after 1918, by lorry.

---

19   *Cooperation in Ireland, Smith-Gordon & O'Brien, 1921.*

20   *Sally the Cope Gallagher Personal Archives – Limerick City Museum.*

21   *'Dawn In Ireland' Marie Harrison, Andrew Melrose Ltd, 1917.*

THE FIRST COMMITTEE OF THE TEMPLECRONE SOCIETY.

These earliest known photographs of the Cope Committee members, outside the shop in Cleendra, accompanied a series of five articles in the Irish Homestead between January 29th and March 19th 1910. It was unheard of for a Co-operative Committee to be featured in this way in the Irish Homestead; clearly the editor, George Russell (*AE*), felt there was a need for the faces of the miracle workers of Templecrone to be seen. The names of the men in this photo are, it is believed: John Gillespie, Paddy the Cope, John Browne, Dan Deery, the last two are not known (Irish Homestead Archive, Feb 5th 1910 issue, ICOS Library, Plunkett House, Merrion Square, Dublin).

The Irish Agricultural Organisation Society: IAOS

The Cope's success in the early years and later could not have been achieved without the support – professional advice, financial backing and moral support – of the IAOS The IAOS archives are packed with correspondence back and forth, with records of visits and advice sought and given freely and warmly. Paddy, John O'Donnell and Daniel Sweeney and the early Cope members received a great deal of help – whether to do with how to transport and sell eggs, keep proper books and prepare accounts. The correspondence between Cleendra and Plunkett House Merrion Square, where George Russell (AE), Robert Anderson IAOS Secretary and others were based was frequent and invaluable. The Cope could not have grown as fast as it did without the help of the IAOS

The IAOS did what they could to help as the resistance from the traders ratcheted up. The Cope applied for a grant of £30 from the Congested Districts Board but was turned down even with IAOS lobbying. They applied for a loan from the Northern Bank with IAOS backing – offered a rate of 5.5%, some 1.5% over normal commercial rates then prevailing, the IAOS recommended they decline. The bank was being influenced by the traders who tried all they could to make

PRESENT COMMITTEE OF THE TEMPLECRONE SOCIETY.

The people in this photo appear to be: John Gillespie, Paddy the Cope, the next three are not known, John Browne, Dan Deery, Denis O'Donnell, not known.

life difficult for the upstarts from Cleendra. In the end, the IAWS discounted a bill for 4% (effectively giving the Cope working capital) with IAOS support – Mr Shaw and IAOS Secretary Robert Anderson were very helpful in this.[22]

In addition to financial advice and backing, the IAOS offered practical help and guidance. A good example of this was with the Cope's first important commercial venture: the gathering, grading and exporting of eggs. Early on, in July 1906, Cope Secretary John O'Donnell asked whether the IAOS could sell their eggs for them or help them find a market.[23] IAOS Secretary, Robert Anderson, directed them to the Manager of the Federated Poultry Societies. A training course run by the DATI (Department of Agriculture and Training) was set up; the Department paid expenses of a shilling a day and a third class train fare. John O'Donnell was put forward for it but it was Paddy the Cope himself who went on the course:

---

22 *IAOS Records, National Archives.*

23 *The IAOS Records in the National Archives are the source of the letters referred to in these paragraphs, between July 1906 and February 1907. The DATI was established in 1900, largely due to Sir Horace Plunkett, the DATI's first Vice President. Plunkett had set up the IAOS in 1894 and the close working relationship between the two agencies was of great help to the Cope in its infancy. A year later and it would not have been as smooth: Plunkett was forced to resign from the IAOS and the new vice president T. W. Russell withdrew support for the IAOS(Appendix 1 has further details on the tensions between the co-operative movement and DATI, who sided with commercial interest, i.e. traders, who wanted co-operation to stop short of the General Stores business that the Cope became).*

There was a list of 11 names entitled 'COMMITTEE' implying these 11 were the 1910 current committee. The Irish Homestead did not identify each member by name – it is possible to work out in part from later (named) Committee photographs who was who:

COMMITTEE.

MR. PATRICK GALLAGHER (Chairman).

,, DANIEL SWEENEY (Secretary).

,, JOHN GILLESPIE.

,, ANTHONY GLACKIN.

,, JOHN BROWNE.

,, THOMAS GLACKIN.

,, DENIS O'DONNELL.

,, MICHAEL DOHERTY.

,, DANIEL O'DONNELL.

,, JOHN DEVENNEY.

,, DANIEL DEERY.

"...the Committee now think that the management of the Agricultural Society is enough for me and they are now desirous that Mr Patrick Gallagher (who already has some knowledge of the business) and has consented to apply, should take my place if the Dept agree..."[24]

Paddy proved to be an excellent student. Richmond Noble, an IAOS organiser who came to Dungloe for a special general meeting in November 1906, said he had:

"...no hesitation whatever in recommending Mr P Gallagher of Cleenderry, Dungloe, for training as a poultry manager...he is a first rate man and just the type we want..."[25]

---

24 *Letter of 5th November 1906 from John O'Donnell to Robert Anderson (R.A.A.) , IAOS records, National Archives.*

25 *Letter of recommendation 19th November 1906 from Mr Richmond Noble, IAOS organiser, IAOS records, National Archives. Mr Noble, in his report of the meeting of the 18th November 2006 added the following in the margin: 'I am seeing Traffic Manager of L&LSR tonight. The traders are boycotting Railway because they won't refuse to carry Templecrone goods'. Clearly, the traders would stop at nothing in their attempts to crush the Cope.*

Robert Andrew Anderson (R.A.A.), close friend and colleague of Sir Horace Plunkett, was appointed Secretary of the IAOS at its inception in 1894. He was of great help – professional, financial and moral - to the Templecrone Co-Operative Society in helping it get started and visited Dungloe many times. The IAOS archive has hundreds of manuscript notes, letters, instructions from Anderson concerning the Cope (Photo from 'My Story' 1946 edition, Mr. Anderson is standing on the steps outside Plunkett House, headquarters of the IAOS, in Merrion Square Dublin)

It took some time to set up but in February 1907, the Dunboe Co-operative Poultry Society wrote to the DATI:

> "…Patrick Gallagher is fully qualified to Grade, Test and Pack eggs and all the duties connected with the management of a poultry society…"[26]

With this qualification, the continued support of the IAOS, the Cope was set up to create a very successful business (see also Appendix 2).

Within a very short space of time, the Cope had established itself and grown rapidly – so rapidly in fact that it had great trouble keeping good accounts and it was again to call on help from its new found friends in the co-operative movement. Within two years of incorporation, it was ready to take the challenge into the enemy's stronghold: Dungloe.

---

26 *Letter 13th February 1907 from Dunboe Co-operative Poultry Society to the Secretary of the Department of Agriculture (DATI), IAOS records, National Archives.*

Cyril Winder (the Cope's General Manager from 1969 to 1993) outside the Cope's Dungloe supermarket in1976 with the 'original' starting capital in 1906 of the Templecrone Co-op: 14 half crowns. Mr Winder collected these in the 1970s to create an eloquent symbol of just how little the Cope was founded on 70 years previously. In 1906, the chances of every member paying with a half crown (rather than a combination of smaller coins) or with the date 1906 are highly improbable (the Cope was registered on 16th January and the first 14 members would have subscribed before this date, it is unlikely that the new 1906 coinage would have reached Donegal by then). It is difficult to give a current day value of a half crown: it was one eighth of a pound (in euro it is only c15 cents as at 2009). In buying terms you would probably have to multiply by at least 300 or 400. (Cope Photo Archive)

The Story of the Cope

Chapter 2

Dungloe

Dungloe is now the major population centre in the Rosses but this was not always the case. In 1824, Dunlo (sic) had 42 houses and a population of 253. There were eleven inhabited islands in 'Templecroan' Parish: Arranmore had 132 houses and 788 people; Rutland, 29 houses, 173 people; Inishfree 25 houses, 171 people; Owey 12 houses, 76 people; Innisceragh eight houses, 47 people; Inniscoo eight houses, 53 people; Eighter seven houses, 42 people; Innisal five houses, 32 people; Eddernish one house, eleven people; Duck one house, five people; and Tully Island eight houses and 44 people. In all, some 236 houses and 1,442 people on the islands, almost six times as many as were living in Dungloe.[1]

> "...Dungloe is a long street running N-S and crossing the Dungloe River by a narrow bridge at the middle. 'It is small', says the Parliamentary Gazetteer of 1846, 'and signally sequestered but possesses a sort of irksome importance from being the only apology for a town within an extensive range of dreary and island flanked sea-board.' Architecturally this is still true, but we have learnt in the 20th Century to value sequestered settings. The only building of any value in Dungloe, the Northern Bank office by the bridge, built in 1886 by G. W. Ferguson, has recently been demolished. It had a bold slate pyramid roof and was boldly detailed in granite. The castle near which Spanish cannons were found in the 18th Century has long disappeared..."[2]

The farmers of Cleendra were happy enough with their 'wee shop', the lower priced, higher quality manures they now had - and the luxuries they were now able to afford from the proceeds of their success as an agricultural cooperative. However, this was never going to be enough for Paddy and Sally. They had seen what was possible at the Pumpherston Co-operative store in Scotland. The real prize was to succeed in the capital of the Rosses, Dungloe, right where the local merchants, who had tried to strangle the Cope at birth, operated. Paddy himself, backed all the way (and shoved sometimes as he admitted) by Sally, was fearless. It helped that they had a bit of money put by from Scotland – but he needed the support and help of others on the Committee – Secretary John O'Donnell, Treasurer Daniel Sweeney, his staunch ally John Gillespie, Johnnie Brown and others. He also had the support of his good friend Jimmy (James Liam) Durnion from the hills of Croveigh on the other side of Dungloe. James was back from working in the States and saw what Paddy was trying to do – he brought good counsel and 14 new members to the Cope from Croveigh.

---

1   Ordnance Survey of Ireland www.osi.ie and 1824 Population Survey.

2   'The Buildings of Ireland: North West Ulster' by Alistair Rowan (Penguin Books, 1979); the Northern Bank actually dates from c1896-98, the architect's drawings are dated 1896.

Paddy and Sally left Dungloe for Scotland after marrying in 1898. Dungloe Main Street would have looked as in this 1890s photograph. Looking down from the Caravan Road towards the Northern Bank and the old Barracks (both fine buildings now gone, the Northern Bank was a huge loss architecturally), on the left is the 'The Tirconaill Bar' (Patrick Johnny Sally's); opposite Patrick's can be seen the Chapel wall and

then a line of single story thatched cottages. Chickens wander freely unworried by traffic and a woman, with a cow and calf, are on a street which appears to be very rough and certainly not uniformly flat. The coming of the motor car in the next few decades would transform the roads (Contemporary photograph, Jim the Cope Archive, Cassie Jock's House).

From KILLYBEGGS to Dunfanaghy.

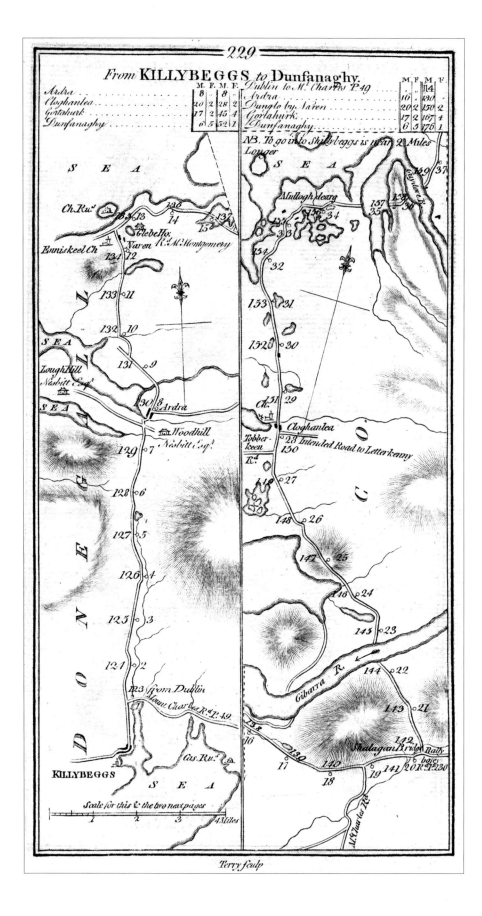

	M.	F.	M.	F.
Ardra	8		8	
Cloghanlea	20	2	28	2
Gortahurk	17	2	45	4
Dunfanaghy	6	5	52	1

Dublin to Mt Charles P. 49

	M.	F.	M.	F.
Ardra	10	"	130	
Dunglo by Naren	20	2	150	2
Gortahurk	17	2	167	4
Dunfanaghy	6	5	176	1

NB. To go into Killybeggs is near 2 Miles Longer

Scale for this & the two next pages
1 2 3 4 Miles

Terry sculp

From the other end of Dungloe, things look a little more prosperous. Again from the 1890s, this is a photo taken by a US relative of Daniel Sweeney NT (Roshine School); Daniel was an important early figure in the Cope and became its Secretary. The extensive notes with the photograph give details of people and buildings. On the left is Sweeney's Hotel: a group is gathered on the steps with a lamp above (possibly fuelled with acetylene gas like the hotel in Burtonport) and a carriage drawn by two horses on the road. Sweeney's shop is next door, a board sign above saying John Sweeney. Jamesie Sweeney's Corner House has a pointed gable and, moving up the left side of the street: Edward Boyle's shop; Owen Doherty's; John Liam Boyle; Condy Boyle (Registrar); Hughie O'Donnell's; and Jim Sweeney's. On the right hand side are: Dan Sweeney's Manor House; the Market House and Court House; Toland's (Tailor); McBride's; and Brennan's Public House (Quay Road); Boyle's Hotel; the Parochial House; and Johnny Bán's (Sweeney) in Castle Row above the Tirconaill Bar, also known as Patrick Johnny Sally's (Photograph courtesy of Cha (Sweeney) Gallagher – who also provided the background details from a record made in 1967 by 'SJD')

Left: This 18th century map shows the route from Killybegs to Dunfanaghy going through Cloghanlea, as Dungloe was then called (on the early British maps - from the 1830s the Ordnance Survey erroneously used 'Dunglow' - it is still printed like this on the current OSi maps). Roads were very poor at this time; people would more often use boats and the sea or shoreline to get around. Travel to Letterkenny – at this stage the road via Doochary was only 'intended' - entailed going up around the coast to Falcarragh, Dunfanaghy etc and getting one's feet wet from time to time, a route very much as the Lough Swilly Railway (& later Bus Service) followed 130 years later (without the wet feet thankfully). At Cloghanlea, just the Church of Ireland is marked. The only other places marked are where there were Protestant settlements such as 'Tobberkeen' and 'Mulloghdearg' (sic). (PB collection, Taylor and Skinner 'Roads of Ireland' 1778)

MAIN ST. DUNGLOE. Co. DONEGAL. 9422 W.L.

In this much higher quality Lawrence photograph from the early 1900s, there is little obvious change. The open drain still runs down the right hand side; chickens wander the street; and street lights (possibly acetylene gas or oil as it is too early for electricity in Dungloe) appear to be only on the left hand side. The turning for the Carnmore Road, on the left, just past the house with the gable end, Mulhern's Corner Bar (as it is called today), is hardly apparent, not much more than a track. Outside Sweeney's Hotel and James Sweeney's shop on the left, a pony and trap – the hotel's carriage or possibly Carberry's mail car to Fintown that Paddy and Sally caught the day after their wedding - is waiting and a policeman is standing by. The Cope's first shop on the Main Street can be seen on the right – it had a rounded, arched doorway. (National Photographic Archive, Lawrence Collection, L_ROY-09422)

But moving into Dungloe was a big risk and the Cleendra people were worried about setting up in the enemy's stronghold. But there was no doubt about its potential – and there was the extra advantage of centralising the operation as Sally, ever the wise counsel, had pointed out:

> '...The more I think of it there is something in what Sally says. If we were in Dungloe, we would save a lot of carting. See yesterday, John had to yoke the horse in the cart and go to Croveigh with two hundredweight of meal and two bags of flour, three miles the other side of the town. We had to cart it first from the station to here, a distance of seven miles, that was fourteen miles in all. If we were in the town, we would be only three miles from the station, and we would only have to cart it another three miles, six miles instead of fourteen. We would also be in the centre

of the parish. We would get a lot of new members and we would show the big guns in the town that we were not afraid of them...'[3]

The move into Dungloe in 1907 was, therefore, in one sense, purely a practical one: Dungloe was a more sensible distribution point. Before the move, everything was hauled back to Cleendra from Dungloe Road Station (Lough Meela), seven miles away on the other side of Dungloe Bay. Most of the Cope's agricultural and other supplies were delivered here by the new Lough Swilly Railway, which had opened in 1903. Fully laden carts would pass through Dungloe town on the way out to Cleendra – and back again with Cope produce for sale, mainly eggs in the early days.

There was however stiff resistance from the people of Cleendra to the moving of 'their' Cope away from its home. Others worried about being so close to the Dungloe traders who resented the Cope's intrusion into the cosy cartel they had been operating. The initial impact on their turnover was limited but the traders could see what it could develop into.

In any event, it had became clear - at least to Paddy, a man with vision and ambition - that continuing to just work out of the 'wee shop' in Cleendra was going to be limiting. Initially, they had opened two nights a week but this was soon extended to five or six nights. Soon, the fledgling Cope began to operate outside its Cleendra base; it began to attract customers from other townlands and traded or bought in their eggs at good prices. The Dungloe traders attempted to squeeze out the upstarts by localising their pricing, i.e. buying in at higher and selling at lower than their normal prices, but just in Cleendra. The Cope responded by expanding their territory by taking a horse and cart (called a 'van' in those days) around the Lower Rosses. The Dungloe traders had to back off as it was costing them too much to lower their prices everywhere the Cope went.

The Cope's horse and cart was the precursor to the much-loved and long gone[4] 'Tea Van' which delivered groceries all around the Rosses. It was a vital service for people who could not get to the shops, in the days before the motor car. The Cope paid more - for eggs that were bought in - and sold agricultural and other supplies more cheaply than the traders. This reversal of the 'gombeen' system proved to be a highly successful and unbeatable business model.

Richmond Noble, one of the IAOS organisers visited Templecrone on 25-27 February 1907; he advised the Cope on how to manage their eggs business, packing etc, commenting that the Cope had imported a new van to carry their growing levels of produce.

---

3   *'My Story' Paddy the Cope, 1939.*

4   *The Tea Van was retired for good in 1979. Cyril Winder, Cope General Manager wrote in 1985: "...Due to escalating fuel prices, van operators' persistence on helpers, yet offering Cope stamps and supermarket prices, particularly with high cost replacement of vans that could not justify themselves as they were losing too much money, we had logically to discontinue this service – nearly as old as the Cope itself..." 'From One Million Pounds to Five Million Pounds : 1975-1985' Staff Bulletin April 1985, Cope Archive.*

"...On the 27th I assisted Mr Gallagher and Mr O'Donnell in looking for a store. Two only seemed suitable – one on the station side of Dungloe, rented 2/6d a week, and the other in Dungloe rented £9 per annum. The latter seemed better, the only defect being that is was opposite John Sweeney's shop which might frighten people on fair and market days from going into the Store. The Templecrone have a profit from their nine months' trading of £30..."[5]

From the middle of 1907, not long after the search for a bigger Main Street store, the new Cope letterhead proclaimed:

THE TEMPLECRONE CO-OPERATIVE

AGRICULTURAL SOCIETY, Ltd.,

EGG and POULTRY EXPORTERS

General Grocers and Provision Dealers

Flour, Meal, Bran and Manure Stores

Boot, Shoe and Hardware Dealers

CLEENDERRY and DUNGLOE[6]

This is audacious stuff – virtually a declaration of war right across the street from one of their main rivals, John Sweeney's shop and little more than a year after starting in Cleendra. The Cope was bursting with confidence.

GROWING PAINS

However, it was not all plain sailing. The growth rate was of course to be welcomed but there are problems with any such rapid increase in trading, as any fast growing small business today would recognise. The Cope people were not accountants and it was their lack of any book-keeping skills which almost saw them go under.

After a year's trading, Cope Secretary John O'Donnell began to get worried and requested help from the IAOS, saying "...our business is increasing very fast..."[7] AE wrote to IAOS organiser Richmond Noble: "...Gallagher seems to be a very fine fellow, and I can only hope that the Society will be able to come out on top without financial difficulties overwhelming it..."[8]

---

5   *IAOS records, National Archives.*

6   *Cleenderry is how Cleendra was recorded on the c1830 Ordnance Survey maps (Dungloe was and still is recorded as Dunglow).*

7   *IAOS Records, National Archives, letter John O'Donnell to IAOS, 18th January 1907.*

8   *Ibid. File note from AE (George Russell) to Richmond Noble, 13th February 1907.*

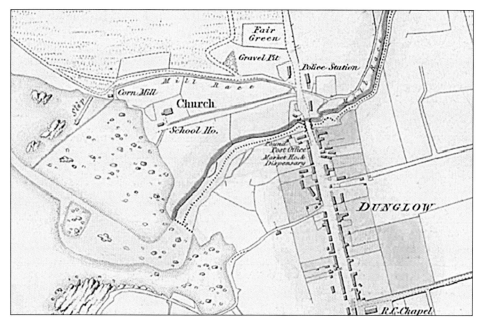

Dungloe from the Ordnance Survey's 1829-41 6" Series – the attractive colour is contemporary; Dungloe was mapped in c1835. At this time there were no more than 40-50 houses in Dungloe (Dunglow) and the population was relatively small compared to the islands (in the 1824 survey, Dungloe's population was 253 compared to the 1,442 living on the 11 inhabited islands off the Templecrone). The Fair Hill is called the Fair Green and just below it there is a gravel pit. The Pound is behind where the Northern Bank was later built and along the street are the Post Office, Market House and Dispensary. Both the Catholic chapel – it was replaced in c1856 and is now a very fine Ionad and Library – and the Church of Ireland by the Mill can be seen clearly marked. (Ordnance Survey of Ireland, www.osi.ie).

After several months of pleading for help with the accounts and getting an audit done, Paddy wrote to the IAOS himself in May 1907:

> "…our enemies they gombeen men is telling our members that (we they committee) are afraid of the auditor and that we do not intend to hold any annual meeting and that it is no Co-op at all that it is purely an ordinary Shop or Store and that the members has nothing to do with it needless to say this is doing our society a lot of injury. I hope you will send us one of your auditors as soon as possible of course our Society is prepared to pay him, Yours Truly Patrick Gallagher…"[9]

Help was not immediately forthcoming. By the end of 1907, the accounts were in a terrible mess. The IAOS appreciated the troubles that the Society were in but had their own worries building with the Department of Agriculture and Technical Instruction (DATI). They were about to lose their annual funding

---

9   *Ibid. Letter from Paddy the Cope to IAOS, 1st May 1907.*

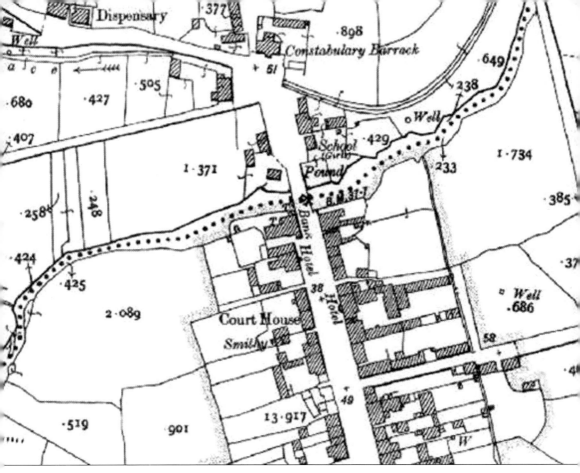

In the early part of the 19th century, the Ordnance Survey mapped certain more important towns – including 'Dunglow' - to a very detailed level: 25 inches to the mile (Burtonport and Maghery were also mapped in Templecrone to this detail). At the North end of Town, can be seen Sweeney's Hotel, Campbell's Hotel, the Northern Bank and a number of buildings now gone – the Girls' School next to where the Bayview is, the Pound, the Courthouse with the Smithy behind and a Dispensary on the road out of town. The early Cope established itself firstly in the garden and then house of Condy 'Klondike' – almost opposite Sweeney's Hotel – and then below the Courthouse in what had been a billiards room. It was starting its Dungloe life right in the middle of and under the gaze of the merchants whose very system it was challenging – bravery indeed! (From the Ordnance survey of Ireland mapping of Dungloe c1906, www.osi.ie)

and Horace Plunkett himself was forced to resign in 1907 from his role as vice president of the DATI. Helping co-operatives like Templecrone develop general grocery stores was very far outside their remit.

Nonetheless, Robert Anderson sent down the IAOS's Miss Reynolds to help but said she could not stay as "…its main business is a co-operative store…" Anderson wrote:

The Story of the Cope

"...It seems a thousand pities not to help these plucky people and save them from the disaster which is sure to ensue if their business is not systematised..."[10]

Anderson asked whether Harold Barbour, IAOS Board member, who had taken a particular interest in Templecrone Co-op, could help. Barbour, staunch friend of Paddy and the Cope, sent to Dungloe, from the Lisburn Co-operative, a Mr S McVeigh who was of great assistance and commented very positively on the Cope:

"...Nothing impressed me more than the spirit of independence displayed by management committee and all its members and their determination to promulgate the gospel of Co-operation in the district..."[11]

Between Mr McVeigh and Mr Swain, sent by the IAOS to do an audit, the accounts were put into order and disaster was averted. Pressure was applied by Anderson as Horace Plunkett was visiting Dungloe on 17th May 1908 and it was important for all to be satisfactory by then.[12]

The Cope had steered itself with help through a rocky period and were now set for steady expansion. Their leader was also becoming more of a public figure too. John O'Donnell informed the IAOS with some pleasure:

"...I am sure you will be delighted to learn that we see from the local paper here that our Mr Gallagher is the only person nominated on County council for the Dungloe portion of County and if the information is correct you may count on one Staunch Co-operator on Donegal County Council..."[13]

Paddy was a councillor for three years from 1908 until he lost in 1911 to John E. Boyle (by 559 votes to 337) in a famously fractious election he recounts in his autobiography. He puts down his losing to a concerted attempt by local traders who slandered the Cope and accused him of associating with Protestants and Unionists (Sir Horace Plunkett who later favoured Home Rule and Harold Barbour being the high profile examples) against the Home Rule cause. Paddy was no Unionist but his lack of prejudice in his business dealings were held against him unfairly. The Cope however was set for even greater success, beyond anybody's expectations.

---

10 Ibid. File note by Robert Anderson, 15th January 1908.

11 Ibid. Letter from Mr McVeigh to IAOS, 16th March 1908.

12 Ibid. Robert Anderson to Mr Swain, 7th April 1908.

13 Ibid. John O'Donnell to Robert Anderson, 17th April 1908.

A PERIOD OF EXPANSION

The Irish Homestead, which had been subsumed into the Irish Statesman in 1923, picks up the story in its 1924 pamphlet on the Templecrone Cope:

> "...The year 1910 saw the Society entrenched, one might say, in a single flat of very small dimensions; the present year sees it ensconced in the finest business premises in the village, and with five prospering branches covering an area extending six or eight miles on each side. In 1910 the business of the Society was confined to buying and selling for its members; since then it has gradually developed an industrial arm which promises soon to become its most important limb..."

THE CENTRAL STORE

> Up to 1912 the premises occupied by the Society were the merest makeshift, and the business, scattered over three or four different buildings, was badly handicapped. The Society this year secured a ten years' lease of a fine, commodious shop and stores, in which a very extensive business had previously been carried on. The new premises not only gave ample room for the rapidly growing business, but also held out inducements to new enterprises. Ample accommodation was provided for the storage of agricultural implements, timber, hardware, etc. A bakery was added in 1913 and continues to serve its members since. A tailoring department was added in 1915, and continued to do steady work for a year or so, when the work of the Society was handed over to a local cutter and member of the Society..."[14]

THE FIRST COPE STORES IN DUNGLOE

The Society's very first buildings in Dungloe were modest. In 1907, they moved to Condy Doherty's house on the Main Street. Condy, a family friend of Sally's, was going to be away in America for a few years. The store was in the back garden of where Doherty's restaurant stands today; it was little more than a storage shed. Very soon they took over a small upstairs room on the main Street, opposite Sweeney's Hotel. In 1909 they signed a lease with the landlord, Conyngham, to take premises in the ground floor of the Old Court House, which had been in use until then as a reading and billiards room. This became a very busy shop and turnover started to accelerate. Here they stayed until 1912 when they moved into much larger premises up the Main Street – what had been James Sweeney's store (James had died some years previously).

---

14 Irish Homestead pamphlet: 'The Templecrone Cope', 1924. Behind this simple statement lies a considerable drama which is developed in the original 1910 Irish Homestead series of articles (Appendix 1).

The tradition of marching bands and the riding of a white horse down Dungloe Main Street on St Patrick's Day is an old one. Indeed, Connie Devenney – Cope Committee member since 1969 – used to ride a white horse ahead of the Maghery band in recent memory. This much earlier image is from an original postcard dating to c1900-02. Sweeney's Hotel can be seen on the left with the light over the door. It is very possible that Cleendra and Maghery people, the future Cope founders, were in this parade as there is a huge crowd following the horse and rider. The St Patrick's Day festival was one of the last in the year before 'droves' of people, children too, headed off for the season to the Lagan or to Scotland. (Postcard, Mícheál O Dhomnaill Collection).

The Cope soon outgrew its first premises:

> "...Progress was rapid. By another change the proportions of the shop were increased by one foot each way, and a room overhead. The miscellaneous stock of boots, groceries and hams so completely filled the available space that the tall member found himself in a wilderness of hams, and for two of the more sturdily built members, passage in the aisle became a matter of nice adjustment! But nevertheless the society grew rapidly. The turnover doubled, membership increased, and non-members found it advantageous to trade. The pig business was taken up on a small scale for the benefits of the members. This was of advantage from the point of view of the member who was a producer and had given up the business as unprofitable, and the member who

The new Templecrone Co-operative Store on the Main Street in Dungloe, photographed in 1912. In comparison to the Cope's first small shop in Cleendra and the previous, rather humbler store further down the Main Street, these are very grand premises. On the left is Harold Barbour, Chairman of the Irish Agricultural Wholesale Society; in the centre, Paddy the Cope and on the right Mr Knox, President of the Belfast Cooperative Society. The shop had previously belonged to James Sweeney of Sweeney's Hotel Dungloe. The old shop name, in cut stone, is underneath and can be seen either side of the new Templecrone wooden board sign. (Harold Barbour Photograph Collection, University College Dublin Archives (UCDA P168).

The Story of the Cope

This postcard dating from c1920 advertises the wares of Barbour & Son. The Cope carried thread from the company's range and would no doubt have obtained the very best terms given the close relationship between Paddy the Cope and Harold Barbour (PB collection).

Harold Barbour (1874-1938), an important name in the Cope story, was elected to the Board of the IAOS in 1906, the year of the Cope's incorporation. Barbour & Son, created by his grandfather, was the largest thread-linen business in the world. Harold's father John helped set up the Lisburn Co-operative Society in 1881 and Harold became its President in 1900. Barbour was of great help to the Cope and became a strong ally of Paddy's. He became an early member of Templecrone Co-op and provided, from the Lisburn Co-op, expert financial help, to set up proper book-keeping, in 1907 when the Cope's rapid rise in turnover threatened to overwhelm them. Barbour was a regular visitor to Dungloe and helped Paddy with business connections and any other help the Cope needed from time to time (Local collection in the Rosses)

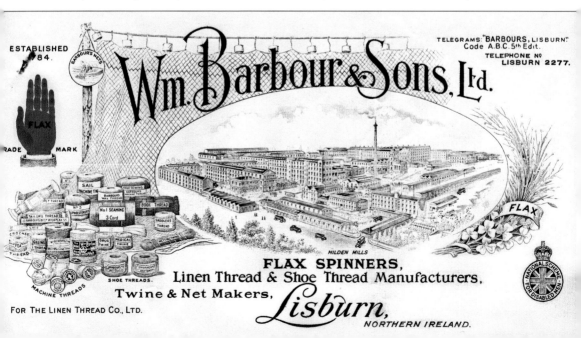

In this c1908 view of Dungloe, taken from the old Barracks, with the mill race running across the foreground, a man is leading a horse and cart laden down with crates. It is very tempting to see this as the early Cope 'tea van' or perhaps a Cope cart laden with eggs heading for Dungloe Road station, some four miles away – but it may as easily be Sweeney's Hotel cart or one from the other Dungloe hotels or merchants. The thatched cottage on the left is gone; the two storey building (now the Bayview) was then also a public house. Beyond the 'Bayview' can be seen a one storey cottage (probably the Girls' School marked on the OS maps), then a gap in the wall

where the Pound was located (straying animals – or ones sold at the Fair – were kept here). At the time, there were no buildings whatsoever over the Dungloe River – these were built on much later. On the right, the scene is also much changed – the slate roofed cottage is gone; the two storey building has been joined by others and Charlie Bonner's shop. Up the street, a postman is passing the time of day with a shopkeeper; the shadows give the time as late afternoon, early evening (Signal Series postcard, posted in July 1910, PB Collection)

One of the first cars to drive into Dungloe was a 1904-made Lanchester, made in Armourer Mills, Montgomery Street, Birmingham. The car's number plate, O-1645, helps identify the place and date of registration; 'O' is for Birmingham and the number gives a likely registration date of c1907. It would have cost c£600, a huge amount then (in modern day terms in excess of €200,000). James Sweeney & Co's shop is the first on the right hand side (behind the blurred figure of a boy) – the Cope moved into these much bigger premises in 1912. Apart from the Revd S A Orr on the left, it has, sadly, not been possible to identify the individuals in the photo for this publication. Perhaps someone reading the book will recognise the faces or the car. Packie Bonner writing in 1981 speculated that the first car in the Rosses was probably brought here by Capt John Herdsman, of Sion Mills, Tyrone, who built the house on Edernish Island as a summer residence (Lawrence Collection, L_ROY_09425, National Photographic Archive)

was a consumer. Likewise the society purchased spraying materials and spraying machines, which they rented out to members. Weeks later the Department and the Donegal Agricultural Committee sent out the same materials, but these came too late to deal effectively with the potato blight which had already appeared. The value of the local organisation over the outside agency was indicated in this practical way. Also a small threshing machine was purchased by the society and rented to members..."[15]

The miraculous progress of the Templecrone Co-operative did not go unnoticed. Word went round and a constant stream of visitors, from other co-operatives

---

15 *Rural Reconstruction in Ireland: A Record of Co-operative Organisation, L. Smith-Gordon and L. C. Staples, 1917, P.S. King & Son Ltd, London.*

The Story of the Cope

and from the IAOS, who also sent researchers, students and journalists from all over the world up to Dungloe.

Sir Horace Plunkett and Harold Barbour visited Templecrone frequently from 1907. From its earliest days, the Cope was admired and praised by the IAOS leadership and held up as a shining example of what could be done with cooperation.

SIR HORACE PLUNKETT IN DONEGAL 1910

Address to Templecrone Society

"...Sir Horace Plunkett, accompanied by Mr. and Mrs. Harold Barbour, and Mr. Anderson, Secretary, IAOS, paid a visit to the Templecrone Society on Monday, 21st ult [March 21st 1910] A meeting was held in the Courthouse, Dungloe, presided over by Mr. Patrick Gallagher, president of the society.

Amongst those present at the meeting were Mrs. Maxwell, president of the Iniscoo Society; Mr. Coppin, president of the Gweedore Society; Mr. O'Donnell, president of the Inniskeal Society; Mr. K. J. Brennan, secretary of the Agricultural Bank; the Rev. Mr. Orr, Rectory, Maghery; Mr. Albert Swain, and Mr. McGlinchy, auditors, IAOS, etc., etc. A letter of apology was received from the Rev. Father Sheridan, C.C., regretting his inability to be present.

Mr. Gallagher welcomed the visitors to Dungloe, and said he was glad to be able to inform Sir Horace and those present that the balance-sheet of the society for 1909 which Mr. Swain had just prepared and which he would read for them, showed that the society was still flourishing.

Sir Horace Plunkett, who received an enthusiastic greeting, said that there were now in Ireland between 900 and 1,000 societies, and with such a large number he and his friends were only able to get into personal contact with those societies which required some special h elp, or for some other special reason. The latter had brought them here. They in Dublin were especially interested in the Templecrone Society, not because it was the most important from a business point of view, but because it had faced and surmounted difficulties greater than any other, perhaps, in Ireland. It was almost incredible that a society in one of the most congested districts should, after three years, be able to show a turnover of £9,000, and with a considerable profit. It was a remarkable achievement, and he never expected such a treat. He was not going to give them any advice in managing their business; they had shown themselves that they understood the needs of the people, and knew how to supply them.

This postcard photograph of Lower Main Street Dungloe, the area called Bridgend, dates from c1920 and shows: on the right, Sweeney's Hotel and John Sweeneys' shop; on the left Campbells' hotel and the Northern Bank; and at the back, the old RIC barracks. Outside Sweeney's shop a dog is sleeping, a horse and cart is waiting and two young boys are loitering. The transition to motor vehicles is under way with two motor cars on the street. The Cope's first premises in Dungloe in 1907 were opposite John Sweeney's shop. By 1912, the Cope had moved higher up Main Street to where it still is today, albeit with a much larger footprint (Contemporary postcard, courtesy Donegal County Museum's postcard collection in Letterkenny)

BRIDGEND , DUNGLOE.

He went on to show why he attached so much importance to the society. They were not so much interested in the profits which they had made. They attached much more importance to the educative effect of the movement. He had been preaching for the past 20 years that no matter what Governments can do for the farmers, they can do much more for themselves by combination, and, moreover, by organising themselves they can get the Government to do more for them. The Recess Committee, appointed in 1895, studied the conditions in nine European countries which were at first oppressed but which are now prosperous. They inquired how far this improvement was owing to the work of the Government and how much to their own efforts, and they invariably found that the Government Departments had done very little in comparison to the work done by the farmers themselves through co-operation.

He looked upon the life of a farming community from three points of view. First, farming is a science. This part of the work is being looked after by the Department of Agriculture. Second, farming is a business; for there is no use in farmers producing better things by the aid of science if they do not market these things better. The Recess Committee had made several comparisons between home and foreign methods of marketing, and came to the conclusion that until the Irish farmer can market his produce as well as the foreigner all his other efforts are useless. But those who look at its purely business aspect will not have altogether solved the problem of rural life. They'd do to supply rural life with some of the amusements and attractions that drew people to the towns.

He was glad to see that they were getting on with the erection of the Village Hall, and he hoped it would do a great deal towards supplying those amusements and attractions. Out of all the 900 societies in all Ireland, he was glad the Templecrone was among the six worthiest of these free grants, and not one of the Selecting Committee ever questioned the decision of placing it not only among the six, but first among them. He concluded by conveying to the meeting an expression from Father Finlay of regret at being unable to be with them.

Mr. Swain read the report and balance-sheet to the meeting, and explained the different items.

Mrs. Barbour, who had come specially to visit the Templecrone Society, expressed her delight at being amongst them…"[16]

---

16 *Irish Homestead, 2nd April 1910. Robert Anderson in a contemporary IAOS file note remarked "…Among the things accomplished we find the following items: a village hall, two horses and delivery vans, a savings bank, sows for breeding and a boar for service, sale of the members' eggs, oats, pigs, and other farm produce, a market for woollen goods and other local industries, and spraying machines kept in stock for members…" IAOS Records, National Archives.*

Growth in Turnover 1906-23

The Cope provided audited returns to the IAOS every year from 1906 onwards; the details were published in the Irish Homestead. Financial returns after 1923 are not as easily got from public records.[17] The Tan War and the Civil War that followed caused massive disruption to the Co-Operative movement; the Black and Tans targeted creameries in particular but the Cope was not excluded from the conflict.

The Cope enjoyed huge prosperity during this period. Wartime (1914-1918) in particular was a boom time for co-operatives like Templecrone: the Knitting Factory was in full production, catering for the British Army and Navy – and Belgian and Indian Armies too); farm produce prices were much higher; and there was much more spending money around.

The new Cope branches and the wartime economy helped turnover increase between 1913 and 1920 by almost 600%, a quite staggering rate of growth. However, the 1920 figure was the high water point for some considerable time; after this, turnover stagnated and then later declined.[18]

YEAR	MEMBERS	TURNOVER
1906	65	£381
1907	101	£5,234
1908	140	£7,048
1909	161	£8,219
1910	187	£11,093
1911	209	£12,063
1912	210	£13,655
1913	219	£13,948
1914	219	£15,573
1915	219	£21,603
1916	359	£34,731
1917	359	£56,616
1918	381	£74,893
1919	538	£78,630
1920	643	£98,393
1921	780	£93,912
1922	804	£91,079
1923	825	£91,361

Note: these audited figures on the left, published in the Irish Homestead, differ slightly, particularly in the earlier years, from figures quoted in various Cope publications, e.g. in Paddy's 'My Story' he has the audited turnover in 1906 as £490 not £381 (Paddy also states the Cope's wages bill was zero in 1906).

At this rate of growth it is no wonder that the local traders were alarmed. Every pound of Cope turnover and every pound of local produce (eggs, woollen goods etc) that the Cope bought in for resale was money that came straight off the traders' bottom line. Within a very short period of time, in excess of £10,000 a year was no longer flowing into the traders' accounts. Significant price competition had also been introduced. The 'gombeen' system, which had existed for decades, had been completely undermined, never to return, by the fearless insurgents who had come down from the mountains.

---

17 *File notes in the IAOS records (National Archives, Bishop Street) do provide additional information for the period 1923-1950).*

18 *In modern day values, the 1920 turnover is £2.6 million using the CPI (€3.9m euro at 2006 exchange rates) or £11.9 million inflated by average earnings (€17.6m euro, ditto).*

A FISHING PARTY AT DUNGLOE.

Dungloe in the nineteenth and early 20th centuries was a popular spot for sportsmen who came for the excellent fishing in the lakes and rivers of the Rosses and Gweedore - and, something that would be frowned upon today, shooting seals off the rocks in Dungloe Bay! Campbell's Hotel was one of several – Boyle's and Sweeney's were others – which catered for sporting tourists. This view of a Fishing Party comes from Edgar Shrubsole's 'Picturesque Donegal: Its Mountains Rivers and Lakes' (1908); this and its sister volume 'The Land of Lakes: Sport and Touring in Co Donegal' (1906) were sponsored by the railway companies (The Great Northern and The Midland) and provide detailed and informative descriptions of the county (PB Collection)

BETWEEN THE WARS AND AFTERWARDS

The Cope exited the First World War in a very healthy position with strong businesses, deposits and a huge confidence in their enterprise. This time of rapid expansion was to come to a sudden end for many cooperatives in the 1920s with the post-war series of Depressions.

The Cope, however, carried on and indeed expanded into new businesses. It bought the mill in Meenmore from the Conyngham Estate in 1921 (transfer of title dragged on for a number of years), began milling and brought electricity to Dungloe. It kept expanding with new branches in Kincasslagh in 1919, Burtonport 1921 and Annagry 1923. It also explored activities as wide as granite quarrying and net-making.

However, the Cope was more fortunate than other parts of Ireland, where the disruption of the War of Independence and the Civil War caused many to go under. The Cope's relative good fortune was commented upon:

> "…In conversation with Mr. Paddy Gallagher the other day, I was glad to hear that the work of the famous Templecrone Co-operative Society has not been adversely affected by the events of recent years. This was particularly welcome when the newspapers of the same day pointed out that some 210 co-operative societies in Ireland had gone out of existence since the Free State came into being.
>
> The fame of Mr. Gallagher has spread far and wide, and it is not by any means confined to Ireland. As "Paddy the Cope" his fame has been spread in books and pamphlets wherever the cooperative idea is practiced or studied. The United States is as familiar: with the name as is India or Egypt; everywhere the name is known but only in Donegal is the kindly, big-hearted man known for what he is…"[19]

Donegal writer Seamus McManus writes of very modern hands-on businessman:

A PRESENT-DAY PICTURE OF PADDY THE COPE

> "…Mr. Patrick Gallagher sitting in his bright office, looking out upon the wild and rocky mountainside to the right, and the crashing, crag-bound Atlantic to the left, suspended his dictation of business letters upon his electric-run Dictaphone. "A mortal fine convenience and time-saver for a busy man." he said, while he called for the books and book-keeper, and had her extract these figures for me. I confess that, though I was prepared for much from what I had heard of the famed Paddy the Cope, the Dictaphone in the wildest corner of our Donegal's wild mountains, dumbfounded me! But after seeing and knowing a little more of this rare genius, Paddy Gallagher, I think that no future developments in connection with him will ever surprise me again…"[20]

Turnover stayed for a number of years at around the £90,000 mark but started to decline by 1927. Profits were hit badly – in 1921 on a turnover of £93,919, there was a profit of just £41. This badly affected the Cope's ability to support the IAOS and the correspondence between the two parties (and between the IAOS and other co-operatives) became very strained. During the good years, the Cope and its members were very forthcoming with special subscriptions desperately needed to keep the IAOS afloat. In 1909, for example, the Cope's

---

19 *Irish Times 15th November 1928. The Dictaphone must have been a godsend to Paddy who had always had trouble with reading and writing since being hired out at the age of 9 and missing his schooling.*

20 *Seamus McManus, writing about Templecrone Cope and Paddy in an extended profile in 'The Catholic World' of New York, subsequently republished in The Derry Journal July 9th 1930.*

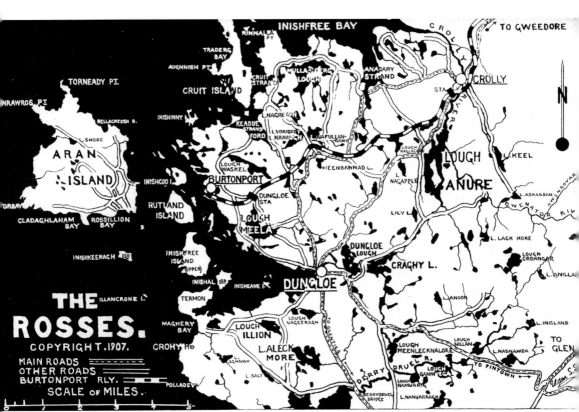

In this 1907 map of 'The Rosses', from Edgar Shrubsole's 'Picturesque Donegal' the key features identified are the rivers and lakes for sportsmen. A ford is marked by Keadue Strand. At this stage there was neither a road around the strand (that came in 1938) nor a bridge into Cruit (1911). Paddy the Cope had a lifelong love of fishing, whether inland or at sea; one of the scrapes he tells of in his autobiography, when he was accused (wrongly) of doing away with the Minister is when he was out fishing above Cleendra. (PB Collection).

140 members voluntarily paid a total of £7 10 shillings over and above their normal registration fees. Voluntary subscriptions continued at this level all the way through till 1920. The Cope did what they could to help, more in proportion than other co-operatives, but these were increasingly difficult times.[21]

Turnover reached a low point of £64,680 in 1932, a reduction of over 34% from 1920.[22] By this time, the world was reeling from the Great Depression and Ireland's Economic War with Britain (over annuity payments) had severely reduced trade between the two countries. An IAOS visitor to Dungloe reported that trade had seen a downturn:

---

21 *IAOS and IAWS records, National Archives, various years.*

22 *Ibid. It may be a coincidence but Paddy was confined to bed with serious knee trouble from March 1932 with as he says "…not much hope a recovery…" He was incapacitated through this year which could account for part of the relatively poor business performance.*

"...During my visit Mr Gallagher had to refuse orders for thousands of pairs of knitted gloves from England for lack of space and machinery to fulfil orders. This is very regrettable as the British tariffs have hampered the sale of Continental goods of this description..."[23]

Through it all, the Cope and Paddy worked hard to keep the businesses going. Paddy, whose salary had by then reached £250 a year, voluntarily cut his pay to £200 to show a good example. He was still always on the lookout for ways to expand, as these two examples, among many, illustrate:

"...We are interested in Angora Rabitts and would like to have a few..."[24]

"...we expect to have 2-3 tons of black face mountain sheep wool, unwashed, for sale..."[25]

The Plunkett Foundation gave a good summary of the Cope's position as it entered the 1930s:

"...This society is the oldest of the Donegal societies and is well known for its striking success and the variety of its achievements. It was formed in 1906 in a congested district on the coast, where farms are extremely small and the farmers are accustomed to eke out their livelihood by harvest work in England and Scotland and in some cases by fishing. Potatoes and a declining quantity of oats are grown locally, and cattle, pigs and poultry are kept. The society now has six branches and serves a strip of country roughly 16 by 6 miles.

After carrying on the business of a general store for some years and also purchasing produce of various kinds from the farmer, the society opened a knitting factory to give employment to girls. It also provides electric current from its own hydraulic plant and provides the village with light. It experimented with flax scutching but conditions were unfavourable.

The members of the society number 800 and there are some 600 non-member customers. Share capital stands at £1,839; there are deposits of £17,553; a bank overdraft of £9,739 and reserves of £3,478. Much of the capital is employed in the knitting factory. Plant and premises are valued at about £9,000.

The largest item in the society's business is the sale of meal and flour, followed by groceries. The trade in seeds and manures is comparatively small. All kinds of domestic goods, hardware and building materials,

---

23 IAOS Records, National Archives, File note 1932.

24 Ibid. Paddy the Cope to IAOS, 23rd January 1928.

25 Ibid. Paddy the Cope to IAOS, 17th May 1940. Paddy was keen to sell through a Scottish wool grower's group and wanted the IAOS to help.

Dungloe. *Co. Donegal.*

Dungloe has a very rural look in this view from the Caravan Road, above St Peter's Church – unlike today, there are no houses along the Caravan Road. Most small towns, certainly in Donegal at this time, c1908, and indeed across Ireland and Britain, would have looked the same, with countryside, tilled land and animals kept in gardens right up to the Main Street (PB Collection, Lawrence, Dublin postcard).

Postcards became very popular in the early years of the 20th Century; every town and accessible scenic area would have been photographed. Islands were much less likely to have been the subject of tourist postcards and are now very scarce. This view, dating from c1908, looks down from the Fair Hill - Sally the Cope's home was just behind where the photograph was taken. Above the town can be seen St Peter's Church, dating from 1856.The town itself is really little more than the Main Street with a few cottages out along what became the Carnmore Road (PB Collection, published by Lawrence, Dublin)

and fishermen's gear are also sold. Heavy goods and some groceries are delivered.

Sales to members represent 90% of the business, but the society also buys eggs, which are collected in the branches and candled and graded in three grades and shipped by the central store. Other purchases are pork on a small scale; wool, which is forwarded to a Bradford broker; and herrings, which are cured and exported to Germany or New York. The society has a mill which is used for maize and also for local oats, the system of payment being the payment of one stone in twenty to the society. There is also a central bakery, from which bread is sent to the branches. Goods are bought both from the IAWS and the SCWS. Heavy goods are usually brought by sea from Liverpool, the society chartering a coaster every six weeks.

The knitting factory was based on a hand-knitting industry and now employs 72 girls. A start was made in 1911 with gloves, but all types of knitted goods are now produced and sold in Dublin, London and abroad. Electric plant for lighting the village was installed in 1923.

The turnover of the society in 1929 was £80,957, of which £12,000 was accounted for by the knitting factory. Excluding this figure the average turnover per member is £80 and per customer £50. Credit is reduced to a small amount. The turnover per £1 share capital is £44, and per £ total capital £2 10s. Running costs amount to not quite 10% of turnover. A profit was made in 1929 and a dividend of 1s in the £ was made on purchases other than heavy goods.

The society has been an important influence on the economic life of the district, which it has greatly changed for the better, an achievement which has not been without social consequences..."[26]

Trading picked up after 1938 and through the Emergency although at nothing like the rate of increase the Cope had seen up until 1920. Turnover in 1945, the year of the devastating fire in Dungloe, was £156,151 and there was a return to profit. The next twenty years saw steady improvement. In 1975, annual turnover breached the £1m mark for the first time and ten years later, turnover exceeded £5m.

The Growth of the Main Store 1969 to the present day

Dungloe Cope in the 1960s, after its founder had passed on in 1966, was still essentially the same frontage as that rebuilt after the 1945 fire. At the back of the shop was a collection of buildings on top of each other, with

---

26 'Agricultural Co-operation in Ireland: A Survey' Nov 1931 by 'The Plunkett Foundation'.

The Quay Road, Dungloe in the 1920s. On the right hand side the first building is the very fine, cut granite Cope Hall. It was built in 1910 with a £200 grant awarded by the Pembroke Irish Charities Fund in 1908 for the 'education and recreation' for the town of Dungloe – Templecrone was one of only six co-operatives in Ireland so honoured, a real accolade for the Cope. The shed next to it contained all the tools, and maintenance spares for the Cope's electricity generation plant at the mill (from 1923). Paddy had the small cottage at the end built for Sally and himself in c1910 – Sally had been lonely in Cleendra when Paddy had moved the shop to Dungloe in 1907. They never lived here though as in 1912 the Cope took over James Sweeney's Main Street shop and Paddy and Sally and their family lived above the shop. The land along this side of the Quay Road was bought from Daniel Sweeney, the Roshine schoolteacher who was also secretary of the Cope. The hall was opened by the Rev Tom Finlay, joint Chairman with Horace Plunkett of the IAOS It was dubbed the 'New Orange Hall' by the Cope's rivals in Dungloe; Harold Barbour and Horace Plunkett, the leading lights in the Co-Operative movement, who with the Rev Finlay had given such great support to the Cope, were both Unionists and Protestants. Rev. Finlay re-assured the assembly at the launch that he had said Mass that morning in Dungloe. (Seán Boner collection, contemporary postcard).

Dungloe Bay

The Story of the Cope

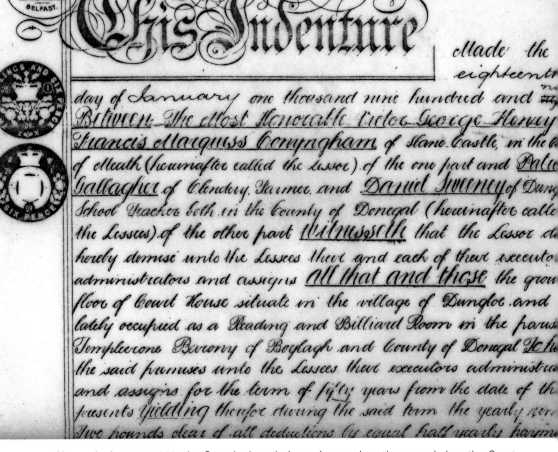

Above: In January 1909, the Cope had made its main premises the room below the Court House opposite Sweeney's Hotel; it had been in use as a Reading Room and Billiards Hall. The lessor was the Marquis of Conyngham, the local Landlord, of Slane Castle; Paddy the Cope and Cope Secretary Daniel Sweeney were the lessees. The rent was set at £5 a year, clear of all expenses, with the Cope required to keep the place in good order and insured against fire. The rent was modest enough (the Cope's turnover in 1909 had grown rapidly to over £8,000), and the lease period was 50 years. However, they were not to stay that long here before moving up the road to much grander premises (Lease courtesy of Dinny Doherty, Meenmore; Dinny found the lease in the premises which he took over and has since developed).

Right Top: The Cope Stamp is a survival from the Dungloe store's very earliest times. It was used to provide an official stamp on sales, which would then be countersigned. It has been preserved as part of the Cope Archive.

Right Bottom: This 'draft' invoice, dating from 1924, is in Daniel Sweeney, the Cope Secretary's hand. It may have been drafted in preparation for delivering a very large order or alternatively represent a list of 'bought in' items from suppliers. The individual prices seem today very low, e.g. oil at 1 shilling and 4 pence per gallon which roughly equates to about 2p a litre (a gallon is about 4.5 litres). Food is in relative terms appears expensive although cheap in today's terms – for both figures, however, one has to allow for both inflation and growth in incomes to make a proper comparison. The Cope's letter heading advertises 'Manufacturers of Machine and Hand-Knit Goods'. The Telegraphic Address is "Co-operative Society, Dungloe" (Cope Letter Book, Jim the Cope Collection, Cope Archive)

TELEGRAPHIC ADDRESS "CO-OPERATIVE SOCIETY, DUNGLOE."

MEMORANDUM FROM
THE TEMPLECRONE CO-OPERATIVE AGRICULTURAL SOCIETY LIMITED.

MANUFACTURERS
OF MACHINE
AND HAND-KNIT
GOODS.

DUNGLOE.............................192
CO. DONEGAL.

To..

Invoice

5½ doz Bread at 5/- per doz
14 lbs Butter @ 2/4 per lb
115 7ot pokes Flour @ 15/9 each
105 gals oil @ 1/4 per gal
1½ doz Globes at 6ᵈ each
1 cwt Cream Tartar @ 1/4 per lb
2 bags Bran at 12/6 each
1 bag onions (112 lbs @ 2ᵃ per lb
8 lbs upper leather @ 3/4 " "
4 boxes cakes (1040) @ ½ᵈ each
4 cwt sugar @ 65/4 per cwt
136 lbs Tea @ 3/8 per lb
12 cwt Indian Meal at 12/6 per c

The Cope's Main Street store was opened in 1912; this image is believed to date from c1918-20. The Cope took out a lease on this building in 1912; it had belonged before then to James Sweeney. We do not have the names of the eight shop staff but their number make it clear just how busy and successful a business it had become in a short time. Paddy is in the doorway, cap on his head. The advert/notice in the window announces a 'Pat McEntee'. (Cope Collection)

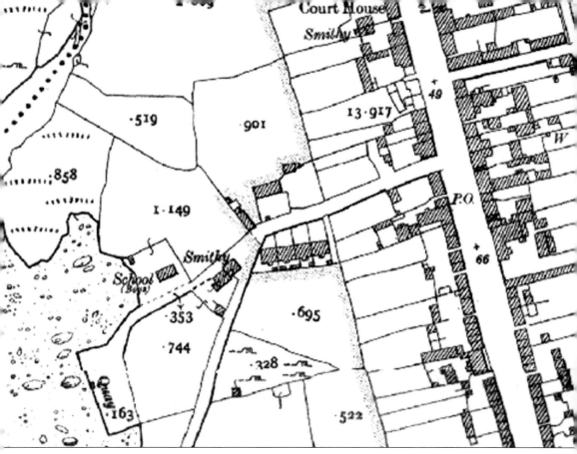

This Ordnance Survey map of the Quay Road dates from c1906 (certainly pre 1910 as the Cope Hall does not appear) and shows where the Cope had bought Daniel Sweeney's land. There is a Boys' School and a Quay (giving its name to the road) just down past the Smithy. '...In order to get a horse shod in those days, it was highly advisable that one should go to the smithy or forge at an early hour, if at all possible. It was known of some men who would make a point of being there between seven or eight in the morning, so that they would be among the first customers of the day. At certain times of the year —say, from March until September — the smith had seldom an idle moment. In the case of Roarty's forge, at the Quay Road, very often there would be a line of horses waiting to be shod, stretching all the way from the forge up to the O'Donnell Buildings...' (Packie Bonner, writing in 1981; map courtesy of the Ordnance Survey of Ireland)

The Story of the Cope

very little room to move. The start of the big expansion was the opening of the Cope supermarket in 1969, a very bold and visionary move at the time, something completely new to West Donegal.

The period 1975-79 was also one of major change. Turnover increased to over £1m a year in 1975 (in fact to £1.17m). The sequence of aerial photos taken in the 1970s and 1980s (illustrated) show the extent of the changes.

Cope General Manager Cyril Winder captured the pace of change and development from the mid 1970s:

> "...In 1975, the Lough Swilly Bus Depot next door was taken over, demolished and rebuilt into the Menswear Department, which is still there today. The next year, 1976, the Cope House next door on the other side was taken over, demolished and incorporated into the old main shop, with a new Furniture Department and offices. The floors were raised and a completely new, long frontage was added to the buildings and the Main Entrance was moved along. A new telephone system was put in, increasing the number of lines from 2 to 28.
>
> In 1980, three sites were bought behind the Main Street premises; these were excavated, levelled to make the Cope Car Park, a very useful addition to both the Cope, giving it a separate rear entrance from Chapel Road, and Dungloe. A dedicated Cope garage for servicing our own vehicles was built at the north end.
>
> In 1982 the property adjacent to the supermarket was bought and incorporated in 1983 with a completely new facia cladding across all the main buildings in the Main Street..."[27]

The closure of the Knitting (1983) and Bakery (1984) businesses allowed the Builders' Providers to expand further to occupy the footprint it had until 2006.

John McCarthy, a writer and journalist who lived at the Rectory in Maghery, described the Cope in the 1970s:

The "Cope": Success Story from the Rosses

> "...SOME 200 MILES from Dublin, tucked away in a remote, barren but beautiful scenic section of North West dour Donegal, lies the Rosses. A romantically rugged, rural, veritable picture postcard area spread from the Atlantic coast towns of Gweedore and Gweebarra and extending inland to include mountainous Doochary.

---

27 *1985 Staff Bulletin: "From One Million Pounds to Five Million Pounds: 1975-1985". Cyril Winder was General Manager from 1969 to 1993.*

Dungloe, a tiny, tidy town with less than a 1,000 people, but with two sizeable year-round hotels and 13 pubs, is the capital of the Rosses. There is located the thriving Templecrone Co-Operative Society Ltd., founded in 1906 by the late Patrick Gallagher, internationally known as Paddy the Cope which was the title of his autobiography, a best seller in a hard cover book years ago and still a salient seller today as a paperback. From its first day in business some 66 years ago with a handful of shareholders, the Templecrone Co-Op, with its present 1,398 shareholders, has been a highly successful operation.

Last year, Templecrone Co-Op did a volume of £600,000. Ordinarily, co-operatives are not supposed to make a profit, but Templecrone not only did make a profit of 1½% but also paid interest to its large share-holding group. Besides, as traditionally practiced, the 1½% profit went back into expanding Templecrone's already large-scale business. The Templecrone Co-op today is a three-fold operation with a manufacturing, a wholesale and a retail division with some six branches which cover the Donegal Rosses like the proverbial dew.

EACH DIVISION and each branch caters to the multiple daily needs and long term requirements of progressive people in enterprising rural communities. Their every want is anticipated and taken care of in a modern, brisk business-like fashion. For instance, in Dungloe, Templecrone has a supermarket of some 20,000 square feet on the Main Street stocked with every conceivable type of merchandise and internationally known brands…"[28]

The last 20-25 years, since the closure of the Bakery and the Knitting Factory and the move of the Builders' Providers to the Quay Road, have been relatively stable in terms of building work. Some modernisations have taken place, for example the new Carpets and Furniture extension, but the latter and the big developments at Sheskinarone Road and in Dungloe, as well as Annagry, Kincasslagh and Lettermacaward have all been developed in recent times.

Fate intervened in 2006 when the supermarket caught fire, necessitating a major unplanned redevelopment. The opportunity was taken to take a radical approach and create a new Sports shop and a fully modernised supermarket. Above the two shops is 16,000 square feet of space for expansion or renting.

The Dungloe Cope is in a strong position with its in-store facilities, including the post office, car park and central position. Despite the radically different trading conditions, compared to 1907 when the first tentative steps were taken in Dungloe, the new stores offer great future opportunities for the Cope and for the people of Dungloe.

---

28 *Irish Times* November 16th 1972.

DUNGLOE, CO. DONEGAL

This is a postcard view of Dungloe from the 1950s with empty crates outside the Bayview on the left and a cluster of buildings now built over the Dungloe River beyond. Opposite, the small cottage built at an angle in the earlier c1910 view is now gone. There do not appear to be many good 'Cope' photographs featuring Dungloe between c1920-1945, possibly these were lost in the fire of 1945. Postcard views of the 1920-30s typically look down the town from around the Boyle's Hotel, Midway area (Mícheál O Dhomnaill Collection)

This view of Dungloe in the mid 1950s has Auctioneer and Fish Buyer James Campbell in the doorway of "C O'Donnell's", where James's son, Paddy Andy, has Campbell's Auctioneer's today. In front is a Ford Anglia (model E494A) number plate IH 8748 and across the road is The Medical Hall where in 1907 one of the first Cope shops was located. (National Photographic Archive, Valentine's photograph VR 8141)

DUNGLOE, CO. DONEGAL   VR 8141.   NO. 2

DUNGLOE, CO. DONEGAL VR 8142. NO. 1

This Valentine's photograph dates from the 1950s. The Cope's Main Street building can be seen on the right hand side. There is a petrol pump selling Esso on the pavement and behind can be seen the Lough Swilly Depot which the Cope was to buy in 1975, demolish and build the then new Menswear department (National Photographic Archive, Valentine's photograph VR 8142)

Dungloe from Upper Main Street with, on the right hand side, the Cope shop, rebuilt after the devastating Bakery fire in 1945 which threatened the whole town. Two petrol pumps can be seen outside the shop – long since gone. Paddy slept in the second bedroom from the right, sharing the house with his son Packie and his family after his wife Sally died in 1948. Paddy lived on for another 18 years (National Photographic Archive).

Outside the shop in Dungloe in 1955 are Michael Wallace, Packie Bonner, Jimmy Brown and Cathal McCole. The occasion was the launching of the Cope as main distributors for Calor Gas. (Photograph by lifelong Cope employee and Cope Committee member since 1973, Hughie McGee, who has taken some very fine 'social history' photographs of the Cope over the years)

Main Street Dungloe 1956. Cope staff Jim Boyle, Cathal McCole and Connie Boyle 'unloading a delivery of goods for the Cope'. The occasion is a cigarette promotion by Player's. The Cope dwelling house, where Paddy lived with his son Packie, Packie's wife Mary and their family, is on the left of the picture. (Hugh McGee photograph)

ST. CRONE'S TERRACE AND MILL ROAD, DUNGLOE VR.8144   NO.B

This postcard view, photographed from above St Crone's Terrace on the road out of Dungloe to Maghery, dates from the early 1950s. The Cope's Mill buildings are across the bay; milling had stopped some years earlier but electricity generation continued till 1956, when the ESB took over the responsibility (Valentine's photograph VR 8114, National Photographic Archive).

Dungloe in the mid to late 1950s, in a postcard photograph taken just above the Bayview. On the left is Charlie Boyle's house, which is just in front of the old barracks. By this time, buildings had been constructed over the Dungloe River. Although still nothing like as busy as today, motor cars had started to appear in more numbers in this decade (PB Collection).

MAIN STREET DUNGLOE

Previous Page: Paddy the Cope is standing outside the Cope in Dungloe in 1949. He is very well dressed for the Irish Times newspaper photographer; a long article about him and the Templecrone Co-op was later published in The Irish Times. One of Paddy's more charming and unassuming characteristics was that he was not normally one for dressing up and caring too much about his appearance. He was certainly no dandy and was quite happy wearing old clothes and 'pumps' as many have commented when remembering him. Next door can be seen the Lough Swilly Depot which the Cope was to buy and extend into in 1975. 'Square Tack', the sign in the window, was a brand of tobacco (Failte Ireland photo)

Right: Before it was officially opened, the new Cope supermarket's very first customer was James McNelis of Purt, Burtonport; here he is, snapped as he wandered past the new store. Later in the day, a huge crowd attended the official supermarket opening. Mary Deery, wife of the then Cope Chairman Dan Deery, did the honours (Mrs Deery can be seen at the door 'with the hat') with Canon O'Callaghan performing the blessing ceremony (Both photographs are by Hughie McGee, current Cope Committee member).

Below: The Cope's supermarket, a radical innovation at that time for West Donegal, opened on 31st May 1969. This newspaper advert has some interesting prices; it was just before the runaway inflation of the 1970s: (converted, without adjusting for inflation, to euro cents at €1 = 80p, for ease of understanding) 2 lbs sugar, 10c; large packet of cornflakes, 12c; a frozen chicken, 59c; 'Banded' 18 piece tea sets, €1.31. The supermarket was a massive success and a good example of a clear vision, well executed; one of the Cope's many fine achievements (Cope Archive)

THE COPE MAKES HISTORY AGAIN — DUNGLOE'S ONLY REAL SUPERMARKET

OPENING SATURDAY, 31st MAY

OPEN
WHIT MONDAY
ALL DAY.

Monday to Friday, 9 a.m. to 6 p.m.   Saturday, 9 a.m. to 9 p.m.

* Two and a Half Thousand Square Feet.
* Twenty-two Feet Refrigeration.
* Well Laid Out for Comfortable Shopping.
* Heating and Ventilation a feature.

* Full Ranges including Catering.
* Barbeque Chickens.
* Low Price Policy.
* All Stocks Clearly Marked.

the Cope

Templecrone Co-Operative Society Ltd.

Dungloe 5.

Supermarket, Drapery, Hardware, Furniture and Builders' Providers.

Opening Offers and Samples of our Price Policy

All these prices available in our Branches too

TEA .... 1/- OFF ALL BRANDS.	FROZEN CHICKENS 9/6	CALVE CORN OIL, 32-oz. 5/-	LARGE DRIVE 2/6
SUGAR, 2-lbs. 1/7	OLD ENGLISH MARMALADE/	BOLANDS RICH TEA / CREAM	RUBBER GLOVES 2/-
BUTTER, per lb. 4/8	CHIVERS STRAWBERRY JAM 2/-	CRACKERS 11d	DELSEY TWIN PACK 1/8
CORNFLAKES (Large) 1/10	JELLIES, Two for 1/6	CHOICE BANANAS, per lb. 1/2	SERVIETTES, Pkts. of 100 ...... 2/-
MAXWELL / NESCAFE, 2-oz. 3/6	S.P.C. PEARS, 1-lb. 3/6	CIGARETTES .... 2d. OFF 20	FIRST QUALITY CUPS 10d
HEINZ BABY FOODS from 6½d	HEINZ SALAD CREAM, Large 1/9	TREE TOPS ORANGE 2/3	BANDED 18-Pce. TEASETS 21/-

ONLY THE BEST

SHOPS ARE

SHOWRAX

— BY —

Johnston & McInerney Lt

There are very few interior shots of cope premises before the big expansion from 1969, when the supermarket opened. This photo was taken in the Main Street store in the mid 1950s. The location is the 'Boot Room' at the back of the Drapery. In the centre, Packie the Cope is hugging his son Jim, with daughter Mary (Logue) to the right of her grandfather Paddy the Cope and Packie's other sons John behind and a young Pat the Cope, future TD and Minister, to his left. (Irish Independent photo; Sally the Cope collection).

Left: Jim the Cope Gallagher holding a copy of his grandfather's autobiography in probably 1969 when it was republished in paperback. Jim was Manager of the supermarket and a respected businessman who was a huge loss to the Cope when he died tragically in 1994. He is remembered with much love by his family, friends and colleagues (Cope Archive).

Dungloe 5 & 102   Tax 8K28400

J. N. Gallagher
(Supermarket Manager)

THE COPE   Dungloe, Co. Donegal.
Templecrone Co-operative & Agricultural Society Ltd.

Jim the Cope's business card and ...

... a page from his employee handbook in 1973 stating what the turnover was when he started in 1969 (£361,915) and that turnover had more than doubled by the year 1973 (Jim the Cope Archive)

NAME ... *Jim Gallagher*

STATUS ....
(temporary/permanent)

I STARTED IN THE COPE ON .... *May* 19 *69*

THE SOCIETY'S
SALES AND SERVICES
THEN WERE

£ *361 915*

£3
million
sales
edition
1973

Housewives Choice

★ ALL REDUCED PRICES and SPECIAL OFFERS galore

★ widest VARIETY OF QUALITY goods and CATERING sizes

★ FRESH fruit/veg daily from the MARKETS and youghart and fresh cream too

★ 22 feet of Fridgeration plus 3,000 cubic feet cold and chilled storage for constant fresh foods

★ fresh BREAD twice daily from our own BAKERY

★ Barbecue Chickens and selection of Choice wines

★ Spaciousness, Cleanliness, ventilation and atmosphere.

★ 3 check-outs now, and TEA ROOMS for your shopping comfort

★ 65 years of service from the Cope; just released 'My Story' by Paddy the Cope, paperback 39p

★ All our reduced prices and special offers are available in all our Branches

★ all this plus GREEN SHIELD STAMPS

★ We Buy Well — You Buy Well at

the Cope DUNGLOE
phone
TEMPLECRONE CO-OPERATIVE SOCIETY   5 or 102

the Cope
DUNGLOE

we say to those who are part of us
who went away to earn
we're fit and well and working hard
and here when you return

we say to those who've yet to find
the beauties of this spot
we're here to help in all you want
there's little we have not

we say to those suppliers who
have served us o'er the years
we thank you in enabling us
to celebrate this year

templecrone co-operative society ltd.

Two promotional 'flyers', executed with wit and confidence, issued by the Cope in 1975. The poem also appeared in the 5th January 1976 Irish Independent article (Jim the Cope Collection, Cassie Jock's house)

Right: Dungloe Supermarket staff in 1975: Jim the Cope Gallagher (Paddy the Cope's grandson), Cathal McCole, Teresa Boyle, Francis Ferry (Boyle), Packie Bonner, Sally McEttigan, Packie Boyle, Mary Grace O'Donnell, Pauline McCole, Eileen Hamilton, Alice Hamilton. The last four named are in the Cope ladies' uniforms of the1970s (Cope Archive).

Above: Jim the Cope cuts the cake with a crush of children waiting for their slice, in a photograph dated to c1975 but judging from the ages of the children, possibly earlier, maybe 1970-71. Along the counter are rows of paper cups filled with orange juice. The boy on the left leaning over and smiling is Tony (Pat) Boyle, then Liam Sweeney, Gerry Brennan, Brendan Bonner in a duffle coat with arms folded, and John Monaghan. (Cope collection, special thanks to Gerry Brennan for providing names and details).

Above: The Cope Grocery Staff in 1981, including: (Back) Bridie Gallagher, Sally McGettigan, Cathal McCole, Jim the Cope Gallagher, Patrick Gallagher, Mary Gildea and Breda Boyle; (Front): Teresa Meehan, Pauline McCole, Liza Hands, Mary Houston and Kathleen O'Donnell (Cope Archive)

Left Top: A busy scene in the Dungloe supermarket in 1975, the year that Cope turnover exceeded £1m a year. At the checkout (in their brightly coloured Cope uniforms) are Mary Grace O'Donnell, Pauline McCole and Alice Hamilton. In the background, Jim the Cope, Manager of the supermarket, is chatting informally to Packie Bonner, arms folded; also in the shot are Cope workers Sally McGettigan, Cathal McCole, Packie Boyle and Eileen Hamilton. The shoppers, alas not identified, will no doubt be well known to Dungloe people. This photograph and nine others featured in a two page spread, including an article by Cope Chairman John J Doherty, in the Irish Independent of January 5th 1976; 36 suppliers took out boxed adverts to congratulate the Cope on its success (Newspaper article in the Hugh McGee Collection, photograph from the Cope Archive)

Left Bottom: Cope Staff in 1975: (Back) Sheila McGettigan, John Joe O'Donnell, Gerald Glackin; Middle: Joe Cronin, Denis Ward, Kathleen O'Donnell, Rose McGettigan, Mary Gallagher, Ann T. Sweeney, John Gallagher; Front: Hugh McGee, Mary Coll, Breid (McCole) O'Donnell, Nancy Shovelin, Susan Doogan. Hughie McGee and Denis Ward are current Cope Committee members (Cope Archive).

Above: The Dungloe Head Office staff in 1981: (Back) Angela Devenney, Thomas Donaghy and Teresa Meehan, "the golden voice on the telephone exchange and PA system" as the caption read in the 1981 commemorative booklet; (Front) Ann Sweeney, Charles Boyle and Sheila Devenney. Regrettable absent for the photo: Dolly O'Donnell, Brigid Bonner and Mary Boyle, the General Manager's secretary (Cope Archive)

Above: Land at the back of the Main Street store was purchased and the Cope car park was opened in 1980; it has been a great asset to Dungloe - as well of course to the Cope. Today it is complemented by the new Cope Street which links the Main Street and Car Park (Cope Archive).

Left Bottom: Dungloe in the mid-1960s, a photograph taken at the bridge, with the Northern Bank still intact but not for much longer (architecturally, the finest building in Dungloe, it was demolished in 1971, a great loss). On the left is Anthony Bonner's garage with three petrol pumps (now The Flower Shop); across the bridge is Anthony O'Donnell's newsagents and sweet shop – Anthony, who was married to Delia (Cannon), Paddy's niece, was fondly called Anthony 'the Cake' (or 'the Bun') and is remembered affectionately by generations of schoolchildren. The old road sign signals left for Ardara and Glenties, down the Carnmore Road. (Dollard postcard, PB Collection)

Next Page: A magnificent aerial view of the Cope from the 1970s before the car park was built in 1980. This is one of a series of aerial photos, commissioned in this very confident decade for the Cope, which now hang near the boardroom upstairs in the Dungloe store. Access to the rear from the Main Street was very tight as the old Post Office was still in place and a cluster of buildings blocked the way behind narrow alleyway. At this stage, before its move to the Quay Road, the whole of the Builder's Provider's was in this crowded back area. "...The building on the right was the Timber yard; at the back, was the Furniture store; on the left the back of the Main Street shop. To the right would have been the Wholesale department..." (Cope Archive and thanks to Jimmy Durnin for providing the detail on layout).

The Story of the Cope

Another aerial view of the Cope showing the new car park from a 1980s postcard issued by the Cope (PB Collection).

Dungloe Post Office was adjacent to the Cope Menswear store until moved to the Quay Road below the Midway in 1993. Prior to this, it had been across the road, where the AIB is today. The McCauley family ran the PO from 1937 to 1992: firstly, Phil to 1960 then Sarah to 1981, after which then her daughter Celine to 1992, aided by her sister Catherine. Catherine married John Columba Boyle who has managed Burtonport PO since 1972. Vince Wehrley has managed the Dungloe PO since 1993; it has now moved back to be inside the new Cope in 2008, a very successful move. The lady in blue is Mary Anne Boyle of Meenatottan, Dungloe; the other two ladies have not been identified at the time of writing. (PB collection from Insight Guide).

Outside the Cope in c1975 – leaning on the petrol pump, John Columba Boyle, postmaster of Burtonport, then Joe Joyce, Guard, and Fred Sweeney. The old post office can be seen at the end of the building (Cope Archive).

Another view of the Cope taken moments later on the same day, John Columba and Fred Sweeney are still at the petrol pump. Arthur's gift shop, still there today, can just be seen on the left of the picture (Cope Archive)

The Main Street store decked out for Christmas in 1975 (Cope Archive)

The Cope supermarket in the 1970s with its new 'Cope' logo, based, it is said, on the handwriting of General Manager Cyril Winder, who managed the Cope from 1969-93 (Cope Archive)

Another view of the Main Street store, showing the unusual fixing of the boards with the shop name (Cope Archive)

Below:
The Main Street store in c1975.

The General Office Staff: (back) Anne Sweeney; Nuala Browne; Breda Langan; Barbara Callaghan; (front) Marguerite McGee; James Greene (Manager), Thomas Donaghy and Bernadette Walsh (Cope Photo, 2006)

Menswear and Sportswear: (back) Denise Ward; Shaun Gallagher; Eamon Hanlon; Mary Brennan; (front) Brian Sweeney; Denis Ward; and Dolores Ward (Cope Photo, 2006)

Ladies, Young Set and Household Departments: (back) Patricia Brennan; Emma Gallagher; Mary Bonner, Rita Rodgers; (seated) Anne Sharkey; and Irene Ward (Cope Photo, 2006)

Grocery and Supermarket: (back) Patrick McCahill, Martin McGarvey, Deirdre Brown, Ann T. Ward, Hughie Mulholland, Pauline McCole, Lisa Barrett, Billy Mooney, Colin Tovey, Mary Ward. Seated: Faye Moulton, Mary F. Ward, Dayna Byrne, Caley McEvoy, Patricia Ryan (Manager), Dolores McMonagle, Lisa (Neary) McGee, Breda Breslin, Catriona Ward (Cope Photo).

Flooring, Furniture and Carpets. Gerald O'Donnell (Manager, Furniture Department); Brendan Gallagher; Eugene McGarvey (Manager Flooring Department) and Donal Boyle (Cope Photo, 2006).

Supermarket: Adina Doherty, John McHugh, Laura Byrne (Cope Photo, 2006).

The Story of the Cope

Eileen Saville in the Gift Department (Cope Photo, 2006).

Ann Davidson, in the Bakery Section (Cope Photo, 2006)

The Story of the Cope

Hardware Department. John Joe O'Donnell (Manager), Kieran Sharkey, Brendan McGee and Martin Glackin (Cope Photo, 2006)

This is the interior of the Agricultural and Fuel Supplies building in 2006. Agricultural is where the Cope started back in 1906 – and where it would have ended if Sir Horace Plunkett and his colleagues at the IAOS had not stuck their necks out to help the tiny cooperative in Cleendra. Today, Agricultural is now a relatively small of the Cope 'Empire'. Photographed are Tadhg Kerr, Joe Dickie, Kathleen Marie Brennan and Oliver Ward (Cope Photo, 2006).

Gerald O'Donnell photographed for the 75th anniversary in 1981. The generator was one of two bought by the Cope in 1979 when felt it could not rely on the ESB. This one was housed in the old Bakery on the Quay Road, the other served the Main Street (Cope photo scanned from the 1981 booklet)

Electrician - Gerard O'Donnell (Cope photo, 2006)

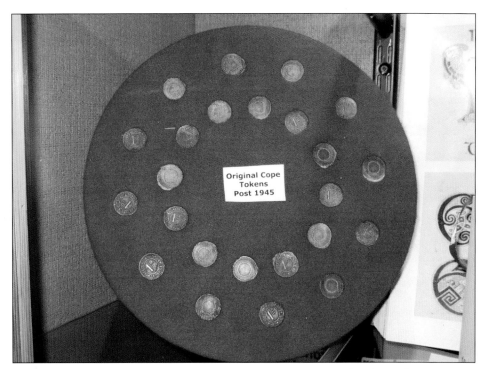

Original Cope
Tokens
Post 1945

When the Cope started off, it followed the model of all the cooperatives by paying a dividend which could be as much as 10% (and even 15%), a very healthy return on purchases which built up very quickly. Paddy the Cope's wife Sally caught on to this when she was in Scotland with Paddy from 1898 and used the Pumperstown Co-op. Today's 'divi' is much less – a 10-15% dividend is now impossible with competition driving net margins for retail to 5% or lower - and sometimes a great deal less. Pictured are the Cope tokens which were issued post 1945, although they do look to predate this era (Cope Archive, Dungloe).

Tokens preceded the Cope stamps which were introduced in 1973. Two examples are shown. The garish, orange coloured ones, which for the first time have an expiry date, are the current stamps. As someone said, commenting on the colour, 'Well you won't lose these ones'. Over time the Cope has had to adjust to this commercial reality; by 1975, the dividend was down to 3.39% and it has had to adjust further since then, to stay competitive on headline prices. (The stamps are in current usage; 1975 data on dividends from the Cope's '£1,000,000 Commemorative Souvenir').

The Story of the Cope

Top: Jimmie Nangle walking the job in 2006 with Jimmy 'Greaves' O'Donnell, now retired but a long term Annagry Cope employee. Jimmie Nangle was General Manager till 2008 and sadly died a few months after leaving. He was only 49 and is much missed by his family and the many friends he made in the Rosses (Cope Photo Archive)

Middle: 'The Man Who Made the Cope What It Is Today'. Phil Ward, of Bel Cruit, but originally from Arranmore, is the master builder, in the foreground, and is sitting down on the job, very unlike him. Behind are Paddy Sweeney, Fair Hill, and Thomas Boyd, Gweedore both of whom work with Phil and his son Adrian. The scene is the building site of the new Cope Supermarket which was opened in 2007. After a fire had badly damaged the building in 2006, it was decided to take the opportunity to rebuild on a larger scale. Phil Ward and his team have worked on every recent Cope development including the new Builders' Providers on the Sheskinarone Road outside Dungloe and the Annagry and Kincasslagh redevelopments (Cope Photo Archive)

Bottom: Phil Ward with his son Adrian in the machine, preparing the ground for the new Cope Supermarket building in 2006 (Cope Photo Archive)

The new extension in Dungloe which houses the Sports Department on the ground floor in a lot more space. Above is sixteen thousand square feet of space available for letting or expansion (Cope Photo Archive)

The new Cope supermarket with its 'Eurospar' branding. The Cope changed its retail partnership from Vivo to Spar in 2008 after competitive tendering produced better margins. The new building, which has a restaurant close by the supermarket, recently added Dungloe Post Office making it an even more convenient place to shop. (Cope Photo Archive).

Chapter 3

The Cope Branches

The Cope developed a branch network of seven stores and added a presence in Killybegs, in connection with its fishing business, from the 1940s. The first branch opened in 1910 in Maghery, close to Cleendra but this very soon after was replaced by the travelling service – the 'tea van', effectively a mobile branch network for the Cope. Maghery re-opened again in 1916, in response to local demand. The next venture was at Lettermacaward (in the Rosses but just outside Templecrone) in 1911, followed in 1914 by Meenbanad. Kincasslagh was opened in 1919, Burtonport in 1921 and Annagry in 1923 – this period of expansion followed the wartime boom and was a very confident period for the Cope. The Cope at Narin was originally the Downstrands Co-Operative Society, founded in 1910. In 1971 Narin was amalgamated with the Templecrone Cope.

The expansion, in branches, in the knitwear business, over the period 1911 to 1923, spanning as it did the First World War helped the Cope increase turnover almost eightfold from £12,063 to £91,361.[1]

Apart from Lettermacaward, the Cope never expanded outside the Rosses, beyond its original Templecrone remit. The Cope's influence did extend beyond Templecrone however – Gweedore (in Glasha, 1909), the Lower Rosses (1909), Inishkeel (1908), all nearby, also set up their own co-operative shops. The West Donegal Fishing Co-operative (1920) based in Kincasslagh had support from Paddy the Cope also.[2]

Hughie McGee remembers the 'Tea Vans' well:

> "…The Tea Vans or travelling Shops were unique to the Cope. They operated from the Main Store in Dungloe and from all branches. They called to all our customers on a set day once a week and covered an area between the Crolly and Gweebarra Bridges [this area, between the rivers, is known as the Rosses]. This service continued until 1979. The Service was provided by a driver and helpers, who formed a great bond and relationship with all our customers and were made very welcome on their weekly visit. And apart from the postman would probably be the only regular visit they might have for the week
>
> How the name Tea Van was derived is debatable - it has been suggested it was because of the amount of tea consumed by the operators. A more creditable explanation is that in the early days most customers were self sufficient in they had their own meal, milk, potatoes and chickens. The only real requirement would be Tea.

---

1   *IAOS records, National Archives, Bishop Street, Dublin; Irish Homestead, various years.*

2   *'History of Co-operatives in Donegal', Patrick Bolger, 1975 (see Appendix 3).*

Derryбеg

Gola I.

Bunbeg

Owey I.

Inishfree Bay

Cruit I.

Gweedore

Annagry

UPPER

Kincasslagh

Inishinny I.

Meenbanid

Aran I.

Burtonport

ROSSES

L. Anure

L. Meela

TEMPLECRONE

Rutland I.

CUSTOM HOUSE

PIER

DUNGLOE

L. Craghy

LOWER

POWER HOUSE

GREENHILL MILL

ATLANTIC

Inishfree

Maghery

Meenatotan

Maghery Bay

L. Aleck More

ROSSES

Cleendra

OWENAMARRE

OCEAN

Roaninish I.

Trawenagh Bay

Lettermackaward

Gweebarra Bay

DUNMORE HEAD

DAWROS HEAD

Dawros Bay

D   O

Dawros Bay

Glenties

Loughros more Bay

OWENA R.

N

Loughros beg Bay

Cloghboy

Ardara

Statute miles

0 1 2 3 4 5

🜨 Branches

to Carrick 7 miles

to Killybegs
8 miles

to Donegal

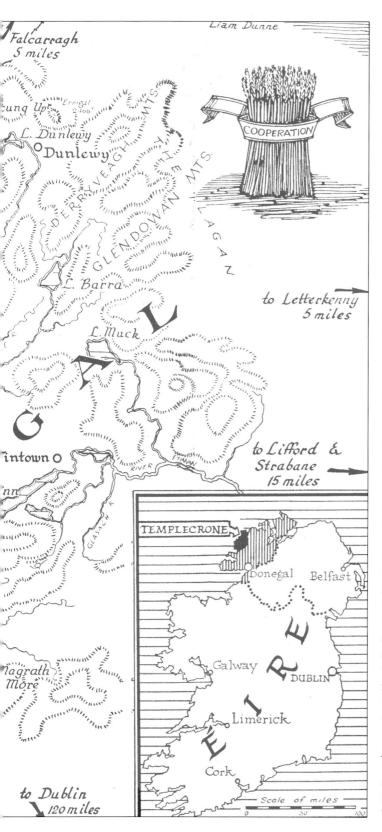

Falcarragh
5 miles

Errigal
2466
L. Dunlewy
Dunlewy

DERRYVEAGH MTS.

GLENDOWAN MTS.

THE LAGAN

L. Barra

DONEGAL

L. Muck

to Letterkenny
5 miles

COOPERATION

intown

RIVER FINAN

GLASAGH R.

to Lifford &
Strabane
15 miles

nn

TEMPLECRONE

Donegal   Belfast

EIRE

Galway
DUBLIN

Limerick

Cork

Magrath
More

to Dublin
120 miles

Scale of miles
0   50   100

This map illustrated the endpapers of the 1942 US edition of Paddy's autobiography 'My Story'. It was designed to show American readers the location and extent of Templecrone Parish as well as the locations of all seven Cope retail stores then trading. At this stage, the Cope did not have a store in Narin or a presence in Killybegs. In Dungloe, the Cope's mill, pier (and yes, a custom house!) are picked out. The Lough Swilly railway line is shown as going through Dungloe – the illustrator (Liam Dunne) and US publisher presumably couldn't conceive of the railway not passing through the main town of the area. Kincasslagh and Annagry are also blessed with stations they never had, it would appear, but Meenbanid has lost the station at Kincasslagh Road. This is all by the way, however, as, by this time (1942), there was no railway service at all in the Rosses. It had all been ripped up in 1940. The 1921 blockade-busting journey of the *SS Better Hope* to Glasgow is marked on the upper left. (Devin-Adair edition 'My Story').

Early on, eggs were another product our customers had in abundance and were exchanged for provisions at the Tea Van. Paddy the Cope found a new market for eggs in the Cooperative in Glasgow and raised the price of eggs; this started another row between the Cope and the gombeen traders..."[3]

MAGHERY (1910, then 1916)

Cleendra, Paddy the Cope's birthplace and the site of the first Cope, looks down towards Maghery from the hills. In 1880, just before Paddy was about to make his first long walk to Strabane for the hiring fair, a journalist from Manchester travelled to Maghery and, in recording the way of life, he helps us today to understand why parents had to take their children out of school and send them away to earn money for the family:

> "...2nd March 1880 – Maghery, near Dunglow, is a small hamlet by the sea coast, where the Rectory is situate, four miles away from the church, which is at Dunglow. It contains forty five families, of whom forty are on the relief list, receiving a regular distribution of meal at the usual rate of half a stone per head per week.
>
> The cabins are fully up to the average, and tolerably tidy; bedding and clothing are better than in the most distressed places we had visited (e.g. Teelin and Meenacladdy). The people had a more hearty and vigorous appearance, as if they had not been reduced so low as in some other places before the relief came. They were, however, all very poor, and are now completely dependent on the "meal". They own less live stock than in any place we had seen. Their holdings are exceedingly small, many have no land, their chief employment being the making of kelp. Large quantities of seaweed were stacked or spread along the walls, and the beach presented a lively appearance, with numbers of the people watching or gathering the seaweed, which after the heavy storms of the last few days was being fetched by the incoming tide. The seaweed is chiefly collected during the winter, but cannot be turned into money until the summer, when it is dry and ready for burning. The price is now extremely low, so that it brings in but little.
>
> A little inshore fishing is carried on. Coracles are the boats employed, and during the stormy winter many of these frail craft had been damaged and rendered useless. One poor man had just been up to the Rectory to beg for some *brown paper* to mend his boat with. A more enterprising man, the Rector told us, had built for himself a good wooden boat, and had done extremely well ever since, and was much better off than his neighbours. The harbour, or bay, is safe and sheltered, and the Rector

---

3   *Hugh McGee, Cope Committee member since 1973, was a lifelong Cope employee, worked on the Tea Vans and became Manager, Hardware in Dungloe.*

The village of Maghery (in c1900-05); Maghery was the Cope's first branch outside Dungloe and opened initially in 1910, closed and then reopened again in 1916; Maghery is the nearest village, a mile or so away, to the hills of Cleendra where the Cope was founded in 1906. The 1780s rectory, one of the finest heritage buildings in the area (still standing but in need of some restoration), can be seen in the foreground. In the distance Termon House, once the Land Agent's House, is now managed for letting by the Irish landmark Trust who have sensitively restored it. (Contemporary postcard published by Lawrence, Seán Boner Collection)

(Rev S.E. Burns) thought that if funds could be got for a few good boats, which could be built by the men themselves, it would be of great and permanent benefit to them *(Assistance was subsequently given and three boats built by the men).*

The women are excellent knitters. Mrs Burns had given them a better class of stockings to do for her than the Glenties firm give out, and paid them 6d a pair for making. A new rectory has been built, and some work is likely to be given in wall building, &c, round the rectory garden and ground.

Near this place (Maghery), some glebe lands had been nominally sold to the tenants at nineteen years' purchase. The history of this transaction, which has been much discussed, appears to be that a man in the neighbourhood, who had some money, came forward and offered to lend, at 4 per cent, to the tenants who had the right of pre-emption, the money needed to buy the land, saying that he could get it from the Commissioners. He afterwards told them he could not so get it and must charge them 10 per cent. They then signed agreements with the Commissioners to buy,

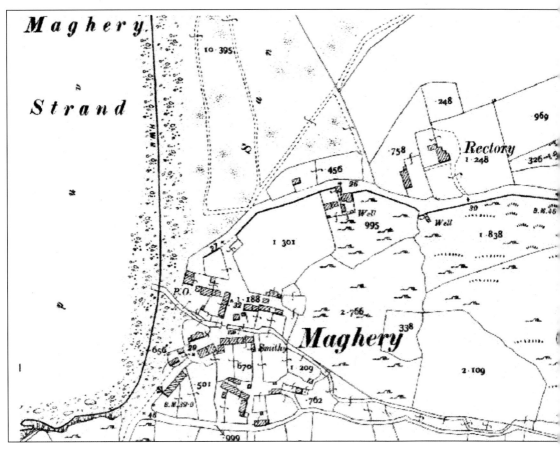

This Ordnance Survey map of the village of Maghery shows the layout of houses, clustered as they would have appeared in c1906. (Image courtesy of Ordnance Survey of Ireland)

which were accepted. The money-lender then brought round a deed for them to sign, making over to him all their rights of pre-emption, which he handed to the Commissioners, and they conveyed the whole to him. The Rector had written on behalf of the tenants - stating that they were entirely ignorant of the contents of the deed, but no redress could now be obtained. The unfortunate men, therefore, are in no sense proprietors, but merely the tenants of the money-lender., with agreements to pay him 10 per cent on the purchase money, or more than double their old rents, which they are now quite unable to pay and have not paid..."[4]

The following description of the Maghery Cope is from the Irish Homestead in 1924:

"...In 1910 a branch store was started in Maghery, a little village about five miles to the west of Dungloe. Here a small, disused shop was secured and some groceries stocked, but it was found after a time that the few townlands it served might be equally well supplied by the Society's

---

4   *The Manchester Guardian, March 16th 1880 – 'The Distress in Ireland'*

The Story of the Cope

Kate Doogan was the manager of Maghery Cope. Here she is receiving an award on her retirement from Dom Bonner, then Chairman of the Cope (Cope Archive)

grocery vans, and the branch was closed. But owing to the persistent desire of the members of the locality the branch was re-opened after a few years. In 1916, a substantial store was built and furnished with all the members' requirements, and notwithstanding that the district had already been served, and it is still catered for, by the ordinary trader, it still does a busy trade, amounting to about £400 per month. Maghery is a beautiful seaside spot. As a watering place nothing is wanted but accommodation for the visitors, and as a fishing centre it only lacks pier accommodation, of which there is none whatsoever. The outlying bay teems with fish of various kinds. Now that the spirit of self-help is abroad, and that the co-operative store has planted the foot of progress on its beach, it is to be hoped that the sturdy men of Maghery will no longer be satisfied with the present voluntary offerings of the ocean. We may with some hope look forward to the day when throngs of summer visitors will ride in safety upon its waters. The place offers every facility for the building of a pier that would give ample and good accommodation for boats..."[5]

---

5 'The Templecrone Co-Operative Society' pamphlet published in 1924 by The Irish Homestead

Maghery Cope in 1981 with an inset of manager Packie McHugh (originally from Arranmore). Packie was one of the first Cope management trainees and worked over the years in many areas of the Cope. He now runs his own store and garage at Burtonport crossroads (Image scanned from the Cope's 75th Anniversary booklet).

The Maghery Cope in c2000, before the decision was taken to close it down in 2004 after 83 years of trading. Changed shopping behaviour – with people prepared to drive past the local shop to Dungloe or Letterkenny (and increasingly as far as Derry) for their 'big' shopping – had made some of the smaller branches of the Cope unviable. Paddy would have been sad to see the branches close – particularly Maghery with its closeness to Cleendra – but he was enough of a realist to appreciate the commercial realities of modern retail business – indeed he closed a number of businesses himself in his time (soapstone mining, granite quarrying and the Cope fishing fleet, to name but three). (Photo courtesy of Frances (Ferry) Boyle).

The Cope made the premises at Maghery available to the Maghery community on very favourable terms and the community shop – Síopa Pobaíl – was opened. However, the venture foundered in 2007 as the costs of running the shop proved too much and community funding was not made available (Photograph from 2006 courtesy Frances (Ferry) Boyle).

John McCarthy, who at the time, the 1970s, lived in the rectory at Maghery, wrote an article about the Cope in the Irish Times:

> "…A year ago, the American Ambassador John D. J. Moore visited Dungloe, and, incidentally, he was the first foreign emissary to penetrate as far as the Rosses since Napper Tandy landed on nearby Rutland Island in a French corvette in the uprising of 1798 with credentials from Napoleon. While inspecting this Templecrone Co-Op supermarket in Dungloe, which has a weekly turnover of £5,000 upward, the impressed Ambassador Moore exclaimed: "Why, it's just like the A and P supermarket in my home neighbourhood on New York's Eastside."
>
> After some years' residence in a 150-year-old glebe house in the small seaside village of Maghery in the Rosses, the American author of this screed can go a bit further than his Ambassador in complimenting the Templecrone Co-Op, by testifying that it supplies its clientele with additional products which the gigantic A and P chain of supermarkets in the U.S.A. is not even aware of. For instance, for the convenience of the some twenty families in Maghery and the others in the environs, Templecrone Co-Op has long had a small branch store, perched right on the banks facing the Atlantic Ocean.

Only a two room emporium, the Maghery branch, is run from early morn till 6 p.m. daily by the capable Kate Dugan, who alone manages to serve a constant stream of customers. Not only can I walk into the Maghery Co-Op store and get my native Maxwell House coffee, Kellogg's corn flakes or Gillette blades, but I can also buy a "grape," a specially designed pitch fork to pile turf, heavy boots which are repellant to the watery Donegal grass, or Bangor slates which are identical with those originally placed on our glebe roof when it was built 150 years ago and still are made by the same English firm. Certainly, the A and P store on the Eastside of New York, as well stocked as it is, would not know what we were asking for if we inquired for a "grape" or Bangor slates but the resourceful Kate Dugan does and produces them pronto..."[6]

At the time of writing (2006), the Cope no longer operates in Maghery but has leased the premises on favourable terms to the local community who continue to operate a small grocery and 'convenience' store there.[7]

LETTERMACAWARD (1911)

"...Lettermacaward is a long, narrow stretch of valley lying between the cosy hamlet of Doochary on the east and the sand banks of Dooey on the west, where it dips into the sea. The Gweebarra River glides smoothly along this valley.

For some years the district formed a kind of neutral zone between the Templecrone and Inishkeel Societies, and had been served by a multitude of little shops. But the people were anxious to join the new movement, and made repeated demands for a branch store in the locality. The opportunity for a start at length arose; disused business premises became available, and a branch was opened in 1911. The Society was fortunate in securing as manager Mr Joe O'Donnell, and under his capable and careful management it flourished from the start, though faced with opposition of the wiliest character by the little combination of local traders. It maintains a steady turnover of about £400 per month. There is no doubt that when normal conditions return, this branch, like its parent society, will be able to stretch its tentacles in other directions. Many of the people of the district are skilled at wicker work, and if some effort were made at osier cultivation, it might become a source of considerable employment..."[8]

---

6   *Irish Times, November 16th 1972*

7   *The store closed in 2007 due to lack of community funding and support.*

8   *Irish Homestead booklet on 'The Templecrone Co-operative Society', 1924.*

John Neil John Gallagher and Colm Melly outside the Lettermacaward Cope in 1981. The Cope opened a branch here in 1911 due to popular local demand – it was not in Templecrone as such but still in the Rosses. John Neil John Gallagher was manager here for many years – he had previously worked in the Burtonport Cope (scanned from the 1981 75th Anniversary booklet, Cope Archive)

Carmel Byrne, Manager, outside the Lettermacaward Cope in 2006. Lettermacaward is one of three branch stores (with Kincasslagh and Annagry) left from the seven stores which the Cope once had (PB photo)

The Lettermacaward staff in 2006: Carmel Byrne, Elma McDyre and Joe Gallagher (Cope photo, by Brian Sweeney)

MEENBANAD (1914)

"…A third branch was opened in 1914 at Meenbanad, about three miles from the central store, and lying in the opposite direction from the other two branches. Meenbanad is placed in the centre of a populous district, and as many of the people had already been members the business of the new branch grew rapidly. The present turnover of this branch is upwards of £600 per month…"[9]

A station was opened at 'Kincasslagh Road', Meenbanad crossroads, in 1913. It cannot be a coincidence that Meenbanad Cope was built one year later, directly opposite. For a while, Meenbanad was an important village with a railway station, school, the large Cope store, a post office run by Charlie Donnachada Rua and Manus O'Donnell's shop opposite the station. Today, all that remains open is Brian Manus's shop. The well-preserved station building, platform and goods shed still attract railway historians and enthusiasts from across the world.

---

9   *Ibid.*

Meenbanad Cope – as recalled by **Timmy the Cope (Doherty)**.

"...The Meenbanad branch first opened for business in 1914. It was the first branch to be established outside of Dungloe and was managed by Charlie Doherty from Gortnasade ably assisted by Sarah Gallagher and storeman Jimmy Mhanuis Bonner, all long gone to their eternal reward.

We are told that before counters and shelving were put in place, it was decided to have a dance to officially 'baptise' it. A big crowd turned up and the dancing was in full swing when In arrived the Big Priest from Burtonport firmly clutching his stout blackthorn stick, dispersing the crowd east and west thus preserving the high morals of the area.

On the first day of business a big contingent of Cruit folk arrived with donkeys and creels, laden down with dulse and carrageen moss to barter for their groceries. There was a big demand for homemade butter and fresh eggs, which were supplied by customers in return for 'a quarter of tea and two pound of sugar'.

On one occasion a local man came in to buy a spade. Having tried the seven spades on display in many different positions, he then enquired of Charlie if he had any more spades. To this Charlie replied ' And about how many spades would you be wanting now?'

Its closure in 1972 left a great void in the locality, not just because of the service it provided but the social side. It was where births, marriages and deaths were told of. But by then, not only had Meenbanad lost its Cope but the school was closed and the station long gone.

Among those who gave sterling service in Meenbanad through the years until its closure in 1972 were John Paddy O'Donnell, Hannah Boyle, Packie Bonner and George Boner, Go ndeanfaidh Dia a mhaith orthu uilig. Others who worked there included Michael Ward, Anna Doherty, Peter Boyle, Owen Bonner, Noreen Bonner and her brother Hughie, Hughie Sweeney and Peter Ward..."

Cathal McCole, later Grocery Buyer for the Cope, worked in Meenbanad for a year in 1953 when he was 17 (he retired after 42 years with the Cope).

"...Charlie the Cope Doherty was Manager. It was very busy; people would come in from the islands (Cruit and Owey) to there to buy stores and trade eggs, other foods and dulse (seaweed) etc. Meenbanad was a big branch with a drapery, grocery and general store. I then moved to Burtonport in 1954/55 – Hughie McGee was there too – and Joe Brennan was Manager. Burtonport was very busy too; lots of islanders, particularly Arranmore, would shop there..."

Meenbanad Cope opened its doors in 1914; one year after the Lough Swilly Railway Company added Kincasslagh Road station at the Meenbanad crossroads. This fine view was taken before 1920; the precise date is said to be 4th January 1918. Above the doorway, the sign reads 'Templecrone Co-operative Society, Licensed to Deal in Tobacco'. In the picture are Biddy Anton Óg Gallagher, Meenbanad (mother of Hannah Anton Óg); Rosina Wilmot, daughter of Annie McAleevey, Keadue: Paddy Joe O'Donnell, Upper Keadue; Paddy's mother, Eilie Joe O'Donnell; Mrs Duffy, Eoin Duffy's wife (her first name is not known); Charlie the Cope Doherty, Manager, who lived in the house attached to the Cope, seen on the left; Jimmy Mhanuis Boner, Upper Keadue; Paddy Coll, Sheskinarone; in the doorway of the house, Maria Doherty, wife of Charlie the Cope; on the rock behind the cart, Mary Doherty, daughter of Charlie and Maria. Meenbanad Cope closed in 1972 and is very fondly remembered still (Cope Collection, with special thanks to Eugene Doherty, Committee member and son of Charlie and Maria Doherty, for the photo, date and identification of the people in the picture).

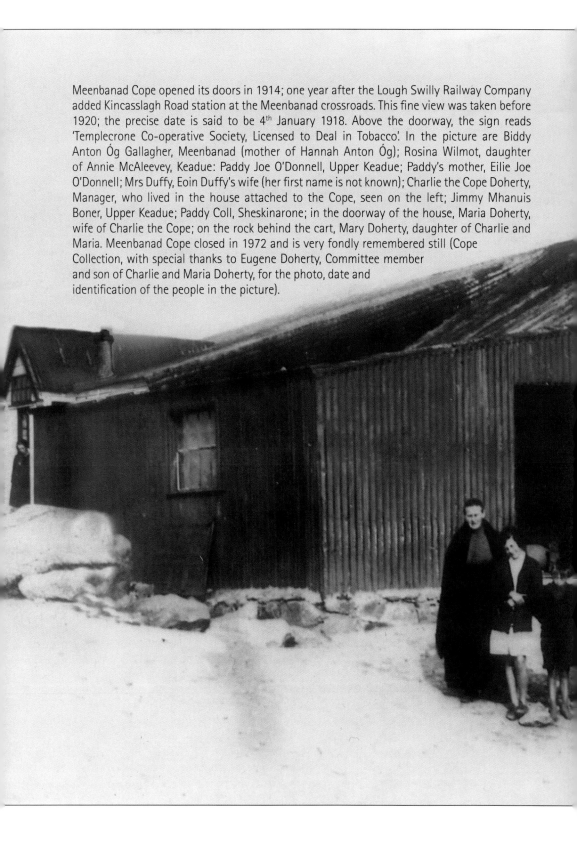

Above: Kincasslagh Road Station – at Meenbanad crossroads – was opened in 1913 and probably a key reason for locating the Cope here in 1914. Store deliveries and dispatch of Cope produce, eggs etc, would have been straightforward; indeed, the Cope may well have taken to treating the station as its own! The station closed in 1940, when the track was pulled up, but the buildings and platform are still in remarkable repair and attract Swilly railway enthusiasts who endeavour to walk the tracks where possible (PB scanned photo).

Right Top: Manus O'Donnell's shop in Meenbanad (pictured here in c1950) was within fifty yards of Meenbanad Cope, on the side road towards Crickamore, just opposite Kincasslagh Road Station. The two shops co-existed successfully. Manus's shop remains today, managed by his nephew Brian Manus, who continues to provide a valued local service. The building is in the same style as the Cope branches – galvanized and painted corrugated iron. (Photograph courtesy of Brian Manus O'Donnell).

Right Bottom: Brian Manus O'Donnell in his Meenbanad shop pictured in November 2006 – and long may he continue to be there. The shop is still basically the same structure, the only visible external change being new windows. The road behind on the left, between Dungloe and Kincasslagh, now has many more houses on it than in the earlier photo. (Photo PB)

Keague St

Keague (Keadue) Strand in 1939. Until 1938, there was no road along Keadue Strand; the route from Burtonport to Meenbanad, Kincasslagh and elsewhere was via Lower Keadue past where the tree nursery is today. Donegal County Council built the road in 1938; the wall seen here in construction was built in 1939 (a new wall was built in 2004 to help prevent flooding of Keadue Rovers' football pitch). Hughie Paddy Óg Ward, seen here on the far right, worked on both; his

Kincasslagh.

father Paddy Óg Ward carted sand and stone for the road as well. The man holding the hammer nearest to the camera is Charlie Paddy Mhanuis O'Donnell, a local stonemason. Joe Mhici Ward, from Keadue, is in between them. On the wall is the supervisor, a Mr Gallagher from Ardara. (Breda (Ward) Smith collection, contemporary 1939 postcard).

Concrete Bridge, Cruit Island,   Kincasslagh. Co. Donegal

The footbridge into Cruit was built by the Congested District Board in 1911, three years before Meenbanad Cope opened. Timmy Doherty's story about Meenbanad Cope records that "...on the first day of business a big contingent of Cruit folk arrived with donkeys and creels, laden down with dulse and carrageen moss to barter for their groceries..." Cruit Island today is well connected with a road bridge to Belcruit [Bel = 'mouth' or 'way in' to Cruit] built in about 1940 – it still keeps its island identity despite being now effectively an extension of the mainland and the location for a spectacular golf course (Contemporary postcard, Mícheál O Dhomnaill collection)

Mary Ellen Bonner (Manny Ann) born in 1923 in nearby Crickamore remembers the Meenbanad Cope well:

> "...it was a tin-roofed building, brown in colour; there were old lamps inside, wooden floors. Charlie Doherty was the manager; he ran it very well, he was very efficient. Noreen (Janey) Bonner worked there and Patsy Brennan, Mary Ellen Brennan's brother..."

KINCASSLAGH (1919)

> "...Kincasslagh is a pleasant little hamlet lying in a gorge of the Atlantic seaboard. The people of the surrounding district are a hardy, industrious, intelligent people and are dependent more upon the sea than on the land. Persistent calls for a branch of the Templecrone Society had come from here, and a deputation at length urged their case before the Templecrone Committee. According to the general desire, a branch store was started

Kincasslagh in c1950. The Cope building is the first on the right after the bridge. Four workmen are repairing the road by the 'spink' on the left. The heart of Kincasslagh village has remained much the same (Brendan Doherty collection, postcard SR Butler, Carndonagh).

Paddy the Cope sent this letter to Neilly O'Donnell, Manager of Kincasslagh Cope, in October 1933. In it he compliments Neilly on the job he has done in Kincasslagh and asks him to take on the Wholesale department in Dungloe. Correspondence like this is a rare survival – much was lost in the big fire in Dungloe in January 1945. The Cope letterhead now refers to it being a "Millers, Bakery and Hosiery Manufacturers" – the Cope's telephone number was Dungloe 5, there were very few phones in those days (Jim the Cope collection, Cassie Jock's house)

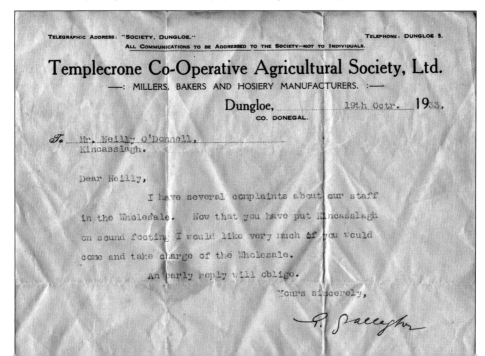

Kincasslagh again in a very fine photograph c1950 with the Cope on the right hand side with the black roof. To its right, the small building is the old Kincasslagh Post Office; across the road is Logue's - now Iggy's Bar. The fine double fronted house in the centre is Dan Ned's house (Dan E. Boyle) – by the chalet next to it there used to be a petrol pump which can just be seen at the end. The thatched cottages which are above and to its left are no longer there; Josie McGarvey's blacksmith's was in the left hand cottage of the group (Mícheál O Dhomnaill collection)

Ann Sweeney and Packie Gallagher outside the Kincasslagh Cope in 1981. Packie worked in the Cope for 21 years; he and Anne married in 1982. (Cope Archive)

In this c1960 postcard of Kincasslagh, the Cope building is just right of mid-centre. The storage shed on the other side of the road by the bridge has now been demolished and in its place is Pa Logue's house where every year there is Irish dancing at the Festival or Community Weekend. The channel leads under the road to Kincasslagh Lake (Postcard by Kiely Ballyshannon, late 1950s, 1960, Packie Bonner Collection)

Kincasslagh, Co. Donegal.

The modernised interior of the Kincasslagh Cope showing the new Post Office and, behind the counter, Branch Manager Geraldine Bonner. The Cope provides everything that the village needs, from groceries, papers, off licence and now postal services (Cope Photo Archive, John Broadbent photo)

Kincasslagh Cope as it is today after a major overhaul and redesign. Kincasslagh is one of three branches still trading successfully - the others, Annagry and Lettermacaward, are both doing well too. The Cope has recently invested in updated the Kincasslagh shop and brought the post office into the same building. The old post office next door, not in use for decades, has been purchased and demolished to make a car park for the Cope (Cope Photo Archive, John Broadbent photo).

in 1919, and the following year a fine shop with stores was erected at considerable expense. The business from the outset went briskly along with a steadily increasing volume approaching £600 or £700 per month. Gortlasade [sic] Pier, which gives good accommodation to fishing and cross-channel boats, is within a mile of the store, and advantage is taken of this means of getting in supplies. It is a rather important fish centre, and a co-operative fishing society was started there in 1920 which, after a short time, became amalgamated with the Templecrone Society. There are certainly great possibilities for co-operation in the Kincasslagh district..."[10]

Johnny Browne, Maghery, a stonemason built the Kincasslagh Cope in 1919. Johnny's daughter is Ann Browne, who is married to James Mickey Gallagher, son of Big Mick Gallagher, Cope Boat skipper. Ann and James live in Burtonport and, after James had finished fishing on the 'Autumn Glory', they started the Skippers bar in 1986.

BURTONPORT (1921)

"...Burtonport is a thriving village lying some five miles from Dungloe. It consists of a straggling collection of two hotels, four or five business houses, five or six public houses, a doctor's residence, a demolished coastguard station, and half a dozen or so dwelling houses. It is the great emporium for the outlying islands of Aran, Rutland and Innisfree and until Gortlasade became a rival port some twelve or thirteen years ago was the only port of call for fishing and trading boats in this part of the county. It is also the terminus of the Londonderry and Lough Swilly Railway. With all these facilities, by sea and land, Burtonport is naturally a busy centre during the fishing season. No sooner had the co-operative store been established in Kincasslagh than the contagion spread in this direction. The prospects of an independent society were discussed, and the promoters received every encouragement from the Templecrone Society, but after a few preliminary meetings it was decided to approach the Templecrone Society with a view to forming a branch society. A central site has been secured, but the work of erecting a store is not yet begun. The Templecrone Society has also leased from the C.D. [Congested District] Board a large store, formerly used as a cooperage, which is used as a store for meal, flour, etc landed at Burtonport Pier..."[11]

---

10   Ibid.

11   Irish Homestead 1924 booklet on Templecrone Cope.

Left Top and Bottom: Kincasslagh Cope in 2006 before modernisation with Una Mulrooney and Manager Geraldine Bonner – behind on the wall are a few photos of Owey and Kincasslagh man Daniel O'Donnell who worked in the Cope here as a teenager. The fortunes of the Cope in Kincasslagh have risen, justifying the investment in updating and modernising the store (Cope Collection, Brian Sweeney photo)

Left Top: O'Donnells' Hotel in Burtonport was built to serve the flood of travellers expected to arrive on the new extension of the Londonderry and Lough Swilly Railway. The station opened in 1903 and the hotel was completed in 1904. The proprietor was James Francis, better known as 'Jimmy Frank', O'Donnell, seen standing here by the motor car. Jimmy Frank and Paddy the Cope were to cross swords on occasion but there was a warm, mutual respect and they remained friends throughout the Cope story. The passenger in the car is James Hamilton, the Duke of Abercorn, a regular visitor to the hotel. The Duke was Lord Lieutenant of Donegal 1885-1913 and in 1905 became the first President of the Ulster Unionist Council. He was strongly opposed to Home Rule but "…he was surprised by the generosity of Wyndham's land act (1903) and was one of the first major landlords to sell to his tenants…" (National Photographic Archive, Lawrence Collection c1907, L-ROY_ 9437; quote from the Oxford Dictionary of National Biography)

Left Bottom: This photograph of Dinny Paddy Johndie's (Boyle) butcher's shop in Burtonport dates from the 1950s; Dinny's shop was almost directly opposite the old Burtonport Cope – sadly no photo of the original Cope building, it had been James Sweeney's shop before the Cope, has come to light (as yet - there is bound to be one out there somewhere). Dinny can be seen standing in the doorway; his lorry, a source of much pride, is a Ford, number plate IH 8318, and succeeded the horse and cart they used until then. The house behind on the left was Joe Brennan's – he was then manager of Burtonport Cope. Dinny's shop, now know as Margaret Dinny's after Dinny's wife (who was from Rutland) who ran it for some years, is still there (although no longer in use). It is now minus the right hand door in the photograph, which was then the entrance to the Butcher's (Photo courtesy of Pat the Butcher (Boyle).

> "…Burtonport is a rapidly growing village, the centre of a granite quarrying industry, and of extensive fisheries. The completion of the railway to the place has done much for its prosperity both as a tourist resort and fishing centre. In the herring season enormous takes of fish are made. They are dispatched sometimes in fresh condition to Scotland and the English Midland, but are more frequently cured for the Continent. Donegal herrings are very popular in Germany, more especially with the Jewish population. A good trade is also done with America. Messrs Sayers, the well known Billingsgate firm, carries on kippering on an island in Burtonport harbour. Burtonport is a great place for boating…"[12]

After much searching (a number of people have said 'ye have me tortured looking for it') no photograph has been found of the pre-1973 Cope. Before rebuilding, the Cope occupied a two-storey building; on its left a ruined long one-storied building in poor repair, no roof and overgrown with briars and grass inside. Originally, the buildings were owned by James Sweeney of Dungloe (the same James Sweeney whose Dungloe premises the Cope would move into in c1912). The two storey building was rented out to tenants (Lough Swilly employees) and James Sweeney's store was in the long one-storied building attached. James

---

12 *'Practical and Pictorial Guide to Donegal and the N.W. of Ireland', Waddington, York, 1937.*

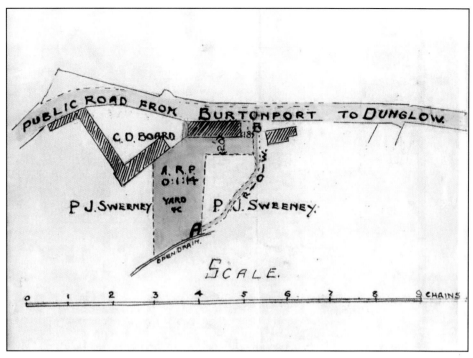

The transfer document from James Sweeney's wife to the Templecrone Co-op contained this map of the shop that became the Burtonport Cope. To the left of the map is the old Cooperage with a long shed extending out – at one stage, Jimmy Frank O'Donnell kept his turf in here. To the right was the bar which is Skippers today and Maguire's in earlier times (Cope Archive)

English railway enthusiast H. C. Casserley took many fine photographs recording Burtonport on his trip from Derry on the Lough Swilly line in 1937. The 'Port', as it is called locally, had many retail shops in the 1930s – on the right is Charlie McCole's tailor's shop. Charlie also had one with very much the same construction in Rutland. Anthony Manny Anne Boner remembers going in to Rutland to get a suit made. The long shed on the far right was used at this time to store carrageen moss; Campbell's Hotel was just behind the shed (Photo HC Casserley 24th June 1937, PB Collection)

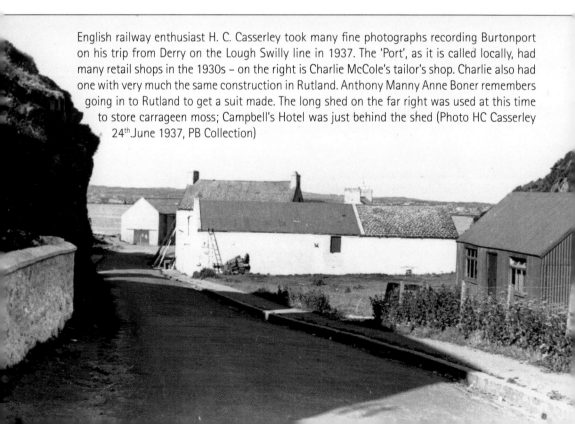

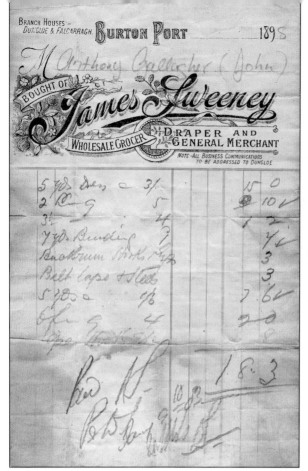

The Cope took over James Sweeney's shop in 1921; it had been derelict for years before this. This very decorative, early bill of sale, dating from 1898, is for curtain-making materials. Mr Sweeney operated out of Burton Port (sic), Falcarragh and Dungloe as a Draper, Wholesale Grocer and general Merchant (Original document from the late Tony Neil Gallagher, Roshine, Burtonport; Tony found it while renovating his house and kindly presented it to the editor of this book).

would have been in direct competition with his brother Johnny Rua across the road.

Burtonport Cope was rebuilt in 1973 and traded up until September 2006 when it closed its doors for it would appear the last time.

Peter Paul Ward, Clougherdiller, interviewed on 24th November 2006

Peter was born in 1937 and worked in Burtonport Cope in the summer of 1952, aged 15.

> "...Joe Brennan was the manager; Michael Ward and John Neil John Gallagher also worked there. John Neil John later managed the Cope in Lettermacaward for many years. The Cope had a number of stores in Burtonport, including the Cooperage where they made barrels. Down at the pier, 20 ton lorries would come in, and need to be unloaded – with cement, flour etc – into the Cope stores, where the Fishermen's Co-op is now. Myself and either Michael Ward or John Neil John would go down to unload the lorries; they were heavy, 8 stone, one hundredweight a

bag. The man driving the lorry didn't help us unload; he was dressed in a shirt and tie, he just drove the lorry.

The shop was very busy; there were three people there all the time. It was a two storey building with either a slate roof or maybe corrugated iron. The building attached next to it was a ruin – no roof and grass growing inside it. The upstairs of the shop had coffins (the Cope in Dungloe made coffins) and lots of eggs. The coffins were empty! The reason for all the eggs was because people would bring in eggs and sell or exchange them for groceries or money [*continuing as late as the 1950s the very earliest Cope business model*]. It sold paraffin for Aladdin, then Tilly lamps. The lighting in the Cope was from a large paraffin lamp like a Tilly, it hung from the ceiling. You had to be careful lighting the lamps. We sold single and double burners; the single used less oil.

Downstairs was a shop with almost everything you'd need (tea, sugar, flour, butter etc) but it did not sell milk. In those days, everyone had a cow or could get milk from a neighbour..."[13]

Paddy the Cope used to say: "...there never was a pennyworth of milk sold in Cleendra and I hope there never will..."[14] Times have changed.

"...You could get bacon, ham, pretty much everything you needed. The ham was sliced with a hand-turned slicer. There was a phone there, not many phones in those days. The counter was on three sides of the shop; as you walked in the door, the main counter was on the right, the till was there and the meat slicer. On the back wall were lots of biscuit boxes with netting across to stop children dipping into them! I would be sent there by my mother after school to get an ounce of tobacco and the Irish Press for my father – and maybe a loaf or tea. Once I brought back the Irish Independent by mistake – my father sent me back with it, saying he was a Fianna Fail man and didn't want that Fine Gael paper. The Cope men would sometimes give me a bag of broken biscuits; they couldn't be sold. They were very friendly people

There was no till, just a drawer with money in it. Everything was worked out by mental arithmetic which in those days was very complicated with the old money: pounds, shillings, pence, halfpennies, farthings – plus half crowns, florins, 10/- notes, sixpences, thrupenny bits, crowns: it was a nightmare. In Dungloe Cope, all that reckoning was done in the office, the counter assistant just sent up the bill and money and it was sent back in the wooden cup/shuttle. Burtonport was too small to have that kind of arrangement.

---

13 *Personal reminiscence from Peter Paul Ward to the editor in November 2006.*

14 *'My Story' Paddy the Cope, 1939*

The Story of the Cope

The 18th Century grain store in Burtonport was built by landlord William Burton Conyngham. In times when cash was hard to come by, payment of rent was made 'in kind' by growing corn. It was used by the Cope as a provisions store and for some time as a place for making barrels (a cooperage), initially by the Congested District Board (CDB, 1895 to 1923). The resurgence of the fishing industry in the 1890s, on the back of CDB investment, generated a huge demand for barrels. Owenie Paddy Ellie (O'Donnell) who used to live in the house where The Thatch Bar was, at Burtonport crossroads, was a cooper in Burtonport along with many others. During the Famine, the building served as a hospital and soup kitchen; an unspecified number of people are buried in the area in front of the building – a memorial is nearby in the front garden of the Medical Centre. No earlier photos than this appear to exist of this historic building (Photograph 1971, courtesy of Alistair Rowan and the Buildings of Ireland Charitable Trust: author of the fine survey 'The Buildings of North West Ulster', Penguin 1979; part of the 'Buildings of Ireland' Record).

Paddy would come down visiting on one of the lorries; he wouldn't have them drive him about, only if they were going to make a delivery. He'd go round all the shops, a friendly man.

The Cope also had a kippering shed next to where the Fishermen's Co-op is now, where the diesel tank is. It was a tall building; the raw herring were tacked up with small nails on rails and hung up high on rungs. There was a lovely smell in there from the burning wood; it must have been a special wood for the kippering..."

Burtonport Cope in 1976 with Eugene Doherty, the manager, on the left. The interior layout and the building itself remained much the same as at its opening in 1973 until its closure in 2006. On the till is Kay (Kathleen) O'Donnell. The two customers in the foreground are believed to be from Inishfree Island. (Cope collection)

Peter Paul has a remarkable memory for detail and remembers the wide range of shops that used to line the street in the Port:

> "...In those days, there were many shops in Burtonport: first as you came in was at Charlotte the Tailor's, then one at Maguire's, where Skippers is today. Across the road – Dinny Boyle's shop, now Margaret Dinny's - was built in my time, not long before I was working there
>
> Maguire's shop, just up from the Cope, was also a bar. In the room below, they bottled their own Guinness. A man from Purt used to do the bottling; he had a special machine for it. There was no electricity then [the ESB came in 1956]. Maguire had a generator and I think a windmill for power at the back.
>
> Opposite Maguire's was Cassie the Flower's small black house, next to Charlie McCole's house. There were no other houses on that side up to the old shed that Sweeney's had once had and then Jimmy Donnachada Rua's house [what had been Sweeney's Hotel].

The Story of the Cope

Patrick Rafferty and Patrick Boyle standing outside the Burtonport Cope in 1981. At this stage Burtonport and this Cope branch were both thriving; the fishing was very good and, at times Burtonport landed more salmon than any other port in Ireland, indeed was one of the top salmon ports in Europe (Cope Archive).

Healey's Drapery shop was in the corrugated iron shed that is still next to Rosehill, where Jimmy Frank lived (Jimmy Johnny and Breege O'Donnell live there now). It sold clothing, material for curtains, suits, skeins of wool. Mr Healey and his two daughters and Eileen Thomas worked there (Eileen later married Charlie Campbell, a tailor in Dungloe); they cycled down from Meenmore every day and back. Later he bought a brand new car – one of the first in the area, it was an Anglia, a green one. That was a big thing in those days. When I was young I thought the place was enormous; it was full of different coloured cloths, material. It doesn't look big at all now.

Campbell's shop was there of course and Charlie McCole's tailor's shop was on the space where Campbell's car park is now.

The Burtonport Cope in 2006, just before it closed, with the friendly faces of Ava Boyle, Lisa (Ryan) O'Donnell, Mairead Ward and Rosemary Gallagher (McShane). The Cope has made available the building at very reasonable rates but at the time of writing, there have been no takers. It is hoped that some use can be made of the building by a community group – it was very sad to see it close after over 80 years of serving the community (Cope Photo).

There were six bars around the Port in those days: Maguire's (now Skippers), John E Gallagher's (now The Lobster Pot), Jimmy Frank's (now Jimmy Johnny's) and Hugh Campbell's bar (The Harbour Bar now closed). Up at the crossroads there was The Thatch (now closed) and behind the church in Acres was a bar owned by a man called Jimmy; he sold it to Francie Melly, who sold it to Micky Connaghan – then a man from Annagry had it and after that Manus McDaid bought it.

There was a long black shed attached at right angle to the Cooperage; it was owned by Jimmy Frank for his turf. At the end of it (next door to JF's turf store) was the first butcher's shop in the Port. It was run by three brothers: Dinny, Pat and Doalty Boyle – the 'Paddy Johndies' [Dinny later built the shop opposite the Cooperage, referred to above]. Pat the Butcher's grandfather was Pat Paddy Johndie. They lived in Keadue and would butcher the meat down there. Later, Dinny bought Lackbeg House from a man called Kelly who bought it from McCarron; they used to butcher meat down there then. I remember they had a delivery bicycle with a large back wheel and small front wheel which had a big basket for the meat. They would go from door to door. Then they had a horse and trap with rubber wheels; it was very quiet on the roads, you could only hear the horse's hooves. After that they had a car for deliveries.

The Story of the Cope

I remember boats – half deckers or yawls – coming in from Arran with a couple of cows swimming behind them. The cows would walk up the slip and then have to walk to the Fair Hill in Dungloe where they would be sold.

And before you got into the Port there was Owenie Boyle's shop at the crossroads and Paddy McBride had one next to where the old girl's school is at the bend in Acres..."

Cope Committee member Eugene Doherty (born in 1923) was Burtonport Cope manager for two years, 1975-77; Kathleen (Kay) O'Donnell also worked there.

Eugene was, in his own words, used across all the branches in his time: he was six months in Meenbanad when Charlie the Cope was there; then three years in Dungloe under Eddie McCullagh. In 1945, he went to Kincasslagh for 20 years, where Packie Bonner and Neil O'Donnell were working too. He then became Assistant General Manager to Cyril Winder until 1989 – he worked one year past his retirement age at the request of the Cope. He has been a Cope Committee member since 1973.

ANNAGRY (1923)

"...In many of the districts in which branches have been established, The Committee of the Central Society have favoured and encouraged the formation of separate and independent societies. No doubt the small society has obvious drawbacks, but against this it has many things to recommend it, and foremost among these is the fact that it brings its members into more intimate touch with the movement, and draws forth the very essential quality of self-reliance. However this may be, the Templecrone Society could not resist the appeal for yet another branch store that has come from the Annagry district, particularly as the district in itself is too small for a separate society, and as it completes the entire area lying between the Gweedore Society on one side and the Inishkeel Society on the other. With this new branch now established, The Templecrone Society has taken in the entire district known as the Rosses, a thickly populated area stretching from the Gweebarra river on the south to the Dore river on the north, a distance of over twenty miles. It is as well perhaps that the Society cannot extend beyond its present compass, as it can better direct its energies to the fuller exploitation of the resources within. Here it has ample scope in the wide areas of peat and granite, with all the possibilities that these and a good water supply afford. And then there are the broad acres of unpastured mountain lying eastward and the broader sweep of the Atlantic to the west filling the imagination with vistas of yet unexplored treasure..."[15]

---

15 Irish Homestead booklet in 1924 'The Templecrone Co-operative Society'.

The old Annagry Cope was built in the then Cope's 'house style', plain with a corrugated iron roof, very similar to Meenbanad Cope (Photo from the late 1970s, early 1980s, courtesy of Vincie John O'Donnell).

Annagry East – a postcard view from the 1950s when housing density was much lower. Returning locals who had worked away and holiday home owners have built new homes and increased the population of Annagry in recent decades (Mícheál O Dhomnaill Collection)

Annagry West in an earlier view from the 1930s. (Mícheál O Dhomnaill Collection)

The Annagry Cope from 1918 to 2006

Remembered by Vincie John O'Donnell,
Meenacreeve, Meenderryinasloe, Annagry

"...In 1918, the Cope started in Neilins Bhrineys O Donnell's house: the lower room was the shop and heavy goods were upstairs. Goods came by train to Crolly and were transported by horse and cart to the Cope. The managers at that time were Anthony Gallagher and John Gallagher from Dungloe. John was married to (Annie Pheigi Ghrainne).

In 1923, a half acre site was purchased from Mici Fheilimi Walsh (the Glen, Annagry). Donnchad (Phadai Sheinin) O Domhnill (my grandfather) from Ranafast with five of his sons and with a few local labourers built the new cope on the site the Cope stands to day but nearer the road. It is said that they started at sunrise and they finished at sunset and had the timber-framed building sheeted and roofed in one day.

Pat Nicholls, a native of Cavan who married Biddy Cannon from Annagry was the next manager (their son, also Pat Nicholls, now lives in Letterkenny). The next manager was Mhici Charlie O Donnell from Annagry Married to Minnie. Their son Danny Minnie (deceased) and wife Terry (also recently deceased) owned the famous restaurant in Annagry,' Teach Killindarragh' better known as Danny Minnie's. During Mhici's time a loom from the near by factory was installed in the shop store. Mhici's sister Sally with Cissie (Phadie Neddie) Sweeney, Annie

The Annagry Cope in 1981, in a scan taken from the 75th anniversary booklet, with Hugh O'Donnell, Margaret O'Donnell and Timmy Doherty, or Timmy the Cope as he is known (Cope Archives)

Annagry Cope 2006: Jimmy 'Greaves' O'Donnell, Catherine Forker, Margaret Sharkey, Sadie Boyle, Patricia O'Donnell, Lee Forker.

"...On 1st December 2006, at the age of 101 years, Biddy (Phadraig Mhor) McGee from Meenacreva, Annagry officially opened the new Annagry Cope. Biddy is our Cope's oldest customer and still likes to shop there almost every day. She loves to meet and have a chat with the people she meets in the shop..." (Words and photograph by Vincie John O'Donnell, Meenacreeva, Annagry).

The Cope has made a significant investment in its Annagry store. The village, together with its hinterland, has a large local population and the results of the new facilities have more than justified the decision to modernise and extend (Cope Photo Archive, John Broadbent photograph)

The new Annagry store has been fitted out to a very high standard with modern facilities, including a new delicatessen which has proved very popular. The bright and welcoming interior, excellent parking and enthusiastic staff have led to a significant increase in turnover (Cope Photo Archive, John Broadbent photograph).

(Neil Pheigin) Duffy, and another lady made hand loomed carpets there.

Dermod Logue from Doochary was manager from 1930 to 1970. Before Dermot moved from Dungloe Cope to Annagry, the shop was divided into three parts, a dwelling house, a shop and a store. Dermot and Mrs Logue lived there till his retirement in 1970 by that time they had a new house built next to the Cope. They had two daughters: Ita who now lives in the U S A and Fidelma who now lives in Coleraine.

Timmy Doherty from Meenbanad took over as manager from Dermot in 1970 until 1993. During his time there he made a lot of changes. Firstly, he requested the dwelling place be removed as he wanted to extend the shop space. The old counter that stretched the length of the shop was removed and replaced with supermarket style shelving and a small counter beside the door that sold cigarettes, sweets and other small items. Business was beginning to expand and in 1981, the Cope got a new face lift: the old tin was replaced with blocks, three big windows were put in and the old slates were replaced with new slates.

Many managers have come and gone since: Joseph Sharpe, Packie Boyle, Brian Sweeney, Anthony Houston and Jimmy 'Greaves' O Donnell from Dungloe. Kathleen Marie Brennan from Drimnaughdig is our present manageress: Kathleen Marie started work in the Dungloe Cope in 1979 as an office girl and worked in many other departments, in 2000 she was promoted to manageress in the Agricultural and fuel department and was delighted to take up the challenge of managing the new and modern Cope in Annagry.

Again in 2006, the Cope has extended the supermarket area into the store, added a new butcher's shop and a hot deli counter; the old vinyl tiles were replaced by new ceramic floor tiles..."[16]

Killybegs

The Cope at one stage had five fishing boats operating up and down the Donegal coast at Downings, Burtonport and Killybegs as well as other ports in Ireland, both north and south, and in Scotland (the story of the Cope Boats and Killybegs is covered in more detail in Chapter 8). The opportunity to buy Coane's Hotel came up as well as the old stores in Killybegs. This suited the Cope and in 1944 they purchased the hotel for £2,200 and the furniture for £275.[17]

The building became well known as the Cope House and still kept this name when it was later sold and turned into a bar and guest house.

---

16 *Memoir from Vincie John O'Donnell, December 2006.*

17 *Cope Minute Book, Cope Archives.*

Downstrands Co-operative Agricultural Society

Downstrands Co-op in Narin became part of Templecrone Cope in 1971 and became independent again in 2003. The Horace Plunkett Foundation commented in 1930:

> "...The society was formed in 1910 in a district of 20-acre mixed farms with a proportion of grazing farms given up to fattening of store cattle. Not all farms are economic and the people are accustomed to supplementing their income by work on the roads and similar employment. The radius served by the society is about three miles. There are 80 members and 180 customers, who include all the farmers of the district. Share capital stands at £107; there are deposits of £732 and reserves of £327. Premises are valued at £100..."[18]

Current Branch Network

At the time of writing, the Cope has three branches outside its main Dungloe base: Lettermacaward, Kincasslagh and Annagry. In all three branches, the Cope has made very substantial investments to bring them up to date, including incorporating the post office in the new Kincasslagh store.

---

18 *Agricultural Co-operation in Ireland: A Survey' Nov 1931 by 'The Plunkett Foundation' George Routledge & Sons Ltd.*

Narin Cope in 1981 with Tony McNelis, Breid Ryan and Owen Bonner (Cope Archives, scanned from the 75th Anniversary booklet, 1981).

arin, Portnoo, Co Donegal

Downstrands Co-operative Society, Narin, in the 1930s; Downstrands was independently incorporated in 1910 and became part of the Templecrone Cope in 1971. It later became independent again in 2003 when the Cope decided to close the branch and has been run locally since then. The photo illustrates just how much cultivation was going on in those days; the field behind the shop is built up into ridges for potatoes (PB collection, D & Co contemporary postcard)

Narin Downstrands Co-op on the right hand foreground, in c1960 with a distant view of Inishkeel island (PB Collection, G Kiely Ballyshannon postcard)

Inniskeel Island from Nairn, Co. Donegal

Peter Paul Ward Clougherdiller and Vincie John O'Donnell from Meenacreeva, Annagry outside Vincie John's house in November 2006 – Vincie, who is a real craftsman, made the distinctive O'Donnell gate. Peter Paul and Vincie John have known each other for over 50 years; they both attended Loughanure Tech back in the mid 1950s. Peter worked in Burtonport Cope in 1952 and Vincie John's grandfather built the first Annagry Cope. Both provided stories and memories for this book – many thanks. (PB Photo November 2006)

Loughanure Technical School (Loughanure 'Tech') was officially opened on 3rd October 1938. Paddy the Cope became a member of the local committee governing the Tech in the same month. (PB Collection; history of the School from John Sweeney's very thorough account at www.loughanure.com/tech.php)

Chapter 4

The Builders' Providers

The official opening of the Cope's new Builders' Providers outside Dungloe on the Sheskinarone Road on 20th April 2007 was a landmark event. The new state of the art building represented the culmination of a century of evolution of the Builders' Providers from a collection of outbuildings behind the Cope's Main Street store in Dungloe into premises the equal of anywhere in Ireland.

The Cope, from its earliest days, has always been in the business of purchasing building materials, for its customers and for its own building projects. One only has to step back and look at the Cope footprint today compared to the 12ft by 13ft stone house where it all started in Cleendra. Over the years, the Cope has built many different buildings and structures: stores in Dungloe and the branches, factories, kippering sheds, the pier in Dungloe, its own pier in Burtonport, etc. It was a natural extension for it to be the provider of building materials for its customers and local builders as well.

In the Cope's early years, there was no standalone Builders' Providers business per se. Materials, building supplies would either be kept out back of the Main Street store in Dungloe or in ad hoc locations as necessary. Supplies would be kept at the Cope branch stores, replenished from time to time by delivery by lorry, and at the nearby stations at Burtonport, Dungloe Road or Meenbanad – wherever, in fact, it was convenient for the Cope and its customers to access.

The Cope was successful in getting important building contracts in its own right. For example, in 1935, it was recognised by the Housing Department and awarded the Gaeltacht Housing Scheme for the area.[1]

Supplies could be sourced from anywhere – Paddy in particular kept a close eye on where the best deals were. He made a trip to Holland in 1936 to secure a large cargo of cement – he also bought a big consignment (400 tons) of artificial manure or superphosphate, on the same trip. Travelling and doing business abroad was of no consequence to him by this stage – his age, he was in his 66th year, did not seem to be a barrier either. He recalls in his autobiography a boatload of cement (1,000 tons) arriving at Burtonport from Denmark. The Cope had become quite the international trading concern by the 1930s: importing building materials, flour, etc. and exporting its woollen goods and eggs and later, in the 1940s, exporting fish to Scotland and England.[2]

In 1938, the Cope became one of two registered distributors of cement (the other was Thomas McBride in Bunbeg) from the newly established Irish Cement company

---

1 IAOS Records, letter from Paddy the Cope to Dr Kennedy, 20th April 1935, National Archives.

2 'My Story' Paddy the Cope, various editions, 1939 through to 2006.

Builders' Providers Staff 1976. At the back: John Boyle, Jamesie Byrne, and Brendan McGonagle. At the front: Connie Boyle, Tony Cannon, Cathal McCole, Owenie Boyle, John O'Donnell, and Josie O'Donnell. This is at the old Builders' Providers at the back of the Main Street shop, prior to its moving to the Quay Road in stages. The building on the right was the timber yard; at the back, the Furniture store; on the left the back of the Main Street shop. To the right would have been the Wholesale department. (Cope Archive; thanks to Jimmy Durnin for providing the detail on layout).

which had been formed in Drogheda and Limerick. Somehow, and it is not clear from the correspondence how he did this, Paddy had managed to have the Cope registered as the only co-operative in Ireland permitted to distribute cement under the new regulations. Paddy wrote to Dr Kennedy, IAOS Secretary, wanting IAOS help in securing further business from co-operatives. He had planned a tour round co-operatives he expected to be purchasing cement: he'd already had orders from Wexford and promises of orders from Lombardstown, Dungarvan, Enniscorthy, Mitchelstown, Drinagh, Knockmeal and Campile. He estimated in total orders to date, or promised, of 4,000 tons – and with luck a total of 15-20,000 tons to all Societies.[3]

Paddy was pleased with the arrangement:

> "...regulated distributors are allowed 1/3d a ton and 7.5% - but must rebate 2/- a ton to any Society or firm that becomes registered merchants and buys 100 tons or over per annum. In any case we would have 2/6d a ton. The IAWS are not distributors..."[4]

This very favourable position does not seem to have survived for any length of time and would have been reviewed in any event once the Emergency began a year later. Wartime meant restrictions and government controls.

After the war, the Cope wanted to formalise its Builders' Providers status and applied, in October 1951, to the Irish Builders' Providers Association (IBPA) for membership. The application was rejected as one of the conditions was that 75% of trade should be wholesale. The Cope seems to have been excluded because it was also a retail store. Paddy was keen to get the discounts but the IAOS could not help in this case as they said "...business associations are a law unto themselves..." They did suggest that membership was not necessary in order to obtain the best discounts but Paddy disagreed.[5] The IAOS records are silent as to how this was resolved.

As the Main Street store grew, there simply wasn't the room in the Cope's back yard so, progressively, the site on the Quay Road, where the Bakery and Knitting Factory were located, developed as a separate Builders' Providers unit. Cyril Winder, Cope General Manager from 1969-1993 described the transition:

> "...In 1977, the Cope bought the land at the back of the Bank of Ireland and built a new store there, called then the Bank Store. In the same year, a new Timber store was built behind the Knitting factory on the Quay Road, next door to the town car park.
>
> In the same year, the Builder's Providers was moved to the Quay Road; the ESB garage was taken over and the old factory adapted. Now only

---

3   IAOS Records, letter from Paddy the Cope to Dr Kennedy, IAOS, 30th April 1938, National Archives.

4   Ibid. IAOS.

5   Ibid. Correspndence between IAOS and Paddy the Cope, 29th December 1951

the Agricultural Department was left behind the Main Street store; this was sub divided into the Agriculture and Fuel departments.

In 1978, the Cement Store was converted into the Household Drapery and Carpet Department (which was a subdivision of Furniture).

In1979, the site behind the Bakery was purchased enabling a further extension of the Builders' Providers (into, broadly, its footprint in 2006 before the big move to Sheskinarone). A further piece of land along the shore was bought at this time also.

In that year too, as a result of industrial trouble in the ESB and their statement that they could not meet capacity, we purchased and housed two Generator plants - one for the Main Street and the other for the Quay Road, both capable of meeting maximum demands even in the future..."[6]

In the early 1980s, when trading conditions forced closure on the Knitting and bakery businesses, it was a natural evolution for those buildings and the surrounding areas to be taken over by the Builders' Providers. Access was available from the town's car park and the Quay Road, making it a lot easier for customers and for suppliers too, certainly compared to the cramped conditions behind the Main Street store. The Quay Road became for the next twenty years, until closure in 2006, a dedicated Builders' Providers, with offices at the back of the old Knitting Factory and supplies spread around the yards and the five buildings

Eventually the level of business grew and plans were drawn up to take the Providers to a new location on the Sheskinarone Road. The Cope linked up with Donegal County Council to develop the foreshore area of Dungloe and the old Quay Road site was scheduled for development along with the town's car park. The plan required the demolition of five buildings, three of little architectural merit (the Bakery, Timber Shed and Bank/Cement Store) and two (Knitting Factory and the Cope's Village Hall) which were of minor architectural interest.

---

6   *Cyril Winder in the 1985 Staff Bulletin: "From One Million Pounds to Five Million Pounds: 1975-1985".*

Next Page: An aerial view of the Builder's Providers yard on the Quay Road in the 1980s showing: at the back, by the town car park, the large white double roofed building with skylights, the 'new' Timber Shed; in front with the 'saw tooth' roof, the old Knitting Factory, which became the office and bathroom/kitchen and other supplies; to the left, the old Bakery, which became a storage area for building supplies; to the right, the Cement Store – or Bank Store as it was called, it being built in the old Bank of Ireland back garden. In the front on the Quay Road, with timber stacked by it, was the old Cope Hall, which became a storage building for light supplies. From 1984 to 2006, the area in the photo housed all building supplies until the move to Sheskinarone Road (Cope Archive - this photo, and other aerial photos from the 1970s and 1980s, can be seen framed and on display in the upstairs corridor by the Cope boardroom, Dungloe)

Dungloe Quay Road: Builders' Providers Yard 1976. Packie Boyle is in the forklift, Barney McElhinney the van driver and Cathal McCole is driving the lorry. This was the Cope's first forklift; it was maintained by Jimmy Durnin, current Cope Committee member, son of Willie Durnin, great friend of Paddy the Cope and grandson of Liam Durnin, Paddy's great ally in moving the Cope into Dungloe in 1907. The location of the photo is at the back of the Knitting Factory, Quay Road, just by where the old Builder's Providers back door was later. The back of the Main St shops can be seen behind (Cope Archives).

The Knitting Factory's 'saw tooth' roof, designed to let in as much light as possible for the workers, had been an interesting part of Dungloe's skyline since 1918. The building had served the Cope and people of the Rosses well, providing employment for hundreds at a time and, for decades, providing the Cope with a strong, profitable export business.

The Cope Hall had had a long and varied history. It began with the Cope winning recognition for their early achievements:

> "...In 1909 another step was taken by the grant of a village hall from the Pembroke Irish Charities Fund, six of which had been offered to the most deserving societies in Ireland. This has offered an opportunity for

1981 Builders' Providers: 1981 Builders Providers Staff: Michael Breslin, John Sweeney, James Byrne, Leonard Hanlon, Josie O'Donnell, Pat Hanlon, John Moore, Mary Boyle, Owenie Boyle, Rose McGettigan, Patrick Sweeney, James A. Gallagher, Jim Duffy, Jim Ward, Hugh McCole, Pat Forker and Daniel McCafferty. (Cope Archive).

young and old to meet for recreation, and new colour and gaiety has thus been introduced into the life of the countryside…"[7]

The architect chosen by the IAOS in 1908 for the Cope's Village Hall was Limerick man Conor O'Brien (1880-1952). Based at 7, St Stephen's Green, Dublin, Mr O'Brien

---

7   *Rural Reconstruction in Ireland, A Record of Co-operative Organisation, by L. Smith-Gordon and L.C. Staples, 1917, preface by George Russell (AE), P.S. King & Son, London. The award was actually made in 1908 – IAOS records have a letter dated 27th July 1908 from Paddy the Cope saying a site had been found – it was one he had bought from Daniel Sweeney, the Cope Secretary. RAA (Robert Anderson, IAOS Secretary) wrote to Conor O'Brien asking that an architect (O'Brien) be sent to Dungloe. The Cope wanted to have the hall up by winter – it was delayed, probably because of legal complications from the lease with the landlord, eventually being finished in 1910. The builder was Thomas Glackin of Tubberkeen.*

Above: Joseph Sharpe and Francis 'Fra' Armstrong are on duty in the office of the old Builders' Providers in its last week of occupation. Bills and invoices were brought here to be paid here before items – timber, cement, other supplies - could be removed from the yard outside. The offices were in the back of the old 1918 built Knitting Factory. (PB photo, November 2006)

Left Top: Paddy the Cope Gallagher, the Copeman's grandson, son of Jim the Cope, and Jamesie Byrne, Builders' Providers Manager are on the roof of what had been the old Bakery. This shot was taken in November 2006, the last week of the Cope's old Builders' Providers at the Quay Road site before its move to Sheskinarone Road, Meenmore. In the far distance can be seen the Fair Hill with the *eircom* mast; in the foreground, the yard is being cleared. The whole area in view, including the car park, is planned for a major development coordinated by Donegal County Council (PB photo).

Left Bottom: The Cope Hall on the Quay Road had served the town of Dungloe well for almost 100 years since it was completed in 1910 – firstly as an entertainment, education and social venue (its original purpose), then as a Knitting Factory as Paddy the Cope gradually took it over. It then became, temporarily, the Main Dungloe Cope Store after the 1945 fire, while the Main Street store was being rebuilt and then for various uses, latterly as a stores building for the Builders' Providers. The building has changed in appearance from when first built: the two lower windows have been inserted and the garage/shed on the right added on – both many years ago (no date is recorded but at least 60 years ago – the windows probably when the Hall was in use as the Main Store after the fire and there was a need for more light and shop window frontage (PB photo November 2006).

had also designed larger projects for co-operatives such as creamery buildings. He probably took on the Cope Hall, a relatively small job, as a favour to IAOS Secretary, Robert Anderson, and also no doubt in recognition of the already legendary success of the Templecrone Co-op. He was an interesting man: as well as an architect, he was a mountaineer, accomplished sailor and a successful writer. In 1914, he sailed his yacht the Kelpie to the Belgian coast, loaded up with guns from Germany for the Irish Volunteers, which were later transhipped and unloaded at Kilcoole Harbour, Wexford – Erskine Childers was running guns into Howth on the Asgard on the same mission (O'Brien's cousin Mary Spring Rice was on the Asgard). In 1923, O'Brien circumnavigated the world in his small yacht Saoirse, leaving from and returning to Dun Laoghaire two years later. His celebrated book about the journey is a sailing classic.[8]

O'Brien, in his capacity as architect, visited Dungloe on a number of occasions. With Richmond Noble, IAOS organiser, he attended and spoke at the AGM on the 5th May 1910. It is not recorded what Messrs Noble and O'Brien said but it can't have gone down badly as a special subscription for the IAOS of 1/- per member was voted for unanimously.

Paddy wrote to Mr O'Brien in October that year regarding the completion of the hall:

> "...Dear Mr O'Brien, Mr Glackin, the Contractor, is now about finished with the Village Hall and I expect he will be writing to you some of these days to come and inspect. I hope you will be able to come as soon as he asks you as we do not want to give him any excuses. If you could have an agreement from the IAOS for me to sign giving them the site free it would convenience me very much, Your Truly (sgd.) P. Gallagher, Manager..."[9]

The Village Hall did not last long as it was originally intended. The story of how it became the first knitting factory is dealt with in Chapter 5.

The Timber Shed has a minor claim on history in that it was where recent Cope events, over the last 25-30 years, were recorded on large panels which divided sections of the shed. Jimmy Duffy took it upon himself to record the comings and goings of Cope people and events in an idiosyncratic way which at times is very humorous. The Cope (thanks to Breda (Langan) Sweeney) salvaged these and they are now stored at the new Builders' Providers site on Sheskinarone Road.

Some examples of the inscriptions from the 1990s:

> "...Dolly O'Donnell and Mary Boyle (Yankee) Last Day in Co-op Sat 23rd June '90

---

8   IAOS records, various dates between 1908-1910; 'In Search of Islands': A Life of Conor O'Brien, by Judith Hill, 2009, The Collins Press.

9   IAOS Records, National Archives, letter dated 12th October 1910

History can be recorded in many ways. The board panels along the wall of the Timber Shed in the old Builders' Providers are a record of events major and minor over some 25+ years. Inscribed by James Duffy they represent a social and humorous recent chronicle of Cope activity, well worth saving – one example: '...Jake Bonner bought THE LAST BAG OF 8 STONE – 50 KILOS – CEMENT, I HAVE CONCRETE EVIDENCE' (PB photo, November 2006).

The Story of the Cope

Gerard Coll started work in the Plumbing Section on Mon 31st Jan '91

Peter's new lorry arrived on Wed 19th April '90

Tony Cannon arrived with brand new Scania on Thurs 4th Jan '96, Wallace took her for test run 9.20am – 96 DL 248

Under a caption 'No Power Sharing': Electric cable cut by council JCB. Power off from 9.45am to 10.53am. Cable cut on Quay Road Fri 8th Nov '96. Gerry turned on the generator.

Theresa purchased new cups, plates, tea towels 26th Aug '96 for Canteen, cups 39p each..."

There are several hundred of these waiting to be transcribed – a future project for someone, a school perhaps. It is probably right not to overstate their importance as individually they are not significant events. However, it is memories like these, which normally are lost, that develop a resonance over time and give us a sense of what was going on day to day in the Cope.

The 'Design Team' at the Sheskinarone Road Builders' Providers in 2005, looking over the plans with the steel frame of the new building in the background: Ben Colangelo, Jimmie Nangle, Phil Ward, John Clarke, Joe Morgan, Jimmy Durnin, Joe McGonigle, Adrian Ward (in the white hat), Shaun Sands, Paddy Sweeney, Kieran McDermott from McDermott's Quarries, Doochary and Kieran Coyle (Cope Photo Archive).

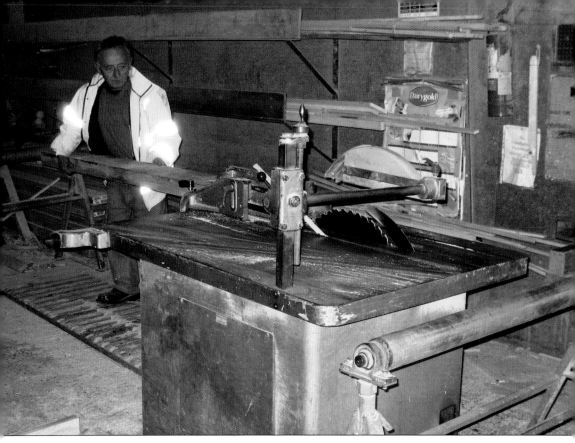

Daniel McCafferty, seen here demonstrating the bench saw, in the old Timber Shed on the Quay Road on the last day before the move to the new premises on Sheskinarone Road (PB photo, November 2006

Anthony Conaghan and Daniel McCafferty are in high visibility jackets in the Glass Room of the old Timber Shed on the Quay Road (PB photo, November 2006).

Robert Elliott and Jamesie Byrne at the counter of the old Builders' Providers in the Quay Road. This was part of the original 1918 built Knitting Factory. Jamesie, Manager of the Builders' Providers, is on the phone coordinating the move to Sheskinarone Road which was happening at the time the photo was taken (PB photo, November 2006)

The Cope's Sheskinarone Road Builders Providers was opened in 2006. In this photo, Cope Committee members Connie Devenney and Dom Bonner cut the ribbon (Marie (Sweeney) McGarvey photo).

At the opening of the new builder's Providers are: Jamesie Byrne, Manager Builders' Providers, Enda Bonner, Mayor of Donegal and County Councillor, Brendan Devenney (Donegal county footballer and Larsen Building Products) , Dinny McGinley TD, David Alcorn, County Councillor, Rose (McGettigan) Gallagher and Marine Minister Pat the Cope Gallagher (Cope Photo Archive)

In the car park outside the new Builders' Providers at the opening are: Gerald McElwee (Chemist), Maureen Doherty, Johnnie Doherty, Cope Committee Chairman, and Pat Dunleavy, James Greene (Cope Photo Archive)

The interior of the new new Builders' Providers – open for business on the day of its opening. Pictured are: Eugene Doherty, Connie Devenney, May Gorman, Dinny McGinley, Dom Bonner and Marguerite (Gorman) McGee (Cope Photo Archive).

The Builders' Providers team at the new Sheskinarone Road site: Back Row: Denis Boyle, Anthony M. O'Donnell, Hugh McCole, Tony Cannon, Brian O'Hagan, Paul Bonner, Anthony Glackin, Paul McGarvey, Patrick Gallagher, Leslie Winters, Fidelma Boyle Ward, Dayna Byrne, Rose Gallagher, Connor McCready, Frankie McGinley, Bobby Sweeney, Teague Boyle, Joseph

Sharpe, Philip Hodkiss, Peter Boyle, Michael Breslin, James Byrne. Front Row: Barry Melly, Kieran McGee, David Conway, Robert Elliott, Rob Fry, John O'Donnell, Fran Armstrong, Eddie Byrne, Vincent O'Donnell, Anthony Ward, Sean Melly, Joe Dickie, Pat Hanlon (Behind), Oliver Ward, Daniel McCafferty, Anthony Conaghan (Cope Photo Archive).

The 'state of the art' new Builders' Providers in Sheskinarone, pictured here in November 2006 just before it opened. The ambitious development has attracted praise from suppliers and peers in the business of serving the construction market. Costing c€4m, it has transformed the Cope's ability to meet the needs of local builders and households to well into the 21st century (PB photo, November 2006).

This is the northern end of the new Builders' Providers, showing the extensive yard and security access. This and the other features in the main building offer easier access, coupled with better parking and modern facilities enhance the value of dealing with the Cope. It has brought a new professionalism to the Cope's operation and positions the business well as the Cope enters its second century (PB photo, November 2006)

Chapter 5

The Knitting Factory

One of the earliest success stories of the Cope was the establishment of a knitting business. In times gone by, *every* girl learned to knit from an early age; 'the knitting' was out at every opportunity, when visiting, at the *airneál* - whenever a spare moment could be got, hands were busy making clothes for family members or for selling for much needed income. Donegal women, Rosses and island women in particular, were renowned both for their speed and for their skill with patterns.

Prices for socks and gloves had stayed much the same for over 60 years. Knitting was a true cottage industry: local women had to buy in the wool, carry it back, knit and then carry back their finished goods. Often they would have to walk as far as Glenties and, before the bridge was built over the Gweebarra in 1896, would have to cross at a ford, which could be hazardous, or take the ferry boat between Lettermacaward and Mulnamina. Paddy the Cope knew well this was a very hard way of making a living – and inefficient too; he saw a way in which women could be freed from the 'heavy lifting' part of the job.

An earlier commentator (James Hack Tuke) noted the same arrangements:

> "...Around Glenties there is a large amount of stocking and glove knitting, and there is an extensive warehouse in the town, where the people obtain the yarn they knit, generally receiving at the rate of per dozen pairs of socks. In some cases it may be more, in others less as a woman said that at Dunglow, where the same firm have a depot, she received 2s 9d for two dozen pairs. The woollen gloves, with coloured plaid backs, so much worn at present in England, are made here by thousands: 3s per dozen pairs is paid. The reason for the low price is that the hand-made has to compete with the machine-made yet low as is the pittance the women gladly earn it. As we drove in the dull wet evening to Gweedore, we saw women, five, six, or seven miles from that place, returning with their small earnings, and with fresh supplies of yarn for another week's or fortnight's work.
>
> At Dunglow, twenty miles from Glenties, where we stopped for the horses to bait, we saw crowds of women, none of whom looked to be in want, waiting at the depot for the supply of yarn..."[1]

Paddy first set up a factory in the Cope Hall in the Quay Road (which was built in 1910, with a £200 grant from the Pembroke Irish Charities Fund, as a recreational and educational hall for the community) – the factory was very

---

1   *James Tuke: A Visit To Donegal And Connaught In The Spring Of 1880*

Knitting was literally a cottage industry in the Rosses in the nineteenth and early part of the twentieth century: gloves, socks, pullovers and other woollen goods were knitted not just for family members but also to order for sale back to wholesalers in Glenties who had provided the raw wool. The money was poor and involved trudging tens of miles across the Gweebarra but it was a vital additional income. The Cope had no trouble recruiting a workforce of highly skilled women, some to work in its factory, others who would be outworkers with Cope machines. It was liberation from grinding, low paid work for many women and young girls (American Stereoscopic Company New York, Donegal Home Industry, PB Collection).

busy, particularly during the war years, and eventually became just too small for level of production .

The IAOS and Sir Horace Plunkett strongly encouraged the involvement of women in the cooperative movement (and promoted this via the Irish Homestead magazine). In 1910, the United Irishwomen were formed with IAOS assistance. Later in the year, one of the very first branches was set up in Dungloe with the help of Mrs Ellice Pilkington, who was appointed the first honorary organiser:

> "…On December 3rd, I started for Dungloe, Co. Donegal, with a diminutive personal equipment, but with the best substitute that good fellowship could give me - an organiser's bag and map lent by the secretary of the

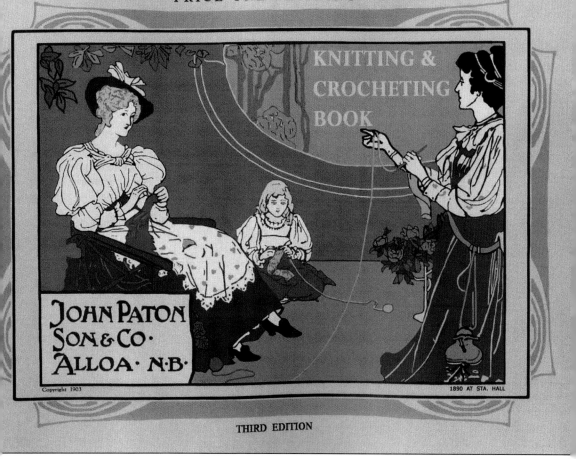

KNITTING &
CROCHETING
BOOK

JOHN PATON
SON & CO·
ALLOA· N·B·

Copyright 1903

1890 AT STA. HALL

THIRD EDITION

Paddy bought yarn from John Paton and Sons, of Alloa in Scotland, in 1911 in order to make some fashionable 'Swiss-style' sports coats which he later took to London to sell. He remembers the company as Paton and Baldwin (Paton later joined with Baldwin in 1920) and always found them excellent to deal with. A pattern book like this would have been a source of ideas for the Cope knitwear business. (John Paton and Sons c1903. Ivy Rose Vintage Reproductions www. ivarose.com. PB Collection).

Irish Agricultural Organisation Society, a thermos bottle and a passport in the old tongue given voluntarily by the president of the Gaelic League [Douglas Hyde, later the first President of Ireland 1938-45]. A herald in telegraphic font was despatched before me by Father Finlay.

On arrival I found an independent capable community, a flourishing cooperative society with a manager who not only knew his work, but held the confidence of his people, a knitting industry in the hands of the women and girls, and all around them great possibilities for cottage gardening, dairying, and jam-making; a village hall for social meetings, a fine healthy race of men and women, bilingual, capable of enjoying intellectual pursuit, and not ashamed to use their hands.

Pictured here are some of the styles that would have been produced by the Cope's Knitwear department up until the end of the First World War. Much of their output in the war period would have been for sale to the British Army and Navy – and the Belgian and Indian Armies too. The war was a boom time for all manufacturers of woollen goods. Illustrated are: a shawl, a boot sock and a sportswear 'fancy' sock for golf or cycling. (PB Collection, Paton's Pattern Book, c1903)

Aonach, 1912

IRISH EXHIBITION,

NOVEMBER 12th to 16th,

Royal Horticultural Hall, Westminster.

The Aonach enables manufacturers to place their goods on the London market—by providing facilities for buyers from various firms to inspect the actual articles and satisfy themselves as to the value offered. Tenth annual Aonach now being organised. Some spaces to let at very moderate charges.

Write for Plan, Prospectus, &c., to

THE AONACH SECRETARY,

77 FLEET STREET, LONDON, E.C.

The Gaelic League organised an annual Aonach in Westminster every year from 1903-13. The outbreak of war prevented the Aonach from taking place in 1914 and, what with the developments towards independence and the later turmoil, it was not revived afterwards (Advert in The Times of London).

And yet there was a silent sorrow here, for the curse of emigration was upon them. The young women and girls were slipping off one by one to the land of promise on the other side of the broad Atlantic, and only some of them came home again to listen mournfully to the sad sobbing of the sea on a dreary shore. The women did not speak to me of this, but the men did.

A meeting was held in the newly-opened village hall, where I gave the message the United Irishwomen had sent me to deliver. The proposal to start a branch of United Irishwomen was welcomed enthusiastically, and the men promised to safeguard the interests of the sister society and free the women from the oppression of the 'truck' system) Members were elected to act on a committee, and within a week the officers of this committee were appointed. I left on December the 5th with these encouraging words in my cars: `A good honest movement like this is sure to succeed.' There is now at Dungloe a busy branch of United Irishwomen with over two hundred members; two instructresses under the home improvement scheme are at work (subjects – household economy, home dairying, cottage gardening); the village hall is a centre for meetings of all kinds..."[2]

The link up with the United Irishwomen and the IAOS gave Paddy the Cope ideas on how he might drum up more business. He became a great evangelist

---

2 *'The United Irishwomen, Their Place Work and Ideals' by Horace Plunkett, Ellice Pilkington and George Russell (AE); Preface by Rev. T.A. Finlay, 1911, Maunsel and Co Ltd Dublin (The United Irishwomen – motto 'Deeds not Words' - was later to become the Irish Countrywomen's Association).*

The Story of the Cope

for the Cope's knitting business, travelling in Ireland, Scotland and England to fairs and making contact with major buyers of knitwear. In 1911 and 1912, he travelled to London via Belfast and Manchester to the Aonach[3] at the Royal Horticultural Society in London. He was invited by Mary Spring-Rice[4] who was an active member of the United Irishwomen.

On his way to sell Cope knitwear at the Aonach in Westminster, Paddy the Cope travelled from Donegall Quay, Belfast (and from there to Liverpool) laden down with samples - and a cooked chicken his wife Sally had packed for him. He travelled in a homespun sports suit (made by Joe Breslin) and wore knickerbockers. He was advised to travel not steerage, as he had done to Glasgow in earlier days, but saloon, where he could make business contacts, and he booked a berth for the first time in his life (he was over 40 at this stage). Paddy was learning slowly how to be a commercial traveller and not a migrant worker.

Paddy, in his autobiography, consistently referred to the Royal Horticultural Hall as the *Agricultural* Hall. One can only assume that what he recalled, from the displays he saw there, were the most useful exhibits, i.e. the ones which would make sense to a Cleendra farmer, vegetables, crops and their like, not fancy flowers that a horticulturalist might also grow.

Thanks to The Irish Homestead, Sir Horace Plunkett and the IAOS, the Templecrone Co-op and Paddy himself were becoming well known. His many visitors at the stall he shared with Mary Spring Rice at the Aonach – most likely introduced to him by Miss Spring-Rice herself as she was well connected - included Sir Roger Casement and Erskine Childers. Paddy dined with the Childers at their house and met other members of their group, keen to meet the man leading the 'revolution' in West Donegal and also to hear his views on Home Rule.

The Cope's knitwear business was going from strength to strength: Paddy wrote to the IAOS Secretary R A Anderson in May 1912:

> "…very good trade, the Army and Navy Co-op Society are pushing our goods…we have opened new premises here in Dungloe and although we made very little profit last year I will be much disappointed if we do not have a record year for 1912…"[5]

---

3   The Aonach (Irish for Fair) was an annual event established in London, by the Gaelic League, to promote Irish crafts and produce.

4   The Hon. Mary Spring Rice (1880-1924) from Foynes, Limerick was the only daughter of Lord Monteagle, one of Sir Horace Plunkett's earliest supporters. Mary and her cousin Conor O'Brien, architect of the Cope Village Hall, both took part in the 1914 gun running for the Irish Volunteers: Mary on Erskine Childers;' boat the Asgard, which came into Howth; and Conor on his boat the Kelpie

5   IAOS records, letter 3rd May 1912.

The Landing Stage at Liverpool Docks as it would have looked in 1911 when Paddy the Cope travelled from Dungloe to London for the Aonach. Paddy made his way from here to Manchester by train. Later in the Cope's history it was to Liverpool that the Cope sent their granite sets; they were badly let down by a Liverpool buyer who never paid them – and from Liverpool or Cardiff that their charter boat *SS Glenmay* travelled with supplies and returned with Cope products to the new Cope quay at Dungloe (Contemporary photograph, c1910-20, PB Collection).

Paddy attended a United Irishwomen's Sale of Work in Fintragh House Shrewsbury Road Dublin; the co-operative stalls were organised by Mary Spring Rice:

> "...Mr P. Gallagher's knitting industry (Dungloe) showed very cheap and remarkably good value in golf jerseys, children's coats, gentlemen's socks etc..."[6]

The First World War (1914-18) led to an upsurge in demand for clothing, socks, gloves, balaclavas etc for soldiers - to use the local Rosses' term, the Cope's knitting business was 'flying'. Paddy had to turn away business as there simply wasn't the room to take on more work. He wrote a letter to a Mr Daniel Tighe of The Glen, Glenties:

---

6   *The Irish Times 13th June 1914.*

"…We are very much obliged for yours re commission. We herewith agree to allow you 5% commission on all goods received through you and also on gloves of your pattern to the War Office. Re socks, I am sorry I cannot undertake the orders as I am booked up for the next four months…"[7]

A purpose built factory was built on land behind the Cope Hall in 1918 and opened in 1919 by the Rev Tom Finlay S.J. of the IAOS – Finlay was a great supporter of the Templecrone Cope and its founder. The new factory, equipped with the latest machines, was a resounding success, leading to work for 150-200 women at a time, in addition to scores and at times hundreds of cottage-based 'outworkers' (The factory remained in business until 1983. The building itself continued in use as part of the Builders' Providers until 2006).[8]

The factory was built by three stonemason brothers from Meenderrynasloe, Loughanure: Con, Charlie and Frank Duffy. During the building work, they stayed with Biddy Hughie O'Donnell on the Main Street, next to where Beedy's Bar is now – in the building where 'Wizzy Brown' the bookmakers were in 2006).

"…Tenders were received from James Gallagher (£60) and from M O'Donnell and Con Duffy (£90 5s 6d). It was decided after discussion that the former tender should be accepted, a bonus to be offered if the work should be completed before 1st August. £3 was added to the amount tendered for the building of the extra door and window…"[9]

Clearly a rethink was done and the Duffy brothers got the contract later.

The War helped fuel the phenomenal increase in turnover that the Cope experienced in the period up to 1920.

Until the new factory was built, Paddy had commandeered the Cope Village Hall full time but it was simply not big enough – he had back orders of six months or more at times.

The Templecrone story was syndicated across America in 1914: in this extract, Paddy is speaking to a party of Americans looking into co-operatives - they had been directed by Sir Horace Plunkett of the IAOS to go to Dungloe to see and learn.

---

7   *Letter dated 13th October 1914, IAOS Records, National Archives, Bishop Street, Dublin. Daniel Tighe complained bitterly to Sir Horace Plunkett that Paddy had not kept to his agreement but had completed a small order and then dealt direct with the customer (the British Army). The IAOS found themselves in a difficult position – Paddy's explanation – that their agreement was only for a small order and not a longer term arrangement - was accepted by Plunkett and the issue appears to have been dropped. In any event, there was going to be plenty of work to go round for the next few years.*

8   *The old Knitting Factory was 'tossed' in April 2009 to make way for the new Dungloe shoreline and road developments.*

9   *The Cope Minute Book, 14th June 1918.*

98527.J.V.   VICTORIA STREET, MANCHESTER.

Paddy didn't travel straight to the Aonach in Westminster in 1911. He stopped off in Manchester and stayed in the Victoria Hotel (room 203). It was his first encounter with a revolving door and he says that he went round several times before managing to get in. He was in Manchester longer than he had intended, seeing buyers (Messrs Byhands and also Smith and Jamieson's) recommended to him by Sir Jocelyn Gore-Booth (of Lissadell House) who was active in the co-operative movement. He had no luck with selling knitwear there but he did receive valuable advice about how to look the part of a travelling salesman; he acted on the advice and bought a business suit in Market Street. The contacts he made were very useful as later on, in wartime and afterwards in the twenties, Manchester buyers placed some very big orders with the Cope (Contemporary postcard, PB Collection; 'My Story')

Irish Lace and Knitted Goods

"…Our co-operative company looks after a good many things besides selling eggs and butter. We are helping the girls market their lace and knitted work. Two years ago we asked the government department to send us an instructor to teach the girls to make hand-knit sport coats (sweaters). They sent a man up. He talked with some of the men here who were not friendly to this cooperative movement. Nothing was done. Our girls were getting one shilling and sixpence (36 cents) for knitting a dozen pairs of socks, using up from three and a half to four pounds of wool. These socks were purchased off the women by an agent of a wholesale trader.

The co-operative society decided they could do better by the girls than these buyers. Since they started buying, the girls get seven shillings six pence ($1.87) from the society for knitting a sweater coat, using only two pounds of wool and taking only one half as long as a dozen pair of socks. Putting it another way, for the same amount of wool and the same time spent in knitting, the girls get 15 shillings ($3.75) instead of one shilling and six pence (36 cents). That is, our society is paying them ten times what they used to get from the other buyers for their knitting. Formerly the girls who knit lace were bound by a bargain under which if they sold to any one privately they were boycotted. The buyer told them unless they sold him all be would buy nothing. Now we are getting fairly good prices for the lace, better than they got before and we, of course, permit them to sell wherever they can. They frequently have opportunity to sell to tourists and others who come through here. While we get fairly good prices for the lace, there is no steady market for it, as there is for the knitted goods..."[10]

American writer Marie Harrison visited Dungloe in 1916 and wrote about the Cope for 'The World's Work' magazine and later a whole chapter of her book 'Dawn In Ireland' was about the Society – this extract gives some colourful detail about the knitting factory:

> "...It was that Jesuit priest of great brilliance and understanding, Father Finlay, who gave Mr. Gallagher the helping hand he so greatly needed. Father Finlay saw at once that the installation of knitting machines would provide work for a considerable number of girls. In June of 1915 the first machine was put up, and as the general affairs of the Society progressed, more and more machines were added until a hundred and forty happy workers are now employed.
>
> It has been my business from time to time to visit factories in England where girls are working. But I have not at any time seen a building where the workers are as pretty, as contented, and as well paid as at Dungloe. With the exception of a few hands who are on time and who finish at seven o'clock after a free meal, the workers are at their machines from 8.30 till 5.30, with an hour off for midday dinner. The hall, which will soon be too small for the growing number of employees, is lit by electricity. It is light and very airy.

---

10   Western Newspaper Union 1914 – the article was carried in score of papers across the States.

Next Page: Paddy brought Cope handknits to the Aonach (Irish for 'Fair', translated as 'Irish Exhibition' in England) in 1911 (14-18th November) and 1912 (12-16th November) at the invitation of Mary Spring Rice of the United Irishwomen He also brought with him the Cope's fashionable 'Swiss-style' handknit sports coats; he was delighted to sell all he brought *and* collect orders for more knitwear. This photograph, taken of the very first show in the Royal Horticultural Hall (or Agricultural Hall as Paddy remembered it) in 1904, shows the inside of the same hall where Paddy laid out his wares. It was a different world to the one he was used to and on the first few trips like this he was, he tells us in his autobiography, very self-conscious (Photograph courtesy of RHS, Lindley Library)

Winds from the sea blow in from the open windows on the girls as they stand or sit at their work in frocks of bright primitive colours.

The average wage is over a pound a week on piece work. In factories in prosperous Belfast women think themselves lucky to get thirteen shillings a week. Here in Dungloe a clever girl can readily make a couple of pounds. "Do you mind telling me how much you got last week?" I asked one girl beautiful in her black hair and in the depths of her grey eyes.

"Not at all," she responded eagerly; "it was two pounds ten."

I chanced on another worker. Ten weeks before, she had come as a learner, making eight shillings in her first week. "It was one pound six last pay day," she told me proudly. Three sisters, on the same day, took home £4 15s. between them.

Erskine Childers took Paddy to the House of Commons (Paddy recalls this was in 1911) where he heard Lloyd George speak; Paddy was very impressed with Lloyd George's oratory. It is possible that he was in the Commons when the 'Welsh Wizard' was speaking on the 1911 National Insurance Bill – the Bill's extension to Ireland was debated on 14th November, the evening of the first day of the Aonach Paddy was attending. Childers remarked to Paddy: 'I have no faith in Lloyd George; I fear he is not the friend of your country he would try to make the people believe'. Paddy added in his autobiography 'He certainly was right about Lloyd George' (PB collection, LL postcard c1905, posted in c1913).

In this view from Dungloe pier in c1930, the distinctive 'sawtooth' roof design of the Knitting factory can be seen. The factory was completed in 1918 and officially opened by Rev Tom Finlay in 1919. The roof was designed to let in as much northern light as possible for the women working there. Behind, on the Quay Road, was the Cope Hall and on the right is a smaller, wooden building which was at one stage a dispensary, remembered by local residents. In later years, Paddy also used it as a cottage for visiting friends to stay in. This whole area later became the Builders' Providers yard in the 1980s after the Knitting Factory and the Bakery had closed. (Mícheál O Dhomnaill Collection, contemporary photographic postcard).

All along the way it was the same happy story...

It happened that afterwards I was waylaid by a gombeener who insinuated that such figures were manufactured, that these girls really made but a few shillings a week. . . . The answer is in the pay-sheets which are kept with careful detail. They are open to the inspection of all interested visitors.

Is there any reason why the girls should not be well paid? There are no employers to demand big profits. The profits that accrue go to the upkeep of the factory, to the maintenance of the Society, to the provision of dividends, but primarily to the payment of first-rate wages. Mr. Gallagher gets no pecuniary benefit beyond a fixed weekly wage. If the factory had been the property of a profit-making business man, lower wages would have been paid, for in a district where there are so few chances of employment it would have been easy enough to engage workers at half the wages given to the Society's girls. But because it is all a co-operative scheme, the workers get the first benefits.

Here in the land where the women once wept tears of bitter sorrow, where even the blessed consolations of religion were powerless to mend broken hearts or heal a shattered faith here there is a great peace and a great happiness. The girls are joyous to see in the colour and radiance of their perfect health. They are well shod and comfortably dressed. They are quick in intelligence and courteous in manner. They have no desire for the artificial attractions of town life. Their pleasure is in bringing comfort to the homestead, in helping their brothers and their fathers, in watching the country grow rich and contented.

Their work at the machines is very good. Were it not so, Mr. Gallagher himself could not keep the factory alive. But it has been a magnificent commercial success. I saw a letter from a Manchester firm giving an order for £5,000 worth of gloves. After two big contracts completed for the Belgian Government, a third is in process of fulfilment. Last year a big order for the Indian Army was executed. Firms in England know the worth of these Donegal goods. May it happen that one day each article will bear in addition to the words "British Made" a distinctive Irish trade-mark so that the fame of the little village may spread afar.

The money paid out in wages finds its way into the stores again, for the girls are great customers of the Society, banking their money or getting useful boots and clothes at the shop. If it so happens that some desired object is not in stock, the knitting girl willingly waits until the Society can get it for her rather than visit the accursed gombeener.

This great movement, as I have indicated, has been accomplished without the help of the clergy of the immediate district. It is typical of the new independence of the Irish people, Catholic to the end in heart and action, but independent of the priesthood on the practical ways of life.

During the holding of a special Lenten mission at the church in Dungloe, Mr. Gallagher started the day's work at a much later hour than usual so that the girls might attend the morning services. But the most heated opposition from that narrow-minded section of the clergy that exists in every church would be powerless to extinguish his burning spirit of progression or to water down his great enthusiasm.

I look upon "Paddy the Cope" this middle-aged man in his workman's clothes, with his reddish moustache and kindly eyes, and a voice so soft and gentle as one of the leaders of the age. No measure of that home government that has been so long delayed could have done as much in North- West Donegal as the enterprise of this man and his loyal band of followers. Very surely he is a token of the new spirit of the land the spirit that is concerning itself less with political abstractions than with the practical every-day fellowship which is the only way to enduring contentment..."[11]

---

11 'Dawn in Ireland', Marie Harrison, Andrew Melrose Ltd 1917 (from Chap 1: The Folk of the Rocks')

The Story of the Cope

R.A. Anderson, Secretary of the IAOS, visited the Society in July 1917:

> "…I visited this Society on the following dates 3rd 4th and 8th July 1917, on the last occasion with Father Finlay and Mr Adams. So much has been said about this remarkable Society that I only desire to note a few points which I have not, so far, seen touched on.
>
> On the date of my visit, to the Society's knitting factory 141 girls were regularly employed and the weekly wages bill was £150. Three sisters told me they had earned over £6 between them the previous week; there other sisters within a few shillings of the same amount, while one girl had received £3 5s for her week's work. Miss McDonnell, the overseer of the work, is paid less than some of the workers and is actually taking the place of three women who preceded her – one of them a Scotchwoman – and doing the work without any friction which was constant before she was appointed. The main work on which the girls were [engaged] was gloves for the Belgian and British Armies.
>
> Mr Gallagher has also taken the precaution of arranging for work for the girls after the war. He has hit on what seems a very promising "line" – ladies' and children's cotton gloves, hitherto imported from Austria. They are made in exceedingly attractive shades and are beautifully finished and made up for sale and are quite different to any cotton gloves I have ever seen. There is practically an unlimited demand for them and Mr Gallagher is able to obtain supplies of the proper thread.
>
> The business is carried on in the Pembroke Village Hall, which has been fitted up for the purpose and lighted by electricity. It accommodates 90 girls and the remainder are disposed elsewhere on the premises. The Factory Inspector has pointed out that the building is overcrowded and does not contain sufficient air space. Apparently the Home Office officials take no account of ventilation for, when I was there, the weather was very warm but the building was quite cool and airy.
>
> I do not know whether the Pembroke Trustees are aware of the use to which the Hall has been turned, but while it is a departure from the purpose for which the Hall was originally intended, there can be no doubt as to the beneficial results from its recent use. It may here be mentioned that the Parish Priest was enabled to erect another Parochial Hall in 1913, which, however, is not available for meetings of the Templecrone Society and seems to be more or less a rival institution.
>
> It is somewhat strange that this cooperative factory, which has brought comfort and prosperity to so many families, is never favoured by a visit from a prominent clerical member of the CDB whose duties bring him frequently to Dungloe. The Board has, however, given liberal assistance to a proprietary Carpet Factory which has extensive buildings at

Killybegs and Crolly, but where I am informed, the average earnings of the girls are considerably less than half as much per head as those of the Templecrone workers. There seems to me something wrong about all this, but possibly the Templecrone Factory is all the better for having had to do without clerical or government patronage.

With sweated labour such a general institution in Co. Donegal, it is worthy of note that there is only one sweated worker in the Templecrone Society – Mr P. Gallagher. The man who has built up this splendid Society with its multifarious benefits; who has evolved the idea of a knitting factory and has made it a success, who night and day spends his time and his tireless energy and devotes his whole heart to the interests of his poor neighbours receives the munificent salary of £100 a year. In any business enterprise of a capitalistic nature his value would be readily recognised and his current salary multiplied by any figure from 5 to 10..."[12]

Anderson's remark about the Congested Districts Board reveals a competitive streak in him; clearly the IAOS and CDB, although working as it were 'in the same vineyard', did not always agree. The CDB had, though, a great deal of respect for Paddy the Cope and his achievements:

"...In only one case was the principle of co-operation applied to female industries, and this was in the parish of Templecrone, or Dungloe, in "The Rosses" district of Donegal. The Society was first established for buying the requirements and selling the produce of the agricultural inhabitants of the district, and subsequently it undertook the ownership of a most vigorous and successful knitting industry. Hand-knitting had existed for generations past in West Donegal; but as a rule an average woman could not in 1891 earn more than 1s. 6d. a week by her knitting, and even this, in the case of some employers (though not the chief, like the McDevitts of Glenties), the workers had to accept payment in tea and sugar of nominal equivalent value. The Templecrone Co-operative Society was fortunate in having as its Manager a local man, Mr. Patrick Gallagher, with an intimate knowledge of the people of the district, with natural business aptitude, and a mind receptive of useful information.

The Board's relationship with this Society were very friendly, and at the starting of it some slight assistance was given by the Board, and advice was always available but the Society speedily became independent in every way and prosperous. As in all concerns the personal qualifications of the managing man is the leading factor for success, but no doubt

---

12 IAOS file note in R. A. Anderson's own hand. Anderson was the Secretary of the IAOS from its beginning in 1894 to 1921. The CDB is the Congested Districts Board – Anderson is referring to Bishop of Raphoe, later Cardinal, Patrick O'Donnell. There would appear to be some tension between the two men – and, sheer speculation here, possibly rivalry between CDB and IAOS as many of their worthy activities overlapped and were in competition with each other.

the wisdom of training an understudy is present in the mind of Mr. Gallagher...".[13]

Ruth Russell, an American journalist interested in the Co-operative movement and Ireland's struggle to achieve independence, was invited to Ireland by Eamon de Valera. In 1918; she came to Dungloe [in the money values below, Russell used an exchange rate of $5 to the £]:

> "...Paddy remembered how his mother used to try to help with her knitting. He saw girls at spinning wheels or looms working full eight hours a day and earning only $1.25 to $1.50 a week. So with permission of the society, Paddy had two long tables placed in the entertainment hall, and along the edges of the tables he had the latest type of knitting machines screwed. Soon there were about 300 girls working on a seven and a half hour day. They were paid by the piece, and it was not long before they were getting wages that ran from $17.50 to $5.25 a week.

> Incidentally, Mr. Gallagher, as manager, gave himself only $10.00 a week.

> When I saw Patrick Gallagher in Dungloe, he was dressed in a blue suit and a soft gray cap, and looked not unlike the keen sort of business men one sees on an ocean liner. And indeed he gave the impression that if he had not been a co-operationist for Ireland, he might well have been a capitalist in America.

> He took me up the main street of Dungloe into easily the busiest of the white plastered shops. He made plain the hints of growing industry. The bacon cured in Dungloe. The egg-weighing - since weighing was introduced the farmers worked to increase the size of the eggs and the first year increased their sales $15,000 worth. The rentable farm machines.

> "Come out into this old cabin and meet our baker," Paddy continued when we went out the rear of the store. "We began to get bread from Londonderry, but the old Lough Swilly railroad is too uncertain. See the ancient Scotch oven--the coals are placed in the oven part and when they are still hot they are scooped out and the bread is put in their place. Interesting, isn't it? But we are going to get a modern slide oven."

> After viewing the orchard and the beehives beneath the trees, I remarked on the size of the plant, and its suitability for his purpose. He said: "It used to belong to the gombeen man."

> The sea wind was blowing through the open windows of the mill. Barefoot girls - it's only on Sunday that Donegal country girls wear shoes and then

---

13 *History of the Congested Districts Board (pp 82-3), W.L. Micks, 1925, Eason and Son Ltd*

The Rev Tom Finlay S. J. opened the Cope Village Hall in 1910 and the Knitting Factory in 1919; he was a good friend to the Cope and to Paddy. Paddy's success in enlisting support from distinguished men of the day created envy locally: he was accused of too close a relationship with Unionists and Protestants (like Sir Horace Plunkett and Harold Barbour). The Cope was accused of siding with forces against Irish Nationalism which enraged Paddy as nothing could have been further from the truth. The Rev Finlay (a Jesuit we should remember) was called the Orange priest, a slur he dismissed by saying mass in Dungloe when he visited. As Paddy recounts in his autobiography, it was Tom Finlay who successfully appealed to Dublin Castle and the Lords Justice when Paddy had been sentenced vindictively to 1 month in Derry jail and had Paddy released immediately (Cope photograph from 'My Story', 1946; for further details on Paddy and Rev Finlay's dealings, 'My Story' is a good and entertaining source).

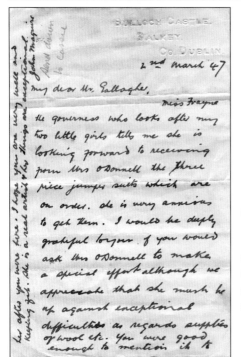

A letter from John Maguire of Bulloch Castle, Dalkey (south of Dublin), to Paddy the Cope in 1947 praising the Cope's fine woollen wear – and Cassie Jock in particular: "...she is an artist and her things are exceptional..." Paddy's note asks that it be sent down to Cassie. There is a reference to post war wool shortages in his letter. (Jim the Cope Collection, Cassie Jock's Main Street house; information on Cassie from Brigid Byrne)

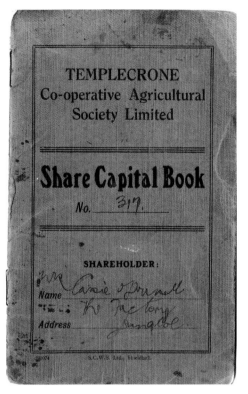

This share capital book no. 317 belonged to Cassie 'Jock' O'Donnell, who managed the Knitting factory for many years. '... Cassie was born in what is now Gay Byrne's house in Tubberkeen; she was there till she was 80 or so...' (Brigid Byrne). Every Cope shareholder had a certificate or later a share book; this one is part of the collection in Cassie's house that was put together by Jim (Packie) the Cope.

Brigid Byrne and Winnie Ward both worked in the Knitting Factory for many years. This photograph was taken in the 1950s in Dublin (Brigid Byrne collection)

they put them on only when they are quite near church - silently needled khaki-worsted over the shining wire prongs. Others spindled wool for new work. As they stood or sat at their work, the shy colleens told of an extra room added to a cabin, or a plump sum to a dowry through the money earned at the mill. None of them was planning, as their older sisters had had to plan, to go to Scotland or America.

"As the parents of most of the girls are members in the society they want the best working conditions possible for them," said Mr. Gallagher as he took me out the back entrance of the knitting mill. "So we're building this new factory. See that hole where we blasted for granite; we got enough for the entire mill in one blast. That motor is for the electricity to be used in the plant.

"Northern sky lights in the new building--the evenest light comes from the north. Cement floor - good for cleaning but bad for the girls, so we are to have cork matting for them to stand on. Slide-in seats under the tables--that's so that a girl may stand or sit at her work..."[14]

FORMAL OPENING OF TEMPLECRONE FACTORY AT DUNGLOE

September 6th 1919

"...The extensive factory, just completed, which has been erected by the Templecrone Co-Operative Society at Dungloe, was opened on Sunday 24th August by Rev. T. A. Finlay, S.J., Vice President of the IAOS Father Finlay was accompanied on the platform by Mr. P. Gallagher J.P. manager of the Society; Mr. D. Sweeney N.T., secretary; and Mr. James Dolan, representative of the Irish Co-Operative Committee. Mr P. Gallagher occupied the chair and after a few well-chosen words explained the object of the meeting.

Father Finlay, who received a very cordial and enthusiastic reception, said it gave him more pleasure than he could express to be asked to perform the function of formally opening this factory. This factory was the most singular development of industry that these islands, or indeed any country in Europe, provided; it was created entirely by the workers and run by them for their own benefit. There may be larger factories; but the principle realised here in Dungloe is unique and is a principle that would go further to satisfy the modern industrial world than any other industry can hope to realise. It is a great pity that the various working classes could not come here and take a lesson from the workers of Dungloe.

---

14 *'What Is Wrong With Ireland' (published in 1920) by Ruth Russell, an American journalist who travelled to Ireland in 1918-19 on the invitation of Eamon de Valera; de Valera later wrote the introduction to her book). This and other free eBooks are available from Project Gutenberg at www.gutenberg.org*

From controversies that we read daily in the papers it is evident that the workers of the world decline any longer to submit to the mere status of labouring men or to be wage slaves; they are urged to rise against the domination of capital and to take the industries under their own charge. Father Finlay dwelt at length on the two theories put forward – namely State Socialism and Guild Socialism; he pointed out the many difficulties in the way of either of these being realised, and said that their factory in Dungloe suggested a third theory which he believed was the real solution to industrial unrest and which was being overlooked. Here we have the workers gradually building up an industry with their own capital which they have laid aside from time to time. They did not confiscate the money of any capitalist, but by their own energies built up their own factory, and he believed if the thousands of pounds which the various trade and labour unions were spending in strikes were devoted to the buying of some industrial concern, whether it be mine or factory, the workers of this acquired industry could show by running it successfully that they could manage industries for themselves, and were thus entitled to consideration in the management of all the various industries they were engaged.

Father Finlay referred to the talent and great business ability of Mr. Gallagher, in whom the people had the greatest confidence, and who spared no effort to make the society and their factory a success. The factory is an heirloom of the future generations who would bless the memories of all those who worked so harmoniously together until it was brought to its current state of perfection.

Mr. P. Gallagher proposed a vote of thanks to Father Finlay, which was seconded by Mr D. Sweeney, N.T., and supported by Mr. James Dolan..."[15]

The following article is from the Irish Homestead pamphlet on the Templecrone Co-Operative Society published in 1924:

"...For generations back the women of the Rosses have been noted for their skill in hand knitting. In former years the knitting gave employment to large numbers of women and girls, but the prices paid

---

15   *Irish Homestead September 1919.*

Next Page: These fine shots are from a series of over 20 photographs (of the same six 'models') taken in 1966 by Denis Tynan, the very fine Glenties photographer. Tynan was commissioned by The Cope to photograph the Knitwear range for promotional purposes, including for a magazine for the American export market. Pictured here are Joe Joyce, Dungloe (originally from Mayo), who was a Guard at the time; Veronica (Bonner) Boyle; Sally 'the Cope' Gallagher; Susie (Rodgers) McGarvey; Kathleen Rodgers (Walsh) plus one woman whose name was not known at the time of writing. (National Photographic Archive, Denis Tynan collection).

for their labour were very small, in some cases as low as one penny per pair for the coarser kinds of socks. Gradually the hand work gave way to the machine-made goods, and the industry dwindled away.

In 1910, the Society entered in a small way upon the making of hand-made garments of various kinds. A few girls had already been employed at these garments, but their wages were low, averaging about 6/- or 7/- per week. Here again, as in almost every other adventure, Mr. Gallagher found himself encroaching upon the preserves of somebody else. He was threatened with legal proceedings if he continued to make certain models of garments for which it was alleged there was a registered patent. The repeated warnings and threats were disregarded, and no further action was taken. Had it been otherwise, this industry, giving employment to hundreds, would have probably followed the way of a few other promising industries that had been strangled in the Rosses in unsympathetic hands.

In a very short time Mr. Gallagher gained a good grasp of the intricacies of the hosiery business, and the work turned out gave every satisfaction to buyers. His next concern was to find a market. The IAOS did much to help him at this stage. In 1911 he secured a stall at the Aonach held that year in London, and his exhibits were much admired by visitors. He secured several small orders as a result, and gradually he was getting into touch with a few of the larger buyers.

The following year he again visited London, and his goods came into still greater prominence. Substantial orders were secured, and Mr. Gallagher was elated with his success. So elated indeed was he that in a moment of fervency he resorted to a neighbouring church to offer his gratitude to the Great Distributor of all good things. On discovering afterwards that his oblation had been made in a Presbyterian place of worship, which he mistook for a Catholic church, he was somewhat exercised to know if it had reached its Objective from this strange angle.

Gradually the Society edged into the glove and general hosiery business. At the suggestion of Father Finlay, who had taken a deep interest in the work of the Society, a new knitting machine of the flat type was purchased, and a lady instructress engaged to teach the girls how to work it. Later on a number of these machines were purchased. The number of workers had now largely increased, and in 1915 the co-operative hall was temporarily used to accommodate them.

At the outbreak of the war the Society secured a number of war orders, and these, with the steadily increasing civilian side of the business, gave full employment to about 150 factory workers as well as to a large number of home workers.

In 1918 a fine factory was erected, fitted with every modern accommodation, and with ample room for 300 workers. A petrol engine was used to drive the winders and brushers, and to supply electric heating and lighting. The necessary power is at present supplied from the electric power station. The output of the factory for this year was £40,000. The following extract from a letter from Father Finlay to the General Annual Meeting in June 1916, will best show the ideal which the manager endeavoured to keep before the workers.

"What you have won up to the present has been gained by steady and persevering work, by fidelity to co-operative principles, and by the ability and disinterestedness with which the business of the Society has been managed. If I could be present I would impress on the members the supreme need for these qualities in the hard times that are before us."

"They have profited by the war expenditure. The girls have, I rejoice to know, been able to earn exceptionally high wages, and their work has well deserved the reward it has brought them. But I appeal to them to make fresh efforts, for their own sake, and for the sake of the whole district to whose prosperity they are contributing so notably. It is only by perfect work, economically produced, that they can hope to hold their market when the normal conditions of competition are restored. Goods without a flaw, produced without waste of an atom of material, will always be in demand, and will enable your manager to pay a satisfactory wage."

"In a co-operative society, careless work, or avoidable waste by one member diminishes the fund out of which all the others have to be paid. The fault of one has to be paid for by the decreased wages of the rest. Let each worker do her work with the conviction that the fortunes of the Society are in her hands; all can then face the future with confidence."

These words were not lost upon manager and workers. The work of the factory has already gained a reputation for its excellence, and the finishing, packing, and putting on the market has won frequent praise from buyers. Machines of up-to-date type have been introduced, and the workers have shown great aptitude in dealing with these and with the novelties and varieties which each new season introduces.

Just as the store had revolutionized prices, so has the factory revolutionised wages. In 1908 there was in the locality a little factory belonging to a Derry firm, and paying 6/- to 8/- per week to its workers. In 1920 the weekly wages ranged from 48/- to 60/-, from 8 to 10 times the former. At present the wages run from 20/- to 35/- per week, notwithstanding a depressed market and the necessity to entice new buyers in the face of keen competition.

Here is a case of the profits of a business entirely at the disposal of the workers, and to those interested in the labour problem it should make a strong appeal in favour of the co-operative solution. At the Annual General Meeting of the Society in 1911 the members, the majority of whom had no pecuniary interest in the factory, voluntarily allowed their dividends to go to finance the new branch of business, and during the prosperous years that followed for the workers they as willingly did their part to provide for the further enterprises of the Society. Thus the Reserve Fund was used to finance the factory, the combined Reserve enabled the Society to purchase the mill and fit it for the grinding of maize, to replace the water wheel by turbine, and the water power by electricity, and these in turn will, it is hoped, help to finance the shipping and other projects..."[16]

The success of the knitting factory in the difficult post Civil War years was noted by journalists and commentators:

"...The most astonishing development in connection with the Templecrone Co-operative Society is its hosiery factory, where 150 local girls are employed in the knitting of woollen gloves, stockings, jumpers and costumes. The machines, driven by electricity, are placed in rows in a large, bright room, which presents none of the factory atmosphere. This enterprise is a regular source of income to the families of the district all year round. By a revolution of industry the girls of the Rosses now earn more than the men and the work is pleasant. Averaging from the expert machinist with 35 shillings a week to the learner with six shillings the all round earnings of those 150 girls would work out to about 22 shillings a week for every week of the year.

The manufacture of gloves is the most important work in the factory. In the months of July and August of this year one New York house received gloves from Dungloe to the value of £1,059. Manchester is the great market. From one firm in that city, there recently came an order for 15,000 dozen gloves. It is strange that that the direct Dublin trade for Dungloe gloves is almost negligible; but a considerable part of the manufacture finds its way to the shop counters of the Irish capital, having, of course, lost nothing in the price to the purchaser from its travels to Manchester and London.

The girls in the factory are particularly smart in appearance, neatly dressed and the picture of health. Quite a number wear gold rings on their fingers. They are all of the class for whom up to the establishment of the factory there was no outlook at home, except the drudgery of work on farms in Tyrone or Derry. It is hard to imagine one of those

---

16 *The Templecrone Co-operative Society, pamphlet published by The Irish Homestead (which by then had become The Irish Statesman) in 1924.*

smart looking girls working in the fields as a common farm labourer for wages not one quarter of what they now earn at home. At the dinner hour they can be seen, when the meal is over, still engaged on the hand finishing of gloves brought from the factory for the purpose. They do not believe in hanging idly round for half an hour until the machines start again..."[17]

Robert Anderson, now Chairman of the IAWS, made another visit to Dungloe in 1928:

"...Visited with Mr Moore and went over the Stores, Bakery, Mill and Factory. The last is now busier than it has been since the war. The large knitting machines are working an extra night shift in order to cope with orders for pullovers, jumpers, women's costumes and golf stockings from New York, Montreal and elsewhere. Sixty five girls are employed at present in the factory and there are about 200 out-workers. A pair of golf stockings - price 12/6d in Dungloe - fetch £2 in New York where the budding Bobby Joneses snap them up and also pullovers to match in most weird and bizarre colours and patterns. "Paddy" told us that the more peculiar and striking the pattern and colour the more certain was a ready sale. The village is now all lighted by the society with electricity except Sweeney's and Boyle's..."[18]

The Cope's knitting business was still thriving in 1930 when the Irish Times reported:

"...With assistance from Father T. A. Finlay, Harold Barbour and others, he not only founded and managed a general distributive store, but founded a knitting factory, which is now one of the finest in Ireland. Here a large number of local people find employment and, in addition, several subsidiary industries have been started. Some of these have been failures, but on the whole the revolt has prospered, and has changed the locality out of recognition. Dungloe knitted goods now go to all parts of the world and the demand is greater than the factory ran at present supply.

The exhibit at this year's Horse Show was something of a novelty for "Paddy the Cope" as it consisted of a display of hand-made carpets and rugs. This is a new industry for the Templecrone Society, but Mr. Gallagher tells me that he is confident of its success. He found carpet-makers out of employment so he just started this industry for them. So attractive was the exhibit that it was purchased outright by one of the leading furnishing firms in Dublin, with further orders to come..."[19]

---

17 Irish Times 17th September 1924.

18 IAOS records – a file note by R. A. Anderson 14th March 1928.

19 Irish Times 14th August 1930.

Brigid Byrne, pictured here in 2006, started working at the Knitting Factory at the age of 14 in 1939 until finishing finally in 1962. Brigid still lives on the Quay Road opposite the old factory and (Brigid Byrne photo).

Brigid Byrne worked in the Knitting Factory from 1939, aged 14, to 1962.

> "...My first job was to wind the wool on to bobbins, using a winder; it came in long skeins of many different colours. There were 20 or so different machine; the factory was filled with them. Each machine was set up to do different types of garment or parts of garments. Some did gloves, others sweaters, cardigans and football jerseys as well. The machine would create the different shapes and they would be put together by the seamstresses, who would sew the seams together and add labels (all with Templecrone Co-Operative Society on them). I moved on to this task when I'd had been seven or eight years in the job. The boss was Cassie (Jock) O'Donnell with

Minnie Roarty as her second in command; they were very strict on the quality of the work, we were all a bit in fear of them.

The shift would be 8.30am to 6pm, with one hour for dinner. All the machines stopped then; it became quiet – it was noisy when they were all operating. Delia and Winnie Ward used to look after the hand knits. There used to be big orders in from America, London, England. There was a big press in the Cope Hall; the finished woollens were put in a shaped frame and pressed for packing, put into boxes and sent up to the Post Office for mailing to wherever they had to go to...”[20]

Bridget worked in the knitting factory till 1958; she had married in 1956 and her daughter Bríd was born so she had nine months off; then her daughter Noreen was born in 1962 and she didn't go back. There were not many machines in there by then; the Cope used to let the machines out to homes, in Loughanure and elsewhere.

Bridget remembers that there used to be another knitting factory behind Sweeney's Hotel; Bridget's mother Nora Biddy Hughie O'Donnell, married to Pat Cannon, worked there. Pat used to turn the sluice gates on and off – to let the water through to power the mill and electricity for the town – he was under instructions from Paddy to make sure the electricity went off before midnight.

The Cope had many outworkers, either hand knit or in later years, machines went out on loan – a real cottage industry. **Mary Ellen Boner** (Manny Anne) was born in 1923 and remembers her mother Madgie knitting at home in Crickamore in the 1930s:

“...I remember my mother used to be knitting at home, gloves mostly; we didn't have a lot of money in those days and the extra helped. I would cycle up to Dungloe or walk if there was no bicycle. I would bring them in to Cassie Jock in the Quay Road, a couple of dozen at least and she would check them and then give me the money in cash. I would go the Cope shop then to buy things we needed. The Cope was a great help to us in those days...”[21]

Mary McCole, originally Mary O'Donnell from Cleendra, not far from Padd the Cope's house there. Her grandmother was Granny McFadden, sister to P Doogan the carpenter who made tables, coffins etc. John O'Donnell v father; he was the seventh shareholder to sign up when the Cope wa⸂

The McCole family have over a hundred years of service betw⸍ the Cope: Josie, Mary's husband 32 years; Mary 5 years ther⸍ outworker; Cathal McCole 42 years in many roles, mainl⸍

225

---

20 *Personal reminiscence from Brigid Byrne to the editor in November ?*

21 *Personal reminiscence by Mary Ellen Boner to the editor in 20ʳ*

Mary McCole worked for five years in the Knitting Factory and then for many years afterwards as an outworker. The McCole family have between them over a hundred years of service with the Cope. This is Mary with Minister of State Pat the Cope TD on the occasion of the Centenary celebrations and launch of the An Post Cope stamp in January 2006 (McCole Family photo).

4 years. This is not atypical; many families have worked with the ral generations.

ert 99 at the time of telling of her days in the knitting factory many thanks to her son and daughter Cathal and Breid for

se 07 and I left school at 14 and started in the knitting from c factory was not long open and we were the first re were 90 girls working there then, it was very making gloves. There was no sitting down all 6pm. We finished the gloves apart from the ke home every night and 'toe' the gloves, hem back in the morning. I would walk back each day carrying the gloves.

Cassie Jock (O'Donnell) and Minnie Roarty were the supervisors. They were very strict; there was no talking. We would be down on the floor working; they were on the stage above us. When we had finished a 'lot' of gloves, about two, sometimes three or four dozen gloves, we would take them up to be inspected. We would stand on a stool and reach them up to Cassie or Minnie on the stage. If the weight of the wool didn't correspond to what you'd been given, it would be deducted from our wages.

Paddy then bought a machine to knit jumpers. It worked around the clock, three shifts: 3am-11am, 11am-7pm and 7pm-3am. Only one person at a time would work on the machine. I often did the night shift; Susan (O'Donnell) Boner (who married Neily Boner, Burtonport), Chapel Road would sit with me on the night shift. There were big bobbins of wool, all colours – the machine would make pieces, fronts, backs and sleeves which would then be sewn together by hand. Paddy got some big orders from the Army and the Gardai – big Government orders which kept us going.

Once when I was on the night shift, Susan and I went to a dance at the tannery where the Pitch and Putt is now. We were terrified that Cassie Jock's housekeeper Mary Niall, who was there too, would tell on us (but she didn't).

I was 5 years in all at the factory then I went to Killybegs to the Industrial School there till 1928. Packie the Cope would give me a lift up in his car or the oil lorry. In 1928, I went to America and came back in 1935; Josie McCole (from Falmore) and I married in 1935..."[22]

The Knitting Factory and the many, many outworkers provided well paid work for the people of the Rosses for well over 70 years until closure was forced in 1983. As Cyril Winder, General Manager of the Cope from 1969-1993, put it:

"...We were forced out of this by Government interference and impositions, and particularly our high rates of pay in a low cost traditional industry. There was an ongoing recession with competition in this industry for a number of years..."[23]

The competition Mr Winder referred to was not in Ireland but totally outside his and the Cope's control; work like this could be done far more cheaply in the newer, low-waged economies, in SE Asia. It was impossible, however much the Cope wanted to stay in this once very important business close to its heart, to compete with the

---

22 *Personal reminiscence by Mary McCole to the editor in November 2006*

23 *'From One Million Pounds to Five Million Pounds In Sales and Services 1975-1985' April 1985 Staff Bulletin, Cope Archive.*

Outside the St Crone Handknitting Centre in 1976, Delia Ward is inspecting an Aran style cardigan. The building is the old Knitting Factory in the Quay Road. This doorway became the Builders' Providers' main entrance from the road. (Cope Archive).

very much lower cost structures in other countries – this trend has continued with the dramatic surge in China's economy and exports over the last 10 years.

In its later years, the Cope Handknits developed a distinctive styling branded 'St Crone' (after the saint from which Templecrone derives its name) which was popular with visitors and the American market. The following is from the c1969-70 'St Crone 'Aran Handknits' brochure:

> "…'ST. CRONE' handknits are still genuinely made in the cottages of Western Donegal on the Irish Atlantic seaboard, and have all the traditional characteristics of these fine garments and people. In these beautifully remote rugged areas handknitting is their only income and pastime in the long winter evenings. From their barren moorland and mountain terrain they sheer their own brand of sheep, spin their yarns and knit designs that have been carried down from generation to generation. They are made with the same pride and loving care that

The Story of the Cope

Delia and Winnie Ward in 1981 with some of the handknit range; on the wall behind is the Aran Handknits brochure (Cope Archive).

went into the protective clothing for their children and loved ones. Their close knit of natural oils braved the winter storms and shed the sea spray and mountain mist. It is almost a miracle that yet no machine can even come close to these authentic garments that are made in the flickering candle light. The patterns are their individual identification and are symbolic of their environment and dreams. The designs to this day have great artistic merit and fit beautifully into garments of practical usage and fashion.

'ST. CRONE' was organised many years ago to help these people maintain this tradition, and see that only this exclusive wool was used, and that all garments came up to a uniform standard so that they could be marketed throughout the world with confidence.

We hope that you too will have a tradition of pride and satisfaction in these fine garments.

Annie Sharkey worked in her house on Upper Main Street Dungloe as a knitting factory outworker; the machine was supplied by the Cope. Annie is remembered locally for ringing the Church bell (at 8am, mid-day and 6pm) every day for over 50 years, from when she was 16 until about 8 years before she died. (Dim Boyle photo).

The Story of the Cope

This Cope 'St Crone' branded brochure advertised handknits made by Cope workers, either at home or in the factory. The date is c1970.

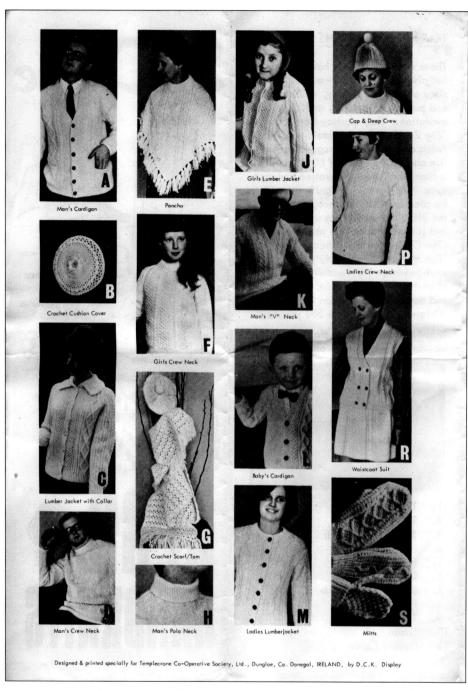

Man's Cardigan — A

Pancho — E

Girls Lumber Jacket — J

Cap & Deep Crew

Crochet Cushion Cover — B

Girls Crew Neck — F

Man's "V" Neck — K

Ladies Crew Neck — P

Lumber Jacket with Collar — C

Crochet Scarf/Tam — G

Baby's Cardigan — L

Waistcoat Suit — R

Man's Crew Neck — D

Man's Polo Neck — H

Ladies Lumberjacket — M

Mitts — S

Designed & printed specially for Templecrone Co-Operative Society, Ltd., Dungloe, Co. Donegal, IRELAND, by D.C.K. Display

Cope people were the models used in the brochure: letters A, D and K: Jim (Packie) the Cope; C, Susie (Rodgers) McGarvey; E, N and R, Eithne Winder, wife of Cyril Winder the General Manager; F, Geraldine McCole; J, Bríd Byrne; L, Pauric the Cope Sweeney; M, Hannah Gallagher; P, Anne Theresa Sweeney. (Brigid Byrne collection).

The Story of the Cope

This is an original Cope Handknits label, one of the last produced, on an Aran style cardigan (Photo, PB Collection)

The old Knitting factory building in November 2006; it has since been demolished as part of a major redevelopment of the shoreline and car park areas. At the time of the photograph, it was still in use as part of the Builders' Providers department which moved here after the Knitwear business was closed in 1983. The building was still in very good order with fine granite work and wooden beams. Until the dedicated factory was built in 1918, the Cope Hall on the Quay Road doubled as a knitwear 'factory' as well from 1915 (and on a smaller scale from c1910-11). The First World War created a huge demand for knitwear for the soldiers at the front and the Cope was working flat out. There also used also to be a knitting factory (not the Cope's) behind Sweeney's Hotel; Nora Biddy Hughie O'Donnell (Brigid Byrne, Cope Knitting Factory worker's mother) worked here early on (PB photo 2006).

TRADITIONAL DESIGNS

These stitches not only have beauty but also a hidden story - a true and real story of reality, fantasy, environment and purpose all ancient tradition and evolution. They portray from the 'Zig Zags' as the mountain paths and twists and turns in the rugged path of life ahead; the 'Tree of Life' symbol of a cherished future generation and many sons; 'The Diamond' signified a wish for prosperity; 'The Honeycomb' was the elixir for continuous endeavours and just rewards for the arduous. 'The Cable' was the fisherman's ropes; 'The Moss and Blackberry' was natures environment; 'The Feather' was a cloak of protection; 'The Spoon' a loving care and hand, and so goes on these 'Originals' known to be 500 years old.

Below are a few of the classics that we would like you to know and appreciate.

The Zig Zag
Tree of Life
Single Honeycomb
Herringbone
Blackberry
Diamond
Double Honeycomb
Feather
Tongs
Spoon
Double Cable
The Hand..."[24]

---

24 'St. Crone Aran Handknits' brochure, c. 1969-70, Brigid Byrne collection.

Chapter 6

THE BAKERY

The Cope started its bakery a year after they had moved to new premises in 1912; these were more spacious, with a bigger back yard, on Dungloe's Main Street (James Sweeney's old store). It was from the first an important part of the Cope, much appreciated by its customers and now much missed. Its closure in 1984 was largely due to spiralling oil prices making the Cope operation uneconomic.[1]

The bakery was part of the Main Street store complex, alongside the drapery and wholesale department. The downside of this proximity became apparent in January 1945 when a fire starting in the bakery destroyed almost all of the Cope buildings and indeed threatened to engulf Dungloe itself (further details of this disaster are at the end of this Chapter). After this, it was decided – in fact their insurance company insisted - to build a stand-alone bakery away from the other Cope businesses. The new bakery contained five True-Way oven heaters and five drawplate ovens (fired by oil), working nine hours per day.[2]

No time was wasted in getting the new bakery building underway: Paddy wrote to Dr Kennedy, Secretary of the IAOS:

> "...To erect the new bakery, we have already taken away one end of the wooden bungalow. I am a bit sorry to have to do this. For this reason, in 1911, I was presented with a magnificent clock there by my cooperative friends amongst whom was Sean [Shane] Leslie and that beautiful girl then Lady Mary Plunkett, she belonged to the Catholic branch of the Plunkett family. The reason I am writing to you now is: if she is still alive or if she has since been married and has any family I would be glad to get their address. I would like to invite her and her descendants to the opening of our new bakery in 2-3 months hence..."[3]

The architect chosen was Charles Vincent McLaughlin, of Letterkenny and Derry. The Cope had a great deal of trouble getting steel and cement for the new buildings, the bakery and the new store on the Main Street. It was still wartime and there were tight restrictions – the IAOS was very helpful and liaised with Irish and British governments to get the Cope's supplies.[4]

---

1   Cyril Winder memoir, Cope Archive

2   IAOS records, 1945 various.

3   Ibid. letter dated 20th February 1945. The clock Paddy refers to cost £16 10s, a lot of money then, and was paid for by subscription: Harold Barbour contributed £5, Horace Plunkett, £2, Rev. Tom Finlay £1, R A Anderson 10s 6d, friends in the Lisburn Co-operative Society £2, the rest being made up of smaller contributions. (IAOS file notes, Oct-Dec 1911)

4   Ibid. 1945 various.

This interior view is of the Old Bakery, which was located behind the Cope's store on Dungloe's Main Street. The Cope's bakery business began in 1913; Paddy brought in a master baker from Derry called Matt O'Hagan to start things off. It was from this old bakery that the devastating 1945 fire spread; Paddy used to dry soapstone bags from the Crohey Head mine on the ovens and it may well have been these caught fire – he always blamed himself for the fire starting – and almost got himself into trouble with the Insurance company for saying so (Sally the Cope Gallagher collection).

Dim (Dominick) Boyle, was born 30 November 1933 and worked in the new bakery opened in 1948 for five years from 1949. He then moved to work on building the new Dungloe Hospital on the Gweedore Road from 1954-57.

"...I was five years in the Bakery in 1949 after I left school. I used to do the Sunday night shift; we got the bread ready for Monday morning when the drivers would take out all the orders. I earned £1 a week to start with; the best wage in the Bakery would have been £2 10 shillings a week. James McGee, Fair Hill, was in charge. The lorry drivers, Neil Sweeney and Cathal McCole, would earn £3 10 shillings a week. The only bakeries in Donegal were the Cope's in Dungloe and another in Milford.

The shift would start at 8pm Sunday night. When we got there, Jimmy Nappy O'Donnell had been there all day getting the ovens heated up; it was turf was used, no electricity used then. Jimmy would get 2 shillings for the Sunday. At that time, there were four ovens and a Steam Press which was used to raise the bread before it went into the oven. The Press was a big room, filled with steam.

The flour was upstairs and came down the chute, straight into the mixer. James McGee (Fair Hill) was in charge of the mixer. The mixer held a big batch, four bags of flour, each was 8 stone in weight. Flour, water and yeast would be mixed together. If it was pan bread, we'd put

The Story of the Cope

in some sugar. Plain bread didn't have sugar in it. The mixer had big blades that went round and round making the dough. The mixer got very heavy then.

Beside the mixer, about ten yards away was the divider which cut the dough into loaves. It was made of galvanised steel which was greased. It made six loaves to a shape. When the whole batch was shaped and put onto the rack then it would be wheeled into the steam press for an hour or so.

The oven was in an alcove on two wheels, fire bricks all around. We'd pull it out, the oven and then put the loaves in and pull the door down; the temperature was 120° Fahrenheit, it would then cool as we put colder dough into it. It would take about an hour and a half to bake. All the ovens would be going all night continuously, twelve batches in a night. There were 13 or 14 men working there. When it was baked, we'd put the bread on racks; there was no wrapping it in those days.

There was a separate area for buns – scones we'd call them today – where two girls worked. The buns would be for the schools mainly.

Dungloe and Milford were the only places with bakeries then.

The men and boys I remember working there are: James McGee, the supervisor; James 'Sticks' Ward, Packie (James) Gallagher, Denis Gallagher, Michael Hanlon, Joe Hanlon, James McDermott, Jimmy O'Donnell, Dinnie Doherty (he drove the Cope van later), Jim McPaul, Packie Gallagher (Fair Hill), Phil Sweeney, Owenie Sweeney (Dobell). All of them were from Dungloe or just outside.

We'd play football in the breaks – outside in the field at the back or sometimes at night we'd play in the bakery while we were waiting for the bread to be baked. We were all young then, it was good fun. There are not many left from those days…"[5]

After working in the Cope Bakery, Dim worked for PJ Walls & Bros Co. Ltd. on the building the new Dungloe hospital for four years (1954-58). He worked later as an ambulance driver for over 30 years (1962-98) until his retirement.

Dinnie Doherty also started in the Bakery in 1949, he was 16; he stayed for two years but had always wanted to get out on the road and in 1951 or 1952 he became a delivery driver for the Cope Bakery.

"…I used to cycle in from Sheskinarone where we lived then. The shift was 8am to 6pm but sometimes it could go on for longer; at Christmas, you could be there till ten or eleven o'clock at night. I worked at greasing

---

5   *Personal reminiscence by Dim Boyle to the editor in November 2006.*

Dungloe, Co. Donegal.

This view of Dungloe c1950 is taken from above the Bayview with the Northern Bank clearly visible in the Main Street. Up the street can be seen the Manor House, one of Dungloe's oldest buildings, and The Medical Hall building to its right. On the upper right, on the Quay Road, the distinctive 'sawtooth' roof of the Knitting Factory can be seen alongside the large new Bakery building, which opened in 1948. Dim Boyle, who worked there (1949-54), remembers

the Cope's priority was the rebuilding of the new Main Street Shop – only then did they set about building a new Bakery, for safety it was built away from the Main Street shop. The Bakery and Knitting Factory became part of the 'old' Builders' Providers yard in the 1980s after both businesses were closed down. (PB collection - Valentine's postcard).

The Quay Road Bakery Staff pictured in 1949: Back: James McDermott, Jim McPaul, Phil Sweeney, Jimmy Ward (Sticks). Dim Boyle, James McGee. Front: Mickie Hanlon (Mosey), Jimmy (Nappy) O'Donnell, Owenie Sweeney (Dobell), Pa Ward, (not identified), Dinnie Doherty. (Dim Boyle collection)

the shapes that the dough was put in or icing the buns. I remember there was a man from Cavan working there then, James McDermott – he was a pastry-maker making fancy cakes. You'd throw sheets over the pastry to keep it fresh.

Anyway, I eventually got to be a driver. I'd drive Paddy down to Killybegs sometimes. The Cope had a maroon van, it was 32 HP and very lively. You would need half a ton on her back to keep her down. Paddy would say to me: 'I'm not going with you unless you promise me you'll drive sensibly'. He was 80 by then; he never used to say much as we drove, he occasionally asked me a question. The van would use a lot of petrol but petrol was cheap then. I remember on the first Monday in August we'd all have to go down to the Cope House, the hotel Paddy had bought in Killybegs, to serve drinks and help out there.

I got to drive the bread van then. It was a huge thing – a Ford, specially built by Doherty's in Lifford. There were several runs. One run, I think it was Monday, went down to South Donegal. The Gweebarra Bridge was

The Story of the Cope

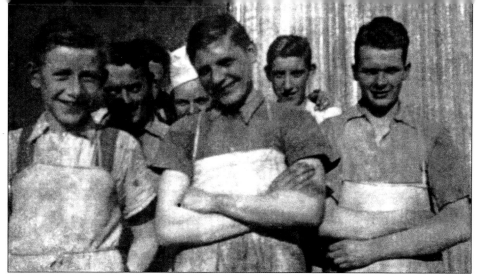

Another group of young workers in the Bakery in the late 1940s. In the back row: Denis Gallagher, Maghery; Anthony "The Cake" O'Donnell, Dungloe; Charlie, surname not given. In the front row: Charlie 'The Yankie' Boyle, Dungloe; Henry Glackin, Cleendra; Packie Cannon ('Ghandi') Dungloe. (Marie (Brennan) Glackin collection)

The old Gweebarra Bridge was built over two years (1894-6) by the Congested Districts Board and opened in March 1896. The structure had been in use as a bridge before in Germany, before being sold and disassembled for shipping to Ireland. As can be seen, Its relatively slender pylons were built from steel sections. Adequate to begin with, It proved to be not up to the task of handling the weight and vibrations from the heavy motorised transport (including the Cope fleet) which came in from the 1920s. Crossing became increasingly hazardous until the bridge was periodically closed to heavy traffic from the mid 1940s – and permanently from March 1950 (1940s Postcard, PB collection; information from James Boyle, Glenties, writing in the Rosses Annual c1995/6)

Corkscrew Hill, Doochary, Co. Donegal

With the Gweebarra Bridge out of commission from 1950, the Cope bread van – a large and unwieldy vehicle – had to make its way to Glenties over the Gweebarra via the bridge at Doochary. One of the challenges the driver (Dinnie Doherty) faced was the 'Corkscrew', which snaked down the descent into Doochary from Dungloe. In bad weather, this was a dangerous stretch of road – and it was tricky at the best of times, for articulated lorries in particular, until straightened in recent years. In the middle foreground can be seen the National School and beyond, fields under cultivation on the other side of the Gweebarra. The first bridge across the Gweebarra was built here in Doocharry in 1786 by the landlord the Marquis Conyngham; he called it Rutland Bridge as it formed part of the road system he had built to access the massive investment he and Irish Government under Grattan's Parliament had made in the Great North West Fishery on Rutland (Inis Mhic an Doirn) (Contemporary postcard c1930, PB collection)

Right: The Gweebarra Bridge was closed to heavy traffic from March 1950 and barriers set up on each side. Bus passengers would be required to walk across the bridge (there were gaps in places where planks had fallen through) to pick up a connection to take them on to their destination. This arrangement lasted until the new bridge was completed in December 1953 (Contemporary postcard, PB collection).

The Story of the Cope

DOOCHARY, CO. DONEGAL

Above: The village of Doochary, here photographed on a Valentine's postcard in c1950. When the bridge further down the Gweebarra became unsafe and was closed in 1950, all the Cope lorries and bread vans had to come this way to get to Glenties and further south. Doochary is right by Rutland Bridge and is a link to Dungloe, Glenties and Fintown, from where the road goes on to either Letterkenny or Ballyfbofey (Mícheál O Dhomnaill Collection).

EBARRA BRIDGE, DONEGAL.

The current Gweebarra Bridge connects Dungloe via Lettermacaward (colloquially shortened to Leitir, pronounced 'Letcher') to Glenties over the Gweebarra and was completed in 1953 and officially opened by Mr Patrick Smith TD on 15th February 1954 (work had commenced in 1948 but there had been construction problems and funding delays). The new bridge was built alongside the old, seen on the left in this photograph taken from the Glenties side. On the Leitir side, workman's prefabricated huts can be seen and the first two piers/pillars are being constructed. Donegal County council received a grant of from the central government Road Fund of £86,000 which represented 75% of the estimated cost (Packie Bonner Collection).

damaged at that time and we had to go round Fintown, a long way round. Then we'd go to Glenties – Frosses – Mountcharles – Dunkineely – Killybegs – where we would stop for lunch. Then we'd go on to Kilcar – Carrick – Teelin – Glencombcille – Malin Mor – Meenacross – Braade –Meenaneery – Killybegs, where we would stop for dinner. In between the towns we'd also stop at shops along the way. It was a long day, often 8am to 10pm.

On Tuesday, the run would be Dungloe – Loughanure – Falcarragh – Ballybose – Ballyconnell College – Meenalarra, there were lots of shops along there – Bloody Foreland – Gweedore where we'd lunch at Friels's. Then on to Crolly and back to Dungloe.

On Wednesday, we would go down to Lettermacaward and Doochary. Thursday was Burtonport – Kincasslagh – Annagry and area. Friday we'd be back down to Killybegs again.

This photograph of Dim Boyle and Owenie Sweeney, both of whom worked in the bakery in the early 1950s, shows them dressed up as Guards at a Fancy Dress party c1950 at the Parochial Hall – "...at the time in the papers there was talk of a 'Gardai Reduction Plan' so we thought it would make a good idea for a fancy dress..." (Recalled by Dim Boyle, photograph from his collection).

I remember one time in Gweedore; it had been notified that bread was going to go up by 1d a loaf. There was such panic buying I had to make five trips there in one day. The price of a pan was 8/11d for a dozen loaves – that was the price to the shop, they would then add on whatever they charged. For plain loaves, it was 8/6d a dozen.

Not every shopkeeper in Dungloe would take the Cope's bread, the only ones that did were Mary O'Brien and John Hughdie Dan, both up the town. Sometimes (often three or four times a week) Paddy would have us call at every house in Dungloe selling bread directly to customers..."[6]

The Gweebarra Bridge referred to by Dinnie Doherty had become very unsafe, in part due to the Cope's heavy lorries themselves which gave it a regular pounding. When it was built, it was not designed for the size and weight of transport that came later. James Boyle of Glenties, writing in the Rosses Annual, tells the story:

"...The first Gweebarra Bridge was completed in March 1896; before this a ferry operated between Mulnamina and Lettermacaward.

This bridge served as the connection between the Rosses and South-West Donegal until large trucks began to appear on the roads in the early 1930s. In the mid Thirties the County Council made an order forbidding vehicles over two tons from crossing the bridge — but they continued to cross until 1945 when it was discovered that the steel sections underneath the bridge were deteriorating badly. Work on the new Gweebarra Bridge began on 14th June 1948. In March 1950 the old bridge was closed to heavy vehicles and gates were erected on both sides —manned by a gatekeeper with two shifts around the clock. The new bridge was completed in December 1953. It was blessed by the late Bishop McNeely and was opened officially by the late Paddy Smith —then Minister of Local Government on the 15th February 1954..."[7]

The Dungloe Fire 1945

The inter-war period was a tough trading environment made worse by the Economic War over annuity payments between the Free State and Great Britain (1932-38). Trading during the Second World War was difficult too – it was certainly not the commercial bonanza that the previous World War had been for the Cope. To make things worse, on January 28th 1945, the bakery attached to Main Street store caught fire and completely destroyed the bakery, the main store and the dwelling house attached where Paddy, Sally and his son Packie's family lived.

---

6   *Personal reminiscence by Dimmy Doherty to the editor in November 2006*

7   *Extract from the 1995/6 Rosses Annual – the full article and the Annual itself is well worth reading for further detail and many other interesting stories about the Rosses.*

Paddy blamed himself for the fire – and it is very possible that he was indirectly to blame: he used to dry the wet bags used to carry soapstone (from the mine at Crohy Head) over the ovens in the bakery

Dungloe on the night in question was bitterly cold with snow on the ground. In Derry, it was reported that there were 17 degrees of frost, a water shortage from frozen pipes and milk was frozen into a sold mass in the city's houses. There was a real risk that the whole town of Dungloe could have been destroyed – but showing admirable community spirit, the townspeople saved the day.

The Derry Journal very promptly covered the story in some detail:

DISASTROUS DUNGLOE FIRE

Templecrone Co-Operative Premises Gutted

POST-OFFICE INVOLVED

WHOLE TOWN THREATENED

"...One of the biggest fires in County Donegal for a very long time, broke out in Dungloe last night, and was still raging in the early hours of this morning.
It was discovered at midnight, and the premises involved were the extensive buildings owned by the Templecrone Co-operative Society.

So huge was the blaze - it could be seen over the Rosses for many miles - that it threatened in its early` stages to involve the greater part of the town. An urgent call was sent to the N.F.S. in Derry City for assistance, and some firemen at once set out by motor-vehicle to make the fifty miles dash to West Donegal over dangerous roads.

Meanwhile the inhabitants of the Rosses' capital were out, and large numbers of local fire-fighters were strenuously working to combat the ever spreading flames, which enveloped the historic Co- operative Stores, whose fame has become nation-wide.

The intensity of the wintry conditions hampered the fire-fighters as they strove to save as much as possible of the premises that housed the great movement started by Mr. Patrick Gallagher (the Cope) more than a generation ago.

The undertaking was the first of its kind in the country, and the pioneer work in local initiative and self-sufficiency - which was attended with most successful results - won national admiration. The remarkable and thrilling story of the movement as told by Mr: Gallagher in a book published a few years ago.

The outbreak appears to have originated in the bakery premises, and these have been gutted.

FOUR BRIGADES SUMMONED

Mr. C. V. McLaughlin, Chief of the Letterkenny Fire Brigade hurriedly proceeded to the scene. The Dunfanaghy Brigade also set out to render assistance. The Dungloe Brigade found difficulty in getting the local trailer-pump into operation, the severe frost acting as a handicap. For two hours the work of fire-fighting was limited to whatever use could be made of buckets of water.

Buckets of Water by Human Chain

Sergeant O'Malley, assisted by other members of the Gardai, organised a number of local people into a human chain extending from the scene of the conflagration to a nearby river. Buckets of water were brought along in this way.

The flames gradually got the Dungloe Post Office in their grip. The postal premises adjoin the Co-operative premises. By means of the human chain the fire-fighters were able to keep the telephone apparatus there intact as long as possible, so that calls for help might be got through.

The Sligo Fire Brigade was also summoned.

No Help Arrived At Two o'clock This Morning

By two o'clock this morning, however, no outside help had arrived. It was then feared that the Cooperative premises had been practically all gutted.

After Three Hours

At half past three this morning the fire was being got under control, to a great extent.

The damage to the Post Office was only partial, but one or two houses suffered badly, as well as a lot of stables at the rear of other premises. A considerable amount of material was saved from the Co-operative stores it is understood.

Sligo Brigade met with an accident on the way, due to a skid, but the Dunfanaghy Brigade arrived all right...”[8]

The article ended with something which would not be acceptable today: a sub-editor had tagged on the end an advert for buildings insurance:

> “...Have you revised the insurable value of Your Premises, Stock, and Furniture in the light of present-day costs? Consult The Hibernian Fire and General Insurance Co., Ltd., Branch Office, 3 Castle Street, Derry...”

Due to the heroic efforts of the townspeople and fire services, much of the town was saved from damage and there were no fatalities apart from Mrs. Grace Doherty, who had been ill and died several days later – it was assumed as a result of shock from the fire.

The Dungloe Fire

Death Of Miss Grace Doherty

How The Local People Saved The Town

“...The death of Miss Grace Doherty Main Street, Dungloe, which took place over the week-end, has a connection with the disastrous fire of last week which destroyed the shop and bakery of the Templecrone Co-operative Society. Miss Doherty's residence immediately adjoins the destroyed shop, and when the fire broke out, she was in bed, having been in rather indifferent health for some time previously. When aroused and taken to a neighbouring house she collapsed from shock and remained unconscious for a period of four days until her death on Thursday, on which day her remains were removed to St. Peter's Church. The coffin was borne to the church and grave by members of the Co-operative staff. The Funeral took place on Saturday following requiem Mass.

The late Miss Doherty's house was gravely threatened in the course of the fire, and it is learned that among the household goods removed at the time was a substantial sum of money in notes, later handed to the Garda authorities. That her premises were not also destroyed is mainly due to the fact that the building is of a lower roof level than the adjoining Co-op shop, and that the fire-fighters took steps to keep the flames at bay. The roof is, however, somewhat destroyed. It is understood th the deceased is survived by a sister in Scotland and a brother in U.S.A., but without any immediate next-of-kin in this country.

That more damage did not result from the fire in question is considered providential, apart from the gallant efforts of the people. In the earlier stages, having regard to weather conditions and regrettable and unavoidable delay in fire brigade help, it looked as if a substantial part of the town was going to suffer severely. It seemed certain all the Co-operative premises and the Post Office would be destroyed. A matter of yards separated the flaming bakery from a timber shed and the extensive wholesale department, and from a petrol tank sunk in the yard. That the flames were confined to the bakery and shop is due, under God, to the great work of the people of Dungloe and district who formed the bucket chain and fought heroically for hours until the fire engines came into action.

The ages of the local fighters ranged from two men of over 90 years (Charles McBride and James Campbell) to schoolchildren, and not least active and heroic were many women and girls. Many of the young men did heroic work in scaling and, cutting the roof tops. In short, the people responded wonderfully, inspired and directed by the Rev. Dr. Molloy, P.P., and the Rev. F. McIntyre, who remained throughout, and the Gardai from the local station, Burtonport and Annagry, under Sergeants O'Malley, Twomey and O'Meaney. Residents in the houses near to the burning premises evacuated with all possible belongings.

Due to the timely messages sent through from the Dungloe Barracks per Garda Clancy, the outside fire-fighters from Dunfanaghy, Letterkenny and Derry made a speedy response in face of difficult weather conditions, and there is great local appreciation for their turn-out, particularly so for the Derry contingent and the gallant but unavailing attempt made by the Sligo firemen.

CARRYING ON

Despite the upset of the fire, the Templecrone Society, under its worthy and undaunted manager, Paddy the Cope, has meantime managed to ʿ ᵗʰᵉ needs of its customers in ordinary supplies An alternative retail ᴵⁿ ᵗhe Co-op Hall at Quay Road. Other bakeries in Milford, are doing 'all possible' to fill the gap as

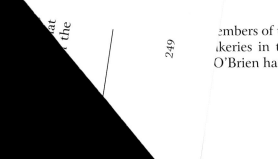

embers of the Co-op bakery are to be transferred ᵢkeries in the extra work, involved, and in this O'Brien has already been transferred to Conlon's

249

Bakery, Bundoran..."[9]
A feature of the fire disaster: which aroused much interest and admiration among the public was the fact that the "Derry Journal" carried a thrilling and comparatively lengthy report of it of the actual morning of the fire. In fact the report was in print and on its way to the public while the flames were still raging in Dungloe.

The story ended rather more happily with a re-opening 14 months later:

Like A Phœnix From Its Ashes

Paddy the Cope Turns Ruin Into Triumph

Great New Co-operative Building Opened in Dungloe

A BIG DAY FOR THE ROSSES

"...The gloomy memory of the almost disastrous Dungloe fire, of fourteen months ago which, at its height, seemed almost certain to ruin the life work of Paddy the Cope, has just given .place to one of gladness and pride, and great expectations for the future, writes our Special Reporter.

From the ashes that littered the frost-bound streets of the Rosses capital on that night of closely averted calamity, an ornate building has arisen, surpassing far in structural lay-out, commodiousness and modern appointments, the premises consumed in the flames. Wednesday was the joyous occasion of the opening of the new emporium, which, fresh from the hands of the tradesmen and decorators revealed itself as a splendid addition to the many fine buildings in this thriving, irrepressibly go-ahead community. It was a big day for Dungloe; it was, in a very special sense, a big day for Mr. Gallagher, to whose courage, industry and enterprise it is a worthy monument.

---

9   *Derry Journal 9th February 1945*

Present at the formal opening were the President and Secretary of the Scottish Co-operative Wholesale Society, one of the biggest concerns of its kind in Great Britain. They flew from Glasgow specially to attend the event,

When I visited the spacious, brilliantly-illuminated stores on Wednesday forenoon, workmen were busy applying the finishing touches to the arrangement of stocks and general tidying-up. The activity was intense and not a moment was wasted. The happy culmination of many anxious months of planning and construction was at hand. The new premises, bigger far than the old, carried a huge stock. Every one of the scores upon scores of shelves was filled: every type of goods had its generous quota. An elaborate central heating plant will soon be functioning in all departments. In for a minute and out again, to attend to some business matter, the beaming countenance of Paddy himself told of the complete satisfaction he must have felt.

Bands in Big Procession

Close on three o'clock the distant sound of music brings Paddy to the street to accord a warm greeting to the first of the bands to reach the town. At the head of a big procession is carried a banner inscribed 'Long Live Paddy the Cope'. The bands taking part were the Derrydruel Pipe Band, the Meenacross Pipe Band and the Maghery Flute Band. In turn, they paraded the street, discoursing national and martial airs.

Blessing and Opening

By three o'clock a large crowd has assembled. The esteemed parish priest Rev. T. Molloy, D.Ph. wearing surplice and soutane arrives and there is an impressive and hushed interlude whilst he prays the blessing of the Church on the new stores. The doors are then thrown open to the public, who quickly fill it to overflowing capacity. Members of the staff sing "Bless This House" as the procession moves to the co-op yard, where a public meeting is held…"[10]

---

10 *Derry Journal April 1946*

A group of bakery workers prepare pastry: Michael Sweeney, Margaret Gallagher, Jim Devenney and Phil Sweeney (1981, Cope Archive).

Michael Sweeney and Margaret Gallagher displaying trays in front of one of the 5 big ovens. (1981, Cope Archive)

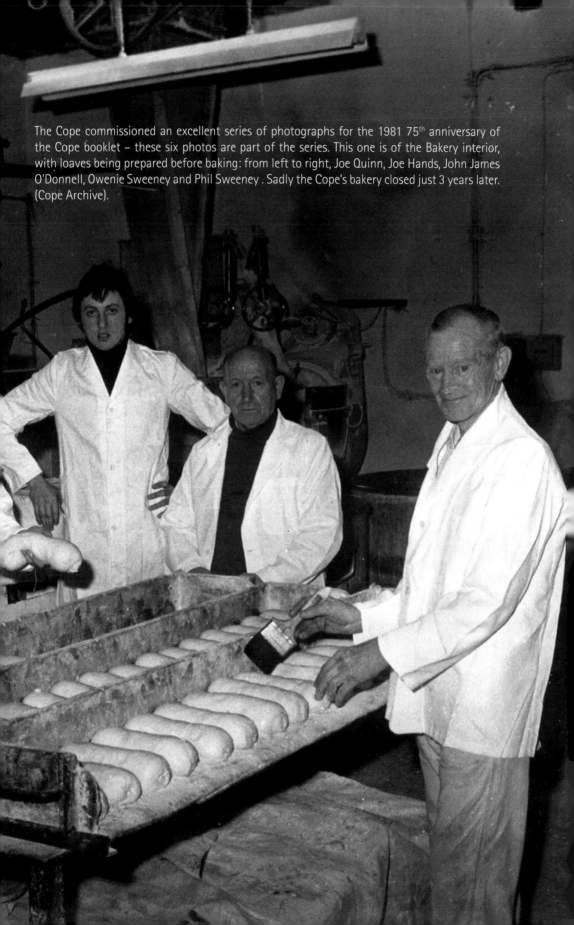

The Cope commissioned an excellent series of photographs for the 1981 75th anniversary of the Cope booklet – these six photos are part of the series. This one is of the Bakery interior, with loaves being prepared before baking: from left to right, Joe Quinn, Joe Hands, John James O'Donnell, Owenie Sweeney and Phil Sweeney . Sadly the Cope's bakery closed just 3 years later. (Cope Archive).

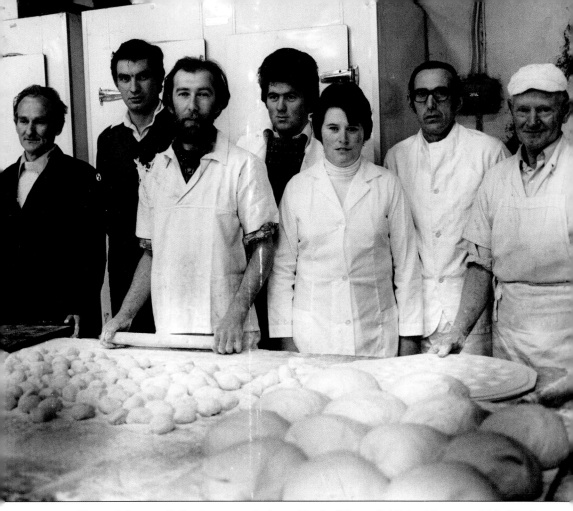

Above: Bakery staff: Jim Devenney, Anthony Martin O'Donnell, Michael Sweeney, Eddie Ward, Margaret Gallagher, Jim Mooney and Phil Sweeney. Jim Devenney also worked on the Cope boats with his brothers Connie and Donald and with his brother Donald in the Cope's Crohy Head Soapstone Mine (1981, Cope Archive)

Right Top: Anthony Martin O'Donnell and Jim Devenney wrapping sliced loaves (1981, Cope Archive).

Right Bottom: Michael Sweeney loads some pastries into one of the Bakery ovens (1981, Cope Archive).

The Story of the Cope

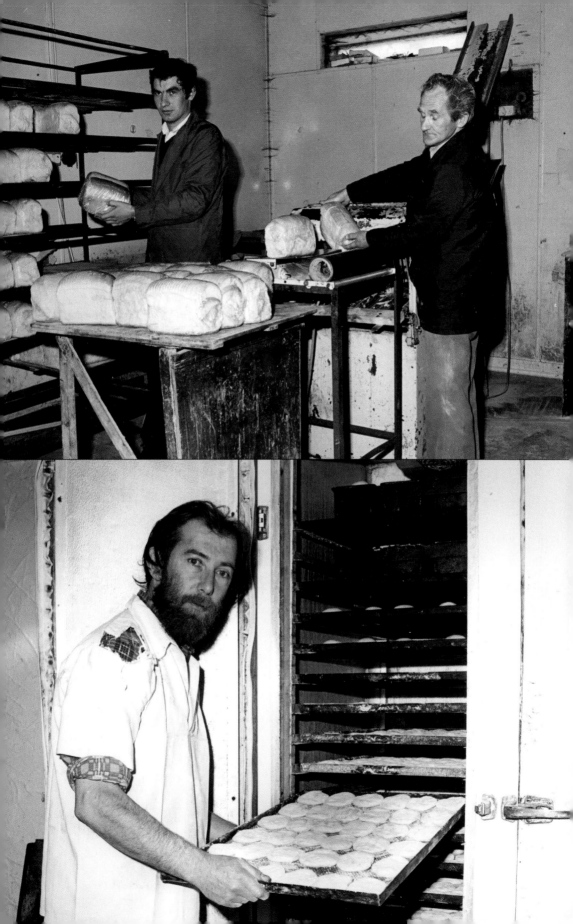

Left Above: This is a view – on the left - of the Bakery building in November 2006, just as the Builders' Providers was moving out to the new premises in Sheskinarone. The large double doors in the side were added later, during its time as part of the Builders' Providers to make it easy to store materials upstairs. Flour was stored upstairs when it was in use as a Bakery; it was taken up via a ramp that sloped up at the far end of the building. On the right is the entrance to the old Knitting factory (PB photo 2006).

Left Bottom: The old flour chute, last used in 1984, is still in situ in the Bakery. Flour would be delivered upstairs and dropped down the chute straight into the mixer (PB photo 2006, Dim Boyle memoir)

The Cope Bakery was successful and popular until its closure in 1984 but the writing was on the wall from the mid 1970s when fuel costs escalated and competition from the North came in. General Manager Cyril Winder, writing in 1975, was still optimistic:

> "...Our Bakery, that lost money in the previous year, justified the capital invested in re-equipping it and engaging an experienced manager, which increased our sales in this end by 70%, and making it once again viable, with greater potential ahead. With progressive reduction in bread consumption over the past years very few bakeries can speak of any increases at all...!"[11]

The optimism was short lived and the capital investment, after good results initially, was not able to arrest a long term decline. The hard decision to close the 70 year old business was taken and the Bakery closed for good in 1984; the building was re-utilised as a storage area for the old Builders' Providers.

In 1985, Cyril Winder lamented the closure:

> "...Due to affluence, people were looking for more fancy breads so we got a more competent Bakery Manager in 1975 who further re-equipped our Bakery, yet as we are often notorious for, we, more than anyone else did not support our own. When we were up against the benefits of high cost capital equipment, Government price controls, high delivery costs and Government bureaucracy and unfair competition from cheaper flour from the North, with growing losses and no prospects, we had no alternative but to close the Bakery..."[12]

---

11 *Cyril Winder 1975, 'Commemorative Souvenir of Our First £1,000,000 in Sales and Service' - The Cope 1975*

12 *'From One Million Pounds to Five Million Pounds in Sales and Services 1975-1985' 1985 Cope Staff Bulletin*

Chapter 7

The Mill and the Pier

The Mill

The following account is from the 1924 revised edition of the Irish Homestead pamphlet on the Templecrone Co-Operative Society.

"...Standing at the end of the pier is an old corn mill, formerly worked by a water wheel, which did the work of the entire Rosses for almost a century back. It was the property of the landlord, who was remunerated by one stone in every twenty of oats ground. Adjacent to the mill are two kilns for drying the grain, one of which continues to do the drying while the other has been improvised, recently, into a custom house.

For eight or ten years previous the purchase of this estate lay at some stage of negotiation, and the Society now felt that when these negotiations were completed the mill should be in the hands not of any individual or section but of the entire community. The landlord was approached, and the mill became the property of the Society in 1921. But it may be mentioned here that the primary object of the Society was to get hold of the water power which could not be acquired otherwise than by purchasing the mill.

The mill continues to do the work of the district, and on the same conditions as heretofore, but machinery and fittings have been overhauled and repaired, and a cleaner and better quality of oatmeal turned out. But the Society had in mind the further utilising of this immense volume of water that rolled uselessly on to the sea. The grimy old water wheel that did good service in its day was torn down in 1922 and supplanted by a turbine wheel, and an electric plant installed. The new power was used to drive the mill and the machinery of the factory, as well as to supply heating and lighting to factory and stores. The Society was thus enabled to dispense with the oil engine used to run the factory, and thus to eliminate a considerable item of expense.

A beginning was also made this year in grinding maize. The experiment proved successful and the quality of meal gave satisfaction, but it entailed frequent changing and adjusting of machinery and fittings to suit the alternate grinding of oats and maize. The present year, 1924, a small Greenhill mill has been installed, which can turn out one ton of Indian meal per hour, while much more efficient methods are employed in handling the grain and output. Formerly bags were hauled about and carried up and down stairways, and the entire building, except the top floors, which were quite inaccessible for any useful purpose, was one confusion of sacks, bags, and dusty men. At present the maize as it arrives at the pier is transferred by lorries to the mill, a distance of forty or fifty yards. There it is turned into a bin and raised by elevators to the top floors, where there is sufficient accommodation for over 100 tons. It is next handled in the ground state, when it is bagged and despatched to the lorries again by means of a slide. The entire process is carried out with admirable expedition and at a mere fraction of the former expense.

In December 1923, a lighting scheme for the village was put into operation, and the electric light was introduced into the shops and principal dwellings at a cost lower than that of the old paraffin lamp. Since then a further scheme gives the new light to the poorer class at a merely nominal cost, and probably before the present winter has passed there will not be a dwelling in the village without its electric fittings. A good reserve of electric power still remains for further developments.

The entire expenditure on mills and electric plant, together with other necessary repairs and fixtures, amounts to a considerable sum, but the investment has already proved not only a useful but a sound one, for as far as present calculations indicate the entire amount standing against it should be wiped off in a very short period.

THE BLOCKADE

Some years ago a local trader, in a platform attack upon Mr. Gallagher, locally known as " Paddy the Cope," referred to him as " This Moses come down from the mountain," the reference being to Mr. Gallagher's former home, which was situated near the summit of Mount Cleenderry. The comparison was rather a good one, though there was an omission of any reference to the commandments the modern Moses had down from the modern Sinai, or that on his descent from the mountain he had found his people worshipping false gods. Recently, however, Mr. Gallagher, who is destined to play many parts, has adopted a new role, that of a modern Joseph. For it came to pass that the land of the Rosses was threatened with a great scarcity of food, owing to conditions of war that existed at that time. Paddy, with somewhat of the prophetic eye of the son of Jacob, foresaw the lean period that was coming, and forthwith set about laying up large stores of provisions therefore. Turning his eyes from the Lough Swilly

This is a fine close up of the Mill and associated buildings in c1905, looking very much as they would have when taken over by the Cope about 15 years later. The Mill Store is to the right with its original three stories. The Cope generated electricity for Dungloe from here from 1923. The store was a versatile building; it had an ice making plant (local people remember ice being made in fish boxes and taken to Burtonport). The Cope also operated a small abattoir here too - Connie Boyle or Connie Conallín as he was better known worked in it. The Cope sold this and the other buildings in more recent times and the subsequent owner demolished the top storey of the grain store and replaced the slate roofs with corrugated steel (the old slate roofs were always being damaged). Templecrone Parish Church (Church Of Ireland, built in 1760 at a cost of £400) can be seen as well as what were once a schoolhouse and a small cottage, both of which no longer exist. Brigid Byrne, now in the Quay Road, who worked in the Knitting Factory from 1939 to 1962, was born in the cottage; her mother was Nora O'Donnell (Lawrence Collection, National Photographic Archive).

The Mill (which dates from c1820) and surrounding buildings and land was purchased for £1,250 in 1920 from the then landlord, Marquis Conyngham; the transaction was handled by Dan Deery (later, Chairman of the Cope, 1966-1972) for the Cope and by Mr Pomeroy for the landlord. Part of the Dungloe River and adjoining land was included in the transaction. This photograph shows Peggy Brennan, Paddy's niece, in August 1942 sitting on the pier (Cope Minute Book 8th January 1920; National Archives, Bishop Street Dublin; photo from Packie Walsh, Burtonport)

Railway, hitherto the food-giving Nile of the Rosses, he bent his steps towards the sea, and after disappearing for a time returned with a great ship loaded with flour. In due time the period of scarcity came, as predicted, and all the people flocked to Paddy for flour, and among those who came were his own trading brethren who, many years ago, would have condemned him to a pit much deeper than that to which his brethren had consigned Joseph. But Paddy pretended to know them not, and, filling their bags, sent them home. Thus by this modern Joseph was a period of dire distress averted in the land of the Rosses. There are details, however, in the comparison lacking. For example, there is no record that his brethren, already mentioned, on any subsequent visit to him, brought back with them presents of their choicest fruits, or that the modern Joseph put the price of their flour in the mouths of their sacks.

The Story of the Cope

This modern day view taken from the pier shows the mill buildings are they are today. In contrast, the large eircom mast, which dominates Dungloe (and gives it the appearance of an early oil town), provides modern communications – for broadband and mobile phones – rather than the basic electricity that the Cope generated from the mill from 1923 to 1956. Times have moved on. The eircom mast was built in 1990 during the time of the First Gulf War – its size, in comparison to the earlier much smaller mast came as a big surprise to the people of Dungloe – in particular those living on the Fair Hill where it is located (PB photo, November 2006)

Leaving aside comparisons, the following are the circumstances which the Templecrone Society found itself up against. On April 20th, 1921, the Londonderry and Lough Swilly Railway, the great food artery of the Rosses, was shut down by a military order, as a reprisal, no doubt, for the acts of the people against the powers that then existed. About the same time all other trains in the county ceased to run beyond Stranorlar and Letterkenny. Dungloe lies about 30 miles from both these towns, and the roads between had been cut up and rendered almost impassable for vehicles of any kind. The whole of The Rosses was, therefore, almost completely isolated, and food and other necessaries were running short. The Society lost no time in coping with the difficulty. Mr. Gallagher set out for Cardiff, chartered a boat there, and reached Burtonport with a cargo of meal, flour, and general goods. During the summer and autumn of this year the entire supplies of the Society came by sea, and most of its eggs and hosiery was got to market by return of boats. During these five months there were twenty-two arrivals and returns of boats at Burtonport and Kincasslagh. The other traders continued to deliver their eggs and get in their limited supplies by cart from Stranorlar and Letterkenny. The strike of Transport Workers, which occurred about this time, produced a serious outlook for the egg trade, which was then the principal source of income of the people. Shipping from Derry had ceased, and it seemed for the time that the large and it seemed for the time that the large consignments awaiting shipment, as well as the large quantities in the hands of other societies and local traders, would be lost. The situation was once more saved by the Templecrone Society, which bought in all the eggs in the hands of neighbouring societies as well as those of local traders, who were anxious to be relieved of them, and shipped them direct to Glasgow.

Seeing the unexpected turn things had taken, that a large slice of their Donegal trade was being diverted and lost to them, the heads of the Derry wholesale houses lost no time in having the military order for the closing down of the railway countermanded. The punitive measure meant for the peasantry and people of West Donegal began to recoil upon loyal heads, and that would never do. The Donegal Railways resumed work after a time, but the Templecrone Society, having once taken to the water, began to feel that its future lay very much that way. It continued to get in all heavy goods by sea, and the saving effected was enough to encourage bigger prospects and new ideas. The Society was easily able to compete in flour (and later on in meal) with Derry wholesale houses, and a great many of the local traders turned to it for their supplies..."[1]

The Cope provided electricity to the town of Dungloe over 30 year before the ESB's Rural Electrification Programme took over the responsibility in 1956. Although, for the most part, the Cope's service was universally welcomed, occasionally there would be an odd complaint. Paddy the Cope wrote to the ESB in 1928, in response to an anonymous complaint about the Cope's way of running the town's electricity supply:

"...A Cara

In reply to yours of the 15th inst. we herewith enclose a List of the names of all of the people in Dungloe who we supply with electric light or heating.

We stop the turbine during the summer months at 1 a.m. and, since the 1st September the turbine is going night and day. Occasionally during the day when there is a heavy load on in the Mill and Factory, we cut off the Town, but this only affects five people who have radiators in which we give them all the current

---

1   Templecrone Co-operative Society, booklet, The Irish Homestead, 1924

The mill race ran from Dungloe Lough to the mill, under the road and across the top of the town. There were two sluice gates to control the flow; these were opened each morning and closed each night by Pat (Cannon) O'Donnell. The Race was used to generate electricity from December 1923 until 1956 when the ESB added Dungloe to the national network. Until then, the Cope had supplied c40,000 units per annum to the two churches, businesses and homes for over 40 years using the water power from the Mill race; as demand from the Cope factories developed they increasingly used oil generated power. This photograph shows a small remaining section of the Mill Race, just up from Connie Devenney's house, before McDevitt's garage on the road out of Dungloe to Burtonport (PB photo November 2006).

they require for the flat rate of £5 per annum and the following are the five – Revd. Father Scanlon, Mrs Sara Brennan, Messrs Daniel Sweeney, Anthony O'Donnell, The Officer Customs and Excise.

We give free light to the Chapel, the Church, and eight free lights to the Street.

We charge 8d per unit to all who have meters, and 5/- per month for two lights and 1/- extra for each additional light to the people who were too poor to have the service installed. We put the service in Free to the poor people. We would therefore feel obliged if you would let us know who made the complaint.

Mise le meas.
Signed P. Gallagher…"[2]

---

2   IAOS records 1088/871/2 National Archives – letter dated 28th November 1928. The letter is included not to highlight a very rare complaint but to give some appreciation of how the electricity supply was managed.

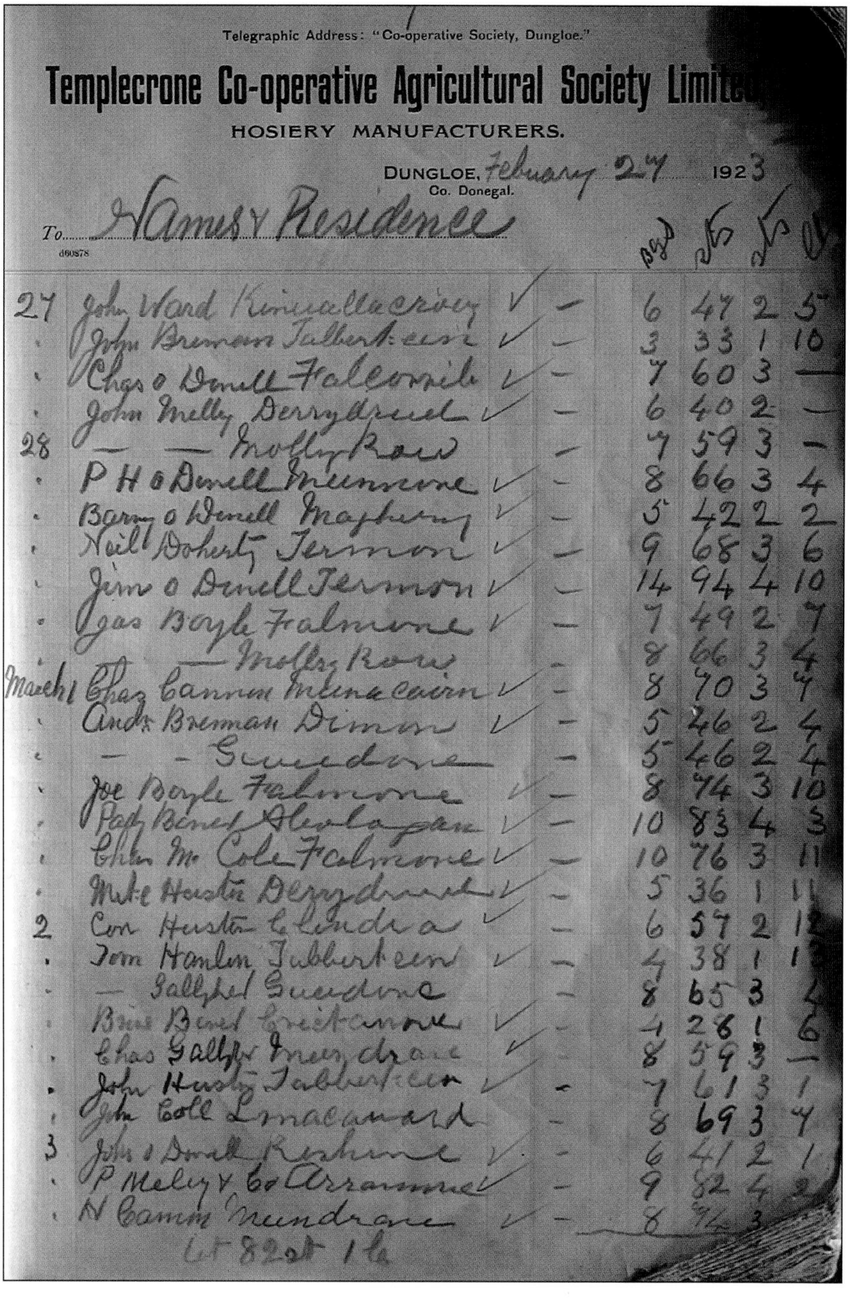

Telegraphic Address: "Co-operative Society, Dungloe."

Templecrone Co-operative Agricultural Society Limited

HOSIERY MANUFACTURERS.

DUNGLOE, *February 27* 1923
Co. Donegal.

To *Names & Residence*

d90978

This page from the Templecrone Mill Book covers the period from February 27th to March 3rd 1923. To take the first person listed - John Ward of Kinvallacruey (Kinballycruey - or 'Kentucky' as it is called locally) brought in 6 bags with 47 stone of grain and gave the Cope 2 stone and 5lbs in payment (47 stone is 299kg - a lot of grain being grown by one person in Kentucky - with 15kgs, 5%, going to the Cope). The farmers bringing grain to be milled are (spellings as written): John Ward, Kinvallacruey; John Brennan, Tubberkeen; Chas O'Donnell, Falcorrib; John Melly, Derrydruel; P H O'Donnell, Meenmore; Barney O'Donnell, Maghery; Neil Doherty, Termon; Jim O'Donnell, Termon; James Boyle, Falmore; Chas Cannon, Meencairn; Andrew Brennan, Diamond; Joe Boyle Falmore; Packy Boner, Aboligan; Chas McCole, Falmore; Mike Houston, Derrydruel; Con Huston, Cleendra; Tom Hanlon Tubberkeen; - Gallagher, Gweedore; Briney Boner, Crickamore; Chas Gallagher, Meendrane; John Huston, Tubberkeen; John Cole, LMacaward; John O'Donnell, Roshine; P Mely & Co, Arranmore; and N Cannon Meendrane (Templecrone Mill Book, Donegal County Archive, Lifford)

Templecrone Co-operative Agricultural Society Limited,

HOSIERY MANUFACTURERS.

DUNGLOE, *November* 1924 2
Co. Donegal.

To *Oat Meal Made*

		Bags	Sts	Sts	lbs	£	S.	d.
28	James F. O'Donnell S. Port	8	60	4	7	2	6	
"	Chas Boyle Arran	4	40	3		2		
"	John Early do	2	20	1	7	2		
"	Hugh Early do	4	35	2	9	2		
"	Denis Bonar S. Port	5	40	3		2		
30	Packie O'Donnell Chapel Rd.	10	50	4		2		
"	Adam Elliott Letter	7	56	4	7	2	6	
"	Chas P McFadden Dungloe	4	25	2	8	2	6	
Dec 21st	Dom Quinn Derrydruel	4	36	2	10	2		
"	Denis Doherty Sheskinorone	3	28	2	2	2		
"	Neil Sweeney Meenacross	7	59	4	7	2		
"	Dan Sweeney Sheskinorone	4	26	2		2		
"	Patrick O'Donnell Arranmore	8	57	4	8	2	6	
"	Hugh Doherty Sheskinorone	3	28	2	2	2		
"	Hugh Sweeney Cronashallog	6	48	5	9	2		
"	Mick O'Donnell Derrydruel	6	48	3	9	2		
22	Paddy O'Donnell Little Bridge	6	48	3	9	2		
"	Chas Salon Derrydruel	7	61	4	7	2		
"	Francis Boyle Chapel Road	6	55	4		2		
26	Jas Sweeney Dungloe	7	51	3	10	4		
"	Paddy McGrath Maas	14	120	9				
"	Adam Walsh Maas	8	64	4	12	2	6	
31st	Jas Sharkey Fair Hill	10	80	6		2		
"	Edward O'Donnell Milltown	5	46	3	8	2	6	
"	Paddy Roarty Carnmore	10	66	5	1	3		
"	John McCarron Diamond	8	88	6	10	4		
						£2	19	-

This is a later page of the Mill Book, dating from November 28th to December 31st, 1942. By this stage, milling was done in exchange partly for cash not just a share of the ground meal. Payment is a mixture of oatmeal (the rate has gone up it appears from 5 to 7.5%) and a flat fee of two shillings or 2/6d. The customers listed are: James F O'Donnell (Jimmy Frank), Denis Bonar, Burtonport; Joe Boyle, John Early, Hugh Early, Patrick O'Donnell from Arranmore; from Dungloe, Packie O'Donnell, Chapel Road, Chas McFadden, Paddy O'Donnell, Little Bridge, Francis Boyle, Chapel Road, James Sweeney; James Sharkey, Fair Hill, John McCarron, The Diamond; Adam Elliott, Lettermacaward; Dom Quinn, Mick O'Donnell, Chas Salon, Derrydruel; Denis Doherty, Sheskinarone; Neil Sweeney, Meenacross; Dan Sweeney, Hugh Doherty, Sheskinarone; Hugh Sweeney, Cronashallog; Paddy McGrath, Adam Walsh, Maas; Edward O'Donnell, Milltown; Paddy Roarty, Carnmore; and John McCarron, Diamond (Templecrone Mill Book, Donegal County Archive, Lifford)

Patrick Sharkey, Dungloe, also wrote to the ESB regarding this complaint – Mr Sharkey was the Collector for the Cope's electricity service and also put in the service for about half the Dungloe houses, including the Guards' Barracks. He stated that apart from Mr James Campbell, the Hotel Dungloe, who thought the unit price should be 6d not 8d, there had been no complaints at all and that in his view the service was excellent.[3]

THE TEMPLECRONE MILL BOOK

The following account and interpretation of the significance of the Templecrone Mill Book was written by Packie Bonner and first published in 1981 in the booklet commemorating the 75th anniversary of the Cope.

> "...To begin with, let me say that the description or title - the Templecrone Mill Book - is entirely my own. This all important record was found in the Old Mill premises in Dungloe when repairs were being carried out to the century-and-a-half old building there, about three years ago. Amongst other things, the repairs entailed putting a new roof on what was formerly the Conyngham Mill, and it was in the process of this being done that the Mill Book was found, hidden away in the old roof structure. Having removed the old corrugated iron roof, the tradesmen doing the job found a well kept ledger tucked away in the rafters, in which was set out the day to day working of the Mill, during the last years of its long life, namely, 1923-1945. Indeed, had it not been for the watchful and discerning eye of Assistant Manager, Eugene Doherty, it is possible that this valuable document would have been committed to the rubble and debris of the job, and that, as a consequence, the information it contains would never have seen the light of day. Our thanks, therefore, are to Eugene, for its recovery and preservation.[4]
>
> In an area where what records there are, are regretfully few and scant, let me say that I would regard the Mill Book as one of the most important local "finds" since the recovery of the 'Templecrone Vestry Book' from the Four Courts conflagration of June, 1922. Both records - the Mill Book and the Vestry Book - are invaluable,

---

3   IAOS records as above – letter dated 28th November 1928 also. Paddy suspected a local politician of being involved: "...I am of the opinion, whether I may be right or wrong, that no person would be capable of making a false complaint, with the exception of Eugene Doherty TD or his Friends, they done their best for the past few years to get the Board of Conservators to obstruct the water supply and, having failed in that, they are now trying to get some other obstacle in the way. I hope I am not accusing them wrongly, but I have a lot of experience of this crowd, and I am confident if they did not complain directly, but they were Behind the Screens..."

4   The Templecrone Mill Book may be found in the County Archive, Lifford where it was deposited, after detailed analysis and study, by Packie Bonner.

each in its own way, toward our arriving at a better understanding of conditions in the Rosses or Templecrone in generations gone by. Both records, too, had the good fortune of having escaped the ravages of two disastrous fires: in the case of the Vestry Book, the fire that enveloped the Four Courts at the outset of the Civil War, and in the case of the Mill Book, the two Cope fires of 1945 and 1951. These two factors, I would say, helped us in our choice of title or description for the record in question - the Templecrone Mill Book, as already stated. It might be said, too, that the Mill Book is of further importance as a Co-op record in so far as that it covers nearly the entire period during which the Mill had been operated by its new owners, the Templecrone Co-operative Society.

The continual flow of corn deliveries to the Mill in those days, serves to bring home to us the great importance of tillage as a means of survival for our ancestors, in those difficult times. Indeed, it could be said that the economy of the entire West Donegal in those days, had three main pillars for support; namely, emigration, fishing and the land. It might be pointed out too, that only about half of the total corn yield of the district, in those days, found its way to the Mill in order to be ground into meal; the other half would be used as feeding for horses, cattle and fowl, and a further portion would be earmarked for seed in the following spring. It is a matter of regret that the Society's records regarding egg exports were all lost in the fires already mentioned, because if these were now available to us, they would testify as to the importance of egg production to our people in the period prior to the outbreak of the Second World War (1939-45).

In the table set out on the next page, I have meticulously copied from the Mill Book all corn deliveries to the Mill for the year 1923. I decided on the year 1923 as the records for that particular year seemed to be more complete, and, besides, the post-War period is further interesting in as much as that is represents a time of very high unemployment and high population as well. The year 1923, too, marked the beginning of the infant Irish Free State, and it might be said that the setting up of the new regime in Dublin brought its own train of difficulties of one kind or another. It was a time then when the people of the Rosses relied considerably on the support they derived from the tillage of the soil, and for that reason, the figures for that year are well worth our attention and study.

Rotation of crops was then the order of the day, agriculturally speaking, so that the amount of corn or cereal grown in any given year provides us with a measure of the extent of the potato crop raised in the following year. Bearing in mind the poor quality of the land in the Rosses, and the primitive methods of cultivation then being employed by those engaged

Mill returns in the Rosses for the year 1923 :

Townland: (No of deliveries made):	No of bags:	Weight in stones:
Inishfree (10)	65	423
Arranmore (16)	162	1,422
Inishaal (3)	21	136
Maghery (7)	39	328
Cleendra (15)	94	808
Loughsalt (4)	20	190
Termon (13)	112	773
Culleen (6)	38	268
Saltpans (14)	89	705
Roshine (5)	33	257
Cronamaddue (14)	100	755
Aboligan (5)	34	259
Meenacross (8)	60	470
Toberkeen (17)	96	768
Marameelin (6)	34	235
Falmore (17)	124	984
Falcorrib (14)	110	956
Crohey (1)	6	55
Dungloe (Fair Hill, Caravan, Carnmore, Little Bridge, Knocknagerra) (21)	144	1,189
Meendrain (10)	74	588
Diamond (17)	109	893
Derrydruel (28)	190	1,531
Drimlaghdrid (19)	102	904
Croheyboyle (7)	41	316
Brockagh & Upper Hills (6)	42	407
Ardveen-Lettercaugh (4)	24	203
Loughanure-Meenamara-Bunwack (8)	52	445
Doochary-Lettermacaward (32)	163	2,258
Meenacarn (14)	111	976
Meenmore (24)	155	1,103
Sheskinarone (12)	79	608
Crickamore (8)	42	326
Milltown (8)	61	434
Other deliveries from Lower Rosses (20)	126	1,011
Corn collected by Co-Op throughout the Rosses ( )	721	7,939
Gweedore (7)	50	425
Total: (420 +)	3,522	31,348

in tilling the soil these figures leave us much food for thought as to the living conditions of our people two generations ago. Fertilisers were not in common use then either, so that maximum use had to be made of seaweed in order to extract a crop from the hungry land that lay between Gweedore and Gweebarra. Oat meal was, then, an important item of diet in those days, and in order to produce eight stones of meal it would be necessary to bring about eleven stones of corn to the Mill in order to have it ground into meal. The drudgery, the sweat, the aches and pains of those days, are now conveniently forgotten by a new generation who, fortunately, live in more happier and prosperous times; but, nevertheless, the figures below speak more eloquently than words and are worthy of our most closest scrutiny and analysis, if we are to fully understand the struggle against great odds, put up by our forefathers in the generations that have passed.[5]

The Templecrone Co-operative Society purchased the Mill from the Marquis of Conyngham in 1921. The affairs of the Conyngham Estate in West Donegal were being wound up at that time, and in a few years hence, the entire property eventually was transferred to the local tenantry. This transfer was actually completed during the years 1925-27. Sometime after the Society acquired the Mill, it was decided to install a turbine there in order to supply power to the Mill and provide light and electricity to the entire town as well. This arrangement held good until it was taken over the ESB, in 1956. While the Cope electricity supply, of necessity, had its limitations, it, nevertheless, showed great foresight and initiative on the part of the man whose brainchild it was; and little wonder then that it was regarded by all as one of the marvels of its time in the Rosses. Bear in mind that the waters of the Shannon did not begin to flow through the sluices at Ard-na-Crusha until the year 1929, and that we had to wait until the year 1950 before the baby of Rural Electrification was eventually born. The Cope venture, then, was more than a quarter of a century ahead of its time..."[6]

The purchase price of £1,250 for the Mill lease included some substantial parcels of land around the Mill and along the Dungloe River (this would prove to be very helpful some 30 years later when the idea of a Dungloe Hospital was being developed. The landlord's agent, Mr. Pomeroy, went to great lengths in the drafting to protect his client's fishing rights:

---

5   *The Cope Diamond Jubilee, 1906-1981 (75ᵗʰ Anniversary) booklet, Packie Bonner (Cope Archive)*

6   *Ditto, Packie Bonner, 1981*

"...FIRST ALL THAT Mill situate in the Parish of Dungloe TOGETHER with the Mill Pool pasture and garden land and outbuildings usually occupied therewith including the strip of land between the public road and the mill race all which premises contain together one acre one rood and four perches or thereabouts and are delineated on the plan drawn on these presents and thereon coloured pink together also with the mill-race gaits dams sluices and Watergates to the said Mill belonging and the right of taking and using the water of the adjoining stream called Dungloe River (usually enjoyed therewith and all rights to the water from the Lakes known as Craghy Lake and the Dungloe lake) save and except the Vendors' fishing rights and subject to any rights of the riparian tenants of the said water AND SECONDLY ALL THAT house and the piece or parcel of land occupied therewith by Dan Deery as Miller which premises contain together thirteen acres one rood and twenty two perches or thereabouts and are delineated on the said plan and thereon coloured green AND ALSO all those pieces of bog land on either side of the Long Lough and all rights of cutting turf enjoyed by the said Dan Deery with the said pieces of land..."[7]

"...The Mill continued to operate until the decline of tillage in the Rosses in our own time, caused it to finally close down. Today, Jackie Brennan's petrol pumps, are, I would say, standing on the spot under which the waters of the Old Millrace once flowed, while further down the road, nearer the Mill itself, the Millrace had been filled in to allow for the widening of the road at this point. The mill wheel, too, is gone and the gurgling waters of the Millrace are now heard no more. Sic transit Gloria mundi. Nothing now remains of the Mill but the name, but as we pass by its storied walls, we should not be unmindful of its story or the part it played in the uphill struggle of our people in the generations that have passed..."[8]

7   Conyngham Papers (Ms 35,382) Manuscript Collection, Kildare Street Dublin; there is a great amount of detail in the lease about the protection of the fishing rights of the Vendor – restricting use of the water for milling, with conditions to stop any possibility of the new owners exploiting the fish.

8   Cope Diamond Jubilee booklet, Packie Bonner, 1981

The Pier

This account of the building of Dungloe Pier is from the 1924 Irish Homestead booklet on the Templecrone Co-operative Society.

"...In the spring of 1922, a grant of £5,000 was made by the White Cross Society[1] to the Dungloe and neighbouring parishes for the construction and improvement of roads and piers. The allotment of the grant to the various contracts and the carrying out of the work was put into the hands of local committees. Of this grant a sum of £1,200 was set aside for the building of a small pier convenient to Dungloe. The village, though within a few hundred yards of the sea, had only a crude little structure which small row-boats could reach at half tide. In urging this expenditure, the Committee had probably in view the possibility of preparing the way for boats of the coasting and cross-Channel type. But the prospect was anything but encouraging. The site and surroundings were shallow and rocky, and the channel winding and shallow in parts. The Committee, notwithstanding, set about their work diligently and intelligently, and under their supervision a neat little pier was built extending about 100 yards into the deeper water. The channel was also straightened, and some slight barriers removed. Whether a boat of the type mentioned should be able to find its way to it in safety now became a question of burning interest. The progressive little town felt that its future prosperity, if not its very existence, depended very much upon its gaining easy access to its markets—it had its eggs, its hosiery, and now its granite to bring to market, and it was eager to get into direct contact with its buyers. Direct shipping alone could accomplish this.

On the 30th April 1923, the Glenmay, carrying about 200 tons of general cargo, glided in the bay without hitch, and cast her cables on to the new pier. It was a gala day for Dungloe, a triumph for the hard-working Committee who made it possible, and a new laurel in the crown of the Templecrone Society. A fortnightly service with Liverpool was established, and continued during the summer and autumn months. The Society during this period collected the eggs of the neighbouring societies, and re-packed and shipped them direct to market with their own supplies. The arrangement was only by way of experiment, and it is expected that when a regular service throughout the year is established the societies along the western seaboard will avail of this cheap and easy means of reaching the market.

---

1   *The Irish White Cross was established on 1ˢᵗ February 1921 and became the vehicle for the distribution of the very substantial funds raised by the A.C.R.I. (American Committee for Relief in Ireland) to assist in reconstruction after the damage to property, businesses and livelihoods during the War of Independence. Its membership included Maud Gonne-McBride who visited Dungloe at the time of the military blockade in 1921.*

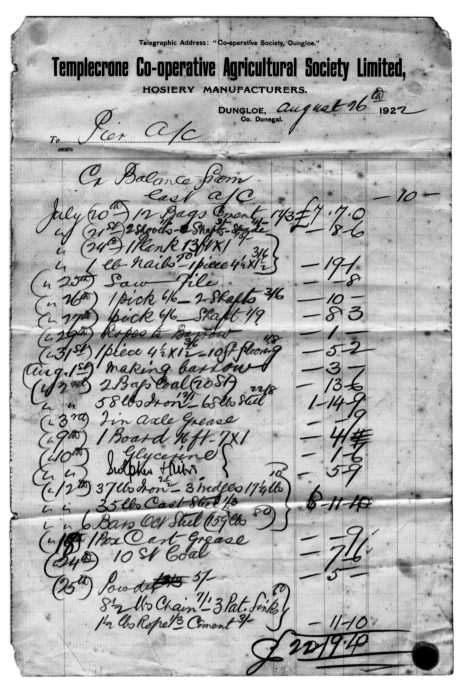

Telegraphic Address: "Co-operative Society, Dungloe."

Templecrone Co-operative Agricultural Society Limited,

HOSIERY MANUFACTURERS.

DUNGLOE, *August 26th* 1922
Co. Donegal.

To *Pier a/c*

d60878

Paddy lobbied successfully for some of the White Cross grant - £1,200 - to be put toward extending and improving the pier beside the Corn Mill in Dungloe: '...for the convenience of the Rosses and island people, to take their corn to the Dungloe mill, and their turf home...' In this invoice for the Pier Account from August 26th 1922, tools and materials for building the pier are drawn down from the Cope store – the Cope's hardware business was therefore benefiting from the grant also (Marie (Brennan) Glackin Collection, Central Bar Dungloe)

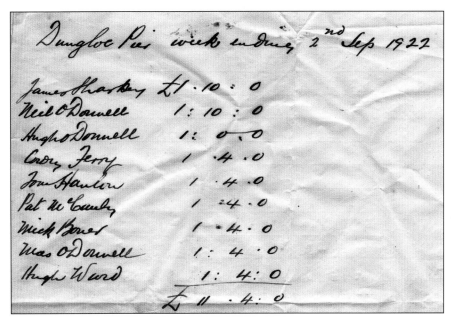

A statement of earnings for the men working on the pier in September 1922. The 'gangerman' was James Sharkey, grandfather of Jimmy Sharkey, who received for the week £1 10s – roughly €2 in today's currency – not a lot now, but of course money went a lot further then when a loaf of bread was only the equivalent of 10c. Also listed are Neil O'Donnell, Hugh O'Donnell, Condy Ferry, John Hanlon, Pat McCauley, Mick Boner, Charles (or James) O'Donnell and Hugh Ward (Marie (Brennan) Glackin collection).

As the winter approached it was found that a boat of deeper draft was necessary to withstand the rough seas around the Donegal coast. If the pier could be further extended 70 or 80 yards it would reach the necessary depth of water. The Committee, with the little balance of funds on hand, set to work again, but the funds became exhausted before the new extension was more than blocked out. In this stage it lies, a mere ridge of rocks stretching out like a gaunt and nerveless arm grasping at the treasures of the sea. Some kindly and patronising Government may some day complete the work so well begun, and when that day arrives the Rosses, with its wealth of granite and the unrivalled handicraft of its workers, will be a better place to live in.

During the first season, from May till October 1923, there were fifteen arrivals of boats at the new pier, carrying a total of 2,021 tons, and valued at £31,455, of which £4,983 was dutiable goods. The service was resumed in May of the present year, and will continue as before during the summer and autumn. A comparatively small grant would complete the pier and enable a regular service to be continued throughout the winter. In freights and prices alone this would effect a saving to the district of thousands of pounds each year..."[2]

---

2   *The Templecrone Co-operative Society, The Irish Homestead, 1924*

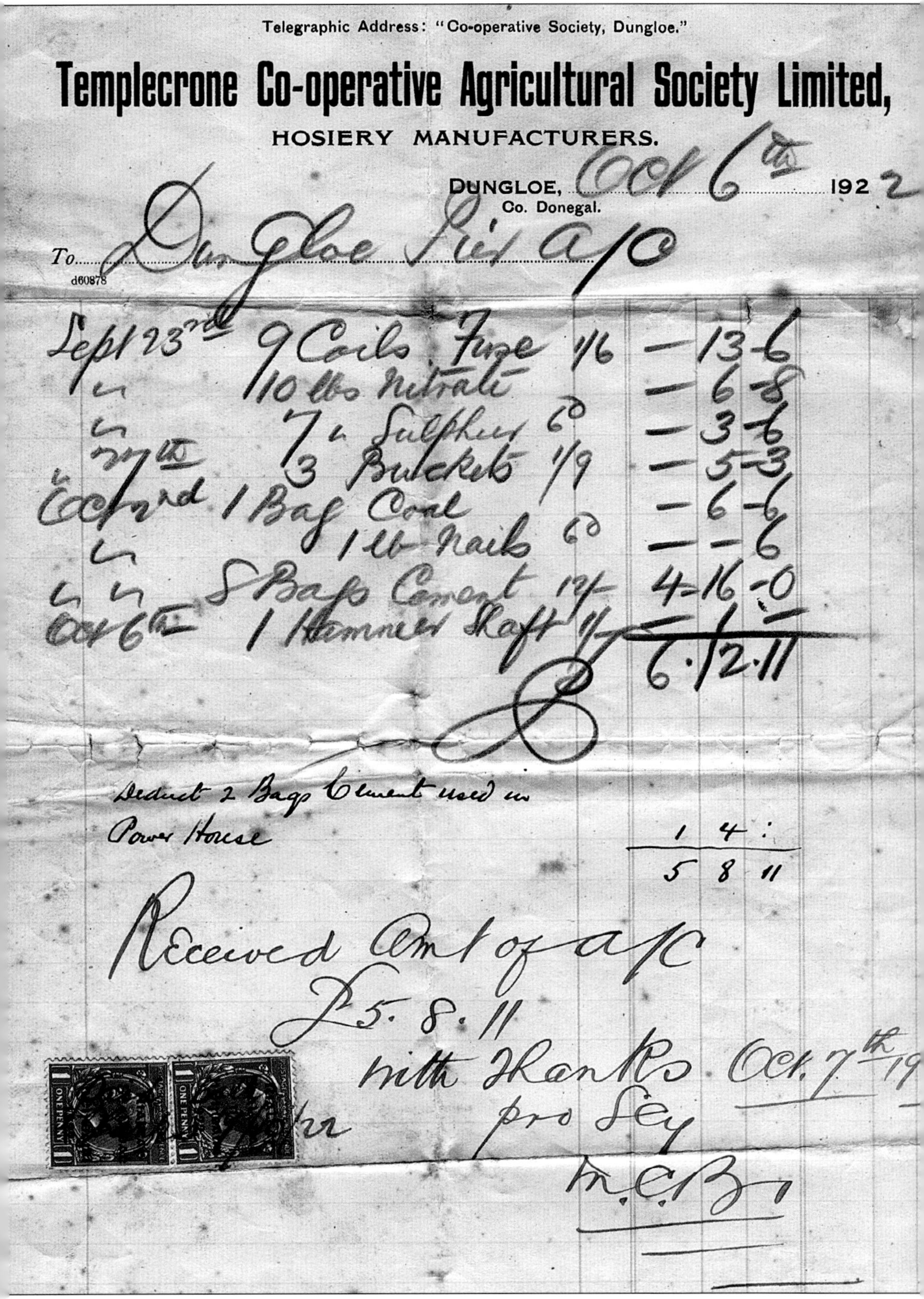

Telegraphic Address: "Co-operative Society, Dungloe."

Templecrone Co-operative Agricultural Society Limited,

HOSIERY MANUFACTURERS.

DUNGLOE, *Oct 6th* 192 2
Co. Donegal.

To... *Dungloe Pier a/c*

d60878

				£	s	d
Sept 23rd	9 Coils Fuse	1/6		—	13	6
"	10 lbs Nitrate			—	6	8
"	7 " Sulphur	6d		—	3	6
29th	3 Buckets	1/9		—	5	3
Oct 2nd	1 Bag Coal			—	6	6
"	1 lb Nails	6d		—	—	6
" "	8 Bags Cement	12/-		4	16	0
Oct 6th	1 Hammer Shaft	11				—
				6	**12**	**11**

Deduct 2 Bags Cement used in
Power House

		1	4	:
		5	8	11

Received Amt of a/c
£5. 8. 11
with Thanks. Oct 7th 19
pro Sey
M. C. B.

Left: This invoice - dated October 6th 1922 for the Dungloe Pier Account - contains some unusual items: nine coils of fuse; 10 lbs of nitrate; and 7 lbs of sulphur. Paddy was more than comfortable working with explosives – he had worked in coal and oil shale mines in Scotland. (Marie (Brennan) Glackin collection)

"...One of the great difficulties to be overcome by those engaged on the construction of the new Pier was the unavailability of explosives at that time. Because of the Civil War, gelignite was then unobtainable so that home-made powder had to be used as a substitute in order to have the job completed. I have heard it said that most of the blasting powder used in the construction of the Mill Pier was made by a man from the Loughanure area — the late Phil Boyle, of Lettercaugh..." (Packie Bonner, writing in 1981)

The stamps on the invoice are overprints of the British George V 1d red – these were the first stamps from the new Provisional Government of Ireland – the overprint reads Rialtas Sealadach na hÉireann 1922. The Irish Free State - Saorstát Éireann - overprints on British stamps began on 11th December 1922; the first Irish stamps were issued on 22nd December (the 2d) and for low value stamps to one shilling at various dates in 1923. High value British stamps with Free State overprints stayed in use till as late as1937.

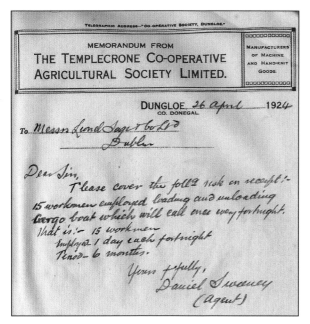

Ever mindful of safety and insurance, Daniel Sweeney, Cope Secretary, made sure that the 15 men working on unloading the Glenmay every two weeks - and the Cope of course - were adequately covered. This letter dates from April 1924. The Glenmay operated from April to September only – the total wages for the 15 men in this period came to £88 9 shillings and tuppence halfpenny (Cope Letter Book, Jim the Cope Archive)

The first boat to come in to the new Dungloe pier on 30th April 1923 was the SS Glenmay. In this picture, Paddy the Cope's close friend Kenny Brennan is sitting on sacks of flour from Liverpool, daughter Marie on his lap, son Kenny next to him and Paddy the Cope standing behind in shirt sleeves on the boat. The hatch doors were being used to unload the ship by sliding sacks of grain down them. Kenny owned the Central Bar in Dungloe just down from the Main Street shop; Paddy was often in the Central Bar of an evening chatting with Kenny by the fire. (Marie (Brennan) Glackin collection, this photo must be later than 1923 as Marie was born in that year and she is about 3 or 4 here).

The SS Glenmay again with Marie and Kenny Brennan in the foreground. The Glenmay was chartered for six months initially. The Glenmay struggled to make it to Dungloe Pier as the channel in Dungloe Bay is very shallow; the skipper had some less than complimentary words about (his words apparently) the madman (Paddy) whose idea it was to bring a ship the size of the Glenmay into Dungloe. The next morning at high tide, the ship just made it back out again – however it proved to be impractical and often cargo was unloaded at the deeper harbour of Burtonport (Marie (Brennan) Glackin collection).

Dungloe Pier was not always navigable and the SS Glenmay, if tides were wrong or it had a particularly heavy load, would unload its cargo at Burtonport, from where it would be stored in the Cope stores there or carried via the Cope's lorries to Dungloe. Here in c1930, a big cargo of timber has been unloaded at Burtonport Pier (the Monument is visible on the left) and one of the early Cope lorries is standing by to transport some of it. These first lorries had a limited carrying capacity – it would have taken a very long time to shift this amount of timber. There is a cine film, by Canon Tommy Doherty, of the Glenmay being unloaded, with Paddy the Cope and harbourmaster Jimmy Frank O'Donnell standing by a Cope lorry (Sally the Cope Collection; North West Film Archive, Letterkenny County Museum).

In 2006, the pier was upgraded and a slipway added:

Pat the Cope officially opens Dungloe Pier and New Slipway

"...Minister of State for Transport Pat the Cope Gallagher TD, officially opened the Pier and New Slipway in Dungloe, on Saturday 21st October. Upgrade works had been carried out on the pier at a cost of €220,000, which Pat the Cope approved during him term as Marine Minister.

Pat the Cope paid tribute to all those that were involved in the project, "The project was led by the Department of the Marine and also received funding from the Department of Community, Rural and Gaeltacht Affairs under the Clar Scheme, as well as a 25% contribution from Donegal County Council and will be an important amenity to the people of Dungloe. I would like to pay tribute to the Mayor, Enda Bonner and all the Councillors and of course Brian Cullen from the Marine Section of the Council.

The new slipway and pier widening was officially opened on 21st October 2006 by Minister for Transport Pat the Cope Gallagher, grandson of the Cope's founder Paddy the Cope. Also pictured are: Delia O' Donnell, Eddie Sharkey, Josie Greene, Eddie Gallagher, foreman with Engineering Division, Department of Agriculture, Fisheries and Food, Pat the Cope Gallagher, TD and Minister, David Alcorn, Donegal County Councillor, Leslie Mc Geoghan, Craftsman with the Engineering Division, Enda Bonner, Mayor of Donegal, Terence Slowey and Virginia Mc Loone (Photo courtesy of Eoin McGarvey).

The cost of the pier upgrade and new slipway was at €220,000, somewhat greater than the original total cost of £1,200, but we need to allow for how much the value of money has changed in 80 years. This aerial view was taken from a helicopter on the day of the launch, Saturday 21st October 2006. The Irish Coastguard Service helicopter had flown up from Sligo on the day to mark the event (Photo courtesy of Eoin McGarvey)

I would also like to thank Gavin Poole, Eddie Gallagher, Leslie McGeoghan and Noel Dorrian together with the Divisional Engineer for the North West John Campbell, whose standard and quality of the work will be a lasting tribute to them, and of course the many locals who demonstrated the benefits of Dungloe harbour for use by fishing boats and pleasure craft.

Dungloe Pier was first constructed in 1923 and it was Pat the Cope's grandfather, Paddy the Cope, who instigated this when, in the 1920s, he was of the view that a pier should be provided to service Dungloe. The S.S. Glenmay would then use the pier to deliver goods for the Cope. The pier had in recent years fallen into disrepair and the upgraded pier now has a slipway for small boats and pleasure craft. This slipway will also allow the use of the pier over a much longer period of the tidal cycle than was possible before and may also be of benefit to rescue services in such an event and for training exercises.

The Minister continued by saying "I am delighted that there are still so many families in the town, whose forefathers played such an active role in the original construction of the pier. In the refurbishment the pier has been improved on its original design, there now is a slipway and turning cycle at the end of the existing pier, a parking area at the upper end and public seating and lighting and I am sure our forefathers would approve of these improvements.

Pat the Cope concluded by encouraging all those who take to the water to be cognoscent of the fact that the seas and our waters are a fabulous natural amenity but can also pose serious dangers if taken for granted. "I would stress the importance on us all, that when we are on the water, whether it be for work or pleasure, to wear a life jacket or other personal flotation device, heed the weather conditions and to avoid the consumption of alcohol. So many lives have been unnecessarily lost by people failing to wear a life jacket and I as Minister for Maritime Safety can only plead with people not to put theirs and others lives at risk..."[3]

---

3   *Press Release, Pat the Cope Gallagher, October 2006, www.patthecope.com*

This is a contemporary postcard from c1960 of the new Dungloe Hospital which opened on Friday 13th June 1958. (Postcard by Kiely Ballyshannon, Mícheál O Dhomnaill Collection)

Dungloe Hospital

When the Cope bought the Mill, there was an additional, unexpected bonus that came with it:

> "…Paddy Gallagher explained the full course of negotiations re purchase of mill and water power. The offer of £1,250 was accepted. Mr Gallagher was complimented on the part he played in the transaction. It has been discovered that parts of the Dungloe River have been included in the purchase…"[1]

Part of the land included was between the Carnmore and Loughanure Roads, adjacent to the river. It was known locally for being something of a swamp. The Cope donated some of the land here to Donegal County Council in 1954 to enable the hospital to be built in Dungloe.

---

1   *Cope Minute Book, 8th January 1920, Cope Archives.*

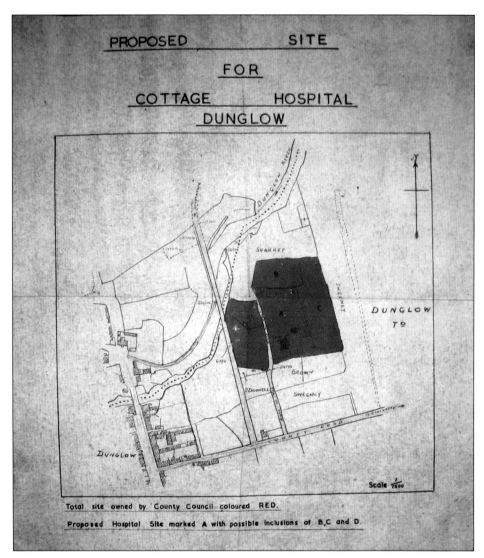

PROPOSED   SITE

FOR

COTTAGE   HOSPITAL
DUNGLOW

Total site owned by County Council coloured RED.

Proposed Hospital Site marked A with possible inclusions of B,C and D.

Above: Dungloe Hospital recently celebrated its 50th anniversary (1958-2008). It was built partly on land donated by the Cope in 1954. The Cope Minute Book (8th November 1958) records: '... The Secretary of Donegal County Council forwarded a letter dated 3rd November 1953 from the County Manager stating that he gave an undertaking to have the Society commemorated in some way in the Hospital in appreciation of the Society donating the field that was used for the site...' On this early planning map can be seen the Dungloe River and the Mill Race above it; it was land adjacent to this which the Cope donated. This land had come into the Cope's hands with the purchase of the Mill from the landlord Conyngham in 1921 (Donbegal County Archive, Lifford).

Right: This is the entrance to Dungloe Hospital being built in c1957; pictured are: Mary (O'Brien) Joyce, Teddy Hanlon, Mary (Ward) McGee and Dim Boyle Dim Boyle (Dungloe), who had been in the Cope Bakery, worked on building the hospital for 3 years from 1954, earning £5 15s and 6d a week. The contractor was P. J. Walls, and Martin's did the terrazzo. Dim worked as a relief ambulance driver from 1958 when the hospital was opened. (Photograph courtesy of Dungloe Hospital, information from Dim Boyle Main Street Dungloe and Cope Minute book).

The crew of *St Theresa* half decker are having their dinner on the whilst out lobster fishing on Roaninish in 1939. In the centre is Big Mick Gallagher, later captain of Cope boats *'Prevail'* in 1941 and later the *'Naomh Eine'* and the *'St Aiden'*. From the left: an unidentified pair of hands; then Tully Leonard, Frank Gracie, Big Mick, Hughie Gracie and Eddie Gracie (Frank and

Eddie were brothers, their father was Hughie). On the deck is a Primos stove boiling a bucket of potatoes, into which small pieces of fish have been dropped to cook. (James Mickey Gallagher and Anne Browne collection).

Chapter 8

The Cope Boats

Special thanks to Connie Devenney and James Mickey Gallagher for the detail and stories about the Cope Boats.

The people of the Rosses had always relied heavily on the sea. Earliest settlements were on the coastal strip and the islands - until very recent times, even the smaller islands had sizeable populations. On maps of the eighteenth and nineteenth centuries, roads were very few and of poor quality. Settlements and churches were built by the sea and the people would get from place to place by boat (currach, yawl and punt) when they could – or of course by 'Shanks' Pony'. Paddy and friends seem to do a lot of walking in the early period covered by 'My Story', Dungloe to Letterkenny or Ballybofey, roughly 36 miles away, being referred to without complaint. In the days before railways and motor cars, there was little alternative.

Commercial fishing in the Rosses had had a number of starts and stops. In the late eighteenth century, after huge investment and a very promising few years, the North West Fishery on Rutland collapsed when the herring disappeared almost completely by the early 1790s. Rutland and Burtonport then went into a long decline for most of the nineteenth century. In the 1890s, with the help of the Congested Districts Board and Fr Bernard Walker, fishing was revived in Burtonport and the pier developed. The coming of the railway in 1903 transformed the industry; fish landed one day could be in British markets the next or following day via Derry. A fishing boom in Burtonport, and the other ports of West Donegal, followed.

> The first 'Cope Boat' Paddy refers to in 'My Story' is the **SS Better Hope**. In June 1921, at the height of the War of Independence, Derry merchants persuaded the military to blockade The Rosses and Gweedore by closing the Lough Swilly Railway, main supply artery by then for the Cope. Paddy secured the SS Better Hope from Bunbeg, loaded her with eggs and made for Glasgow. He was given a warm welcome by the Scottish Co-Operative Wholesale Society in Morrison St near the docks. The boat was loaded up with much needed provisions and they returned to Burtonport. The Derry merchants, fearful of losing trade permanently, reversed the illegal blockade quickly after.

Burtonport born General Joe Sweeney confirmed just how successful Paddy's action had been:

> "...On 10th June, the competent military authority issued an order prohibiting the passage of large fishing boats between Derry and Burtonport and was prompted, evidently, by Paddy the Cope's action

cottish Co-Operative Wholesale
ldings in Morrison St., Glasgow

The Scottish Cooperative Wholesale Society was a great friend to Paddy and the Cope. When the Derry traders persuaded the military authorities to blockade West Donegal in June 1921, Paddy chartered the *SS Better Hope* from Archie Dunlop in Bunbeg; loaded up with eggs, they headed for Glasgow. Paddy records in his book: '...Here again the Scottish Co-Operative Movement came to our rescue. They gave me everything I asked for. They loaded the ship and did not ask me for a penny of cash. I could not then, or now, find words to express my great gratitude to the Scottish Co-Operative Movement. Once again they showed their human element and their honesty, no bargaining about prices, and everything of the best at the lowest possible figure...' (PB collection, contemporary postcard; 'My Story' by Paddy the Cope)

Bunbeg is where Paddy chartered the *SS Better Hope* in 1921 (note the boat against the quay, SO 240). The pier has recently been substantially extended and can now cater for more and larger vessels. (PB Collection, Valentine's postcard c1950)

Right Top: Burtonport harbour needs dredging regularly or the channel between its pier and the nearby islands becomes very shallow with the build up of shifting sand – at low tides, areas of the bay outside the channel dry out completely. In the 1940s and 1950s, the era of the Cope Boats, a 'bucket dredger' called the Sisyphus, but remembered locally as the 'Sissy Puss', was deployed by the O.P.W. (Office of Public Works) to keep the channel open. Sisyphus is a very apt name for a dredger: in Greek legend, Sisyphus was condemned in the underworld to push a huge stone up a steep hill, but each time, the stone always rolled down before he reached the top, and he was forced to begin all over again – much as the 'Sissy Puss' had to with the shifting sands of Burtonport bay (Mícheál O Dhomnaill Collection).

Right Bottom: The Sisyphus was built in 1908 and scrapped in c1972 – it and its sister vessel the Saxifrage were in big demand for dredging harbours all round Ireland – this photo would appear to be Dun Laoghaire. From the records, the Sisyphus worked in Burtonport in the early 1950s - Burtonport harbour was not dredged again till the 1990s. (Photograph courtesy of 'The Secret Bookshop', Wicklow St Dublin; information Jimmy Johnny (O'Donnell), Burtonport and from The National Archive Bishop St Dublin)

in hiring trawlers to bring goods from Derry to the Rosses. Paddy immediately took a trawler to Glasgow where he enlisted the support of the co-operatives so successfully that the blockade was lifted...”[1]

Later, in 1923, the Cope commissioned the shallow draft SS *Glenmay* to bring goods into the new pier at Dungloe and export Cope produce back via Liverpool (Chapter 7 has more detail on the new pier).

The Cope had cause to charter other boats when the Economic War developed between the UK and Ireland from 1932. The 'war' flared up over the Irish Government's decision to cease the payment of land annuities. Fianna Fail, elected for the first time in 1932, were determined to make Ireland self sufficient. The outcome in the short term was a series of 'tit for tat' import and export tariffs – initially 20-30% but some later as high as 50-75% - imposed by both Irish and UK governments. Trade slumped so badly that Guinness opened up its brewery in Park Royal in London in 1936 to protect its British market. This curtailed trading between the UK and Ireland, until 'hostilities' ceased in 1938, and meant that the Cope had to look for new, internal markets for its produce:

> “...‘**A Donegal Project**’: The traders of the Rosses, Donegal, are pushing ahead with their scheme for confining their business to the Free State. The “Rosses Traders’ Association”, which was recently formed, is composed of representative local merchants, and two of these, Mr. P. Gallagher and Mr. J. E. Boyle, of Dungloe, have chartered a local steamer, the *Nora* for plying between that town and Sligo. The vessel, capable of carrying about 100 tons, has begun her experimental trip,

---

1   *Capuchin Annual 1970, ‘Donegal and the War of Independence’, Major General Joseph Sweeney*

Burtonport Harbour, Co. Donegal. 798

and after bringing her cargo of goods from Sligo, will take back on the return journeys quantities of Donegal products, including knitted goods, from Mr. Gallagher's Dungloe factory, where a large number of hands are busy at present, some being engaged on overtime. There is much optimism in the Rosses about the project, and similar movements are on foot in other parts of Donegal. It is hoped to open up trade with other Free State ports later..."[2]

The Cope Boats, as they are remembered, came later, in the 1940s. Packie Bonner wrote an appreciation of the first Cope skipper, Big Mick Gallagher, explaining how the Cope got started in the fishing business:

"...Following the settlement of the Economic War between Ireland and Britain in 1938, a gradual return to normal trading conditions followed and the position continued to show improvement until the onset of World War II in September, 1939. Because of the war conditions then obtaining around the English and Scottish coasts, fishing had become curtailed and restricted there in the years to follow and because of the scarcity of fish at that time, it meant that Irish fishermen got better prices while hostilities lasted.

It was during the Second World War that the late Paddy the Cope, Patrick Gallagher, entered into the fishing business for the first time. Born as he had been at Cleendra, overlooking the bays of the Rosses it was but natural that Paddy the Cope should have an innate interest in the sea and that he should be alive to its great potential as an obvious source of human food. As well as that, in the Rosses when there were so few natural resources, the urgency to develop what few resources that were became all the more obvious to him. While the Templecrone Cooperative Society had been in the fish-curing business since the 'Twenties, it was not until the War years that the firm first embarked on getting fishing boats of its own. These boats, Paddy felt, would have the effect of creating employment for families at home and thus making a contribution towards reducing the plague of emigration that had bedevilled the countryside for generations back. I don't suppose Paddy the Cope would have learned much history from his old master, Mickie Neddy, long ago at Roshine School, but shrewd man that he always was, he would have learned by then the obvious truth of the dictum that England's difficulty was Ireland's opportunity. I would say that Paddy had this in mind when he purchased his first fishing boat a few years after World War II was declared.

Having got the approval of the Co-op Committee before doing so, Paddy bought his first fishing boat — the "Prevail" — early in 1941. Soon afterwards, he purchased his second boat — the "Celine" — and in the

---

2   *Irish Times 12ᵗʰ September 1932*

following year (1942) he bought a third vessel, the "Naomh Einne". The latter was originally a Congested District Board boat and was built in Baltimore, Co. Cork, in the year 1914. Big Mickie was first employed as skipper on the "Prevail", but later transferred to the "Naomh Einne", and it was on the latter boat that he worked for most of the time. The other Cope skippers at that time were Ned Heraghty of Downings, and the late Neil Ward, Burtonport.

Looking back on those years now, if one were to attempt an assessment of the late Paddy the Cope, what would it be? Before saying anything, it would he well to begin with the premise that it is better to have tried and failed than not having tried at all. It is often said as well that the person who does nothing in his life seldom does anything wrong. But, Paddy the Cope didn't fail. On the contrary, his life-long efforts - employment wise, morale wise, economy wise, etc. - brought their own reward. It might be said of Ireland in Paddy's time that it produced more than its due share or proportion of the type that we regard as being of the hurler-on-the-ditch category; but certainly the late Cleendra-man was not one of these. He at least made the effort. He tried to get things done. With the slender resources at his disposal, he tried to do in the 'Forties what Bord Iascaigh Mhara (BIM), with the financial backing of the State behind it, tried and succeeded doing in the 'Sixties, namely, the setting up of a modern fishing industry in the Rosses. We cannot ignore facts, and we must apportion credit and praise where such is due.

During the ten or more years they remained in operation, the Cope boats, for the most part, fished from both Burtonport and Killybegs. As a fishing port, Killybegs was only in its infancy then, with less than a dozen boats using the harbour there. There was a RNLI lifeboat stationed there as well while the War lasted. This was considered necessary in order to cope with all shipping emergencies that might arise between Erris Head and Glen Head in those years. The lifeboat might also be asked to render assistance to aeroplanes using the Allied Air Base at Lough Erne and Enniskillen in the Six Counties. During the War as well, the British had a surveillance ship, the "Robert Hastings" based there.

As readers of the older generation will recall, times were really hard here in Ireland during the War. Ireland was neutral in that conflict so that we usually refer to those years as the Emergency years. Food shortages and rationing of one thing or another became the short supply and what there was of it had to be used sparingly. Because of the difficult fuel position of those years, petrol was strictly rationed and hackney drivers and other essential personnel were given a small ration in order to enable them to get around. Although the public were inconvenienced by these measures, they seldom complained. Of course the petrol shortage didn't hurt so much in those times as it was not until the 'Sixties that cars became popular and in general use. In the 'Forties, young people either walked or cycled. Fishermen were given an allocation of oil for their boats in those days and that was all. There were few private cars in pre-War days and any there were had to be left in the garage while the War lasted. As I've said Big Mickie and his men had been fishing out of Killybegs in those years and their great problem was getting home to the Rosses at the weekend. As there were no cars, then, they used to cycle home on a Friday night and cycle back again on Sunday evening. I merely mention this so that the youth of to-day should have an understanding of the hardships and inconveniences which their elders had to endure in days gone by…"[3]

Operating out of Burtonport and Killybegs, the five Cope boats were the foundation of later success in commercial fishing in West Donegal; their importance has been to a great extent underestimated or ignored. They were the training 'ground' for many of the skippers who later came to prominence in the 1950s and 1960s, men like Connie Devenney, whose boat, the Ros Mhuire was commissioned on 15th August 1954. Connie was the first skipper in Donegal of a modern style BIM sponsored 50 ft boat. James 'Mickey' Gallagher and his brother 'Red' Michael Gallagher skippered the boats Autumn Glory and Darnette respectively. Their father, Big Mick Gallagher ('Mickey Maire'), was a skipper of the Cope boats.

> "…I would say that more than anybody else in his tune, Big Mickie's knowledge and understanding of the waters of Boylagh Bay was indeed outstanding. He had been fishing in these waters all his life so that nobody knew the many reefs and shoals there better than he. We must bear in mind that most of the older generation of fishermen seldom used charts and yet they knew the "fouls" and shoals amongst which they worked, as they did the back of their hand. Most of their knowledge in such matters was acquired through experience or from their elders down the years…"[4]

Pictures of the Cope boats are sadly very hard to come by, but they are no doubt out there somewhere. Those in this book came to hand slowly over an extended period. When the question is asked, the answer is often:"no-one had cameras in those days". What images that do survive were taken by visitors, passing enthusiasts and occasional shots by professional photographers for publication. Fishermen, even skippers it seems, were not that sentimental then about their boats. Time aboard could, at times, be very hard work, much like being on board a floating factory. There was little time to be wasted taking photographs.

---

3   *Derry Journal, January 1986, Packie Bonner, writing as 'Islander' an appreciation of Big Mick Gallagher on the occasion of his passing.*

4   *Ibid.*

Paddy wrote to the IAOS, informing them that the Cope was thinking about buying a boat. The local boats were too small, only 30 ft or so. The cost would likely be about £3,000, with another £1,000 needed to fix them up with nets etc.[5]

A month later, Paddy was in touch again with the IAOS, saying he was interested in installing a small ice-making plant for keeping fish cool in summer. He estimated they would need 5 cwt of ice a day for "fish sent across the water". His query continued, explaining that they had an engine for generating power for such a plant, "...we supply town with electricity – a 60 H.P. National Engine and a 50 H.P. turbine (turban), also a 25 H.P. engine we have no use for..." In a lengthy correspondence, the IAOS, as usual, were very helpful in advising the Cope and putting them in touch with manufacturers.[6]

Connie Devenney and James Mickey Gallagher remember the boats well:

> "...There were five boats in all, four in operation at any one time, the first in 1940, the last in 1953. Paddy got them all from Scotland; they weren't new boats to begin with and after a hard working life with the Cope, they ended their days rotting up in Kelly's Quay in Killybegs.
>
> The masts were not stepped (that is, they were not lifted up into position), as no cranes were available in those days.
>
> Also, no one thought to collect the associated tonnage on them; valuable though it was, it was left with the ships as they rotted away in Kelly's Quay, Killybegs..."

Some of the dates below differ between some earlier ones that Paddy the Cope details in his book 'My Story' and those recalled by the men who worked the boats.

Paddy is very precise about the dates he purchased the boats, implying he had to hand some documentation when he wrote this section of his book:

MB (Motor Boat) Prevail -	15 February 1941
MB Celina	16 May 1941
MB Naomh Eine	5 September 1942

The **Shamrock (1940) D183** was a 30ft boat built in 1919. Its crew were: Connie Devenney, Maghery; John Doherty, Tearmann; James Bonner, Falmore; and Sean Dinny Doherty. It was based in Tearmann and worked out of Rosbeg and Killybegs. It had an inboard engine of 13/14 hp, using petrol/paraffin – a Gleniffer engine, then an Atlantic, from the west of Ireland. It was started on petrol by pouring on the plugs, and then turned over to paraffin. It had a swing

---

5   IAOS Records National Archives, letter dated 27th January 1941 from Paddy the Cope to Dr Kennedy Secretary IAOS

6   Ibid. 25th February 1941

start, much like starting a car with a starting handle. It fished herring, whitefish, lobster; the fish was salted in the Cooperage in Burtonport.

The **Prevail (1941)** was a 60ft boat with Big Neil Ward from Tully Island as skipper. Paddy the Cope says in his book that it was bought in February 1941 with Big Mick Gallagher as skipper and a 44hp engine. Paddy rigged her out with herring and trawler nets. The shares deal was that after all costs, oil, repairs, etc, the proceeds were split 50:50 between the Cope and the crew. Heavy storms, unusually from the south east, in December 1951 sank her while in Killybegs harbour and although partially refloated, this signalled her end.

Joseph Kyles, originally from Killybegs now living in Tully Island, was born in 1937 and remembers the sinking:

> "…Divers came in from Derry to lift the Prevail, you couldn't leave her where she was, she was blocking the harbour and boats couldn't get to the east side of the pier. Myself and Cathal Mooney, who later became a priest in The Divine World Missionaries, were hired to work the hand pumps for them. We had to keep the pressure steady at 32 psi (pounds per square inch) – they paid us 10 shillings each, which was great money then! They couldn't lift her completely but put straps underneath and then got her off the bottom; two trawlers towed her half in half out of the water with ropes out of the way to where she ended up, in Kelly's Quay…"

The **Celina (1943 or 44)** was 45ft or 48ft in length. An old Scottish boat, it had a new keel put in by a man called Dixon (from Meenalaragh or Tory). The keel was built at the pier in Dungloe with the boat up on blocks. Paddy state that the Celina has a 44 HP engine. Ned Herrity from Downings was the skipper.

The **Naomh Eine (D46, 1944)** was 56ft in length. John Cannon from Downings was skipper; and Big Mick Gallagher also skippered her. It had a 60 HP Bolander engine. Paddy has the Naomh Einne starting in 1942 and with a 64 HP engine. During the war, the Naomh Einne was used to transport soapstone (grey, white and blue varieties) from the mine in Crohy Head to Sligo; this continued until after the war. Up to 20 men worked at the mine at any one time. She fished out of Portavoggie and Ardglass in County Down as well.

> "…During the war, you couldn't fish with lights as the British convoys and German submarines were about, so you had to get the nets in daylight…" (James Mickey Gallagher)

The **Naomh Eine** was the famous boat that went to Girvan on 23rd November 1945. There had been a glut of herring but no ship to take the catch away. Paddy's son Jim wired the Scottish Co-Operative Wholesale Society who replied: "SHIP TO AYR. WE WILL TAKE ALL". James Mickey Gallagher, son of skipper Big Mick Gallagher, picks up the story:

Below: The 64 HP engine *'Naomh Eine'* at Burtonport, in a photograph taken from the south steps, where the ferry slip is now, on 21st November 1945 just before Paddy, Big Mick Gallagher and his crew headed off to Ayr in Scotland. Pictured are: Georgie Buchan, Downings; Big Mick Gallagher, Rutland, skipper; John Cannon, Downings; The Copeman himself; the fifth man is not known, thought from Downings; John Bán Gallagher , Point; again, not known, Downings; Jim the Cope, Paddy's son; and Ned Herrity, Downings. (Cope collection and James Mickey Gallagher family photograph)

"…I was 11 at the time. I remember it well. I left my father out from Rutland where we lived. The wee flat boat on the left in the picture above is the boat I took him out on. The Naomh Eine had several round 'manholes' on each side of the deck; men were carrying baskets of herring to the boat, spreading them on the deck while another man scooped salt on them to 'roil' them, so that they reached Scotland fresh. Another man had a long 'hoe' like stick or rake to move them around and then sweep them through the manholes. Then they were taken below, where they would be stacked high behind pond [pronounced 'pawn'] boards that were slotted home as the fish were loaded (at Ayr, a basket would be held at the base of the boards, the board lifted, basket filled and board closed). They had no chart so they used my school atlas, which had maps of Ireland on one page and then Scotland on the next. The wheelhouse was small, only the width of one man, there was no seat in it. There was a wheel and a compass and that was all there was…"[7]

---

7   *Personal reminiscence from James Mickey Gallagher, Burtonport, to the editor of this book. James was very generous with his time. His knowledge of boats and local history has proved to be invaluable.*

Kelly's Quay in Killybegs in 1958. Behind the two large boats – *Ros Donn* D 55 (built Killybegs 1955) on the right, *Kilros* D 424 (Portavogie, 1942) on the left - having their keels scraped and de-fouled before repainting - are what remained of three of the Cope boats: the *Celina*, *St Aiden* and the *Prevail* – the *St Aiden* is the larger boat on the right. A sad end: an easterly gale destroyed all three boats, the *Celina* ended up on her wheelhouse. By the time of their demise, they were old boats that no-one was interested in updating and repairing (A Donald Martin photograph, from his excellent 'Killybegs Then and Now', published by Anvil Books).

Killybegs in c1950, showing D.173 the *Jeannie Gardiner*. Although not a Cope boat itself, it would have been very like the Cope boats of the 1940s period. Apart from the classic image of the Naomh Eine, no 'intact' photos of the other Cope boats have come to light. The boat alongside is the *Mulroy Bay* SO 88, skippered by Martin Moore from Kerry; it has an unusual 'goose' keel and a chain for the rudder. She was an old sailing boat that had been converted. Note: 'D' indicates a Dublin registration; 'SO' Sligo (PB collection, contemporary postcard).

Kelly's Quay again in the late 1950s with, on the left, the three Cope boats (Celina, Prevail, St Aiden) rotting away and a distant view of the pier. Joseph Kyles' father Harry was a blacksmith and made all the ladders and steel for the new pier in 1952. The little white boat is John McGilloway's; he built it himself. Joey Murrin's punt is to the right of the quay; Liam Kyles built the white caravan on the shore (Photo courtesy Micheál O Dhomnaill, additional information Joseph Kyles).

Killybegs in the late 1950s, just after the last of the Cope Boats and after the BIM (Bord Iascaigh Mara) 50 ft boats came; the pier is flanked by 60 and 70 foot boats: visible are the blue keel Evening Star D251, green keel Mulroy Bay SO 88, the rest have not been identified (PB Collection, contemporary postcard)

They sailed 4.30pm Wednesday, arrived in Ayr 11.40 am Friday (after some adventures which Paddy recounts in 'My Story'), departed Ayr 12.45pm Saturday morning and were back in Burtonport 1.15pm Sunday. They came back with the boat filled with salt for curing herring.

The **St Aiden** was a big boat (72 ft) with a new 120 HP (or 136 HP possibly) Kelvin engine put in at Dungloe. Manus Herrity was engineer, Big Mick Gallagher was skipper. Connie Devenney took over as engineer and skipper when Big Mick left in 1948; Connie stayed to the end of the Cope boats in 1953. Paddy Hunter of Maghery was a regular crew member. It became increasingly hard to find crew; as people left to fish in their own boats and their friends and family would go with them.

Fisheries Harbour, Killybegs, Co Donegal.

Two views of Killybegs from about 60 years ago, taken by SR Butler of Carndonagh and published as postcards in the late 1940s. The old wooden pier dating from 1897 was provided by the Congested Districts Board was in existence until 1952 when replaced with a concrete pier at a cost of £70,000. The rails embedded in the pier used to connect to the County Donegal Railways station in Killybegs (closed in late 1959), collecting fish straight from the boats (PB collection).

This photo is of Killybegs in c1950-52 and shows a number of boats tied up alongside the old pier. The two outer boats are of similar style to and could be Cope boats, but this is not certain. From the left, not known then D 412, D39, and SO 149 and on the right the *Máiréad*, D206, owned originally by James Mcleod, over 90 now and in his time a great moderniser of fishing practices. Tommy Watson then bought her; Cope Boat man Jim Doherty of Tearmann fished with him (BIM photo, from Ireland's Fisheries by John de Courcy Ireland published 1981).

A Killybegs postcard from the late 1950s with the *Brothers Hope* D247, SO21 name not known, the *Mulroy Bay* SO88 and the *Mary Buchan* D168 (skippered at one time by Cruit man Seamus 'The Captain' Doherty) along the west side of the pier. On the right is local man Danny Brennan, not connected with the fishing (Mícheál O Dhomnaill Collection; postcard by T Cassidy and Sons Donegal)

Brothers Connie, left, and Donald Devenney, right, pictured in Maghery in 1949. Their father Danny Devenney was a blacksmith and kept two stud horses. Connie skippered the Cope boats the Shamrock and, from 1948, the St Aiden (after Big Mick Gallagher left to fish in his own boat). In 1954 Connie got his own boat, the famous 50 ft BIM Ros Mhuire. He fished on her for almost 30 years till 1983. In band competitions, or at festival time, Connie would ride down Dungloe Main Street at the head of the Maghery band dressed as St Patrick on a white horse. Donald fished on the Ros Mhuire for a short time with his brother and before this worked in the Cope's soapstone mine in Crohey in 1946/7 (Noel Delaney, Collection, New York).

AFTER THE COPE BOATS

Big Mick Gallagher left to fish in his own boats; he got a half-decker in 1950, the Irene 2, built by McDonnell in 1948. Manus Herrity went to the boat yard in Killybegs in 1947. Among many others who worked on the boats were: Owenie Paddy Oinin, Paddy Hunter from Maghery and Jamesie Boyle.

George Buchan, who was on the Naomh Einne to Girvan, drowned (with four other men) off Dunmore East on 10 February 1958 when a freak wave overturned his boat, the 'Jack Buchan', just 300 yards outside the harbour.

Seamus 'the Captain' Doherty had the sister ship the 'Mary Buchan'.

Jim Doherty, Tearmann fished with Tommie Watson on his boat, the 'Mairead', ringing herring.

　　　　　　　　　　　　　　　　　　The Story of the Cope

FISHING FOR LOBSTER

After the Cope Boat period, many fishermen would fish for lobster off Roaninish:

> "...Fishermen from Inishfree, Inishkeeragh, Rutland and the other islands of the Rosses fished for lobster in yawls off Roaninish from April to August. They'd come back to Burtonport on Saturdays to sell the lobsters; the typical weekly catch was 50-60 dozen, our best week was 94 dozen! When not fishing, we'd live in huts (there were seven of these in the 1940s and 1950s) on Roaninish itself: stone built, about 10-12 foot square, these consisted of a fireplace with two or three beds each side, the base typically made up of old hatches from boats. The roof would be thatch on top of turfs laid on lattes; the 'doorway' would be at the side, you'd need to stoop to get in – no door, just a tarpaulin over the door-space. A bench would be at the other end for storing supplies, a change of clothes etc. As it was the summer months, there was not much of a requirement for lighting; there'd be an oil lamp if necessary. The island men had a programme of work for the year: turf, hay, cows, lobster fishing and then later in the year, herring..."[8]

There is an interesting modern day parallel with the fishing that James Mickey's son Jim does. He too is often away from home fishing but not for a week at a time like his father and grandfather. At the time of writing (November 2006), Jim was skippering over a thousand miles off Chile in a vast 'factory' boat with a crew from mainly Russia and China. Supplied with fuel and provisions by other boats, the boat doesn't go into harbour for months on end. Jim himself is away from Burtonport for up to four months at a time and to reach the boat it takes him four days with several flights, a long bus ride and a helicopter or ship. But he is, however, able to keep in touch with family and friends via satellite phone – unlike the fishermen on Roaninish fifty years ago.

In earlier times, fishing off Roaninish could be a hazardous business:

FISHERMEN MAROONED.

A FORTNIGHT ON ROANISH ISLAND

> "...Four Donegal fishermen who have been stormbound on Roanish Island for the past 14 days were able to return to their homes last evening. While lobster-fishing a fortnight ago the men were blown out to sea, and when they did not return within a few days they were given up as lost. The sea continued to be very rough, but the crew of the Arranmore lifeboat, which went out in search of them each day, saw

---

8   *James Mickey Gallagher, son of Big Mick Gallagher, who fished lobster in this way from 1953-1970, (when he got the 56 foot 'Favourite') off Roaninish with his father and brother Michael, who fished from 1953-60 (when he got the 'Rath Osan').*

them on Thursday last sheltering on the island. Owing to the state of the sea the lifeboatmen were unable to land, but they succeeded, after two attempts, in floating ashore a barrel of provisions, and yesterday, when the sea went down, the fishermen returned to the mainland in their own boat.

This is the second occasion on which these men have been marooned on the island. Three years ago they went there to fish for lobsters and were unable to return as a gale sprung had up; the lifeboat put off to their assistance and succeeded in reaching them with much difficulty. The island is overrun with rabbits, so that in no circumstances could the men have starved…"[9]

THE BURTONPORT FISHERMEN'S CO-OP

Then came the era of the bigger boats, what was in retrospect a golden age, when big money was made through the 1960s and 1970s. Boats included the Ard Dallan (Joe Bán McBride); the Ard Macha (Joe McGinley); Ard Mhuire (Willie McBride of Gola, then Gweedore), skipper Tony Owenie Manus, Cloughlass; the Ros Mhuire, Connie Devenney's boat; the Rath Osan, Red Michael, son of Big Mick Gallagher, brother of James Mickey. Red Michael and James Mickey fished together, James Mickie's boat was the Autumn Glory. Then there was Stabat Mater (Owenie Kavanagh); and many others.

It is not too fanciful to link the Cope Boats to the later successes of the Burtonport Fishermen's Co-op. John McCarthy, in an Irish Times article from 1970, would have pleased the founder of the original Fishermen's Co-op:

Co-operating for fish provides a handsome return in Donegal

"…UP IN THE ROSSES section of County Donegal, there is a tradition of exceptional success for co-operatives. Family feuds, frictions and failures in production and profit - which have scuttled not a few Irish cooperatives - somehow have been surmounted in that remote section of the country.

Today in the Rosses are two thriving co-operatives. The Templecrone Agricultural Co-Operative Society Ltd., founded in 1906 by Patrick Gallagher, widely-known as Paddy the Cope, whose autobiography was a best seller years ago and still is in print. Templecrone now has branches all over the Rosses with a variety of successful operations including a modern supermarket in Dungloe. The other is the Burtonport Fishermen's Co-Operative Society Ltd., just two years old, but already a model of a tightly-knit organisation, whose turnover and sales last year were up 50% with a record volume and profit.

---

9   *The Times, 7ᵗʰ February 1914, spelling of 'Roanish' preserved.*

Though Burtonport, with its fine, almost land-locked harbour, is rated the fifth largest fish landing port in Ireland, more salmon and lobsters are landed there than at any other port in Ireland or Britain. Last year, total sales for the Burtonport Co-Op were £196.491. In spite of unfavourable fishing weather plus currency complications internationally caused by the prolonged bank strike and the economy let-down in Britain and on the Continent, volume and sales this year have held up remarkably well.

During the past season, some 60,000 salmon were landed which resulted in sales of more than £120,000. In a recent week, over 20 tons of lobsters, worth £26,000, were taken. On one day alone, 4½ tons of lobsters bringing £5,700 were caught, a record for a single day.

Co-operatives are not supposed to make a profit. Their main purpose is to make a good living for the members. However, the Burtonport Co-op not only operates at a minimum profit for itself but provides a maximum profit for its individual members. Charging a mere 5% commission for selling the member fishermen's entire catches and in return for this furnishes complete organisational facilities, a trained staff and office space, the Burtonport Co-op still managed to turn in a net profit of £4,824 last year.

The commission total or the gross profit from sales was £10,071. Hence for wages, rent, rates, insurance, freight, travelling expenses for the Burtonport Co-op operation came to only £5,247. That small total evidently made no allowance for fancy salaries for the president, executive secretary and other expensive personnel often present in co-operatives; such stipends are not to be found in the Burtonport Co-op. Its president, secretary and the treasurer, all able administrators, are not in the fishing industry. All are prominent Donegal citizens, actively engaged in other pursuits, who volunteer their services to the Burtonport Co-op. Since these officers of their Co-op are independent, capable men of understanding, judgement, with no salary and no stake in the industry, the rank and file of fishermen members obviously respect and appreciate their opinions and abide by their decisions.

Each year, these non-salaried volunteer officers of Burtonport Co-op automatically resign at the annual meeting in May. In the past two years of the Co-op's existence, all of these same officers have been unanimously re-elected. Incidentally, attendance at the annual meeting is large. Last May, more than a 100, practically the entire membership, were present to listen to the annual reports, elect officers and make suggestions.

As to the annual earnings of the Burtonport Co-Op fishermen, the captain of his own trawler (56-footers), of which there are some fifteen, took in for himself between £5,000 to £6,000 in 1969, while each of his four-man crew got between £1,500 to £2,000. Considering that the Rosses is in the depressed Donegal agricultural area, here, according to the comprehensive survey released last spring by the Agricultural Institute, the average farm income for holdings under 50 acres was £138 per year, the fisherman's financial take yearly is truly handsome when compared to his Donegal neighbour farmer.

Since fishing activity is limited to 35-40 weeks a year, the Burtonport Co-op fishermen's income still is better by far than the average Irish labourer or factory worker. In fact, some high-powered Dublin executives might even envy the skipper's annual take of £5,000 to £6,000 and certainly his being his own boss, completely free of capricious chairmen and nosey directors. They'd like, too, the skipper's weeks of time-off during the year.

Following the recent salmon season's landings realising mere than £120,000, the Burtonport correspondent of the Donegal Democrat reported enthusiastically that "the village of Burtonport has a population of less than 100 and its residents are now reputed to have the highest income per capita of the population in Ireland". What he failed to consider was that not all the skippers and their crews are from Burtonport. Only two skippers, Tony and Mike Gallagher live there. The others come from all over the Rosses.

All the skippers own their boats worth more than £15,000 to £20,000. For the purchase, they usually secure a loan from the Bord Iascaigh Mhara after putting down 10% of the total cost, and paying off the rest in instalments over the years. Not a few skippers are able to do this within six or seven years. Then, like all proverbial boatowners, they usually sell their crafts and buy bigger ones. For gear and supplies, the Burtonport fishermen patronise the Co-op, which handles such at a tiny mark-up over the wholesale price.

The crux for making a success of a co-operative is getting its members to sell all their production through it, thereby strengthening the co-op's bargaining power to get higher prices. If members even deal directly for only portions of their production with buyers, they are weakening the co-op's selling position. Being fiercely independent, competitive and whose heritage has been farming rather than seafaring, Donegal fishermen are not easy to organise into a tightly knit project.

For the past several years, Killybegs, the largest fishing Port in Donegal, has been trying to put together a complete co-operative but has not achieved it as yet. Buyers there continue to deal directly with individual fishermen there and have the advantage of bidding on more than one single source of supply which can and does adversely affect prices of Killybegs landings.

President Patrick Sweeney, of the Burtonport Co-op, is adamant that the members sell their entire catches through the Co-op or else. Normally, a genial gentleman with a regal legal manner, and born in the Rosses, Mr. Sweeney is perfectly capable of local Billingsgate in telling off fishermen and buyers alike when they attempt to circumvent the Co-op's strict selling rules. And they listen, too.

The seeds that the Cope Boats and their skippers had planted in the 1940-50s flowered in Burtonport in the 1960-80s. Here, in a photo from the 1960s, before the new, much extended pier was built in 1973-4, is Joe McGinley's *Ard Macha D 207*, Red Michael Gallagher's *Rath Osan D 208*, behind is the white hull of Joe Bán McBride's *Ard Dallan*, on the end is an unidentified boat (Bord Failte photograph, cropped)

Consequently today the leading buyers, such as James Campbell and Sons, the British firm of MarinPro. Michael Boyle and others, fully recognise the collective bargaining of the Co-op, and confine their Burtonport bidding to its daily morning auction right on the pier. The result has been that the Burtonport fishermen are satisfied with the prices secured for their entire catches. Certainly, the Co-op's selling arrangement is a far cry from those days not so long ago when the Burtonport fishermen had to seek out the buyers themselves and take what they were offered for their catches or be stuck with them.

With this new Co-op's exclusive businesslike selling procedure, the buyers too have prospered. Profitable markets for Burtonport herring have been built up in Holland and Czechoslovakia; lobsters in France and Belgium; salmon in Britain, Belgium; and white fish in Dublin.

To serve local family needs in the Rosses, the Co-op has its own retail store on the Burtonport pier. A similar store is planned by the Co-op to be opened in Dublin to bring white fish, plaice and other seafoods at economical prices to the city's families…"[10]

---

10 *Irish Times 15th September 1970*

Above: The Cope bought a store (on the left in this photograph) next to Murrin's First Class Spirit Store in Bridge Street (also called the Back Street), in Killybegs. Known locally as the Corn Store, the river backed on to it and at high tide boats used to come up and unload flour etc. The man by the old water pump in front is Tommy Rowan. Captain Hood, who skippered the 'Robert Hastings' (a British surveillance vessel which operated out of Killybegs in World War II), lived in the house next to Murrin's; next door is Cassie Kennedy; then Jim McIntyre's and James Toland's house (Mícheál O Dhomnaill collection; Killybegs' memories Joseph Kyles).

Right Bottom: The Cope bought Coane's Hotel in c1942 for £2,250, the furniture was an extra £275. At the time the Cope's fishing fleet did a lot of business in Killybegs and it seemed a natural extension, a base for Paddy and for his captains and crew when on land (National Photographic Archive, Cope Minute book for details).

Above: The new pier at Killybegs was opened on the 2nd October 1952 by Sean Lemass, future Taoiseach (1959-66); at this time, he was Tanáiste and Minister for Industry and Commerce. Also present and in this photo were Dr William McNeely, Bishop of Raphoe from 1923-63, Paddy the Cope and (it is believed) Senate member Michael Óg McFadden. The pier came too late to be of any benefit to Paddy and the Cope boats, they were over by this time, but it helped the rise of Killybegs to become Ireland's premier fishing port (Jim the Cope Archive, Cassie Jock's house, Dungloe)

BURTONPORT FROM THE FERRY V

Right: The *Ros Mhuire* D51 at Burtonport in 1956 - on the pier are ESB supplies for the Rural Electrification Programme. The *Ros Mhuire* D 51 was the first, on the Donegal coastline, of the BIM 50 foot boats. It was built in Killybegs and cost £8,500 (£850 deposit). Skipper Connie Devenney, Cope Committee member since 1969, came up through the Cope boats in the 1940s, including skippering the *St Aiden* from 1948. Alongside is the *Girl Christina* SO 607, owned by the Brown Brothers (James and William) from Inch - this boat is still operating today; in the background is the Cope Kippering shed. Jimmy Johnny (O'Donnell) Burtonport was 8 at the time "...I remember the ESB had poles for the whole of The Rosses piled high opposite where Kelly's (The Lobster Pot) is now, in Campbell's car park. Campbell's had a wild lot of chickens then and they would be laying out amongst the poles; we used to be out looking for the nests in the poles. Next to them, where the chalets are now, was a high hipped shed filled with carrageen moss. The boat that brought in the poles was the Galtee ..." (Valentine's photo V.R. 8115 courtesy of the National Photographic Archive, Dublin).

The Ros Mhuire in the mid 1950s with from left to right: Connie Devenney (skipper), his brother Jim Devenney, Paddy Hunter, Jamesie Boyle, Joseph Kyles and Charlie Murrin. The photograph was taken off Gweedore where the *Ros Mhuire* was ringing herring and taking great hauls. Local drift net fishermen were strongly opposed to the then new innovation, which they felt was 'cleaning the sea of fish'; they let the crew of the Ros Mhuire know how they felt by surrounding the boat with half-deckers and throwing dorlein stones at them (Photo courtesy Conal Hunter, son of Paddy Hunter; Conal is himself a fisherman out of Killybegs, still living in Roshine between Maghery and Dungloe)

Left: Paddy Hunter of Maghery in oilskins with a big skate in his hand. The photo is dated 1950, with Connie Devenney named as skipper, which would make the boat the *St Aiden* (but some have said the date is wrong and it could be the *Ros Mhuire*). Paddy who passed away in March 2007 was a much loved character who had a great sense of humour both on and off the boat. Joseph Kyles remembers Paddy well – he recalls that Paddy always felt that the St Aiden was haunted – he was lying in his bunk one night, heard the chain running out with a sound of heavy breathing and jumped up with a start, bumping his head (Noel Delaney Collection, Joseph Kyles memories).

Right Top: The hold of the Ros Mhuire in one of a series of photos taken in 2007 in Greencastle and Moville by Ian Whittaker whose website on the 50 footers (and other boats) is a treasure trove of photographs and information. On the right can be seen the pond [pronounced pawn] boards which were slotted in and the fish were stored behind in compartments so that they didn't move around in heavy seas. The Ros Mhuire, although now in poor shape with its engine and wheel removed, would have been a good candidate for renovation as a centrepiece for a heritage centre in Burtonport but it has now deteriorated so much that it has been scrapped (photo courtesy of Ian Whittaker: http://www.sol.co.uk/i/iangwhittaker/rosdonn/asiad19.htm)

The remnants of Paddy the Cope's pier are showing above the waterline and the Cope's Kippering Shed can be seen behind what became the Fishermen's Co-op Hall. The roof of the Cope's Kippering shed (erected 1941) had vents to let out the smoke; a large, tall diesel tank is standing near there now. The building on the end of the fairly dilapidated looking shed is the old toilet. The old bogey from the railway can be seen clearly here – it is remembered fondly by children growing up in the Port at the time as great for playing on especially at the weekend when grownups weren't around (National Photographic Archive, Cardall Collection, CAR 213/10, cropped).

Below: Burtonport Pier in the 1950s with in the distance the old station, when Charlie John McBride, the last stationmaster, was living there. The Cope owned stores along the quay from the left. The lorry being unloaded is very likely one of the Cope's; it appears to be carrying either flour or cement. What remains of Paddy the Cope's pier is sticking up out of the water where the ferry boats now come in (it was later to become something of a hazard and was removed). Paddy recounts in *My Story* his disagreements with the harbourmaster at Burtonport [Jimmy Frank O'Donnell] which led him to build his own pier in an attempt to escape paying harbour dues. He argued that the pier was inadequate for the draught of the boats he was chartering from the continent. It was all settled eventually and payment of dues resumed. The pier conveniently led right on to the Cope stores and the old bogey on rails – dating from the Lough Swilly Railway era - which can be seen on the pier edge (National Photographic Archive)

Jim Devenney, brother of Connie, in the wheel house of the *Ros Mhuire*. Jim later worked in the Cope Bakery on the Quay Road. There are four Devenney brothers, Connie, Jim, Donald and Paddy, a fine singer, who lives in the States but is back so often to Maghery he is called there 'The Commuter'! (Noel Delaney, New York, Collection).

Paddy the Cope is sitting outside O'Donnell's Hotel and Bar in Burtonport with his old friend, occasional adversary and local legend Jimmy Frank (O'Donnell) – one of JF's many claims to fame was that at the age of 7 he met the man, postmaster Harry McNelis, who had met Napper Tandy in 1798. Jimmy Frank was harbourmaster when Paddy was in dispute about paying harbour dues for the landing of cargo from Holland. Between them is Jimmy Frank's sister, Maud; on Jimmy's lap, his grandson Jimmy Johnny (O'Donnell), the current owner of O'Donnell's ; on Paddy's lap his grandson Jim. The year would be about 1950, judging by the ages of the children (Cope Family Archive)

Next Page: A marvellous photograph from c1967, by Glenties photographer Denis Tynan, inside Campbell's Factory, Burtonport with a huge salmon on the table. In the centre is Paddy the Cope's grandson Pat the Cope Gallagher, now a TD and MEP, then about 19 years of age. From left to right: *front* Joe Bonner, Dinny Doney Owen (O'Donnell), Charlie Healey, Robert Sweeney, Pat the Cope, Paddy Sweeney, Paddy Joe Forker; *middle*: Liam Reilly, James 'Big Ward' the Post (Ward), Dom Sheila O'Donnell; *back*: Ray Hamm, Charlie Sweeney, Big Jim O'Donnell (son of Dinny Doney Owen), Terry Boyle, John Mickie Nancy Bonner, Hughdie Hunt. Robert, Paddy and Charlie Sweeney were brothers (National Photographic Archive, Tynan Collection)

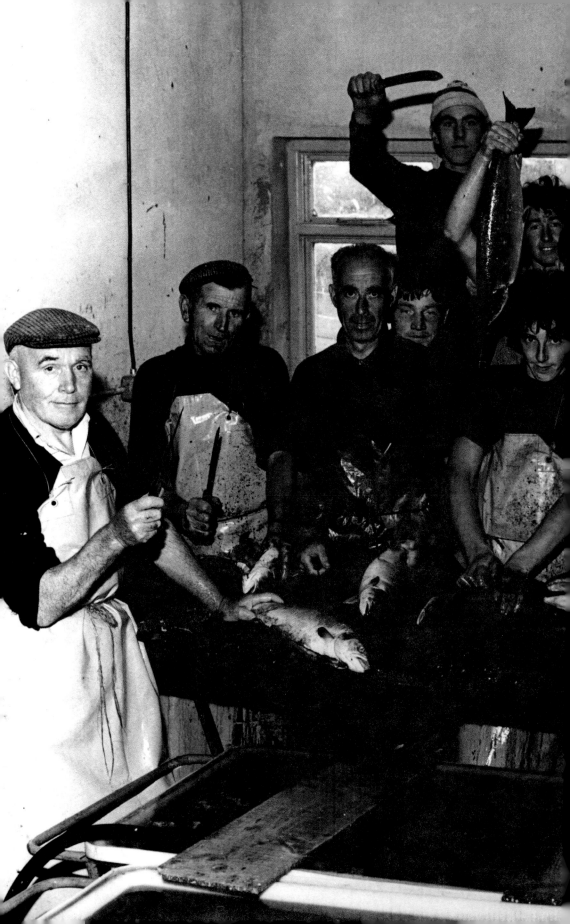

The *'Eleftherios M Tricoglu'* – locally known as the *'Elfinoris'* or just 'The Greek' - ran aground off Arranmore on January 28th 1926. The ship was built in 1894 by Palmer's Shipbuilding and Iron Co. Ltd in Jarrow, Newcastle; 2,633 tons and just over 300 feet long. She was carrying a large cargo of grain which would have been lost if she had sunk – Paddy the Cope saw this as a big opportunity and decided that the Cope would salvage the cargo. The houses immediately below at the shore are the Post Office where Charles Boyle and family lived; Jack (Charlie) Boyle, coxswain of the Arranmore lifeboat grew up here (Seán Boner Collection)

The following account is by the Rosses historian Packie Bonner (he also wrote in Irish as Pádraig Ua Cnáimhsí and was affectionately known around the Rosses as Packie Manny Anne). Written for the 1981 Cope Diamond Jubilee booklet, it gives an insight into Paddy the Cope as a man of action, ingenious, opportunistic and - to use a modern turn of phrase - a 'hands-on' manager.

> "...Nowhere in this book does Paddy mention his salvage of the cargo of the Greek steamer, "Elfinoris" which was wrecked at Arranmore on January 28th, 1926. Yet, it will be admitted, that great credit was due to him for handling of the salvage job, so we think the story should now be told, even though he himself didn't think it worthy of mention.

[Editor: the ship's correct name was 'Eleftherios M. Tricoglu', local people called it "Elfinoris" as the Greek name 'Eleftherios' which means 'Freedom' in Greek was difficult to pronounce – "Elfinoris" is used throughout here for consistency]

GREEK SHIP IN DANGER.

ASHORE ON DONEGAL ISLAND.

The Greek steamer Eleftherios M. Tricoglu went ashore at Arranmore Island, County Donegal, on Friday. She has a cargo of Indian corn and is bound for Sligo.

A message from Burtonport on Saturday night says that the captain and officers are still on board. The Greek crew of twenty-three are being hospitably entertained on Arranmore Island.

The ship is expected to become a total wreck. The salving trawler Carrigart is standing by.

Mr. Patrick Gallagher, manager of the Templecrone Co-operative Agricultural Society, Dungloe, has bought the ship's cargo of over 4,000 tons of maize. Arranmore fishermen and all the carts in the Rosses are removing the cargo.

The Elfinoris was a Greek vessel of 5,000-odd tons, bound for Sligo, with a cargo of maize from the port of Braila, on the Danube. She first called into Belfast, where she took on about 300 tons of coal in addition to discharging some of her cargo of maize. This is understandable as her next port of call was to be Sligo, and as the latter port is tidal, it would be in their best interests that the ship would be lightened somewhat in order that she would be in a position to berth at Sligo, later on. However, as fate would have it, the vessel never got as far as Sligo at all. When west of Arranmore Lighthouse, the ship sprang a leak, and her captain, in the interests of safety, decided to leave the open sea and try for a harbour where he might be able to beach his ship, or possibly summon assistance. The nearest harbour capable of accommodating a ship of this size would be Derry, Lough Swilly, or Killybegs; but she was making water fast, so he couldn't risk running to any of these ports. Thus it was that the Elfinoris entered Arran Roads and was beached at Leabgarrow, about a hundred yards out from the pier. As her name was beyond the capability of the ordinary people

The Arranmore lifeboat crew, here pictured in c1929 at Aphort with the new lifeboat, were on alert and at sea as the *'Elfinoris'* made its way into Arran Roads. The crew, renowned for their skill and bravery, were responsible for a number of heroic rescues in the sometimes treacherous seas off the West Donegal coast. In the foreground is Johnnie Bán Byrne, assistant coxswain, sitting on the canopy is Hughie McGill, mechanic, in the suit and hat behind is Hughie's father Barnie McGill, Secretary of the Arranmore Lifeboat Committee, Jack (Charlie) Boyle, coxswain. The two men on the left are believed to be from Aphort. (Seán Boner Collection).

around, pronunciation wise, locally she was simply called the "Greek". There is little point of us to-day trying to re-live or detail the last moments of the Elfinoris. Obviously, her position was rather serious from the very beginning, as otherwise, her master, Captain Alif M. Tricoglu, wouldn't have attempted to enter the narrow waters of Arran Bay with a ship of her size and draught. In addition to all else, the fact that she was cargoed rendered the leak far more serious than if she had been travelling in ballast. I would say that water had been pouring into her at an alarming rate and that the point was fast approaching, when with her entire pumping system going at full capacity, it would have been impossible to keep vessel afloat much longer. Faced with this unhappy situation, her Captain decided to ignore all offers of assistance made to him by a local pilot boat, and to try to enter the upper approaches of Arran Roads unaided. This in itself was no easy task. Further damage to the ship's hull was encountered by striking submerged rocks on the way, so that the ship began to take in water in alarming proportions. It only remained for the Captain then to try and beach the ship in shallow

Paddy bought a Fordson tractor - the first tractor in the Rosses - in 1926 in order to power the winch he had ingeniously rigged up as a makeshift grain-elevator on board the 'Elfinoris'. (Packie Bonner, writing in 1981). The Fordson Model F Tractor was produced between 1917 and 1928. Initial production was at Dearborn in the U.S.A. with production commencing in Marina, Cork, Ireland in 1919. (This photo is not from the Rosses but from the island of Jersey and is courtesy of the Pallot Museum – many thanks to Richard H Huelin for his help in sourcing. Judging by this photo, the ridged metal wheels on the tractor would have done the roads of the Rosses no favours).

waters, as otherwise the vessel would have sunk in a very short time. Thus it was that the Elfinoris finally grounded at the spot that was to be her resting place and grave ever since.

We will now leave it to Phil Byrne to describe that night of drama, excitement and tension on Arranmore, the night the "Greek" struck. Phil would be about ten or eleven years at that time, and he has a vivid recollection of it all. Phil, who is a former coxswain of the Arranmore lifeboat, is also a man of great local knowledge and experience. He was amongst the eight members of the Lifeboat crew to receive medals and decorations for rescuing eighteen crew members of the Dutch steamer "Stolwyk" at Inishboffin, in December 1940. A fisherman and a man of the sea, Phil has a prodigious memory as well, so that if somebody would like to know about something that has happened in the past, Phil is their man. He tells us about that night in January 1926: "We were all sitting around the fire, doing our home exercises, around seven o'clock. My father was having his tea at the table, as he had been to a funeral that day. Funerals in those days left to go to the church and graveyard around two o'clock in the afternoon, and there was no funeral Mass as there is today.. Somebody came running in to tell us that there was a big ship coming up the bay. All hands went to the door to see. Father left his tea and came out as well. He knew every rock for miles around and he became scared, when he saw the course the ship had taken. I remember well his words to my mother and to us all out at the door — "Tá sé dul a bhualadh An Chloch Chaoch". No sooner had he the words said than we heard the grinding impact of the ship's hull as she tore her way along the submerged reef. Our house is high above the sea and harbour, so that we had a grandstand view of it all. My father then left us and ran to the beach in the hope of rendering some assistance. With full lights on, the ship edged her way up towards the anchorage, leaving the trouble spot at the Blind Rocks behind.

The Captain then proceeded to drop the ship's anchor as the vessel approached the Narrows, that is, the entrance to Rutland Harbour and Burtonport. Things were beginning to move faster then, which gave us to understand that all wasn't well aboard. Nine or ten staccato blasts on the ship's siren only confirmed what our fears had been. Boats had begun to converge on the big ship then from all directions. Charlie Tony, from Eighter, and my father seemed to beat the others to it - they got there first. They clambered on to the ship and made their way to the bridge. The Captain and his officers were there trying to cope with the dangerous situation in which they had found themselves. They had a top-level discussion as what would be best to do. There was very little time left. The leak that had developed west of the Lighthouse and the damage sustained at the Blind Rock, were rapidly taking their toll. They could see it as a race against time. To make matters worse, there was a serious difficulty in communication. The Captain had scarcely any English and any decisions he made had to be done through the First Mate, who acted as his interpreter. He wanted the ship beached and he left the choice of location to the men of local knowledge, my father and Charlie Tony. They decided to run her in at Cladagh Bawn. In their opinion, it was the most suitable place. The signal, "Full Steam Ahead", was then passed on to the engine room, ignoring the fact that the ship's anchor was still out. However, the ship got under way, snapping the cable as she went, and leaving the anchor behind. But their troubles were then only beginning. The ship's steering was now defective, because of the damage caused half an hour before, so that she careered along without being under proper control. They did what they could in the circumstances, but it became obvious to them that they couldn't make it to Cladagh Bawn. Under partial control, the big ship finally struck out behind Carraic An Chléibh Mhóir. It was high water by then and the ship's bow rested on a rock there that prevented

The Taoiseach Eamon de Valera visited Arranmore in July 1947. The welcome address was given on the pier at Leabgarrow by Packie Bonner N.T. (the author of the story of the 'Elfinoris' and many other passages in this book). The people of Arranmore, unlike the islanders of the Aran Isles Dev had just visited, were not impressed with Dev's wearing of *báinín* (woollen homespun clothes traditional in the Aran Isles, a gift from the islanders to their Taoiseach). They expected their Taoiseach to be wearing something somewhat 'smarter'. From left to right, seated: de Valera, Fr McDevitt, Packie Bonner N.T. (standing), Cormac Breslin (Gweedore) local TD 1937-77; standing behind, Mickey Boyle N.T., Liam Conaghan, Derry Journal correspondent, Mr J McHugo, Assistant Private Secretary to de Valera, a Burtonport Guard (believed to be Guard Keown), James Ward (son of Kitty Ward), Pat Gannon, Paddy the Cope, John Gillespie (from the Hills), de Valera's Chief of Staff, in uniform, Lieut.-General D McKenna, Sheila Jack Boyle, Paddy Edward Gallagher (sole survivor of the Arranmore Disaster) and Johnny John Boyle, a local builder on Arran. (Derry Journal photo 21st July 1947).

The Taoiseach arrived in Arranmore on the LÉ Macha naval vessel, one of three corvettes bought from Britain in 1946/47 (the others were names LÉ Cliona and LÉ Maev; Ireland's naval vessels are named after women in Irish mythology; LÉ stands for Long Éireannach, Irish Ship). This view of the LÉ Macha is at Killybegs behind the old pier, so dates from before 1952. After leaving Arranmore, De Valera travelled to The Hebrides and then the Isle of Man where he endowed an Irish college (photo courtesy National Photographic Archive, Cardall_160_10).

her going any farther. The stern and midships portion was still afloat, so that the entire ship swung around with the ebb tide and finally settled down alongside the Rock. There she was to remain".

The late Paddy the Cope, intent on getting the maize cargo of the "Greek" for his mill at Dungloe, decided to buy the salvage rights of the doomed vessel from the underwriters, and in this he was entirely successful. Although the ship was badly holed, the upper portion of the maize cargo in the holds was still undamaged by the seawater, and the question of salvaging this part of the cargo became Paddy's first priority. It was a race against time, but the Copeman was more than equal to the task set out before him. As the ship's winches, etc., were all useless without the ship's boilers being in operation, it was decided to install a mechanically operated winch, above the ship's holds, in order to have the cargo hoisted out of the holds, for transport by boat, to the Mill at Dungloe.

Boats from Arranmore and the mainland were employed to take the maize thus salvaged from the steamer to the Mill, for milling into Indian meal. Dungloe Bay, as we know, is rock-strewn, so that it was not always

The Story of the Cope

easy for boatmen to negotiate the difficult channel to and from the Mill. Yet, though there may have been some near mishaps, that was all. The salvage work was brought to its successful conclusion without a hitch.

While the salvage work lasted, Phil Byrne's father, the late John Byrne, and another islander, Nohar Bonner, were employed by Paddy the Cope as watchmen on the Elfinoris. Phil informs me that they had beds on board as well, so that one of them stayed there overnight always. It was then that Phil told me a story that helps to give us a rare insight into the type of man Paddy was. Not being contented with having given Johnny and Nohar specific instructions as to what they should do, he decided to check in order to see if his instructions were being complied with to the letter. He decided to go in himself at night and see for himself how things were progressing. For reasons of his own, he decided not to bring the punt with him. Instead, he employed a Burtonportman, the late Dan Bonner, to take him in. Phil goes on: "My father was this night walking about the deck of the ship, in furtherance of Paddy's instructions, when he thought he heard the splashing of oars, making towards the ship. He challenged them to stop but they seemed to ignore his words and kept rowing on. Then my father shouted to them a second time, telling them to stop, or failing that, that he would sink their boat. It was then that a voice shouted to him, from the boat approaching in the darkness: "Oh Johnny, don't. It is only me". It was Paddy the Cope coming to inspect his charge, at the witching hour of night! He was pleased when he saw that everything was alright. Next day, Paddy came again and he handed a bag or sack up to Johnny Byrne, telling him to handle it with care. Johnny asked him what the bag contained, but Paddy made him no reply. It was when they entered the ship's galley that Paddy disclosed his secret. He went on: "It is not right for you, Johnny, to be here all by yourself at night, without some kind of protection". He handed Johnny a double-barrelled shotgun and a whole box of No 12 cartridges. When Johnny saw the supply of ammunition he brought him, he said to Paddy: "Where are you going, Paddy, with that much stuff? Sure less would do". But Paddy was adamant: "You'll want them all, Johnny. You can have practice firing in order to let everybody knows you're armed, warning shots fired in the air, and what not". Johnny Byrne took the gun from Paddy, but the need to use it, never arose. When I told the story to somebody who knew Paddy well, he wasn't at all surprised at Paddy making the midnight visit to Arranmore. He went on: "That was the kind of him. He always made a point of checking on the work, if at all possible... If you were cutting wrack for him at Inishfree or paring bogs for him at Tangavane, he would try to pay you a visit before your day was in. He took nothing for granted".

Phil Byrne, of Arranmore, tells us this story of Paddy's boating days during the "Greek" salvage operation: "My mother had a business this day to Dungloe and she volunteered to go up with Paddy, when he'd be returning home from the ship in the evening. She would stay in Dungloe overnight and return again with Paddy a day or two after. They left Leabgarrow in the evening, in the punt, with Paddy steering and operating the outboard. My mother had gone up Dungloe Bay very often in her youth — with boats that would be going to the Mill with corn —but she never before made the journey in a motorboat. She had a notion that it was more dangerous travelling in a motor boat because of the rocks there. Even if a rowing boat hits a rock, it wouldn't do much harm, as the impact wouldn't be so serious. But in the case of a motor-boat, it could be entirely different. When they left the open bay and proceeded to wind their way up along Milltown and Meenmore, she didn't feel at all happy, and she said so to Paddy: "Paddy, a dheárthair, go a little bit easier here — this place is full of rocks". But Paddy assured her that he had things well under control. "Madgie", he said to her. "Don't have the slightest fear. The tide is high now and any rocks that are around here are deep flags. If we do happen to bump against any of them, the punt will glide over them". It should be pointed out that Paddy always took about ten bags of maize back with him in the punt, on his journey homewards. When Mrs. Byrne returned home, her husband, Johnny, asked her about her trip with Paddy to the Pier at Dungloe. Phil remembers her story still: "Paddy was trying to be talking to me on the journey, but his voice was drowned by the noise of the engine, so that we had to sit there without saying a word. I left home to go to a dentist but when I arrived in Dungloe, I felt as if I should go to an ear specialist as well, because of the noise and vibration from the engine"!

Our sincere thanks, therefore, to the Byrne family, Madgie and Phil, for all their painstaking assistance to us in filling in the gaps about the events of more than fifty years ago. It entailed a long night's airneail, during which many stories were told and many questions asked. And what could be more befitting or appropriate end to it all, than to sit around a blazing fire drinking a cup of coffee, using the cups from the Elfinoris of fifty-five years ago. They were souvenirs from Captain Tricoglu to his hosts of that time! To me it was unbelievable that mementoes such as these could have survived all these years. Once all the undamaged grain was taken off, they then directed their efforts towards salvaging the maize that had by now been damaged by the sea. This damaged maize was sold at the ship for about threepence a bag and re-sold by boat owners throughout The Rosses and even to buyers from places further afield. In many respects, the "Greek" harvest was something in the nature of a windfall or a Godsend. The damaged grain was dried everywhere and given as feeding to cattle and fowl. One old man to whom I talked about the "Greek" had this to say: "It was a great year in the Rosses, the year of the "Greek". Cows calved that year that didn't have a calf for years, and even the oldest hens in the pen kept laying throughout the entire winter, until St. Patrick's Day". Yes, seemingly it was a year of plenty. It's an ill wind

Little wonder, then, the Cope did a colossal business in eggs that same year, so that the "Greek" helped in more ways than one. Having removed all the undamaged maize from the ship's holds, Paddy the Cope then decided to take some of the damaged maize to the Mill, as well. The damaged grain was bulkier and heavier and for that reason more difficult to take by boat to Dungloe. At the Mill, it was necessary to have the maize dried before it could be ground into Indian meal, so that it was left out in the sun for some time to dry. The fields where Ostan na Rosann now stands, was originally part of the Mill Farm, but sometime in the mid-twenties it was sold to the Boyle family, who were later to sell it to the Hotel authorities. Paddy the Cope rented this field soon after the "Greek" became shipwrecked, and it was in the Mill Field that the damaged maize was dried therefore.

The late Paddy the Cope, the Lord have mercy on him, would have been 55 years of age when the "Greek" was wrecked, but he certainly worked hard while the salvage work lasted. He had men from Dungloe assisting him in the work - operating the winch, keeping accounts, filling bags, etc - but he also made a point of being aboard the ship each day himself, if at all possible. He used a punt, powered by an outboard engine, to bring himself and his workmen to and from the "Greek" daily - from Meenmore or from the Pier at Dungloe. He must therefore have been a pioneer in the use of outboard engines in the Rosses, and when I come to think of it, a very noisy outboard it was! We can still think of him cruising up and down by Rutland and Inishfree, "breaking the silence of the seas", as the poet had it, at a time when there was no other mechanical sound to be heard. Apart from all else, it must be said of the Copeman, that he was a man of courage, and, added to that, his knowledge of the sea was far from being elementary.

The Captain and crew of the 'Elfinoris' remained on the island for more than a week, that is, until all hopes of having their ship refloated were finally abandoned. As there was no hotel on the island in those days, the Glen Hotel dates from about 1928, the ship's officers and crew were given accommodation in houses around the village of Leabgarrow. As only the ship's mate could speak English, the other members of the crew had difficulty in communicating with the people of their new surroundings, during their stay on the island. As one old man informed me, "Only Dr. Doogan could speak to them, as he knew their language." Thus it was that the good priest became their friend and interpreter during their brief stay on Arranmore. [Dr. Doogan was Curate of Arranmore during the years 1921-26]

The remuneration paid to those who boated the Indian corn or maize from the "Elfinoris" to the mainland was small accordingly. Five shillings a ton was the rate paid to Burtonport, while those who brought it all the way to the Mill at Dungloe were paid ten shillings. In the 'Twenties, too, prior to the setting up of the Fianna Fail tariff wall of 1932, the Co-op. used to import flour direct from both Cardiff and Liverpool to the harbour at Burtonport. The "steamer days" were always big days around the Port, with all the young men of the entire locality coming there to the Pier to look for a day's work. As there were always twice as many men there as there were jobs to offer them, it was often a source of great embarrassment for all concerned. In order to get over this embarrassing situation, the decision was then made that members of the Co-op. would have first claim on what jobs there were to give away. In other words, the Co-op. customers were to be given preference in recruiting workers to unload the ship. And we remember, too, that the wages being paid there were nine shillings for a nine-hour day...!"[11]

THE COPE'S KIPPERING AND GUTTING BUSINESSES

Paddy the Cope travelled to the Scottish Cooperative Wholesale Society in Aberdeen in December 1940 to learn about kippering after a Cope consignment of herring had arrived there in poor condition. Paddy's trip, which then took him to London via Manchester (where he sold some Cope knitwear – stockings) was very eventful, taking place as it did in the middle of the Blitz (September 1940 to May 1941). Ten days after he left Manchester, his hotel, the Victoria, was flattened by the Luftwaffe. London was also being bombed while he was there – Paddy was nothing if not courageous!

Connie (Ellen John) Boyle has a marvellous memory for detail and recalled in November 2006 both the kippering and gutting work in Burtonport in the 1940s:

> "...I did three winters (October to the end of March in 1944/45, 1945/46 and 1946/47) in the Cope's Kippering Shed in Burtonport; I was sixteen when I started. I worked on the night shift which was 8pm-8am. The herring were tipped onto a bench with a wooden board along one side and salt rubbed in to 'catch' the fish – they were too slippery otherwise.
>
> Unlike with curing, the fish were split down the back, run out to the tail, then the reverse, up to the head. They were opened up, guts taken out and any blood on the bone washed out in a nice clean pickle (made out of water and salt).Unlike the curing, there was no selection with the kippers – in the winter there were mainly big herring anyway. They were put into a tub with 45-50 per cent proof (salt) pickle with a dye added to make them brown (Mallaig and the Isle of Man were the only places then to *smoke* them brown, they didn't use a dye).
>
> After half an hour they were put in a different trough still wet. The herring would be hung on a 'tenter stick ', a long pole about 5 feet wide

---

11 *Packie Bonner, 1981 writing in the Cope's 75th anniversary booklet.*

with two Y-shaped ends for hanging up. You'd pull the herring down on to nails in the sticks to hold them. Then when each pole was full, we'd take them into the kiln and, legs wide apart, we'd hand them up to each other; there would be 24-25 sticks high. There were three kilns (two single kilns, one double) in the shed, in total about 40-50 rows of sticks I think – in all over a thousand herring kippered a night at a time.

All this was done by the day shift, ready by the time we got there. We then got the fire going; we used sawdust but it was scarce, there was very little sawdust to be had in the Second World War and afterwards. The fire was not a great blaze, just enough to generate the smoke. You could tell they were ready and smoked by looking to see the last drop on the tail; when you ran your finger and thumb down each side, it would be dry. Towards the end of the shift (8am), they were taken down and put onto the trusses on the stacking frame in the packing shed for the day shift who would pack them into wooden boxes, a stone weight of them in each [14lbs, c6 kilograms]. In my time, all the kippers were bought by one man: Harry James Fish Merchant, Belfast came in with his lorry and took them all away.

The boxes would be marked with a stencil on the lid, with the name of the curer and the place – black polish would be rubbed over the stencil to leave the marking .My mother remembers seeing in a shop in Bayonne, New Jersey in the Twenties a box marked Doherty and Doherty, Kincasslagh.

The day shift would split the herrings and put them up on the poles; our job would be to keep the fires and smoke going and to take them out to put on the stacking frames. The kippering was done in the winter; there was no herring to speak of in the summer.

Between October and the end of March, weather permitting, lots of boats were fishing them: Paddy's boats of course and the 'Bolanders' (half-deckers with Bolander engines) too. There was Owenie Manus, Pride of Rutland, Charlie Sharkey, Pride of Lackbeg, Jimmy Boyle, Pride of Keadue, Pat the Yankee Bonner, Pride of Arlands and many others from the islands, with yawls as well as half-deckers. Dinnie Boyle of Keadue lost his boat with a load of herring coming in I remember. Yawls would be fishing too: four men rowing; John Nellie Andy Boner, first cousin of my mother, from Lochaseantie pier and Manus Charlie Boner..."[12]

---

12 *Personal reminiscence by Connie Ellen John Boyle to the editor in November 2006.*

HERRING GUTTING

Connie Ellen John also worked at gutting herring after the 'Emergency' (Second World War)

"...When the herring were in, the gutting would be on all the time. I remember even one Christmas Day; they were curing herring at the back of Campbell's – where the car park is there now. The herring were selected into seven different barrels: Large, Fulls, Madth Fulls, Matties, Small Matties, Dead Smalls, TBs ('torn bellies'). There were three in a gutting crew: two gutting, one packing – both men and women were at it. The gutters would stand in front of a farlan (a trough like a table on four legs) filled with herring with salt tipped on them for gripping, otherwise you couldn't catch them as they would be too slippery; behind each crew would be seven tubs, and there was a cog, a barrel for the guts. The gutters were very skilful: one dab and gills and guts were cleaned and the fish flicked behind them into the correct tub without looking.

The packers put salt into the bottom of the barrel. Each packer had a big square 'rousing' tub on four legs next to the barrels. The herring, selected into the different barrels, would then be tipped into the tub and salt was rubbed into them, they were given a good 'rousing', turned over and over in salt.

Burtonport women gutting herring early in the 1900s. The location is behind where the Fishermen's Co-Op has their long buildings today. Gutting was an important seasonal work in Burtonport and Kincasslagh and many local men and women, from the islands and mainland Rosses, also travelled across Ireland (e.g. to Ardglass) and to Scotland as far up as Wick for gutting work (Mícheál O Domhnaill Collection, postcard published by Hugh Campbell Burtonport c1906, posted 1908).

GUTTING THE HERRING AT BURTONPORT.

The coopers [barrel makers] would look after the barrels. They had a big tub of water and would beam the barrels in it, swirl them round, turn them upside down to see if there were any bubbles. If there were, they'd tighten the hoops to make them airtight. [Marjorie Bonner N.T. (Manny Anne) of Acres remembers that Owenie Paddy Ellie (O'Donnell) who lived where The Thatch is now, was a cooper in Burtonport]

The packer would salt and pack the first layer, then shout 'Bottom!' to the cooper to check them. The bottom layer would be packed with all the heads going the same way; the next layer would be reversed so they'd lie on each other better. Between each layer would be another layer of salt. When it was full, the lid would be put on but not tightened. After 2-3 days, the barrel would be opened and there would be a loss of about a quarter of a barrel as the fish shrank in curing ['pined] and the salt was absorbed. The barrel would be topped up (called 'laying over') with other already cured herring of the same selection (Large etc). The top was put back on and a 'spile' put in a hole in the lid (a spile was a long plug about ¾ inch diameter).

The barrels would 'lay over' for a week to ten days, stacked in two tiers. Then came the filling up; this was done when there was no herring waiting to be gutted. All the tiers were taken down, the plug taken out and the pickle [salt and water] would come out. The barrels were emptied again and washed into pickle and then repacked, branded and ready to go. The fish on top were always 'melt' herring; this was done just before shipping (customers in Germany, Russia etc liked it this way). The name of the curer and place were put on the lid with a stencil and polish rubbed into it leaving the markings. My mother once saw in a shop in Bayonne, New Jersey in the twenties a box with Doherty & Doherty, Kincasslagh stencilled on it.

The inspector would then come, open up the barrels and check they were packed right. The lid would go back on, the spile banged in and the end of it pruned, using a tool called an 'each' (like an adze or an axe but with a rounded head on it)..."[13]

Connie Ellen John was born on 28th November 1928 in the USA. His mother worked in Sweeney's Hotel Dungloe 1922-24. She was then going to the States but the cook in Sweeney's Hotel, Burtonport was ill, so she did six months there before leaving. Connie's father, who worked in the mines, died six months before his birth.

---

13 *Personal reminiscence by Connie Ellen John Boyle to the editor in November 2006.*

This is Burtonport in a very early photo, c1900 or possibly even earlier, judging by the style of the boats, the old shed and the clothes that the fishermen are wearing. After a century of decline, fishing was regenerated in the 1890s with the help of the CDB. The coming of the railway in 1903 further boosted the industry, creating a bonanza for local fishermen but also for Scottish boats which were larger and more able to exploit the plentiful herring in the seas around the Rosses and Gweedore. The barrels in the foreground would be filled with herring that had been gutted and packed locally and sent across Britain, Europe and the United States (Photo courtesy of Irene James Mickey and Nigel Blaney, Skippers Restaurant, Burtonport).

A c1967 photo by Denis Tynan, Glenties, of the Fishermen's Co-op in Burtonport, with Burtonport Co-Op fish boxes filled with salmon stacked around – those days are long gone sadly. *In the front* sitting from left to right: Bernard Ward, Hughdie Hunt, Connie Ellen John (Boyle) who provided the descriptions of gutting and kippering in this book; sitting on the right, Liam Reilly and Ray Hamm; *middle*, left to right, Willie Alcorn – father of Donegal County Councillor and ex Mayor David Alcorn, (behind, in the hat and turned away, is Jimmy Johnny O'Donnell), Red Dinny Francie Ward (Keadue), Manus Bhrianey McGonagle, (believed to be) Sean McGuinness, Killybegs, and one other man from Killybegs behind; (just behind Ray Hamm's head, Johnny JF O'Donnell, father of Jimmy Johnny), harbourmaster; *at the back:* not known, John Johnnie Bonner (uncle of John Mickie Nancy), Aloysius Bonner and John 'Mickie Nancy' Bonner (National Photographic Archive).

The Cope's Kippering Factory Burtonport was built in 1941, after Paddy's trip to Aberdeen in wartime 1940 to learn about kippering. *Paddy's first recorded flight was on his return via Belfast to Glasgow.* This scene is from 1956 and taken from a Denis Tynan photograph. The kippering shed had a very distinctive look, with ventilation shutters to let the smoke out. Where it stood is now a large, vertical diesel tank (National Photographic Archive)

Paddy the Cope and the St Aiden

The following story, written as a play, is a short extract from Sally the Cope's own stories, written in the 1940s for her grandchildren. Discovered recently, they present a new perspective on the Cope story and Paddy and Sally in particular. Both of them come out of the stories enlarged and with even greater humanity.

The context is that Paddy, about 76 at the time, had been invited to America in 1947, in Sally's words:

> "Well, one day he handed me a letter from Johnnie Curran, of New York. It must have been lost in the burning along with many others. It was sometime in July 1947, and it was an invitation for Paddy to be the Guest of Honour in Croke Park, New York on the 31st August, at a field day between Donegal and Fermanagh".

Paddy had some difficulty getting a ticket and so decides on another tack.

> Paddy goes down to the pier. The Cope boat the *St Aiden* was there for overhauling. They were after installing a new 136 h.p. "Kelvin" engine in her. Paddy called Manus Herrity; Manus came to the pier.
>
> PADDY: Manus, when will she be ready for the sea?
>
> MANUS: I expect tomorrow night.
>
> PADDY: Hughie Doogan and I want to get to New York before the end of August. We cannot get a passage by air or sea. Do you think will she be able to make it?
>
> MANUS: Why the hell wouldn't she. She will be ready for any sea tomorrow night!
>
> PADDY: Call the crew.
> (Manus did so, and they all came to the pier.)
>
> PADDY: Boys, Hugh Doogan and I want to be in New York on or before the 31st August. We have been trying for the past few months to get a passage by air or sea. Manus says the Saint Aiden will be ready for sea

tomorrow. I was asking him if he thinks she is fit for New York, and he says she is.

JOHN: Paddy, you must get a skipper that can read the chart and box the compass. Mick Gallagher is your man.

PADDY: If Mick goes, will all of you men go, any that want to go, put up their hands. (All hands went up like shooting stars.) Now boys, I'll run up and phone Mick, but for heaven's sake, don't one of you leave the boat tonight, and don't mention America to any person for your life, if Sally heard it that would finish it.

Paddy went to the Post Office and asked to call up the Cope Hotel in Killybegs. After a short time he got through to Killybegs.

PADDY: Hallo, Hallo: Is that you John?

JOHN: It is.

PADDY: Run down to the pier and tell Mick to come on the 'phone, if he is not in, wait until he comes in.

(After a few seconds)

MICK: Hallo! Hallo! Is that you Paddy, do you want me? You will be glad to her that we have fifty boxes of good stuff, I am sure we will get £80 for them.

PADDY: Mick, the Saint Aiden is now in first-class repair. Hugh Doogan and I want to go to New York, we cannot get a passage, Mick, and the crew are willing to go if you go with them. If you agree, hire a car and come immediately, don't tell any person and when you come to our house, for your life don't say where you are going

MICK: All right, I'll tell Neil to take charge of the boat.

(Some time later in the Cope House)

PADDY: Sally, you are tired, we will go to bed, it is nearly ten o'clock. Off we went.

At 10.30 p.m. there was a knock at the door.

SALLY: I wonder who is there?

PADDY: I suppose it is some of the fishermen; I'll run down and see what they want.

(Paddy goes down and opens the door, and takes the fishermen in.)

PADDY: Mick, you were not long, come in to the room. Speak low. I don't want Sally to know until we are away. We will sail to-morrow night. Go you down and go aboard and don't let any one of them come up to the town. If they went into the pubs they won't be able to keep their mouths shut. I'll go down to you in the morning. Don't move until I get there.

(Paddy was up early and went down to the pier and wakened them.

PADDY: It may take us three or four weeks. Now, boys, you must give me a list of the goods we will want for at least four weeks or better, take five weeks' supply. I'll tell Jim, I did not tell him yet. For heaven's sake keep a shut mouth!

JOHN: We had a chat last night and we came to the conclusion that Mick had not enough experience. Sure Scotland was not out of sight all the time. Let Mick speak for himself.

MICK: Paddy, we had a long chat and examined the chart for over two hours, and none of could make a damn thing of it, after we would lose sight of Arranmore. I think I would steer her straight west to America, but the wind and the tides might carry me off the straight line. After a long chat we decided not to go unless you get us a man that brought ships to America before, and we have the man if you take him. We will all be delighted to go. The man is Captain Dominick (Mickey Kitty) O'Donnell, of Eighter Island. He travelled the whole world and he is a friend of your Sally's. He won't refuse you, there is not a harbour in the world that was worth going to but he was in, but sure the sailing in the sea is in his veins; sure his father hardly left the sea, but what am I talking about, sure Paddy you know them better then me. Sure only for his brother Charlie you would never have bursted the blockade. How could you bring in and out the Dutch boat, only for Charlie Mickey Kitty that had the guts to pilot her in and out.

PADDY: Give me your hand, Mick. God bless you. I am a stupid man; that I never thought of Captain O'Donnell. It is a shame for me. Now make out a list of the goods you want, and don't move from the boat until I come back again. I'll run up and get Jim to take me to Burtonport; I'll be back in less than two hours. Don't for your life leave the boat until I come back.

(Paddy and Jim went down to Burtonport and called on Charlie Sharkey.)

PADDY: Charlie, will you run me in to see Captain O'Donnell? I have a message that I want to give him.

CHARLIE: Mr. Gallagher, the sea is rough for you. I'll give him whatever message you want. Oh, there is the Captain on the pier.

(Goes down to the pier to the Captain; he is about to step into his boat, going home; his brother Charlie was sitting on the taft, with an oar In each hand.)

PADDY: Hallo. Captain, will you please come over here, I want to speak to you.

CAPTAIN: (Caught Paddy's hand) You are welcome, Mr. Gallagher. I have not seen you for a long time. How is Sally?

PADDY: Fine, Captain, Hugh Doogan and I want to be in New York not later than the 30th August. We tried to get by air and by sea but failed to get a berth. We have just installed a new 136 h.p. engine in one of our boats, the "Saint Aiden" and Big Mick is down from Killybegs, all the crew are willing to leave Doogan and me in New York, if you go with us.

CAPTAIN: (Laughed) Mr. Gallagher, it is quite impossible for a small craft like yours to cross the Atlantic, and if you did, you have no idea of the formalities you would have to contend with.

PADDY: Sure, Big Mick took us over to Scotland, through Tory Sound, we had no chart, no Compass or Customs papers and we landed a cargo of herrings and got back home again without any trouble with our wee Naomh Eine. If the Scottish people, who are foreigners would let us load and unload and load up again, surely our American friends would not stop us landing. We'll have no cargo with us.

CAPTAIN: Mr. Gallagher, the tide is leaving. (Steps into his boat and took one of the oars out of Charlie's hand, and they rowed away.)

(Paddy and Jim came up to Dungloe again; on their way up they stopped at the Pier and. Paddy went over to the fishermen.)

PADDY: Hallo, boys: Come up here, I want to speak to you. (They all came on deck.) Stand there a minute. I saw Captain O'Donnell and he says that this boat would never make New York. He knows what he is talking about; I never saw him looking better.

MICK: What will you do now, Paddy?

PADDY: I hope we shall get a passage by air or sea yet, Mick. Jim will you run back again to Killybegs, Manus when the boat floats let you and the crew go to Killybegs, the day is good and the fishing is good…"

Paddy and Hughie Doogan eventually made it to America on the 'Marine Flasher' sailing from Cobh on 23rd August 1947. The Marine Flasher was built as a WW2 troopship in 1945 and converted for 914 tourist class passengers in 1946.

Most unusually, Paddy's trip was recorded for the Derry Journal, demonstrating what a celebrity he had become since his book had been published:

'Paddy the Cope's' Barefooted
Voyage to America
Here Is a Soliloquy Recorded on Board the Ocean Liner

"…'Paddy the Cope' has done some peculiar things in the course of his chequered career, but never did he personify his flair for the unconventional in such marked fashion as when he paraded barefooted the deck of the liner which carried him to the U.S. to figure in the "Smash the Border" demonstration at Croke Park, New York, under the auspices of the Donegal-Fermanagh Associations.

Passengers regarded his unorthodox behaviour with a certain amount of misgiving, but just because it seemed to annoy some that were distinctly prudish "Paddy" persisted and got a kick out of it.

By special arrangement Mr Gallagher has forwarded us a day-by-day diary of his doings since he embarked on the liner at Cobh, accompanied by Dungloe men, Messrs, James C O'Boyle, John Sharkey and Hugh Duggan.

Following are extracts from the travelogue written in Mr Gallagher's inimitable style, which made his book "My Story" such a romantically appealing volume.

Inishcoo Island off Burtonport was the home of the Mickey Kitties (O'Donnell) in the middle of the last century. Captain Dominick Mickie Kitty, his brother Charlie and their father Captain John O'Donnell were highly experienced sea captains. It was Dominick that Big Mick Gallagher recommended to Paddy the Cope when Paddy wanted to sail to America on the St Aiden (Sally the Cope's short play tells the story). In 1901, the combined population of Inishcoo and Eighter was 44. The house on Inishcoo is one of the oldest in the Rosses (National Photographic Archive, Lawrence Photograph R9449).

Burtonport in the 1940s at the time of Paddy's attempt to get Big Mick Gallagher to take him to America on the *St Aiden*. On the right is O'Donnell's Hotel and Bar then run by Jimmy Frank (O'Donnell), a celebrated local character and grandfather of the current owner Jimmy Johnny (O'Donnell), who was born in 1948. Burtonport Post Office was originally located here. On the left is the Harbour Bar (without its later addition of a covered porch) and in the centre, attractively covered with creepers, Campbell's Hotel; both of these latter two premises are now sadly closed due to the downturn in business, closure of the fish factories and end of large scale fishing in Burtonport (Mícheál O Dhomnaill Collection)

Again Burtonport in the 1940s – up the street is John E Gallagher's bar (now The Lobster Pot, but known locally as Kelly's). The harbour has since been partially filled in to make a very useful car park – it is said that before this the path used to be wide enough (just) for a horse and cart to go past the Harbour Bar and round the back (Mícheál O Dhomnaill Collection).

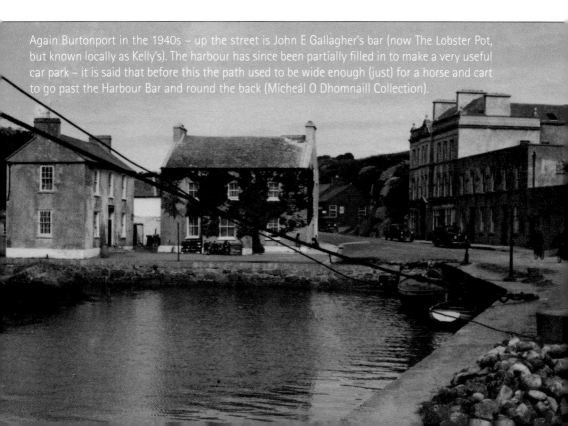

The Marine Flasher was built in 1945 and sailed between Bremen, Le Havre, Cobh and New York between 1946 and 1949. It was originally built as a naval vessel and, although converted to carry commercial passengers, it remained fairly basic.

Photo courtesy U. S. Maritime Commission

MARINE FLASHER

Length, overall	523' 0"	Gross tons	12,420	Propulsion	Turbine
Beam	72' 0"	Speed (knots)	17	Passengers	3,485
Draft	29' 0"	Radius (miles)	12,000	Cargo (cu. ft.)	53,000

Built in 1945 by Kaiser Co., Inc., Vancouver, Wash.
Operated in World War II by Matson Navigation Co.

August 23, 1947 (Saturday) – "We went aboard the tender at 8 o'clock and sailed out to meet the United States liner. We met her, The Marine Flasher, at 10.30 p.m., outside Spike Island. When I went to look for my baggage, two parcels were missing. Some lousy devil pinched them. I should have told you that it was pleasant in one way and in another it was very sad. While they were singing, many were also crying at the parting of dear ones. There were at least 400 people on the pier and all of them singing. Among the songs they sang were 'Come Back to Erin', 'Paddy Fagan', and 'Off to Philadelphia in the Morning'. Jimmie Boyle, Hugh Dugan, John Sharkey and myself were standing together and, just as they about to take in the rope they started to sing 'The Hills of Donegal', Jimmy Boyle thundered above them all and Sharkey too, but Boyle drowned them all. Dugan and I could only cry a wee bit. The Marine Flasher sailed at 11.45. We got a good cup of coffee and a bit of cake. We were then shown to our bedroom. Oh! Such a bedroom: 108 beds, most of them on top of the others. I was in luck, for I got one of the bottom ones and I did not care how many were on top of mine. The bed was good enough.

August 24, 1947 (Sunday) – I went to 9 o'clock Mass in my bare feet. I was the only one that was barefooted. It is many, many years, near seventy, since I was at Mass in my bare feet. Then we went into a queue for our breakfast. There was a big jug of tea on the table and a teapot of coffee. Funny, isn't it! There was plenty of sugar, milk, and the best of white bread and butter. It was a grand breakfast. Lunch at 12.30: it was good but I was sorry to see at least as much left behind as was eaten. I wish I could pick it up and send it to the hungry creatures in the Six Counties to keep them in their own homes so they would not have to cross the Border to Donegal for a bellyful so often. It is grand that no one in Donegal or, as far as I know,

The Story of the Cope

in the Twenty Six Counties begrudges them a bit. I recalled that morning, February 4th 1944, when I read from the 'Derry Journal' that Mr. W. Lowry, the Minister of Home Affairs, had said in that wee Parliament that Lloyd George gave to our Six Counties "...that a Mass was celebrated for the American soldiers in the Portrush Orange Hall and that he was making preparations to have the hall fumigated..." That was when the Twenty Six Counties had 200,000 fighting for the Allies. At that time they had won nine Victoria Crosses and not any Orangeman won any yet. The one which was won in the Six Counties was won by a Catholic. And imagine a British Labour Government making a judge of Mr. Lowry!

August 25, 1947 (Monday) – The weather has changed to rainy. The sea comes up, but none of our fishing vessels would have any difficulty for there is no sea like that we had in Big Mick's boat when we took the cargo of herrings from Burtonport to Scotland. We meet much heavier seas going past Tory. Dinner at 5.30 – as usual, it was very good.

August 26, 1947 (Tuesday) – I am still in bare feet. A few women said 'Sir, I would advise you to put on your shoes or you will get pneumonia'. I paid no attention; just said 'Thank you' and walked on.

August 27, 1947 (Wednesday) – The sea is flat. The wee Shamrock could make it. It is a pity that neither Big Mick nor I could read a chart. We would come flying through with the St Aiden. There is a fog on and we are only doing only fourteen miles an hour, sixteen yesterday. I am beginning to worry, fearing that I'll not be in time for Croke Park on Sunday as guest of honour of the Donegal and Fermanagh sportsmen. But more than me are worrying. You should feel sorry for Boyle and Sharkey worrying about the girls they left behind them, but don't say I told you.

August 28, 1947 (Thursday) – The sea is flat but there is a heavy fog. The Flasher is going well, doing 16.23. My hopes are rising a wee bit, but poor Boyle and Sharkey have not yet recovered. Boat drill. You would break your sides laughing if you could see some of the powerful big men and women trying to put on their lifebelts. The sea is very calm. I could make it in my wee flat.

August 29, 1947 (Friday) – We are only 716 miles from New York. I might be in time for Croke Park. I sure hope I will.

August 30, 1947 (Saturday) – Not a move in the sea. It is getting very hot. I had near to burn my feet on the starboard side of the ship to-day. You could fry a roast on the deck. It is an all iron ship, even the tables. The port side wasn't as hot. Noon: only 329 miles from New York. I sent a radio message to Mr. Curran and my sisters telling them we would land tomorrow.

August 31, 1947 (Sunday) – Alongside the Statue of Liberty. I never enjoyed a trip better. The attendance, food and beds of the best. 11.50: A loudspeaker says: 'Patrick Gallagher wanted in the Purser's Office'. Up I went, said 'I am Patrick Gallagher'. A very handsome man came to me and said 'Are you Patrick Gallagher?' I said 'Yes'. He said 'I have a radio message from Johnnie Curran to say that he will meet you; have you your passport and landing card?' I said 'Yes'. 'Come with me'. He took me into another office where there were half a dozen clerks. He aid to one of them; 'Please fix up Mr, Gallagher's papers. He is one of the greatest Irishmen. I'll be back shortly.'

My papers were fixed up in less than five minutes. That handsome man came back and said lunch was at 12.30 'and when you take your lunch come up to the lounge and remain there until I bring Mr. Curran into you'. I did as I was told up to a point. When the ship was coming close to the dock, I went on deck and saw Johnnie Curran, heard him shouting 'Paddy'. Who do you think was the next one I saw? It was Bridgie. Well that was a happy sight. Boyle, Sharkey and Dugan were on the bridge. Boyle said American citizens were to get off first, but we will wait for you Paddy. It will be an hour at least. As the ship docked, I went into the lounge and started to write my impressions. In comes the handsome man and Johnnie Curran. The porter came along, took my case, bag and parcel with him and landed us outside the barrier and who do you think was there? Our Margery, Lizzie Tully and her husband John Trainer and Jack Feeney, the singer. Well, I was the first man out. Boyle, Sharkey and Dugan were left. I got into Curran's car for Croke Park, Margery with me. John, Lizzie and Bridgie followed until we came to Mr McGuire's. Had some refreshments there. The next stop was Croke Park. The games were already started. Curran was introducing me to everyone we met, a great many from home. After a time, Father McDermott, Curran and I were placed in position, two banners in front of us and three Irish colleens in between them. Two pipes and a flute band after us. Then a loudspeaker announced that the procession was going to march around the field with Father McDermott and Paddy the Cope, the guests of honour. Off we went, the band playing 'The Hills of Donegal'. When we came to the grandstand, as instructed by Mr McGuire, I put up my hand. The cheering started and continued till we halted it. I never dreamed that such honour would be paid me. I hope God will forgive me; it is the first time I became proud. The number of people who came to me and kissed me! My book was on sale; I must have autographed at least forty of them. Then Curran and Bridget, Margery, Trainer, Lizzie, John, Jack Feeney and I left for a turkey supper..."[14]

---

14 *Derry Journal, September 17th 1947. 1947 was the year when the All Ireland was played in New York, the only time outside Ireland. It took place on 14th September between Cavan and Kerry (Cavan won 2-11 to Kerry's 2-7) in commemoration of the hundred year anniversary of the Great Famine in 1847.*

Chapter 9

The Cope by Road, Rail and Overseas

Horse and Cart – the first 'Tea Van'

The Cope's only means of transportation in 1906 was the horse and cart – very, very few individuals or businesses had cars (these were an expensive luxury purchase at the time) and lorries were still some way off. Supplies would come in to Dungloe Road station, at Lough Meela, by rail or to Burtonport by boat. This meant a round trip from Cleendra to Burtonport of 18 (slow and bumpy) miles. One of the main reasons that the Cope moved into Dungloe was to cut down on some of the wasted miles they were doing; it made no sense at all to haul goods all the way back to their 'wee shop' in the hills for sorting and then send the cart out again to Croveigh or Meenbanad and elsewhere where they had customers.

The first tea van was a horse and cart which brought provisions all around Templecrone and collected eggs as payment. The Cope developed a very loyal customer base outside Cleendra before they moved in to Dungloe: their goods were keenly priced; they delivered to the door or nearby at least and they collected eggs as payment, giving good prices for these. The Cope's egg business became very professional and an important part of their early success (Appendix 2 gives an American journalist's contemporary account of how they went about things).

The Letterkenny and Burtonport Extension Railway

Three years before the Cope's beginning, the Londonderry and Lough Swilly Railway came to the Rosses with the livery of the Letterkenny and Burtonport Extension Railway (L&BER). Oddly, it did not go into Dungloe or the other main seaboard towns of West Donegal. Its scheduled journey to Derry was five and a half hours – it often took a lot longer.[1]

Edward M. Patterson, railway historian, writing in 1964 describes the course of the Lough Swilly Railway as it entered the Rosses:

> "…Leaving Gweedore, trains turned south across to the Gweedore River valley, in sight of the sheltered cottages of Dore and the island-studded coast at Inishfree Bay. Curving around from south to south-west and on falling gradients the train entered Crolly, a single platform, with a small carpet factory as the local industry.

---

1 For a very detailed, well researched and highly entertaining account of the L&BER, Frank Sweeney's 'That Old Sinner' (Irish History Press 2006) is highly recommended

The Cope's first transport was the horse and cart, often called a 'van'; supplies were picked up from Lough Meela (Dungloe Road) station and hauled back to Cleendra and, from 1907, Dungloe. Early photos of the Cope's horse and cart do not appear to have survived; this is one of Barney Bhrianey Sweeney in Burtonport in the 1920s – it is very like how the Cope's first transport and 'tea van' would have looked. Barney worked for Johnny Rua Sweeney, Burtonport, delivering groceries, sugar, flour and other supplies all around the Lower Rosses, Glenahilt, Keadue, Meenbanad and back to Burtonport. Behind the cart is the small black house where local character Cassie the Flower lived; she used to walk around the Lower Rosses and beyond in her bare feet with a basket of paper flowers she made herself for selling. Charlie McCole's house can be seen in behind her place. (Photo courtesy of Barney's granddaughter Peggy Barney (O'Donnell)

Burtonport Station in 1937. The station opened in March 1903 (less than three years before the Cope started) and the line was closed and track pulled up just 37 years later in 1940. During its relatively short existence, the Londonderry & Lough Swilly Railway (L&LSR) was a vital supply line for the Templecrone Co-Op: it brought in supplies from Derry and beyond and was the principal way in which the Cope goods reached the outside world. During the troubles in June 1921, Derry traders blockaded the Rosses and Gweedore in an unsuccessful attempt to quell insurrection. Paddy was forced to charter a boat – the aptly named *SS Better Hope* – to bring in much-needed supplies to the Rosses. Paddy from then on never relied wholly upon the Swilly line or the Derry traders. (Mícheál O Dhomnaill, HC Casserley photo)

For the last ten miles to Burtonport, the railway was in the district known as the Rosses, consisting of some 60,000 granite-strewn acres, intersected by streams and with more than a hundred lakes filling hollows in the almost treeless landscape. The population is scattered, with only two centres of any size: Annagry in the north and Dungloe on the south coast. With characteristic perversity, the railway ignored both these places, heading to Burtonport as directly as the land surface allowed. The traverse was unsheltered, gradients varied, and short rock cuttings alternated with low embankments laid across patches of waterlogged peat bog. Just over half way across the Rosses a halt, Kincasslagh Road, was opened in 1913 at No. 21 Gates in Meenbanid townland. Here the railway passed between two small loughs, a mile inland from the intricately indented coastline at Keadue Strand.

Dungloe Road [opened 1903] was at the nearest approach to the village, but was four miles north-west of it, at the north end of Lough Meela.

A classic H.C. Casserley photo from the 1930s, this one shows just how busy a station Burtonport could be. On the right, a train leaves the station for Derry; in the far distance the old pier. The seven tracks seen here were for shunting goods and passenger carriages and for taking on loads from the pier and road. There was only a single track leaving the station carried over the sea inlet by a narrow causeway and on past Nad-na-Geadh by Purt Inismeal (PB collection, postcard, photo by HC Casserley, c1937 – Mr Casserley's brilliant photographic record of the Letterkenny and Burtonport Extension of the Lough Swilly Railway is by far the best available and much thanks are due to him and his son R.M. Casserley for permission to reproduce these photos)

Now on low ground, the train passed the last pair of crossing gates, and half a mile from the terminus the railway emerged from the rocky wilderness to the coast, running past weed-strewn creeks, and by short rock faces of warm red granite. A level course brought the rails past the distant and home signals, the turntable and the engine shed, and alongside the single platform of Burtonport station.

The terminus was something of an anticlimax. There was little but the harbour at Burtonport. The station accommodation was of the simplest, a two-storey, stone-built agent's house, backing on a granite bluff, with a little waiting room alongside. The goods store and the loading bank faced out to sea, and the line serving them continued close to the edge of the water, past fish packing and curing sheds to the head of the pier. The entire area occupied by the terminus and sidings was laid on an uneven rocky shore, and required great quantities of rock material to fill

The train bound for Letterkenny is passing the old engine shed – one of the few remaining 'Swilly' buildings still left standing in Burtonport. The windows have now been filled in and the old 'shingle' style slate roof has long since been replaced. In the background are a number of goods carriages/vans which the Cope would have used to receive supplies and send their produce off to other markets in Ireland, Britain and beyond (HC Casserley Collection)

and level it. Today, even after a quarter-century of neglect, the massive stone pitching is still perfectly sound..."[2]

The coming of the railway, and its perverse avoidance of the town of Dungloe, led to some strange decisions regarding the postal system – it was quicker to send a letter from Burtonport than Dungloe! It was still the case in 1911, when local MP Mr. Hugh Law attempted to get this anomaly changed:

"...Mr Hugh Law asked the Postmaster-General whether a petition was received by the secretary, General Post Office, Dublin, from the residents of Dungloe, county Donegal, in September, 1910, headed by the signatures of the parish priest and the business men of the town, requesting that the mails should be permanently conveyed by the Burtonport mail train to Dungloe Road Station, three miles distant, instead of as at present by the Glenties train to Fintown Station, twelve miles distant over a hilly road; whether he is aware that the mail car from Dungloe to Fintown has been unable on several occasions to complete its journey owing to floods, etc., thus causing inconvenience by the

2   *The Lough Swilly Railway, Edward M Patterson, David and Charles 1964, 1968*

delay; whether he is aware that Burtonport, which was formerly served from Strabane, via Fintown, has now two outgoing and two incoming mails each day, giving from twelve to twenty hours' quicker service in home correspondence, and up to forty-eight hours' quicker service in cross-channel correspondence than Dungloe obtains; and whether, with a view to a more economical and satisfactory service, he will have Dungloe connected in the same way as Burtonport, thus securing the same postal facilities?

Mr Herbert Samuel responded: The petition was duly received. It was found, however, that the change asked for would have resulted in an inferior service at a large increase of expense, and this was explained to the petitioners by the postmaster of Letterkenny. I will have further inquiry made into the possibility effecting any improvement in the Dungloe services and communicate the result to the hon. Member..."[3]

Very quickly, the railway became *the* vital supply line into the Rosses and the most important export channel for the resurgent fishing industry. The railway had an initially quite spectacular positive impact on the local economy, creating a boom time for fishermen in the early years of its existence (Frank Sweeney, Op. Cit.)

The Swilly's arrival in the Rosses in 1903 and the Cope's rapid growth after its beginning in 1906 is no coincidence. It is no exaggeration to say that the railway was a vital part of the early success of the Cope. It allowed them to order increasingly large quantities of materials and have them delivered to Burtonport, Dungloe Road or to their new store in Meenbanad – this made for a very useful distribution network - as well as servicing the Cope's growing export businesses (eggs, knitwear, etc).

When things turned bad, during the War of Independence and after, and rail services were interrupted, the Cope and Paddy in particular felt that they could never rely on the service exclusively ever again and turned to the sea and the roads.

The Burtonport extension of the Swilly staggered on through the 1920s and 1930s and closed forever in 1940. Burtonport, Dungloe Road, Kincasslagh Road were all closed in this year and the track pulled up; a service from Gweedore to Letterkenny survived between 1941 to 1947. High maintenance, low capital investment and increasing competition from road transport made the service uneconomic – disruption during the War of Independence[4] and after didn't help either.

---

3   *Hansard December 11th 1911*

4   *The trains were often disrupted, derailed by the local I.R.A. as they were used by the forces of the Crown to move men and materials. It is said by one wag that Joseph Sweeney's election campaign slogan should have been 'Vote for Joe and walk to Derry'. Joe Sweeney, from Burtonport, the late Major General Joe Sweeney, commanded the local brigade in West Donegal.*

This close up of the 8.30 morning train about to depart for Derry was taken in June 1937 when HC Casserley, the photographer, made his journey along the Lough Swilly line. Although its reliability left a lot to be desired, the loss of the railway was a crushing blow to the people

and businesses along the line. The roads that the replacement buses travelled along were very poor for many years, at one stage getting so bad that the line reopened to Crolly for a time (HC Casserley Collection).

OUR LOCAL EXPRESS
Londonderry to Burtonport
and back in 48 hours

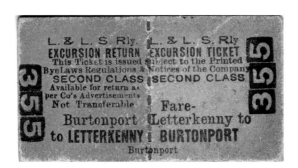

These three colourful items give a brighter sense of the railway than the old black and white images. The second class railway ticket reminds us that there were three classes of travel – travelling third class on bare bench seats in an unheated carriage was to be avoided at all costs Anthony Boner (Manny Anne), Crickamore still remembers going to Letterkenny Hospital to have his tonsils removed in the 1920s – it was very cold and uncomfortable and the journey seemed to go on forever. The 'Wilds of Donegal' poster dates from before 1910 and showcases Portsalon, Rosapenna, Gartan Lake and Burtonport. It would have been displayed in stations and waiting rooms across Britain and Ireland, looking to attract tourists searching for both scenery – and sport: the huntin' fishin' and shootin' fraternity. Lastly, the comic postcard exaggerates (some would have said only slightly) the extended journey times. Generic postcards like this were produced for many railways with the line name and comment added afterwards (PB Collection)

A very unusual photo of a the L&BER train at Burtonport station. The train driver on the right here is Hughie Boyle father of Maggie 'the Thatch'. He is *reversing* the train into Burtonport, shunting, i.e. to add on or take off carriages on one of the other six tracks, and keeping an eye on the line as he goes. The Cope goods and supplies would be carried in goods vans and

attached to the train in this way. In the background can be seen the islands of Inishfree and Rutland. Hughie was the last train driver on the Burtonport route (This is almost certainly another fine photo by H.C. Casserley in 1937. Mr Casserley would need to have clambered up on the rocks adjoining the track to take the photo, Mícheal O Dhomnaill Collection).

Burtonport station in c1950, ten years after the track was pulled up and the line was closed as far as Gweedore. The stationmaster in its last years and resident afterwards was Charlie John McBride who kept the building in very good order. The building was 'tossed' (a Rosses colloquial term for demolished) in 2003, coincidentally almost exactly 100 years to the day after it was opened, to make parking spaces for trailers and boats. Since then, the Port has seen both factories closed, their processing equipment sold and gone – and a complete end to Burtonport's once mighty fishing industry (crabbers, seasonal lobster fishing and sea angling, small boat fishing continue). The demolished station was a lost opportunity for a Lough Swilly Railway Heritage Centre which would have complemented well the marina development it is hoped will soon be in place (Derry Harbour Museum collection).

Donegal is now one of the few counties in Ireland with no railway service at all. The others are all border – Ulster - counties too: Cavan, Monaghan, Tyrone, and Fermanagh. It is not the only factor but, in part, the complete absence of *any* railway lines in these counties has to be a direct result of Partition: a nationally directed transport plan would not have left these counties completely bereft of a train service of any kind.

Louie McBride's father, Charlie John McBride, was the stationmaster at Burtonport. Louie remembers some of the other men working on the railway right to the end: Hedley Connell (Derry), engine stoker; Jimmy Sharkey, linesman; Pat Connaghan; Jimmy Boyle, engine driver; Hughie Boyle, engine driver; Johnny Hannigan; John McCole; Condy McNelis, guardsman, ticket collector; and Paddy Tierney (Derry).

Connie Ellen John Boyle remembers the old station in Burtonport:

> "...Me and Manus McGonagle were asked one day to demolish the waiting room to make some space for the Fishermen's Co-op. When we

The Swilly railway became the L&BER – the Letterkenny &
Burtonport Extension Railway - for the stretch between Letterkenny
and Burtonport. In these photographs are the third class carriage,
an open topped freight car and a wagon for transporting livestock.
The Cope's produce outwards and supplies inwards would have
been carried in wagons like these (PB collection, probably H.C
Casserley photos, c1930s).

LETTERKENNY HIRING FAIR

FRIDAY, 14TH MAY, 1937.

-----:-----

On above date, PASSENGER TRAINS will run as under:-

A.

Burtonport	dep.	6. 0 a.m.	Letterkenny	dep.	5. 50 p.m.
Dungloe Road	"	6. 6 "	Kilmacrenan	"	6. 39 "
Gweedore	"	6. 41 "	Creeslough	"	7. 7 "
Creeslough	"	7. 43 "	Gweedore	"	8. 18 "
Kilmacrenan	"	8. 14 "	Dungloe Road	"	8. 55 "
Letterkenny	arr.	8. 55 "	Burtonport	arr.	9. 0 "

B.

Londonderry	dep.	9. 0 a.m.	Letterkenny	dep.	4. 30 p.m.
Newtoncunningham	"	9. 45 "	Newtoncunningham	"	5. 10 "
Letterkenny	arr.	10. 30 "	Londonderry	arr.	6. 0 "

(A) - This Train will replace the usual 8. 30 a.m., and will leave LETTERKENNY for DERRY at 10. 30 a.m., running correspondingly earlier throughout.

(B) - This Train will replace the usual 10.0 a.m. as far as LETTERKENNY, but will run at usual times from LETTERKENNY to BURTONPORT. Connects at DERRY with 8. 0 a.m. Bus from MOVILLE, and at BRIDGE END with 8. 10 a.m. Bus from BUNCRANA.

THE USUAL CHEAP FARES WILL BE IN OPERATION.

NOTE. --- In addition to the usual BUS SERVICES the following BUSES will run:-

GORTAHORK to LETTERKENNY at 7. 0 A.M. returning from LETTERKENNY to GORTAHORK at 3. 30 P.M.

LETTERKENNY to CHURCHHILL at 4. 45 P.M.

--

FOR FURTHER PARTICULARS SEE TIME TABLES.

JAS. WHYTE,

Londonderry,
30th April, 1937.

MANAGER & SECRETARY.

B/S.

Paddy at the age of nine in 1880 and many others before and after made their way to Strabane or Letterkenny to the hiring fairs. When Paddy left, he walked all the way. They were an unfortunate way of life in the nineteenth century for children and young men and women - astonishingly these fairs survived well into the 1940s. This special 'Letterkenny Hiring Fair' timetable for the Lough Swilly railway dates from 14th May 1937 (PB collection)

got there, we found that the interior was panelled with narrow boards/ planks on each of which there was the name, with dates, of someone who had left from the station, some never to come back. My mother was there, uncles, aunts etc. I felt it should not be knocked and said so but the decision was to go ahead. The timber was burnt, none of it kept. It was a very sad thing to do and I felt so at the time..."[5]

At the date of writing, very little remains of the old railway in Burtonport: the last remaining station building was demolished in 2003, ironically the centenary year of the line and Burtonport Station opening, to make way for parking for trailers and boats. The old platform is still there and one engine shed which has had its windows closed in; the old single railway line out of Burtonport via Purt is a single lane road across the old causeway built by the Lough Swilly engineers. Further down the line, there are better preserved remains at Dungloe Road Station and Kincasslagh Road (Meenbanad), and several of the gatehouses.

Photographer and railway historian Henry Cyril Casserley travelled the line in June 1937:

> "...A short account of a trip to Burtonport may prove of interest to any reader who contemplates taking a trip over this line whilst the opportunity exists.
>
> In company with a friend we duly arrived at Letterkenny shortly after 5pm one evening from Strabane; this is necessary to avoid having to travel by bus between Letterkenny and Londonderry, owing to there being only one through train on the Lough Swilly line. Except on certain fair days, indeed, it is not possible to do the return trip from Letterkenny to Burtonport in a single day; there are only two trains each way, and the second one back leaves before the arrival of the first one outwards.
>
> We found our train, consisting of one coach and several vans, waiting at Letterkenny, and a brief inspection of the accommodation simply confirmed my resolved intention of travelling first class. The return first class fare from Letterkenny to Burtonport is 9s 5d, about three shillings more than third, and considering that one is going to spend at least seven hours on the journey, it is emphatically worth the difference. The first class, in addition to its privacy, is naively upholstered and quite comfortable, but the third has bare wooden seats.
>
> In due course we started off, a fine sunny evening, and were soon climbing towards the hills. The scenery over the route is very wild and fine, something after the style of the northernmost stretch of the old Highland Railway. In places one does not see a cottage or sign of human habitation for miles.

---

5   *This is a personal reminiscence by Connie Ellen John to the editor of this book.*

Dungloe, the most populous town along the Swilly's L&BER route, never had its own railway station. The financial – and political - rationale behind this act of folly is well laid out in Frank Sweeney's excellent history of the Letterkenny & Burtonport Extension 'That Old Sinner' (Irish History Press 2006). Dungloe Road station (originally called Lough Meela – a more accurate description than Dungloe Road) some three and a half miles away was the nearest point.

Carriages would meet passengers – there was even a Lough Swilly ticket for 'Sweeney's Car' to take passengers to Sweeney's Hotel in Dungloe. In this Cope photograph from c1930 the "Pratt's" oil lorry is probably the Cope's. It is standing in the yard of Dungloe Road station, the station platform and waiting room were behind this and the gatehouse on the Burtonport-Dungloe road can be seen on the left (Cope Collection)

There is very little passenger traffic, but quite a fair amount of goods, which took some time to unload at each station, this, added to various shunting movements to detach vans caused us to be half-an-hour late arriving at Burtonport, the time being then 9.30 pm. Visitors being few and far between at this veritable "back of beyond", our arrival caused some little upheaval, but Sweeney's Hotel – the one and only – at Burtonport, did us very well, and the place was very comfortable.

The following morning we caught the 8.30 am train back; she proved to be a fine puller and an excellent steamer, judging from the number of times the safety valves kept blowing off. It seems strange that the sister engine, No. 11, has been scrapped.

We continued to Londonderry, the 4-8-0 working throughout. Much time was lost in shunting at intermediate stations, and we did not get into Londonderry until 2.15 pm, nearly six hours' journey. We arrived with a tremendous train, two passenger coaches and about twenty vans of various sorts, but the engine seemed to have no difficulty in handling it; another train was at Letterkenny waiting to take the mid-day train to Burtonport. At Tooban Junction two more engines were shunting, but we were unable to get out owing to the solicitous guard having locked us in to prevent unauthorised gate-crashers. Still, one cannot have it all ways.

In spite of rumours to the contrary, there was no indication that the line will be closed at present; indeed, the railway appears to be the only practical means of communication with Burtonport, such roads as there are being extremely poor..."[6]

Mr. Casserley was right about the roads but his optimism about the railway proved unfounded: less than three years after his visit, the Rosses section of the line was closed and the track ripped up. Not one engine survived, all were scrapped. Today, a line like the Burtonport Extension would be a world famous tourist attraction, taking in spectacular coastal and mountain scenery as it skirted the seaboard and Errigal. Such anachronistic considerations would never have occurred to people in the 1930s of course, when the more important issue was how people would get from A to B.

MOTORISED TRANSPORT

The Cope's first lorry was bought in 1918 for £205. It was a Model T Ford. In 1924, there were two drivers working for the Cope (Owen Sweeney and John Cannon); their wages were £1 10s a week (1924); the general mechanic earned £2 a week, making the combined wage bill £5 a week for keeping the lorries on the road.[7]

---

6   'The Londonderry and Lough Swilly Railway' The Railway Magazine, May 1938 by H C Casserley

7   The Cope Letter Book 1924-25 (Jim the Cope Archive).

Packie Bonner recalled the Cope's first motorised transport:

> "...Besides grinding corn from all over the Rosses, the Mill was used now for grinding maize as well. The maize was shipped direct to Burtonport and sometimes even to the pier at Dungloe; but when it was not convenient or practical to have this done, it was brought by rail from Derry and taken to the Mill by lorry or tractor from the Railway Station.
>
> We still remember getting lifts on the Cope lorries on their way from Lough Meela Station [Dungloe Road Station] to the Mill, with a load of maize, or maybe oats. The drivers of these lorries were the late James O'Donnell and Owen Sweeney, but the tractor in use at that time (a Fordson) was always driven by John Ward, who, thank God, is still hale and hearty and now living in retirement on the Main Street. The first lorries in use by the Cope were Fords of the Model T type, and I would say their load capacity would be about one ton or thereabouts. The tractor, on the other hand, would be capable of pulling a load of about 3 tons. The tractor, a 25 H.P. petrol/paraffin Fordson, was originally bought in 1926 in order to drive or power the winch or grain elevator on the "Elfinoris" at Arranmore. After the salvage job had been completed, the tractor was used for the haulage of meal from Dungloe Road station at Lough Meela, to the Mill. John Ward tells us that he drove it once as far as Ardara, but for the most part its use was confined to The Rosses.
>
> As there were no tarred roads in the Rosses until early in the 'Thirties; traffic at that time was very light. As John Ward the driver put it to me one day: "It was easy driving in those days. Hadn't we the roads all to ourselves?" The first Cope lorries had solid tyres on the rear wheels, and I can still see the impression or print left by them in the muddy roads of that time. Because of the very poor surface of the roads in those days, punctures had become the order of the day; but by using solid tyres on the rear wheels, it meant that puncture repair work was reduced by half..."[8]

The Cope Letter Book, a chance survival of letters written by Cope Secretary Daniel Sweeney in 1924-25, records a number of road accidents in the early days of motoring on the empty roads of The Rosses:

> "...Motor Accident 8th August 1924. Lorry travelling between Dungloe and Burtonport about 11 o'clock Friday 8th August. The Driver pulled up to Rev Father Sweeney C.C. Acres. A motor car belonging to Daniel Walsh came up behind and unable to pull up in time, ran into the lorry causing damage..."

---

8   *Cope 75th Anniversary Booklet, 1981, Packie Bonner (Cope Archive)*

954

Gweedore station reopened in 1941 as the substitute bus and lorry services were no match for the roads, which at that stage were in very poor repair. The line closed for good in January 1947. The train shown is no. 3; the trains were colloquially called 'An Muc Dubh', the Black Pig – they made for quite a sight as they laboured their way through the difficult terrain, belching out clouds of black smoke (Original photograph on a postcard, PB Collection).

In February 1925, there was another accident. This time the driver was John Cannon and in the lorry as well was Hugh McPaul. The lorry hit a stone, the steering locked and the lorry ran over a fence with the result: windshield, wheel, steering gear, tyre and tube destroyed.

Motor transport became the Cope's main supply and distribution progressively from the 1920s, even though the roads were poor and in some cases treacherous and impassable at certain times of the year. The disruptions and increasing unreliability of the Swilly line gave them no other alternative. Attempts were made to transport supplies in and produce out (e.g. eggs, soapstone and herring – not all together we hope) by boat. However, from the 1940s, after the Emergency, after the Swilly had closed and the Cope boats were given up, it was to lorries and vans that the Cope turned.

Petrol rationing (introduced in October 1939) during the Emergency made it difficult to keep vehicles on the road. Paddy came up with an ingenious solution, recorded in the following letter to the Department of Industry and Commerce on 31st December 1940:

"...A Cara

During the present emergency, I suggest for your serious consideration, that a saving in Oil and Petrol would result in a reorganisation of Vans and Lorries.

Take for example the distribution of bread. It is often seen in small villages, 5 or 6 bread vans, some travelling long distances, while one van would be sufficient. We have a bakery here and we have 4 bread vans going out, some of these vans are going as far south as Donegal Town, and going east to Ballybofey, Stranorlar, Convoy, Lifford and Letterkenny. Then there is the Milford Bakery, which we think is bigger than ours, they must have about 9 vans, distributing bread all over the county, as far as Bundoran. There is also a bakery in Ballyshannon, Bundoran and Buncrana, and I think there is one in Moville and in Letterkenny.

There is probably in all 30 bread vans. In my considered opinion 8-10 bread vans would do, if the areas were confined so that no motor van would be allowed to go no more than 10 miles from the bakery and that no bakery should distribute bread within 3 miles of the bakery by motor vans, as this could easily be done by horse vans. If this were done the savings in Oil and Petrol would be enormous. I would say a similar rule should apply to all other merchandise.

We have in West Donegal at the present time, the best herring fishing which we have had for the past 20 years. We have lorries carrying the fish from here to Derry, Belfast and Dublin with the result that the consumption of petrol must be enormous, and unfortunately today some of the boats are held up for want of Oil and Petrol. If you prohibited the lorries carrying the fish beyond the railway stations there would be a large amount of petrol and oil saved. In my opinion, there would be no difficulty in getting a connection if the herring were handed in to the Donegal Railway Co at Killybegs, Glenties, Fintown and on to the LLSR at Letterkenny.

If you confine the bread service to the areas convenient to the bakery of course you would have to insist that no bakery would take advantage of such a position by insisting on a very heavy penalty, the min being £100. I think that if such a scheme were adopted the price of a 4lb loaf could be reduced by 1 penny..."[9]

The Suez Crisis in 1956 caused fuel rationing to be re-introduced; the Cope's fuel requirements had to be sanctioned by the Department of Industry and Commerce, Petroleum Oils Division, D'Olier St Dublin. The Cope had five vehicles at this time:

---

9   *IAOS Records (1088/871/8), National Archive Dublin; letter from Patrick Gallagher to the Department of Industry and Commerce, 31st December 1940. It would also have occurred to Paddy that the Cope would benefit from the creation of such local monopolies!*

Dungloe Road Station, in a photograph taken in c1950. The line, from which the track which had been ripped up ten years previously, can still be seen clearly. Photographs of Dungloe Road station cannot convey of course just how busy the station was in its heyday, nor how important it was to the Cope for delivery of vital supplies and exporting Cope goods, e.g. eggs, and knitwear (Derry Harbour Museum Collection).

Crolly Bridge station was also closed in 1940; this fine photograph dates from the 1930s. Crolly is on the borders of the Rosses, just on the Gweedore side. It was at Crolly station that Paddy, being escorted to Derry Jail by Sergeant Kirk and Constables Healy and Moore, was joined in his carriage by the manager of the Crolly Hotel, Paddy Gallagher (no relation) and Mr Thomas Hamilton, the excise officer at Dungloe. A bottle of whiskey was produced and...best to let Paddy tell the story in his far more entertaining way, including how he, a Justice of the Peace at the time, had been sent to Derry Jail by his fellow J.P.s (Photograph Micheal O Dhomnaill Collection; 'My Story', Paddy the Cope, Templecrone Press, 2006)

This photograph was taken in c1950; the Dungloe Road station building is still in a very good state of repair today (Derry Harbour Museum Collection).

- two petrol lorries: a Ford ZP678; Ford ZP 952 (2.5 tons unladen);
- two diesel lorries: ZP1801 (6 tons); ZP1584 (2-3 tons)
- a Morris Van ZP 2907 (half a ton)
"...100 gallons a month were required for transport of dairy produce (eggs)..."[10]

John McCarthy, living in the Rectory, Maghery, wrote about the motorised tea vans in the 1970s:

"...Besides the Maghery outpost and supermarket in Dungloe, Templecrone Co-Op has other branches in Burtonport, next in volume to the Dungloe supermarket, Annagry, Kincasslagh, Lettermacaward and Meenbanad. In addition, there are three mobile shops mounted on trucks which travel daily to distant points in the Rosses and serve those rural areas where the population is too sparse to support a branch store. These travelling marts carry groceries, clothing and other necessity items. In addition to the three mobile shop trucks, the Templecrone Co-op owns five other large lorries which are used to deliver supplies to their branches, to their other wholesale customers and farm implements and bulky building materials ordered by their retail rural customers..."[11]

In the Seventies, the Cope expanded the fleet significantly; the size of the lorries would necessitate a shift away from the back of the main Store – it was getting

---

10   *IAOS records as above*

11   *The Irish Times 16th November 1972*

The Cope Minute Book, 11th October 1918, records that "a motor lorry should be purchased, cost £205". The first one was a Ford Model T Lorry; the example here is in a very well preserved state in Cork at the premises of Flemings' Motors. The battering that the roads of the Rosses gave the Cope's lorries has resulted in none surviving locally in any state. The three photographs here show what the Cope's Model T would have looked like and are courtesy of Flemings' Motors in Boherbue, Mallow, Co Cork (www.flemingsmotors.ie).

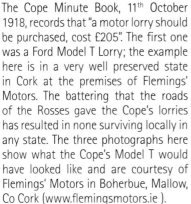

very hard with the bigger vehicles to reverse down the narrow alley by the post office. Cyril Winder, General Manager, writing in 1975 explained the rationale behind the expansion:

> "...Last year we not only replaced 4 vehicles but we increased their carrying capacity as it was identified that overloading from increased trade was a major factor in repair costs. Also there were predicted economies in large scale vehicle operation. Our 25-ton Hino is opening new opportunities not only in better buying and transportation but also in access to better sources of supply. To this end we spent money in enlarging and improving our warehousing towards greater accommodation and efficiencies in handling bigger loads. We have recently acquired our first fork lift for even greater use of the Hino and also for better space utilisation and handling in our stores..."

(Note: a 'Hino' is a Japanese truck manufacturer. J Harris Assemblers of Naas Road Dublin have been importing and assembling Hino trucks since 1967 and supplied the 25-ton Cyril Winder refers to above. Chapter 4 has a photograph of this Hino and the Cope's first forklift, a Henley Hawk)

Mr Winder continued:

> "…Few people are aware of the enormous cost of transportation in this remote corner of Ireland and the dispersed areas we serve with poor roads. Transport costs last year were our second biggest expense item, amounting to £45,000, covering our nine vehicles. Yet they are an essential part of our service and means of acquiring the goods we want at the right time, more particularly in these days of external transport rationalisation. At this juncture, I would compliment our transport staff for their performance in a difficult exacting job, as there is hardly any reference to them in our sales reports…"[12]

In 1975 the nine vehicles in the Cope Transport fleet were:

Hino Lorry	1975
Ford Lorry D800	1972
Commer Walk Through, 2 tons	1972
Commer Walk Through, 2 tons	1975
Commer Walk Through, 3 tons	1975
Ford Transit, 25 cwt.	1973
Ford Transit, 25 cwt.	1974
Ford Transit, 35 cwt.	1975
Ford Escort Van, 15 cwt.	1970

Note: 'cwt.' stands for 1 hundredweight which is 112 pounds or roughly 51 kilograms, so 25 cwt. = 1,270 kilograms.

Trading Overseas

Paddy saw the potential for selling Cope wares abroad very early on – in 1911 and 1912, he was in Scotland and England, ending up in London at the Gaelic League's Aonach, where he was very successful (Chapter 5 gives further details). If he had access to the facilities we have today, an airport at Carrickfin and international travel being that much easier, Paddy would have been travelling all over the world selling Cope produce and the Co-operative idea.

Paddy made a number of trips, three in all, to the States, ostensibly on business (he always used every opportunity to sell the Cope's wares) but as much to do with having a break and seeing his many friends and relatives over there. There was also the attraction for him of his growing celebrity which preceded him. He was well-known - a legend almost - among the Irish community there, particularly with Rosses people but he had also become known through American journalists and researchers visiting Dungloe; speakers visiting the

---

12 *'Commemorative Souvenir of our first £1,000,000 in Sales and Services 1975', Cope Archive.*

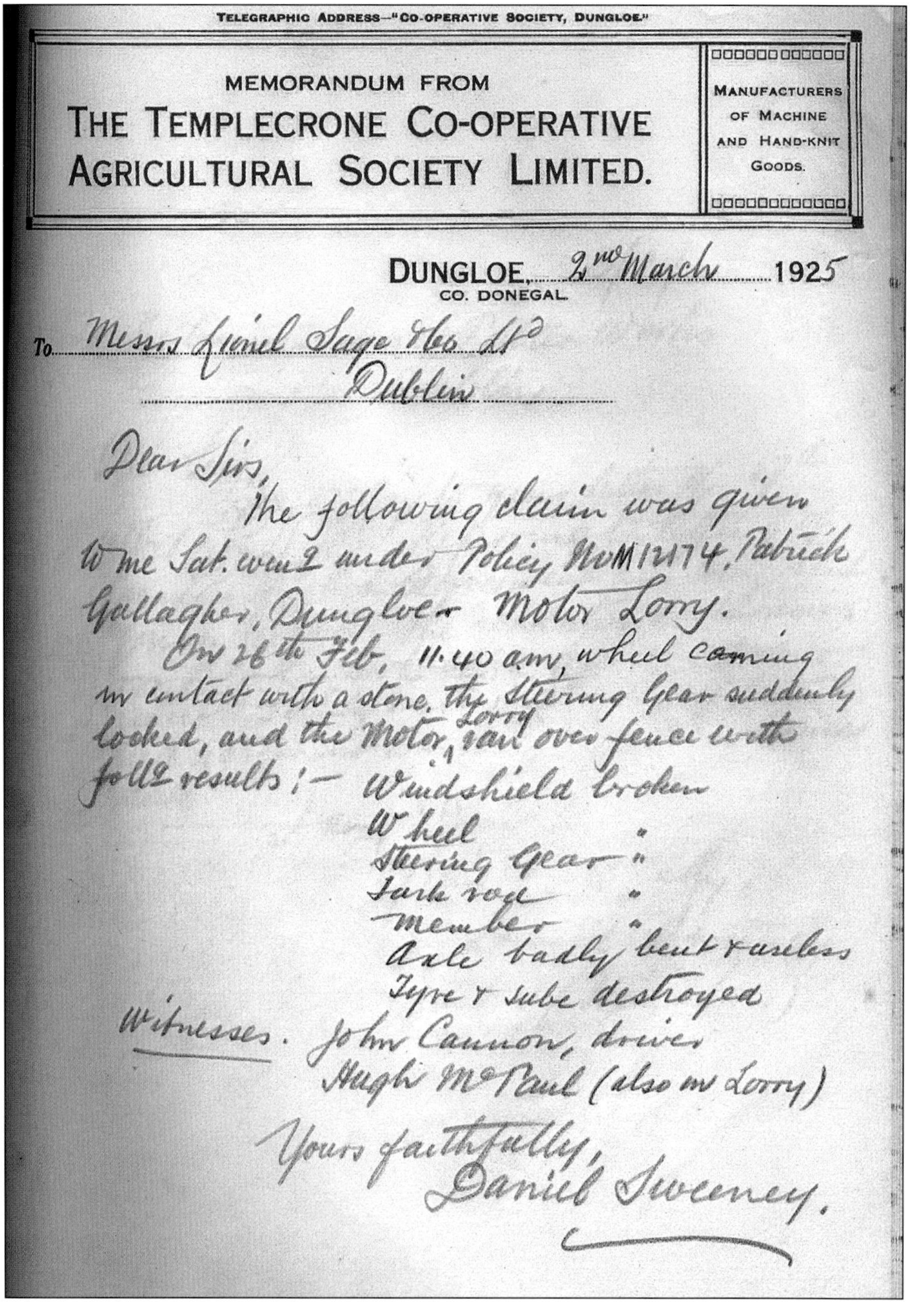

TELEGRAPHIC ADDRESS—"CO-OPERATIVE SOCIETY, DUNGLOE."

MEMORANDUM FROM

THE TEMPLECRONE CO-OPERATIVE AGRICULTURAL SOCIETY LIMITED.

MANUFACTURERS
OF MACHINE
AND HAND-KNIT
GOODS.

DUNGLOE, 2nd March 1925
CO. DONEGAL.

To Messrs Lionel Sage & Co Ltd
Dublin

Dear Sirs,

The following claim was given to me Sat. wen2 under Policy No M12174, Patrick Gallagher, Dungloe Motor Lorry.

On 26th Feb, 11.40 a.m, wheel coming in contact with a stone, the steering gear suddenly locked, and the Motor Lorry, ran over fence with foll2 results :— Windshield broken

Wheel "
Steering Gear "
Sark rod "
Member "
Axle badly bent & useless
Tyre & tube destroyed

Witnesses. John Cannon, driver
Hugh McPaul (also on Lorry)

Yours faithfully,
Daniel Sweeney.

Insuring men and vehicles was very important to the Cope – they were very diligent about this, with just cause. In this claim letter to Lionel Sage & Co Ltd, the Cope's Insurers in 1924, Daniel Sweeney, Cope Secretary, reports a traffic incident against policy number M12174. Driver John Cannon, with Hugh McPaul also on board, hit a stone on the road, the steering gear locked and the lorry crashed (Cope Letter Book 1924/25, Jim the Cope Archive).

The Story of the Cope

States and Canada, like AE, Horace Plunkett et al, would reference Paddy and the Templecrone Cope as an excellent example of what could be achieved in the most difficult of circumstances with grit and cooperation.

> "…The famous Patrick Gallagher, better known as "Paddy the-Cope" was in Cork yesterday, on his way to Cobh, to embark on a liner for his third visit to America. Energetic as ever, despite his 76 years, Paddy intends combining business with pleasure on his trip to the United States…"[13]

Sally the Cope's memoir has Paddy going to Dublin in 1947 to get a passport:

> "…Paddy said, "Well, the first thing I had to do was to go to the barracks and ask for a passport. The Sergeant took a sheet of paper from his desk and asked me my age. I said, "Seventy-six years last Christmas night." He then said, "Give me your birth certificate?" I said, "I never had one and I was in America twice before, and they never asked me for it." He said, "The regulations are very strict now, you must have a birth certificate." After a good deal of trouble I got a copy of my birth certificate. My father and mother's name and Cleendra as the place of birth was there all right, but my name was down as Pat, and the date of my birth was down as the 23rd. May, 1871…"

Sally's account continues with Paddy's friends (Donal, Denis and Gracie) giving their views on this date of birth:

Donal:	That is a damn lie. I am ten years older than you Paddy, you were never called Pat, and you were born on Christmas night.
Denis:	I'll swear on the book that you were born on Christmas night. Sure I was at your Christening. It was Charlie Given and Rosha that stood for you. I remember Rosha handing you to your mother saying: "Nancy, that is your wee Pat, God bless him, he is a fine child!" Now I remember your mother saying, "We shall call him Paddy, that's what they called Pat's father, and if he is half as good a man as his grandfather, I'll be content."
Gracie:	Paddy, was it in writing that you were born in May
Paddy:	It was. The sergeant has it now.
Denis:	The hell with the writing, sure some people will write anything that fits them…"[14]

---

13 *The Irish Times 23rd August 1947*

14 *Sally the Cope Gallagher, Personal Memoir, c1947, Limerick City Museum Archives*

The Transport Staff photographed in 1981 with some of the Cope vans and lorries behind them. Back: Casmir McGill, Patrick McCahill, Packie Boyle, Jimmy Sweeney, James McDyer, Eamon Boyle. Front: Barney McElhinney, Jimmy Durnin, Jimmy O'Donnell, Peter Healy, Patrick Ward (Panda), Michael Wallace, Peter Boyle, Michael Breslin (Builders' Providers) and Pat Boyle. Tony Cannon was regrettably absent when the photo was taken (Cope Archive)

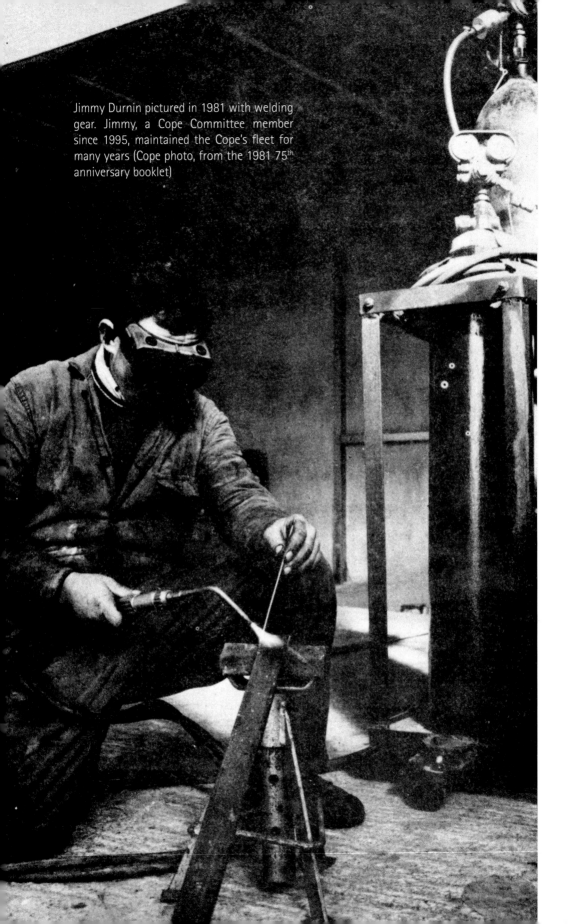

Jimmy Durnin pictured in 1981 with welding gear. Jimmy, a Cope Committee member since 1995, maintained the Cope's fleet for many years (Cope photo, from the 1981 75th anniversary booklet)

Jimmy Durnin and Peter Boyle pictured in 1981, outside the recently built maintenance shed for the Cope transport fleet, at the end of the new Cope car park (Cope Photo Archive)

Jimmy Durnin again, some 25 years later, still working – he is next to a digger engaged in breaking ground for the Sheskinarone Road Builders' Providers (Cope Photo, 2006).

Charlie Gallagher, Cope Transport Department, standing next to the Cope's delivery van, outside the new Carpets and Furniture department (Cope photo, 2006).

Paddy's precise date of birth is not easy to pin down: in the 1939 edition of 'My Story' he says he was born on Christmas Day 1873; in the revised edition (1948) he changes this to Christmas night 1871. His birth certificate (found by Lawrence Scanlon, who wrote an academic study of Paddy's autobiography) gives Paddy's date of birth as 23rd May 1871 (the birth was registered on July 7th 187!). It seems pretty clear, from Sally's account and Paddy's family's memory, that this is wrong in one respect anyway – it is incontrovertible that Paddy was been born on 25th December and not the 23rd May – but what year?

Professor Scanlon and historian Packie Bonner, conversing in October 1990, came to the conclusion that the actual date must therefore be 25th December 1870 – there were penalties for late reporting of births and it may have been difficult for the family to get to Glenties to report the birth in the winter of 1870/1.[15] Paddy's passport for travelling to the States in 1929 has yet another date: January 1872 - giving five different dates in all!

---

15 *'The Story He Left Behind Him' Lawrence Scanlon, 1994, University Press of America*

TELEGRAPHIC ADDRESS—"CO-OPERATIVE SOCIETY, DUNGLOE."

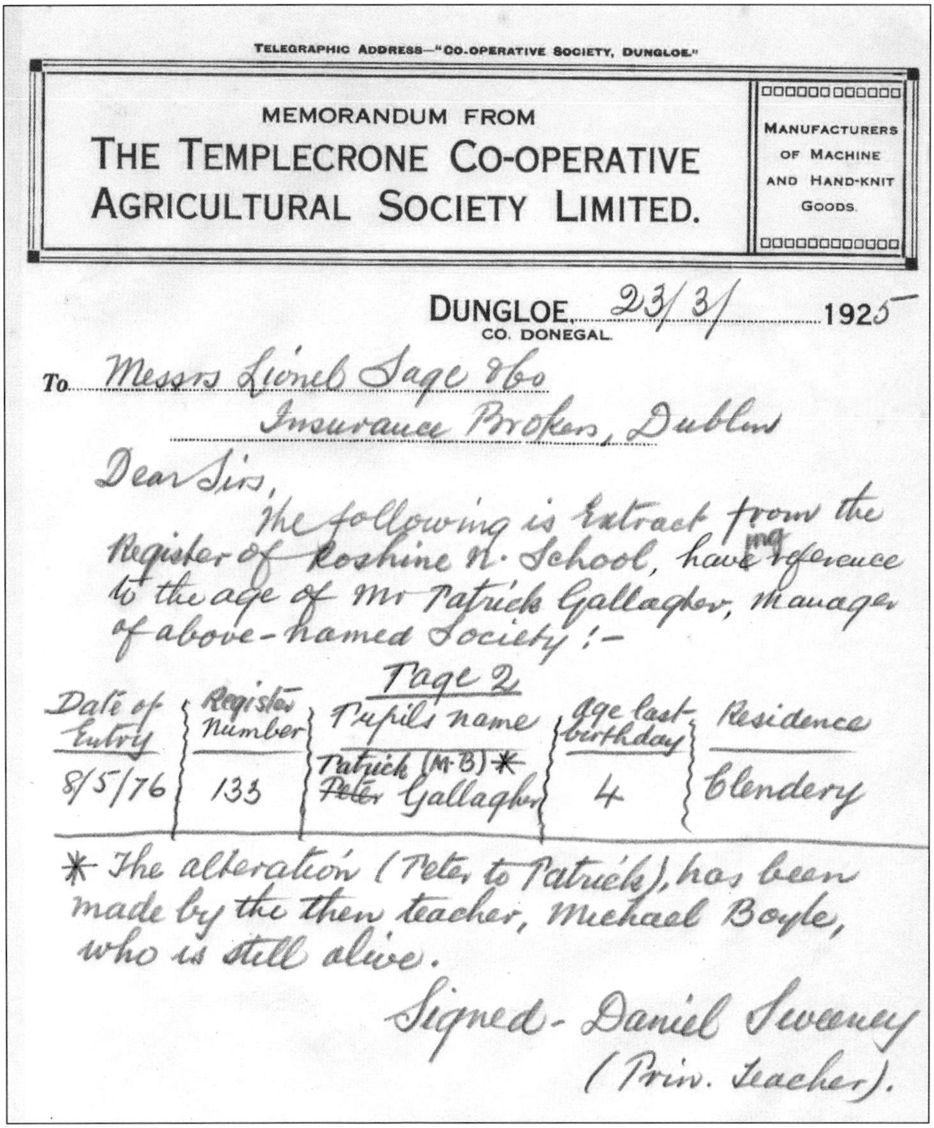

MEMORANDUM FROM
THE TEMPLECRONE CO-OPERATIVE AGRICULTURAL SOCIETY LIMITED.

MANUFACTURERS OF MACHINE AND HAND-KNIT GOODS.

DUNGLOE, 23/3/ 1925
CO. DONEGAL.

To Messrs Lionel Sage & Co
Insurance Brokers, Dublin

Dear Sirs,

The following is extract from the Register of Roshine N. School, having reference to the age of Mr Patrick Gallagher, manager of above-named Society:-

Page 2

Date of Entry	Register Number	Pupils name	Age last birthday	Residence
8/5/76	133	Patrick (M.B.)* ~~Peter~~ Gallagher	4	Clendery

* The alteration (Peter to Patrick), has been made by the then teacher, Michael Boyle, who is still alive.

Signed - Daniel Sweeney
(Prin. teacher).

Pinning down Paddy the Cope's birthday for his passport and life insurance purposes proved to be very difficult. This is an extract from the school register for Roshine School which gives Paddy's name as Peter (Cope Letter Book)

The date arrived at by Laurence Scanlon and Packie Bonner, 25th December 1970, seems the most plausible; it would make Paddy about 9½ years of age when he was first to the Lagan.

When the Cope was trying to insure Paddy's life in 1924 for £10,000, a huge amount of money then (equivalent to well over £1 million today), lack of certainty about his birthday caused some headaches in getting a quotation. Not only was it difficult to pin down his date of birth, it appears that he was in the Roshine school register as Peter not Patrick Gallagher.[16]

16 The Cope Letter Book, 1924-5, letters by Daniel Sweeney, Cope Secretary.

COMHARTHAÍ SÓIRT.
PERSONAL DESCRIPTION.
SIGNALEMENT.

		A BHEAN CHÉILE. Wife. Femme.
Gairm / Profession / Profession	Co-Op Society Manager	
Ait agus dáta beireatais / Place and date of birth / Lieu et date de naissance	Donegal Jan 7 1872	
Ait chomhnaithe / Domicile / Domicile	Irish Free State.	
Aoirde / Height / Taille	5' 6"	
Aghaidh / Face / Visage	Round	
Dath na súl / Colour of eyes / Couleur des yeux	Blue	
Dath na gruaige / Colour of hair / Couleur des cheveux	Grey	
Comharthaí fé leith / Special peculiarities / Signes particuliers		

LEANBHAÍ - CHILDREN - ENFANTS.

Ainm / Name / Nom	Aois / Age / Age	Innscne / Sex / Sexe

DÁ MHNAOI CHÉILE. WIFE - FEMME.

issued. *Patrick Gallagher* — 3. JAN. 1929

PAS. PASSPORT.

SAORSTÁT ÉIREANN · IRISH FREE STATE ·

Mc Patrick Gallagher.

Paddy first went to the United States in 1929 (he was to travel there three times in all, again in 1939 and 1947). It was, as he said, "...his first holiday in 22 years since he started in the Cope..." It was both a business trip, to show samples of Cope knitwear to American buyers, but in reality it was an opportunity to see friends and relations who had left the Rosses long before. His passport, no. 104552, was issued by Saorstát Éireann, The Irish Free State, on 3rd January 1929. In those days, the Irish passport still had a reference to 'His Britannic Majesty' and James McNeill, the Governor General of the Irish Free State. The American Visa was stamped at the American Consulate in Dublin on 8 January with $10 worth of 'fee stamps'; it allowed Paddy a four week stay in the States. We learn that Paddy was 5' 6" in height; he had blue eyes and grey hair (he was in his late fifties by then). His birthday is given as January 1872. (Passport courtesy of Sally the Cope Gallagher, Gallagher Family collection)

VISAS

mitted at _New York_
.... 19__ under Para-
ph .... Section ___ Immigration Act
1924, for _____

Immigrant Inspector

VISAS

AMERICAN CONSULATE
at _Dublin_ _Ireland_
     (City)   (Country)   No. 150

SEEN
for the journey to the United States

via _any port_

_____ _January 192_

American $1.00 FEE STAMP

America $39.00 FEE STAMP

Visa granted as
Non-Immigrant under
Section 3 (2) of the Act of 1924

Temporary

_____ **Vice Consul**

---

imid-ne, Seamus MacNéill, Seanascal Shaorstáit
...........Shoillse Briotani, a iarraidh agus a éileomh
...........mbaineann leigint don tsealbhóir dul ar
.......gan cosc agus gach cuinamh agus caomhna is
          do thabhairt d'_____

James McNeill, Esquire, Governor General of
Free State. Request and require, in the Name of His
ric Majesty, all those whom it may concern to allow
...er to pass freely without let or hindrance, and to afford
.... every assistance and protection of which
.... may stand in need.

...us, James McNeill, Gouverneur Général
t Libre d'Irlande, prions et requérons les Autorités
...tes au nom de sa Majesté Britannique de permettre
...eur de passer librement et de lui donner toute aide,
...ce et protection partout et en toute circonstance où
...era.

1

Tá 32 leathanach sa phas so.
This passport contains 32 pages.
Ce passeport contient 32 pages.

PAS.
PASSPORT.
PASSEPORT.

SAORSTÁT ÉIREANN.
IRISH FREE STATE.
ÉTAT LIBRE D'IRLANDE.

140552

Uimhir an PHAIS
No. of PASSPORT }
No. du PASSEPORT } : 140552

AINM AN TSEALBHORA
NAME OF BEARER } : _Mc Patrick Gallagher_
NOM DU PORTEUR

Agus a bhean chéile lena chois, i.
Accompanied by his Wife } : ....
Accompagné de sa femme

                mar aon le } { leanbh
                and }........... { children
                et de } { enfants

NÁISIUNTACHT
NATIONAL STATUS } : Citizen of the Irish Free State and
NATIONALITÉ   of the British Commonwealth of
                       Nations

662/47

MOVILLE PIER.

Below: American Liners at Moville c1905. Moville was the nearest pickup and drop off point for passengers for America, boarding ships that would start from Glasgow; tenders would deliver passengers and freight to the ships in deeper water. Paddy travelled this way on his way to America in 1929. Many of his friends and relations emigrated to the States in this way, some never to return (PB collection; Valentine's Dublin postcard).

American Liners at Moville, Lough Foyle

Left Top: Passengers are collecting around the pick-up point in Moville, waiting for the tender, which can be seen at the end of the wooden jetty, which would take them out to the waiting liners for America. Paddy made the journey in this way in 1929, his first trip to the States, leaving on 26th January on the way to New York. After driving from Dungloe, he had called in on the way to see his son Jim who was at St Columb's in Derry (Contemporary 1920s postcard, courtesy PJ Kelly collection and thanks to Helen Windsor for her help).

America was where many of Paddy the Cope's family and friends had emigrated, in the nineteenth and early part of the twentieth century. When Paddy travelled to America for the first time in 1929, he was almost 60. His trip was as much about seeing them all again before it was too late, as it was to sell Cope wares. This postcard of New York Harbour dates from the 1900-1910 period and has a mixture of steamships and sail boats, reflecting a period of transition in ocean-going travel (PB Collection).

"...At our Committee meeting on the 11 January 1929, I told them that I would like to go to America. I had a nice range of samples to show the American buyers. I said that since I started the Cope in 1906, twenty-two years ago, I had never had a holiday, and that would like to see my sisters, cousins and other relations again. None of the Committee spoke, for what I thought, a long time..." (Paddy the Cope, 1939).

The Committee were none too happy about Paddy going; he was indispensable to the Cope's success. However John Gillespie sided with Paddy, agreement was reached and Paddy made the trip, promising to look up relations of and bring gifts from Committee members.

ANCHOR LINE—TURBINE TWIN-SCREW STEAMSHIP "CAMERONIA."

The Anchor Line's SS "Cameronia" steamed between Glasgow, Londonderry, Halifax (Canada) and New York. Passengers were picked up from the tender from Derry. Paddy travelled to New York on this boat on 26th January 1929, arriving in Halifax, Nova Scotia, Canada on February 2nd and then New York on February 5th. Paddy recalls that the reason that the Cameronia stopped off at Halifax was "to discharge 4,000 cases of liquor" (not from the Cope!) which would then have been smuggled into the States, then in the Prohibition era (1920-33) (PB collection, Anchor Line official postcard).

Name of Ship "CAMERONIA"

Steamship Line—ANCHOR.

NAMES AND DESCRIPTIONS OF **BRITISH** PASSENGERS EM

(1) Contract Ticket Number.	(2) NAMES OF PASSENGERS.		(3) LAST ADDRESS IN THE UNITED KINGDOM.	(4) CLASS. (Whether 1st, 2nd or 3rd.)	(5) Port at which Passengers have contracted to land.	Pr Occu Ca Pa
L1819	Mary	McGuire	Dungloe. Co.Donegal.	R2	NEW YORK	Hou
L1820	Patrick	Gallagher	Dungloe. Co.Donegal	Do.	Do.	Mar
				Do.	Do.	
				Do.	Do.	
				Do.	Do.	

The Story of the Cope

Paddy is silent as to what he got up to on the Cameronia but it is unlikely he took part in the various 'high jinks' that used to be part and parcel of life on board the long and otherwise monotonous journey by sea to the States before air travel (PB Collection, SS Cameronia postcard, c1920s).

Date of Departure _____ 26th JANUARY _1929._

HALIFAX &

Where bound—NEW YORK.

THE PORT OF LONDONDERRY.

(7)						(8)						(9)
.GES OF PASSENGERS.						Country of last Permanent Residence.†						Country of Intended Future Permanent Residence.†
12 years wards.		Children between 1 and 12.		Infants.								
Not Accompanied by husband or wife.						England.	Wales.	Scotland.	Northern Ireland.	Irish Free State.	Other Parts of the British Empire. Foreign Countries.	
Males.	Females.	Males.	Females.	Males.	Females.							
	46									7		Irish Free State
45										1		"
1	1	•	•	،	،					2		U.S.A

This is the entry recording Paddy's travel on board the SS Cameronia – he is listed as a "British" passenger boarding at Londonderry. Travelling with him is Mary McGuire from Dungloe. Paddy's age is given as 45, but he would have been 59 at this time. Paddy recalls how the trip came about in his autobiography: '...In December, 1928, Miss Mary Ann McGuire, a great friend of ours, who was then living in Dungloe, and who is now proprietress of Carrigart Hotel, decided to go to the States. She had previously been there. She was also interested in knitting. I made up my mind to go with her, if the Committee would agree. In fact I had made all arrangements before I asked permission from them...' (Anchor Line records and Paddy's 'My Story').

NEW YORK HARBOR AT NIGHT

Above: An atmospheric contemporary postcard showing a liner arriving in New York in the 1920s. (PB Collection)

Paddy would book his business and pleasure trips overseas via his sister Sarah who was a shipping agent; here Sarah (Brennan) is standing outside the Bridge End Bar (now known as Cannon's) with her daughter Mary Ellen Brennan (Walsh) who helped Paddy put together 'My Story' and typed up the first manuscript published in 1939. (Photo courtesy Packie Walsh, Burtonport)

Left Bottom: Paddy's second trip to America was on the Anchor Line's TSS "Transylvania". He travelled to New York on 19th August 1939 (just before war broke out between Britain and Germany on 3rd September), bringing Cope knitwear samples for the American market. This was the Transylvania's last commercial journey from Glasgow-Moville-New York before being requisitioned as an armed merchant cruiser. On 10th August 1940 the German submarine U-56 torpedoed her, 35 miles west of Inishtrahull, Northern Ireland and although taken in tow, she sank with the loss of 48 lives. Paddy was lucky not to share the fate of those on the SS Athenia (going from Glasgow to Montreal) which was sunk off Inishtrahull 3 hours after war was declared (PB collection, contemporary postcard).

First Class · CABINE DE LUXE · SMOKING ROOM · LOUNGE · DINING ROOM

SMOKING ROOM · Third Class · STATEROOM · LOUNGE

LOUNGE · Second Class · SMOKING ROOM · DINING ROOM

Left: The TSS Transylvania, launched in 1925 at Govan, Glasgow, was a well appointed ship. Paddy's cousin Neil O'Donnell was on the same crossing, but had booked in First Class. Neil said Paddy should travel with him but Paddy could not justify to himself the expense; eventually they compromised and both travelled Second Class. Seamus McManus, the celebrated Donegal writer, alerted the Captain that Paddy was on board and he was invited to dine at the Captain's table (PB collection, on board letter-card of TSS Transylvania)

> *"...On 18 October 1939, I did go to New York, met Johnny Curran who introduced me to that famous artist, Terry Long, who put me sitting in front of the microphone, saying: 'Now Paddy, fire away.' I made a wee speech. When I had finished I was sure I made a hell of a mess of it, but Terry and Johnny said I put it over swell..."* ('My Story', Paddy the Cope)

Paddy returned from America on the USS Harding on 25th October 1939, after war had broken out. Paddy's sister Bridget in Rockaway New Jersey said that nothing could happen to Paddy, that no German would dare touch the SS President Harding, named as it was after an American President. Later on, the USS Harding was drafted into war service and on 14th May 1940, she was attacked by German aircraft in the River Scheldte in Holland, was beached and burnt out. In 1952, she was taken apart for scrap. (PB collection, official postcard of shipping company).

LONDON: CHARING CROSS AND STRAND.

Paddy travelled to Holland in January 1936 to buy a cargo of cement and other goods. He stayed at the Charing Cross Hotel (on the right in this photo from c1910-20) in London, where he would catch the boat train to Dover, then on to the Hook of Holland. On his way to the hotel, he met Rosses man James Doherty, who had business experience 'out foreign' as Paddy puts

it. After a good long talk about friends back home, James gave him sound advice and sorted Paddy out with boat train tickets with some Dutch currency (Photochrom real photo postcard c1920s, PB Collection).

Rotterdam. Hotel Atlanta ad Coolsingel

On his buying trip to Holland, Paddy stopped off in Vlaardingen where he bought 400 tons of artificial manure, called superphosphate, for the Cope, saving £225 in the process, from Co-Operative Superfosfaatfabrieken. He then travelled on to Rotterdam, where he chartered a steamer, the 'm.v. Beta'. While in Rotterdam, Paddy stayed at the Atlanta Hotel, illustrated in this contemporary 1930s postcard.(PB Collection)

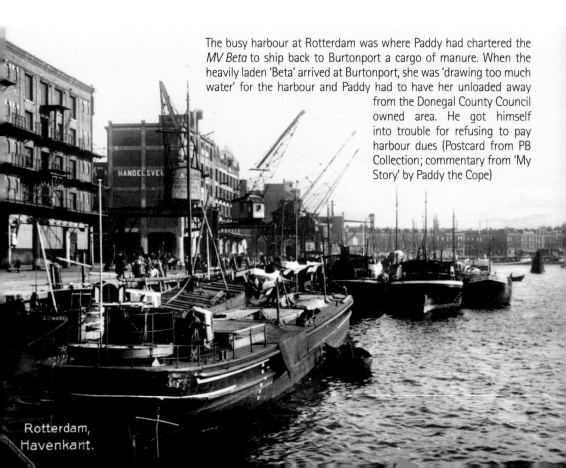

The busy harbour at Rotterdam was where Paddy had chartered the MV Beta to ship back to Burtonport a cargo of manure. When the heavily laden 'Beta' arrived at Burtonport, she was 'drawing too much water' for the harbour and Paddy had to have her unloaded away from the Donegal County Council owned area. He got himself into trouble for refusing to pay harbour dues (Postcard from PB Collection; commentary from 'My Story' by Paddy the Cope)

Rotterdam,
Havenkant.

Chapter 10

GRANITE and SOAPSTONE

"...If a traveller visits the district he wonders how men ever came to settle there, what necessity drove them to make their homes in a region where the rocky ribs of earth stick everywhere through its skin..." (AE, George Russell)

Mining and quarrying were never a major long-term component of the Cope's business. However, Paddy was always on the lookout for ways to make use of the local assets of the Rosses: the various ways he exploited the plentiful water supply (the mill, electricity, and fishing) are a clear example of his way of thinking. He also turned his thoughts to another abundant local 'resource': the ubiquitous rocks, which were mainly composed of granite but with local seams of valuable soapstone at Crohy Head. Both had been tried before by others but Paddy could see opportunities both for employment and extending the Cope's business.

CRICKAMORE GRANITE

Granite quarrying had been under consideration in the Rosses since at least the middle of the nineteenth century; a prospectus for Donegal granite was issued in 1887 which was fulsome in its praise for the "practically inexhaustible" granite of the Rosses. This deposit was especially prized for its colour and particular hardness: "...The unquestionable beauty, rare quality, great variety and exceptional abundance..."[1] A narrow gauge railway was built to a quay on the shore at Milltown; the line of the track can still be seen.

Just before the Cope period, granite was being quarried and exported:

> "...Yesterday the Duke of Abercorn witnessed at Burtonport, County Donegal, the ceremony of lowering into the steamship Turtle the first block of granite of the first consignment from the recently reopened quarries. The quality of Donegal granite is celebrated, and the highest hopes have been formed regarding the new venture. His Grace congratulated the workmen on the successful start. Later the Duke visited the fish-curing stations on Rutland and Inishcoo islands, and was presented with a memorial from the fishermen praying him to use his influence to have the railway extended to Burtonport. His Grace reminded the deputation that he was not a member of the Government. He would, however do all he could..."[2]

---

1   *Prospectus for Donegal Granite Quarries 1887*

2   *Irish Times, Sept 17th 1896*

Next Page: This 'Bird's Eye Sketch' is an artist's impression of Dungloe by Philip Brannon of the Geological Survey. It dates from 1887 and is possibly the earliest view of the town. It was included in a prospectus for Donegal Granite which was designed to draw in investors (PB Collection).

W.B.JONES & CO. LIVERPOOL.

LAKES

BIRDS' EYE SKETCH OF THE DONEGAL GRANITES; THEIR &

Note.—THE DOTTED LINE IN I

SOUTH.

IN DUNGLOE BAY, LOOKING WEST TO ARRANMORE ISLAND.

INDICATES THE DEEP CHANNELS.

The granite deposits in Dungloe gained publicity across Britain – and also in the United States:

IRISH GRANITE

"...Donegal now threatens the supremacy of Scotland in the matter of granite. Experts, who have been paying extended visits of inspection in the neighbourhood of Dungloe, in West Donegal, report immense formations of granite, which for variety of shade, durability and general beauty are said to rival the famous products of Aberdeen and Peterhead. The Dungloe granite, it is stated, embraces almost every variety of color and texture, the predominating shade being red and flesh-colored stones of medium and coarse grain. A still more beautiful variety of stone, which is found in Dungloe, is the very dark micaceous granite, closely resembling the handsome "Labrador," with which many London buildings are pillared. When it is remembered that one firm alone In America imports $95,000 worth of polished granite yearly from Aberdeen and that the demands for the highest class stone in all shades is ever on the increase, there should be thriving times for Donegal in the near future..."[3]

James Sweeney, whose shop in Dungloe the Cope was to make their long-term base in 1912, also tried his hand at making something out of the local granite.

"...By 1908, after six years of railway transport, the granite business had still not produced anything. James Sweeney, a local businessman, lost £1,000 by investing in a company, which intended to develop the granite and make the Rosses district the envy of Aberdeen, but it all came to nothing. A load was shipped out from time to time by sea but lack of investment capital and the reluctance of the CDB to invest the vast sums required for initial development left the granite in the ground. The Burtonport Extension and the L&LSR were both blamed for not co-operating with the proposed development and were further blamed for not quoting much lower prices for carriage but, in reality, without substantial funds to open up the quarries, there was never much chance of the quarries' success and the railway became an easy target to blame..."[4]

The reissued 1924 edition of the Irish Homestead pamphlet takes up the story as the Copeman decided to develop the Rosses' most plentiful 'asset':

---

3   From the Iowa newspaper the Dubuque Telegraph December 20th 1901 (articles like this were syndicated across America).

4   Extract from Frank Sweeney's excellent book on the Letterkenny and Burtonport Railway "That Old Sinner", Frank Sweeney (Irish History Press 2006): The CDB was the Congested Districts Board (1891-1923). It was set up to alleviate poverty and "congested" living conditions in the west of Ireland by paying for public works, such as building piers for small ports, to assist fishing, or by setting up local factories to give employment and help stop emigration.

"...There are vast possibilities in the excellent granite supplies of the district. Within a few hundred yards of the pier lies a practically endless supply of granite of the finest quality. A small start has already been made at dressing and set-making, and a convenient market procured for the output. With ample electric power at hand for drilling and polishing purposes, and with the boat leaving, as at present, practically empty, there are all the facilities (pier accommodation excepted) for making the undertaking a great success

THE GRANITE

Lying to the north of the village of Dungloe and about a mile inland, there is a long stretch of beautiful red granite, and in the immediate vicinity of the village to the south and west there is a still larger area of grey granite of the finest quality. Some 20 or 30 years ago the former was leased by a Newry company, and a considerable sum expended in machinery and other equipment, but after a few years the work ceased from some unaccountable cause. About 30 years previous an attempt was made to work the grey granite, but this was also dropped after a time.

These failures, however, were not enough to deter the Templecrone Society from a further attempt to exploit what must be considered as the only natural wealth of the Rosses. The Society here, as in all its other undertakings, treads with cautious steps. No flowery prospects are held forth, and no capital is subscribed or sought from workers or others. As in the case of the factory, the Society begins the quarrying operations in a modest way, falling back on its Reserve Fund for the initial funds necessary to start off, and aiming to make the work pay its way from the outset. A small piece of land with a quarry face was purchased for a few pounds, and half a score of men set to

Next Page: The Cope was not the first to try its hand at making money from the Rosses' most abundant asset: in 1887, a prospectus was issued for "The Donegal Granite Quarries Dungloe Co Donegal" which offered investment in 70 square miles of 'The Most Honourable The Marquis Conyngham's estate. "...The unquestionable beauty, rare quality, great variety and exceptional abundance of these granites, in combination with the very favourable circumstances under which they can be quarried and manufactured, *in situ*, into every possible form which granite can by manual skill or mechanical appliances be wrought..." – many people were seduced by such words and lost big money. Paddy and the Cope also lost money later – he was never paid for consignments sent to Liverpool This illustration, an extract from the 1887 prospectus, is a highly imaginative representation of the developments proposed at the Conyngham Mill in Dungloe with an aqueduct, railway and new buildings; the Church of Ireland church can be seen on the right with two thatched buildings now gone (PB Collection)

ISOMETRIC SKETCH OF THE PROPOSED DONEGAL GRANITES WHARF & W

TO BURTON PORT

High Road

Present Malt House

Present Dungloe Flour Mill

Existing Lime Kiln

PLAN

OF THE PROPOSED WORKS AT DUNGLOE,

FOR THE DRESSING AND POLISHING OF

THE DONEGAL GRANITES

With the existing and proposed new Buildings and Conduits, the Tramways from
Lefinn, Crocknegeerah, and Toberkeen Quarries, the Channel as cleared, Wharf, &c.

W. R. JONES & CO. LIVER

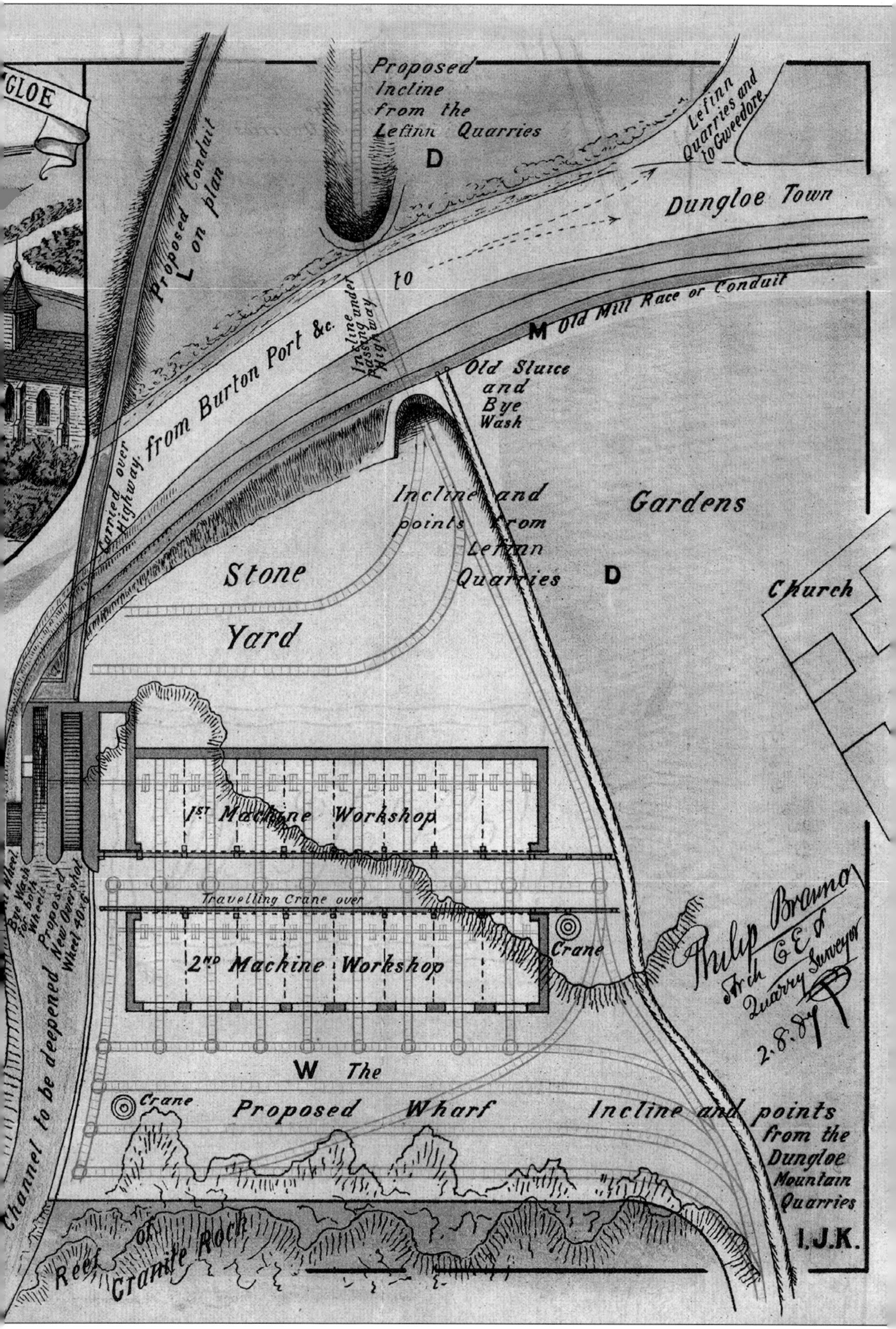

GLOE

Proposed
Incline
from the
Lefinn Quarries
D

Lefinn
Quarries and
to Gweedore.

Dungloe Town

Proposed Conduit L on plan

Incline under passing Highway

to

Carried over Highway from Burton Port &c.

M Old Mill Race or Conduit

Old Sluice
and
Bye
Wash

Incline and
points from
Lefinn
Quarries

Gardens

D

Church

Stone
Yard

1st Machine Workshop

Travelling Crane over

2nd Machine Workshop

Crane

Bye Wash for Lock Wheels

Proposed New Overshot Wheel 40'6"

Philip Bramo
Arch G E &
Quarry Surveyor
2.8.89

Channel to be deepened

Crane

W The

Proposed Wharf

Incline and points
from the
Dungloe
Mountain
Quarries

Reef of Granite Rock

I.J.K.

MEMORANDUM FROM

THE TEMPLECRONE CO-OPERATIVE AGRICULTURAL SOCIETY LIMITED.

MANUFACTURERS
OF MACHINE
AND HAND-KNIT
GOODS.

DUNGLOE, *26th Apr* 192 *4*
CO. DONEGAL.

To *Messrs Lionel Sage & Co Ltd*
Dublin.

Dear Sirs,
    Please cover under E I Insurance
4 workmen employed in quarrying & set-making.
no machinery employed.
    I am instructed to have the above workmen
covered at once. These works are just started
to-day, and it is expected to number may increase
to 40 n 50 workmen, of which I shall give you
particulars as work develops.
          Yours faithfully,
            Daniel Sweeney
              (agent)

work. Leading members of the Government have expressed their high appreciation of the spirit of self-help that pervades the district, and the Board of Fisheries have provided a competent man to teach set-making to the local workers.

After some weeks a first consignment of sets, mainly the work of the learners, has been shipped to Liverpool, where it has found a ready market. The dressing of the sets was satisfactory to the purchaser, and the quality of the stone was considered excellent. A quantity of lintel and pillar stones has also been dressed for local use. This is something encouraging to show for the few months the quarry is in operation. If the industry succeeds, and there is no reason to doubt that it will, the workers, in conjunction with their fellow-members, will find themselves in the unique position of being their own employers. There will be no capitalist to dispute their share of the profits, and whenever they desire a higher wage all they have got to do is to strike for more, and the harder the better. It is to be hoped that in these conditions it will grow and prosper, and afford another example of co-operative methods and co-operative ideals as applied to industry…"[5]

The Cope, in particular Daniel Sweeney the Secretary, was very mindful of its responsibilities to the people working for it. A surviving letter book (saved by

---

5   *Irish Homestead 1924 pamphlet on the Templecrone Co-op.*

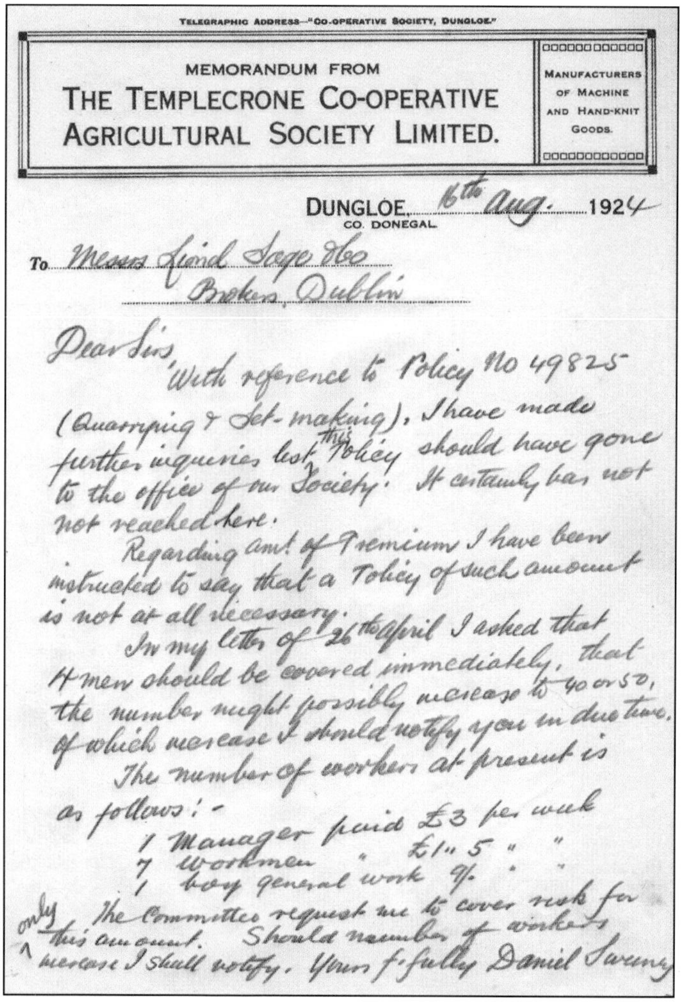

Memorandum from

THE TEMPLECRONE CO-OPERATIVE AGRICULTURAL SOCIETY LIMITED.

TELEGRAPHIC ADDRESS—"CO-OPERATIVE SOCIETY, DUNGLOE."

MANUFACTURERS OF MACHINE AND HAND-KNIT GOODS.

DUNGLOE, 16th Aug. 1924
CO. DONEGAL

To Messrs Lionel Sage & Co
Brokers Dublin

Dear Sirs,

With reference to Policy No 49825 (Quarrying & Set-making), I have made further inquiries lest this Policy should have gone to the office of our Society. It certainly has not reached here.

Regarding amt of Premium I have been instructed to say that a Policy of such amount is not at all necessary.

In my letter of 26th April I asked that 4 men should be covered immediately, that the number might possibly increase to 40 or 50, of which increase I should notify you in due time.

The number of workers at present is as follows :-

1 Manager paid £3 per week
7 Workmen " £1. 5 " "
1 boy general work 9/- " "

only the Committee request me to cover risk for this amount. Should number of workers increase I shall notify. Yours f.fully Daniel Sweeney

These two letters were written by Daniel Sweeney, Cope Secretary. They inform the Cope's Insurers, Messrs Lionel Sage and Company, of the start of granite quarrying in April 1924 with initially four workmen (and no machinery employed – it must have been tough going for them). The expectation was that up to 40-50 men would be employed there. The second letter in August that year has nine men working, a manager (Michael Kavanagh from Dublin) at £3 a week, seven workmen at £1 and 5 shillings, and a boy earning nine shillings a week. (Cope Letter Book; Jim (Packie) the Cope Gallagher Collection, with further detail from Irish Times September 17th 1924).

Jim (Packie the Cope) Gallagher) has 101 letters from February 1924 to April 1925 – all written longhand in pencil by Daniel Sweeney - on a wide range of subjects; there is much correspondence to the Cope's Insurers. The Cope was at pains to ensure that, in starting off the dangerous work of quarrying granite, its workers were well insured.

Paddy's dreams, of turning the Rosses granite into gold, fell foul of an unscrupulous trader: Paddy in good faith sent two boat-loads of granite sets but was never paid for them:

> "…We sent out two cargoes of sets to Liverpool and we never got a cent for them. This was the only English firm that ever let us down over our twenty years' dealings with the English people. Some time ago I was told that he was not an Englishman, although he could speak English fairly well. Would you believe neither 'AE' nor any other writer ever wrote a scrap about this big blunder on my part, and not one of the Committee ever blamed me…"[6]

This was pretty much the end of the Cope's granite business. However, Paddy, ever the business optimist, had not given up. He wrote to the IAOS in early 1939: "…We intend starting a granite quarry here…".The IAOS were not at all keen, they felt it would be a drag on the rest of the Society's business.[7] The Copeman was undeterred: the Derry People reported that "…Paddy the Cope had departed for the West of Ireland to purchase machinery for the opening of the Crickamore Granite Quarries and men were being recruited to work in them…" The war which broke out later that year and the closure of the railway in 1940 put paid to any prospect of the granite business being developed.

Today, Paddy would be surprised to learn that granite is being 'mined' for even bigger profits. Recent years have seen (and very much heard) rock-breakers working the granite to make sites for housing, something Paddy and many others from those times would find astonishing, given how many houses were deserted through emigration and the abundance of land in the Rosses.

SOAPSTONE AT CROHY HEAD

Commercial mining had been going on in Crohy since before 1886 and possibly as early as 1863 when an analysis of Donegal soapstone was published in the British Association Journal. In 1826, a professor from the Royal Dublin Society noted:

> "…At Croey, eight miles from Arranmore, you find extensive beds of talc slate, with imbedded, somewhat ironshot common pyrites. Common talc, asbestos, steatites, and jade occur in nests and globules. The mica slate is partly of a silver-white, partly of a pearl-white colour. The latter

---

6   *My Story, Paddy the Cope, Jonathan Cape 1939*

7   *IAOS records National Archives, letter dated 6th February 1939, and file notes at this time.*

A modern day photo (2006) showing the granite workings in Crickamore, on the Pole Road (so called because of the electricity and telephone poles erected along it in the 1950s – this used to be the main road from Burtonport to Dungloe – the Swilly bus still follows this route). The quarry is now very dangerous to visit, particularly in wet weather; there are large slabs of rock strewn about, it is very overgrown and there are hidden, deep pools of water. Not for the faint hearted – in fact to be avoided (PB Nov 2006 photo).

A small tray of polished Crickamore granite made for Paddy the Cope as a memento of the quarry (Sally the Cope Gallagher Collection).

variety passes into talc slate. The beds of talc slate run along the coast, and are very much decomposed, being washed by the tide..."[8]

In 1896, the North Of Ireland Mining Company, Dungloe, whose local agent was J.N. Warburton, were mining soapstone at Crohy Head with 19 underground workers and two on the surface. The Orchard Refinery Company of Harland Rd Belfast took over the soapstone mining rights for Crohy before 1918. Their Donegal agent was Burtonport's John Sweeney (Johnny Rua), a local merchant who established Sweeney's Hotel in 1904 for travellers and business people using the Lough Swilly Railway. In 1918, he repeated that he was mining between 20 and 40 tons of soapstone a week at Crohy Head.

Paddy the Cope will have been well aware of the Crohy mine from his childhood growing up in nearby Cleendra. When the mine closed, he would have had it in the back of his mind that the Cope might one day re-open it. A.M. Flagg writing in 1979 got Paddy's status slightly wrong: "More recent workings were undertaken by 'Paddy the Cope' an enterprising priest who raised soapstone for use in storage heaters up to about 1945" That would have amused Paddy!

Soapstone (scientific name 'steatite') is used for a variety of purposes: as talcum powder, in storage heaters, tailors' cloth markers and today, carving of ornaments etc. It is sometimes used for fireplace surrounds because it can absorb and evenly distribute heat while being easy to manufacture. The same heat-trapping property makes it suitable for the manufacture of woodstoves. It is also used today for griddles and other cookware. It feels soapy to the touch, giving it its name, and was found in mineable quantities near the surface in two other places in Donegal: Carrowtrasna, near Gartan Lough and Inishkil, near Glendowan. Paddy (Jim) the Cope remembers a big and very heavy old radiator containing soapstone in their house on the Quay Road, Dungloe.

Rex Herdman, from the family who built the fine house on Edernish, writing in 1970, recalls visits to Maghery in 1908-1911:

> "...There were also the ruins of an old soapstone quarry, and grinding mill. This is the only place soapstone exists in the British Isles. It is ground up to make French chalk. We collected bits of soapstone, and it felt just like soap. It is the colour of golden sandstone. This is one of the many industries that have died out in these parts. There had also been a granite works at Dungloe, and one could see great square blocks of pink granite on the quay there..."[9]

---

8   Account of a Mineralogical Excursion to the County of Donegal, Charles Lewis Giesecke, (1761-1833, Professor of Mineralogy, Royal Dublin Society, 1814-33) 1826, Royal Dublin Society (the professor deposited 7 samples from Crohy and Maghery in the RDS museum). Note Crohy appears in this other reports in this chapter with a variety of spellings which have been kept as quoted.

9   'They All Made Me' Rex Herdman, S.D. Montgomery publisher, 1970 – the book is notable for its stories of life on Arranmore, Edernish, Rutland and the other islands). Soapstone may be found in many locations in Ireland and U.K.

Before the Cope took it over, Johnny Rua (Sweeney) of Burtonport was the local agent for the soapstone mine in Crohy Head. Here he writes in 1918 to the Geological Survey in Dublin, telling of his involvement in mining some 20-40 tons a week at Crohy and requesting information on more soapstone locations. It was clearly a business worth being in. Johnny Rua was the brother of the late James Sweeney in Dungloe (James had also operated in Burtonport) and been a successful businessman in his own right. (Letter courtesy of The Geological Survey, Dublin).

By the time the Cope restarted tunnelling and mining after September 1942 it was the middle of the 'Emergency', as World War Two was euphemistically called in the Republic. Exporting proved difficult with the shortage of shipping caused by the U-Boat War in the Atlantic and the operation closed soon after. However, there was still enough of the better quality white rock to mine three tons a day of it in 1946 when the mine re-opened. Mining continued until 1947. Competition after the war – as French sources with abundant supplies re-emerged – and a collapse of the main undersea tunnel to the valuable white soapstone source meant that the Cope's main was no longer comercially viaable.

A geological report, written nine years before the Cope began operations, may well have been influential in persuading Paddy to re-open the mine:

> "...On the advice of Deputy Hugh Doherty I got in touch with Mr Patrick (Pa) O'Donnell of Roshine, Dungloe, Co. Donegal, who conducted me

Johnny Rua was the local agent for the Crohy Head soapstone mine before the Cope began mining in the 1940s. His house in Burtonport, believed to have been built in the 1880s but possibly the 1890s, was converted in 1904-5 to a hotel after the Lough Swilly Railway was extended to Burtonport in 1903. The front part of the house became Sweeney's Hotel with six bedrooms and built on to the back was a house with four bedrooms where the family lived. On the left is Johnny Rua's shop, a corrugated iron affair that the Cope may well have used as a model for its branch buildings in Meenbanad and, later, Annagry. Johnny's brother (James) had a smaller store further down the street; this became the Burtonport Cope in 1921. Johnny's store was multi-purpose – it housed a drapery, a grocery and a bar. Behind the house, on the right, can be seen a flagpole and the roofs of the eleven houses of the coastguard station. These were built in 1895 and, in 1921, after intelligence had been received that soldiers were to be billeted there, were burned down on the orders of Johnny Rua's son, Joe (later Major General) Sweeney (1897-1980). Joe was the only Donegal man in the GPO in the Easter 1916 Rising and was the youngest TD in the First Dáil Éireann in 1918, after winning a seat as a Sinn Féin MP for West Donegal at Westminster in the 1918 General election. All the Sinn Féin MPs declined to take their seats and formed the First Dáil instead. Visitors to the house and hotel

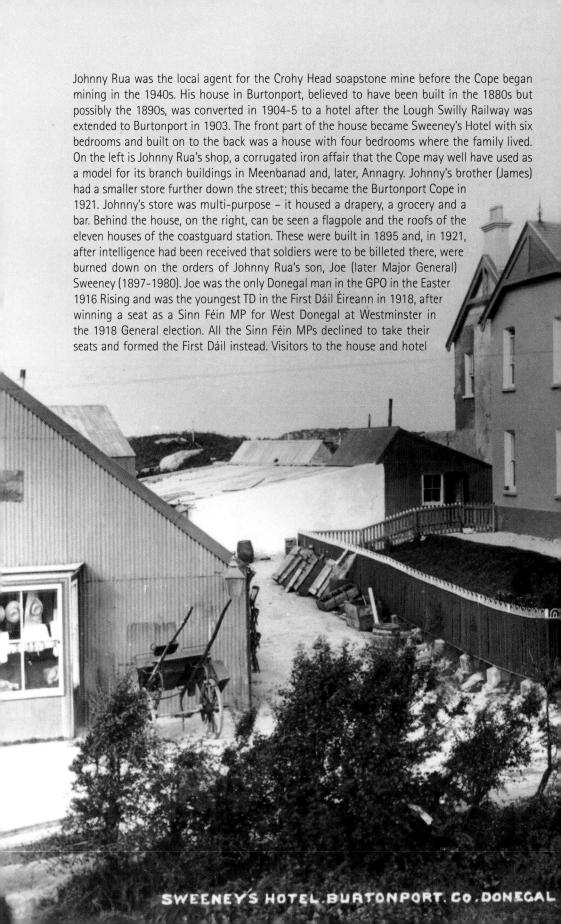

SWEENEY'S HOTEL, BURTONPORT, Co. DONEGAL

included, at various times, Maud Gonne, Patrick Pearse (who taught Joe Sweeney at St Enda's Dublin) and Eamon De Valera. Source: Alice Sweeney memoir – Alice was Johnny Rua's second wife, they married in 1911 and she lived on to be 107; Johnny Rua died in 1939. (Lawrence Collection Photograph c1905, courtesy National Photographic Archive, L_ROY_9439)

This is Crohy Head in 1905–10 looking towards The Breeches, the arch and 'stags' rock formation in the foreground, with the island of Arranmore in the far background. On the top of the cliffs, where soapstone has been mined since the at least the nineteenth century, and possibly very much earlier, can be seen the winch tower used for pulling up the bogey (trolley cart) in which the soapstone was carried. The seams worked by the Cope in the 1940s were on the cliffs facing the The Breeches (Lawrence Collection L_ROY_09430, National Photographic Archive)

over the occurrence of soapstone and marble in the Crohy Head and Maghery district on the 30th September. In the cliff at Crohy Head, about 200 yards north of Tullard Breeches, some seven or eight veins of soapstone occur which dips SW between 65° and 80°. A number of rough drivings on these veins were formerly made on the cliff-face and a considerable quantity of material was removed. These workings were made in such a haphazard fashion that many of them are now collapsed and have helped to weaken the cliff-face to such an extent that fairly large landslides have taken place. Consequently very little of the outcrop material can now be clearly seen. The average thickness of the soapstone veins appears to be about two feet, but I was informed that in some of the drivings they were found to widen in places to as much as five feet.

The worked soapstone was formerly carried up a pathway cut in the side of the cliff to a rolling mill situated on the cliff-face over Tullard Breeches. The mill has been dismantled and only the foundations of the

The Story of the Cope

structure now remain. The pathway has disappeared in places due to landslides and the descent to the workings is rather perilous. However I managed to secure sample from some of the level. These were of the massive variety of talc, light pearly-grey in colour and possessing a foliated structure.

Some 250 yards along the cliff, to the north east of the workings, we have some further veins of soapstone, which appear among mica schists and quartzites dipping at 80° to the SW. These veins are apparently thin and owing to the precipitous nature of the cliff they are more or less inaccessible. Some 600 yards due east of here an occurrence of soapstone was found inland, and soapstone was also found about 550 yards due east of the old workings.

From an economic point of view, this soapstone is apparently of good colour and quality, but the quantity yet available for exploitation is a doubtful factor. From the meagre evidence at present available, it is impossible to make a confident statement as to the continuity and extent of the veins. The fact that the rock has been discovered nearly as much as half a mile inland from the cliff would lend one to infer that there may a fair amount of the material in the intervening ground.

In Maghery bay, at the northern end of the strand, I was shown the marble deposit. This consists of a band of limestone containing irregular laminae of serpentine. The bed dips at about 80° to the south and is about 8 feet thick. The sample I was shown polished easily and well and the colouring contained a pleasing mixture of light and dark greens. However, this bed is too narrow and jointed to be of any economic importance as an ornamental stone...”[10]

The following report was done just before the Cope restarted mining. It would have been a very useful guide for Paddy had he seen it (it is not known for sure, but it seems very likely he would have collared anyone visiting the site and got them to send him a copy of the report). He would have been encouraged by the upbeat tone and the prospects it saw for a profitable venture.

“...On the 3rd August 1942 I visited the Steatite workings at Crohy Head. Michaél O Baoghaíll, Fál Mór, Cruaiche, who was employed there at one time, pointed out the old workings to me. The Steatite occurs in veins up to 12 feet wide with a strike in a SW direction and a varying dip of from about 45 degrees to 70 degrees. A large amount of Steatite seems to have been extracted by an open cut working (area A), down the cliff face. Further along (Area B), small drifts were driven into the cliffs about 20 feet above the beach and about 90 feet from the top of the cliff. It was not possible to ascertain the extent of these drifts

---

10 *Geological Survey of Ireland Archives; report by J. McCluskey 11th October 1933,*

C.572　　　　CROHEY TOWER, DUNGLOE

The Breeches at Crohy Head (in an early postcard from c1906) can be seen nearby to the soapstone mines. It is a spectacular setting, difficult to see from the road but well worth the attempt. (Seán Boner Collection, Lawrence postcard c1905)

due to the lack of light and negligible timbering in the drifts themselves; but from the way they wander, they were apparently tapping the richest sources of the deposit at this point. The soapstone was hauled up the cliff in buckets. There are two other good seams of Steatite (area C), neither of which shows signs of having been worked.

Proposals for Working: A good amount of Steatite could be profitably be extracted from area 'A', although previously worked. It would be necessary to work the open cut here in tunnels of about five feet each, forming these from the top and the bottom. As at present, the working is steep and dangerous. The soapstone could be hauled to the top in buckets by a hand windlass. 15 or 20 men should be able to extract about 6 or 7 tons per day after a little preparation. That figure would be greatly influenced by the quality of the Steatite required. At 'B', the older workings seem to have tapped some good Steatite and it would be well to have these explored further. These would be more difficult to operate, however, as a good deal of cleaning up and timbering would be needed. The drifts are rather small, about 4ft by 3ft and run in all directions.

The road from Crohy to Maghery – about 1.5 miles – is bad. From Maghery to the railway at Crolly – about 20 miles – is fairly good, however, and from Maghery to Burtonport – about 9 miles – is also good. Shipping is available at Burtonport…"[11]

A further more negative report, which questioned the long term commercial potential was produced in December 1942 – by this time the Cope had restarted mining:

"…In the North area, there is a small showing of Steatite in the cliff face in a very inaccessible position, which has not been worked but is of limited extent. In the South area only the remnants of the Steatite veins remain, owing to cliff erosion by wave action, and these remnants appear to have been pretty well worked in the past.

It would no doubt be possible to get from this coastal area a small tonnage of fairly high-grade Steatite by carrying on some of the old cliff workings in a small way, but owing to the high transport and other charges that would have to be met the business could hardly be regarded as a sound undertaking.

There is little doubt that a considerable amount of Steatite occurs in the portions of the veins below sea level but to reach this would necessitate sinking a fairly deep shaft and it is more than doubtful whether the value of the Steatite won would offset the cost of this and deeper workings involved…"[12]

Paddy wrote to IAOS secretary, Dr. Henry Kennedy, in spring 1943, letting them know what he was up to and implicitly asking for their help to get licenses sorted out:

"…We are mining the soapstone and have 60 tons already, we will send that 60 tons to Sligo as we want Walshe's cooperation in getting the licence. We have just installed a mill (The Miracle Mill) in Dungloe. We got it for seaweed but are now advised by the makers that it will grind soapstone. We are drying the stone (it must be dried) in our mill kiln today…"[13]

Paddy, clearly frustrated with officialdom continued:

"…I called in the Industry and Commerce, Kildare Street, on the 20th, met Mr. Clarke who is in charge of the licence for mineral. I have been

---

11 Geological Survey of Ireland Archives, Dublin; report filed 8th September 1942 by John C. Meavy.

12 Geological Survey of Ireland Archives, Dublin; report filed December 1942 by H.G. Dixon:

13 IAOS records 1088/871/1-8 National Archives – letter dated 30th May 1943.

looking for a licence for the soapstone at Croghey for the past six months. He stated to me that there was an application in before ours; that he would give us a licence for a place in Falcarragh, that we ourselves located; and that he thought one place would be enough for us.

If he persists in refusing us, a greater injustice could not be done or a greater disappointment to the people of the Rosses. There was no word of any other person looking for a licence until I got the locals to take out 25 tons as a sample. The sample has been approved by the British Government. They want all that we can produce. This information leaked out. In addition to Croghey Head soapstone there were two other mines in the county, one at Fintown, the other at Gartan. We would like to get the rights to all of them. We can work them and know how. When our men at Croghey heard that we were not getting a licence, I had the greatest difficulty in keeping them from going to Britain where they can earn big money and our Society is now paying them clearing a way to get to the bottom of the 300' cliffs and a passage for our boats to come in and lift the stone.

We are now missing the tide as it will not be possible to work at Croghey Head in winter.

I am not a betting man but I'll bet ten to one that no other firm will work at Croghey Head and make it pay. Two other firms already burst there. I am expecting the licence for the Falcarragh place any moment.

I am sure it is not Mr. Clarke's fault. There must be some others. If you can help, please do..."[14]

Donald Devenney, interview 5th November 2006.

Donald Devenney from Roshine, 80 in 2006, is one of two surviving miners from the Cope's soapstone mine in Crohy; the other, his brother, James (Seamus) Devenney 97 at the time of writing, lives in Dungloe. Both are in the 1946 Irish Press photographs accompanying the article – Donald is named (erroneously) as Danny in the photos. Both Donald and Jim later worked on fishing boats with their brother Connie Devenney, Cope Committee member; Jim worked in the Cope Bakery till its closure in 1984.

Donald was born in December 1926 in Maghery; he was 16 when he worked in Roshine School, which was rebuilt in 1942, almost wholly with Cope labour. Donald remarked that it could be said that the Cope built the school – Roshine was where Paddy went to school for his few short years – and where Mary Campbell, his daughter in law, taught (Mary's children all went to Roshine School too).

---

14 *IAOS records 1088/871/1-8 National Archives – letter dated 30th May 1943.*

Donald Devenney worked in the Cope's Crohy Head Soapstone Mine in 1946-47, its last days. Donald's memories of working at Crohy are very vivid. He was also a member of the Maghery Band and is pictured here in the 1950s in band uniform with drum on bicycle in a typical pose (Noel Delaney, NYC Collection).

Donald's father had worked for the Cope from the very early days in 1906. He used to collect supplies from Dungloe Road station with a horse and cart and deliver to Cleendra before the move into Dungloe in 1907.

After Roshine School was completed, Donald then spent a couple of years working in the Cope in Dungloe. He was to have been out in Fintown cutting trees when a fatal accident occurred; Donald was on a week's holiday and Jimmy O'Brien (who was tragically killed by a falling tree) had taken his place.

After this, he went to work out at the Cope's soapstone mine at Crohy. The money was good, £2 a week, his father had died in 1946 and they were eleven of a family. Wages in the 1940s for the hard graft associated with such work were relatively good: for stripping and excavating £2 a week; barrowing etc £1 10s a week; and the gangerman would be paid £2 10s a week.

Editor's note: Donald very kindly accompanied me in November 2006 to the main access point to the mine he worked in. He is a very fit man for then almost 80 and had no trouble with fences, ditches – indeed he was hard to keep up with. He also has, I learned, a very mischievous sense of humour. The route we took was very safe until the very last few steps when Donald stepped aside to reveal a precipitous drop only feet away with clear evidence of rock having broken away very recently. He then was doubled up with laughter at my reaction and it was some time before we could continue with any questions.

Donald remembers mining the soapstone as if it were yesterday, it was a hazardous activity:

> "...The best - and scarcer, more valuable - soapstone was white; it was used particularly in cosmetics (e.g. in face cream). Coloured soapstone was more common, used in paints, not cosmetics.

When it came to starting off something, The Copeman was in the lead. He had a group of fifty men who were called 'The Flying Column'; if he had a big job to do, he would round them up and bring them along. They re-opened the mine, built the track and put in place the transport bogey. When they were done, Paddy would say 'Come on now boys, we've something else to do'.

The most productive mine was out under the sea – it contained very fine white soapstone, the most sought after kind. Mining it required building shuttering and concreting to create a shaft some 20ft down below the sea level. Water would seep in at night or splash over with the waves; there was a small petrol engine to pump water out. The tunnel went along under the sea for a hundred yards or so; the air was bad and there was no pump to keep fresh air circulating. Lighting was by candle or small oil lamps. Picks were used to break off the soapstone; the white variety was easily worked. Bags were filled at the face and dragged back along the slippery surface to the shaft where they were transferred to the track alongside and to the bogey for taking them up using a hand winch. Francie Boyle and Donald used to work the winch together. It was 'slow in the gear'; six bags were taken up at a time (about 5-600cwt). The lifting wasn't hard but it was slow. The lorry would be loaded and take away the stone to Sligo, a bumpy ride in those days – and the heavily laden lorry would not have helped the state of the roads either.

During the war, you had to be careful with explosives. Sea mines, which occasionally floated into the bay, could explode; there was a fear they would detonate the gelignite stored in caves.

Sometimes, the soapstone would be taken away by boat. The Naomh Eine, with Big Mick Gallagher skippering, would wait out away from the beach and rocks. Smaller boats would be loaded with bags of soapstone and rowed out to her. When filled she would head for Sligo.

The shift was 9am to 6pm to start with; then, to maximise the yield from the undersea mine, two shifts of 8am to 4pm and 4pm to 12pm were created. One morning, the shift arrived to find that the spink above the mine had collapsed and thousands of tons had crashed onto the shaft and undersea mine entrance. Fortunately, it had happened after the second shift the day before had finished.

That put an end to the white soapstone mining; it would have been in 1947, not that long after the Irish Press article came out. There was no point continuing with only the coloured soapstone as it was very common – it was worked in Sligo off Ben Bulben – and less valuable. It became uneconomic to just work coloured stone to transport or ship to Sligo where it was plentiful…"

The following article, describing the Cope's soapstone mining, appeared in the Irish Press. Spelling of local place names has been left as in the original article.

So This Is How We Get Talcum!
Reporter Liam Robinson

"…Paddy the Cope pointed to a bleak mountain on our left. Beyond it lay Claoin Derry and the birthplace of "The Cope" and his co-operative movement.

Here Michael Powell will come in spring to shoot the film of the organiser's life. Our car bumped and twisted along the road for six miles.

The lurching reduced conversation to gasps.

Maghary, a tiny village of weathered thatches, loose stone walls and scattering hens, fell behind.

Soon we were on the mountain road. On one side lay the Atlantic and on the other Croughy mountain. A scramble down a stony track to the corrugated iron shed brought us to what seems like the edge of the world.

Below, the Atlantic bashed against jagged rocks. Like swallows' nests in a sandpit, the entrances to the mines showed in the cliff beneath.

Here was the only working steatite mine in Ireland, with France the nearest rival. Soapstone, as the mineral is called, is refined to make talcum powder; tailors use it for marking cloth, and long ago hedge-schoolmasters around Croughy use it for chalking their slates.

When a boy, The Cope had mined it beneath this cliff. In 1942, on his suggestion, the Templecrone Co-Operative Society opened the mine. It worked satisfactorily. But the acute shortage of shipping killed the export of the product and the mine closed.

THREE TONS A DAY

Six months ago it reopened and now yield three tons a day. The stone is conveyed by road to Glenties and then by rail to Sligo, where a commercial firm buys the total output. There it is refined and prepared for export.

Stacked inside the iron shed on the cliff-top were sacks of soapstone. At the side, two men slowly wound a winch. Inch by inch cable appeared over the edge of the cliff. Then a bogey came into view loaded with small grey bags.

DONEGAL SOAPSTONE MINE

PADDY THE COPE and IRISH PRESS Reporter Liam Robinson ascending the cliff face on the bogey, after visiting the mine below.

This series of photos is from The Irish Press and were used to illustrate the article 'So This Is How We Get Talcum' in 1946: the first shows Paddy (then 75) with reporter Liam Robinson going back up to the top on the bogey. (Irish Press). Five of the men working at the mine are pictured: Donald Devenney (erroneously named as 'Danny' in the caption), James Bonner, Patrick McCole, Tom Boyle and Seamus Devenney (Copyright 'The Irish Press', Merrion Square, Dublin).

TOM BOYLE (right) and Seamus Devenney drawing out the soapstone.

PATRICK McCOLE—propping the roof of the mine—also has experience in American mines.

DANNY DEVENNEY (aged 19) hacking soapstone seam in the mine.

FOREMAN JAMES BONNER spent 15 years in the Pennsylvania anthracite mines.

LOOKING DOWN from the entrance to the mine. A snap of the winch-cable would send the bogey down there.

We glanced over the edge. A narrow gauge track swept sheer down to where the Atlantic roared 1,000 feet below. "How do we get down to the mine?" I asked. "Down on the bogey" said Paddy. "Not for fifty quid" muttered our driver, and stepped back. We decided to descend on the rope.

The cliff face was slimy, and the wind roared round us, swinging the photographer's camera in wild circles. From the top the driver roared warnings against landslides and surface cracks.

Foreman James Bonner met us on the ledge, where the small openings led into the mine. A shaft could not be sunk from the top he explained, because the seams of soapstone were vertical and narrow. To avoid striking them when boring would be an easy matter. By mining them from underneath, passages could be bored in any direction in which the mineral veins ran.

One by one we filed into the tunnel. Bending double, we walked with a shuffle. Ahead, the carbide lamp of miner Paddy McCole bobbed. The floor was thick with a soapy slime, and at least two of us advanced with the motion of a weird Cossack dance.

At the end of a shaft Danny Devenney picked a seam through to the hard rock behind. The stone came away easily with picking. In the hands, it could be chipped or flaked easily but not broken.

Walls felt soft to the touch. Seams of white, blue and yellow soapstone shone around us, and "diamonds", or mica-flint, glinted.

The Cope explained that the yellow and blue seams were of inferior quality, and only the white was being worked.

After twenty minutes, we two began to know the meaning of miners' cramp, and sacks of stone at shaft junctions tried to trip us in our race for air. Tapping of picks became fainter, and the passages echoed with the soft boom of sea against shore.

Outside miners were dumping waste matter over the ledge into the Atlantic. The bogey rattled down from above. "Coming up?" roared a winch hand.

Seated on the bogey with Paddy, the foreman blasted his whistle, and the bogey started to crawl up. I looked down at the sea and the rocks, then at McGonagle with the camera to his eye. He grinned and bellowed after us: "If that cable breaks, what a scoop!"..."[15]

---

15 *Irish Press 26th November 1946*

The Cope's mining and quarrying activities were short lived and apart from a brief period of success with soapstone, not commercial. If it had been at all possible, Paddy would have kept both going – they were very much his ideas – but his hard headed business side knew when enough was enough.

A later reference to the Cope's soapstone business came in an article in the Irish Times, well after mining ended at Crohy Head:

Invention by Doctor to Keep Guards Warm

"...A hot brick, invented by an Irish doctor, may beat the cold feet 'bogey' for the Republic's traffic policemen. An experiment — to be carried out to-night at about 7 o'clock in College Green, Dublin can quite possibly make their lot a much happier one.

The idea is that when a Civic Guard goes on point duty he will take with him a thermal heater in the form of a 'brick' which has been charged overnight. As he directs the traffic, come rain, come snow, the heat will drain off slowly supplying a constant temperature.

Dr. John Brennan, who processed and produced the invention, has the enthusiastic support of the police. If the idea is a success, an 18-inch high brick will be part of the standard equipment of the Guards.

Storage heaters on this principle are considered economic, because electricity sold at night is cheaper - the costs of current for these heaters works out at less than a halfpenny a unit.

An Irish firm, Lumite, which has put storage heaters on the market, with the backing of the ESB, will supply the bricks. The brick is built from soapstone, mined in Donegal from a quarry owned by "Paddy the Cope." The trade name is Copestone, in honour of Paddy..."[16]

---

16   *Irish Times 23rd November 1950 – the article reads so strangely that one expects the date to be 1st April!*

Chapter 11

Events, People and Memories

The Cope has been many things in its existence, a Main Store and Branches, a series of businesses like fishing, baking, milling, knitting, mining, quarrying and many smaller enterprises. But to the people of the Rosses, it has been a lot more than this. Both Paddy himself and the Cope people have had a wide impact on the cultural development of the area. It's probably true to say that there is not one aspect of life that it has not become involved in, whether it be Politics, Religion, Sport, Entertainment or just everyday life.

In this chapter are collected some of these events and the memories people have of the Cope and Paddy himself.

POLITICS

The Cope grew and lived through a turbulent century; through the Home Rule era, then 1916 and the War of Independence, the Free State and the Republic and beyond. Paddy's own views developed too – and certainly there were differences of opinion, reflecting the national divide, between local people along the way.

Packie Bonner captured Paddy and the Cope's political dimension in the Cope's 75th anniversary booklet in 1981:

> "...If I were asked to single out one of Paddy the Cope's many public appearances, during his long life, I think I would decide on the occasion of De Valera's meeting in Dungloe, in the late summer of 1937. There was a General Election pending at that time and Dev came to Donegal in support of the campaign that was then getting under way. It was a memorable election too, in as much as that the referendum for the new Constitution was being held on the same day. During his five years in office, De Valera had got rid of the Oath of Allegiance and the office of the Governor General, so that the way was now clear for a referendum on the Constitution issue. It was the occasion, too, of the late Cormac Breslin's first appearance in the political arena as the new Fianna candidate for West Donegal, following the standing down of the late Deputy Hugh Doherty.
>
> It was decided that the Election rally or meeting should be held outside Patrick Johnny Sally's, and Paddy the Cope was the unanimous choice as meeting chairman. It was further planned that Paddy should receive Dev at the town's boundary. This was what was done. The town wasn't as big then as it is now, so that Paddy and his associates awaited Dev's arrival at Dinnie Greene's garage. From there, Dev and his host walked

Taoiseach Eamon de Valera visited Dungloe on a number of occasions and always made sure to visit Paddy in the Cope House. Here he is seen walking up Dungloe's Main Street with Paddy; they are just passing Edward Boyle and Sons on their way up to a huge Fianna Fail rally to be held outside Patrick Johnny Sally's where Paddy and others spoke. The date is 29th June 1937, two days before the election. Paddy campaigned all over West Donegal for Fianna Fail and his hero de Valera. His speeches in Arranmore, Falcarragh, Dungloe and Meenacrosh helped get TDs Cormac Breslin and Brian Brady elected (Cope Archive, probably from the Derry Journal).

up the street, and the scene, as I recall it to-day, more than forty years after, was not at all unlike the procession described in Browning's "Pied Piper of Hamelin"! The men of the Rosses were surely there, but there were women and children go leor as well. There were no 'Mary from Dungloe' Festivals then, and apart from the political significance of the day, it had its social side as well.

Dev had been Taoiseach now for more than five years, so that he was not only a national figure but a world figure as well. Paddy, too, had reached the peak of his fame by that time. Although his book, "My Story", had not yet been published, he had travelled extensively in both Europe and America; he had given many press interviews and had spoken on Radio

Rutland Barracks, Meenmore, dating from the early part of the 19th Century, was burnt down in 1920 by a group led by Frank O'Donnell, ex Cope employee and brother of Meenmore man, Peadar O'Donnell, Republican, Socialist and Writer.

General Joe Sweeney, writing in the 1970 Capuchin Annual, recalled: "...Documents, captured in the post in mid-July 1920, apprised us that the British intended to put a garrison into the old Rutland Barracks at Meenmore, near Dungloe, then a summer residence of the Maudes, a landlord family near Clondalkin Co. Dublin. We burned the building immediately, as a post at that location would have interfered seriously with our communications..."[1]

The local people seen here, some of whom would have been involved in the action, are posing for a photograph issued as a postcard by O'Donnell, Dungloe. Very little evidence remains now of this substantial three storey building – it is said locally that much of the stone was used to make roads.[2]

"...From 1918 to 1921 I had a miserable time of it. The Black and Tans were worse than savages let loose. They were murdering, ravishing and burning. There were £28,000 deposits in our Society, all Rosses' money. Some people had £5, others from £50 to £300. Every day when I

---

1   1970 Capuchin Annual: 'Donegal And The War Of Independence'

2   Contemporary local postcard published in Dungloe, Packie Bonner Collection

opened the paper I would read of Co-operative Societies being burned out. I did not know the minute the Cope would be set on fire too, and as the ordinary insurance did not cover us against military acts, I felt most miserable. I got out a special insurance policy against military destruction. It only covered us for three months and the premium was £500..."[3]

The War of Independence hit the cooperatives hard – particularly creameries which the Black and Tans devastated right across the country as they were seen as hotbeds of Republicanism. Post 1922, the Cooperative movement went into a steep decline. Donegal was not as badly hit as some counties – casualties and damage to property were relatively light in comparison. Decisive actions by local IRA columns, led by Burtonport's Joe Sweeney and Meenmore's Peadar O'Donnell discouraged Government forces, leaving them no base or place where they could be billeted. In the period 1920-21, barracks in Dungloe, Arranmore and Meenmore were burnt as was the coastguard station in Burtonport.

"...A report from Donegal states that on Monday night the fishing lodge called Rutland Barracks, the property of Capt. Maude, of Dublin, was destroyed by fire. The mansion, which is situated near the sea coast not far from Dungloe, was purchased by Capt. Maude some years ago, and he and his family invariably spend the summer holidays there. Captain Maude is very popular in the district and it is supposed the barracks was burnt to prevent its being used by the military. It is stated that early in the last century the place had been used for military purposes..."[4]

The course of the war was followed across Europe and America:

"...LONDONDERRY, Ireland – Several hundred Sinn Feiners last night successfully blocked the running of a mixed passenger and freight train through Letterkenny because it was carrying a dozen armed soldiers and food for the military barracks in Dungloe. No actual fighting took place, but the crowd was so hostile that it was decided not to proceed with the train and the 200 passengers to sit aboard at the station all night. The soldiers were taken to the police barracks to avoid the crowd. Conditions quieted after three hours. Meanwhile, the troops in Dungloe were in desperate straits for food, the Sinn Fein inhabitants refusing to supply it and trains with consignments being raided. The troops have been without food for many days..."[5]

---

3   Paddy the Cope in 'My Story' 1939 Jonathan Cape (and editions 1946 to 2006)

4   Irish Times, June 13th 1920

5   New York Times, 27th July 1920.

Eireann as well. The radio talk I remember best was one in which Paddy was being interviewed by Liam O Conachain, of the "Derry Journal", regarding various aspects of life here in the Rosses. Amidst cheering and flag-waving, Dev and Paddy mounted the platform and the meeting started. All the Old Guard of Fianna Fail seemed to be there that day, many of whom, alas, like Dev and Paddy, have been called to their reward since. Amongst them were: Anthony Delap, Johnny McMonagle, Anthony Doogan, Phil McCauley, Peadar Greene, Willie Durnin, and others besides. As you see, there are very few of that number alive today. The years surely take their toll.

To open the proceedings, Paddy made a few introductory remarks before calling on Peadar O Ceallaigh to read an address of welcome. Peadar, a native of Doochary, was at that time teaching in Roshine School. Believe it or not, snatches of what Peader said, or read, still keep ringing in my ears: "A Thaoisigh, níor loic tú, níor shéan tú, ní dheachaigh tú riamh ar gcúl orainn; ní dheachaigh tú i dtréas riamh ar Éirinn ná ar mhuintir na hÉireann. Bhí tú dílis i gcónaí...". Then in conclusion, Peadar said a few words in English. I can never forget his opening sentence: "Pardon us, Oh Chief, if in order to show you the universality of our welcome, we should have recourse to an alien tongue..."

Political feelings were running high in the Rosses at that time and the people had turned out in their thousands to hear Dev. The meeting was held on a Sunday afternoon and many of those present — the menfolk at any rate — hadn't gone home since Mass time. I would say, too, that many of them too had partaken of the good Patrick's hospitality so that they were feeling a bit merry by this. I can still remember an old fellow standing up on the churchyard wall, cap in hand, waving it to the crowd, and exhorting his audience to "Vote for the good old Davie and get more gravy". I need hardly explain that this was an obvious reference to the Free Beef Scheme of the days of the Economic War. After Dev. and the running candidate, the late Cormac Breslin, had spoken, it then fell Paddy's turn to speak. Certainly the good Copeman had no difficulty in getting his points across, but, of course, he had little practice at oratory, so that when he became emotional or worked up on some point, there was a danger of his becoming tongue-tied. All things considered, I must admit that he spoke very well.

I can still recall the things he spoke about. He mentioned Dev's fight for the Retention of the Land Annuities and drew a comparison between Fianna Fail's ambitions in this regard and the efforts of Peadar O'Donnell towards that same goal in the decade gone by. His mention of the Cumann na nGaedheal government of 1922-23 drew from him an outburst about the Cumann na nGaedheal leader, William T. Cosgrave. "Aye, auld Cosgrave. What did he do to poor Biddy Doherty, of Marameelin, and to James Durnin, of Croveigh? Did he not give them terms in Sligo Jail, for doing nothing at at all? Aye, and he wanted to transform the role of the Guards too. Did he not want to make them bailiffs' auxiliaries, if he would get his way...but, thank God, he didn't get his way and he never will"

In a reference then to the Gárdaí Síochana, he drew a comparison between the new forces of that time and the R.I.C. of the British times. "Long ago, I remember that barracks down there full of police. There was the D.I.; the Head Constable; the Sergeant; the constables and the devil knows what. There must have been about a score of police there at times and now the Sergeant there and his four Guards are doing the same work without any fuss at all. . . Yes, the Peelers are gone at last, and as we used to say, a good year after them. We don't want them back ever. We'll get on grand without them". Yes, that was Paddy the Cope; Patrick Gallagher; Paddy Pat Bawn — the man from Cleendra. He said to me once: "You know, I often feel the want of better education. As I told you before, I was only in the third book the day I left Mickie Neddy. I could be doing with a lot more, if I only got it."

It behoves me now to say a word or two about Paddy's political involvement. Like all his contemporaries in the Rosses, he was a staunch Nationalist in his youth. By this is meant that he was a follower of the Parnellite tradition during Parnell's lifetime and after the days of the Split, later on. Then, after the wounds of the Split had healed, we witnessed the United Ireland Parliamentarianism under the leadership of John Redmond. Then, as we know, the Irish Party finally finally crumbled under the Sinn Fein avalanche of the 1918 Election. From this crushing defeat at the polls, the Irish Party never recovered. During the Treaty debates, later on, it would seem that that Paddy was on the side that thought that the Treaty should be accepted — "as a stepping stone to a Republic", as Collins had said. It should be pointed out, too, that this was the view held by the majority of Rosses people at that time, so that Paddy was not alone in his view. County Donegal was one single constituency at that time, and, as we all know, two local candidates were successful in the 1923 General Election, viz., Peadar O'Donnell (Anti-Treatyite) and Eugene Doherty (Pro-Treatyite). Peadar O'Donnell, being an abstentionist, declined to take his seat in the Dail.

As there were less than a dozen motor-cars in the Rosses at that time, the transport of voters to the poll created problems for the two major political parties, especially as there were few polling centres in those days. To help out on Election Day, Paddy sent out his lorries on polling day in order to bring out the voters to the polls. Then the year 1927, saw an estrangement between Paddy and prominent Government figures in the Rosses, so that each went their separate ways. Then, to use a racy expression, there followed a slack-water period, during which the Cumann Na nGaedheal government of the day found fit to

Taoiseach Eamon de Valera, outside the Cope House in Killybegs with a local Fianna Fail group in the late 1940s. The Cope bought Coane's Hotel in 1942 after which it became known locally as the Cope House – it was still referred to by this name years after it was sold. Standing with the Taoiseach are Paddy the Cope (third from the right) and a group of local Fianna Fail politicians including Joe Brennan (TD between 1951-80), Brian Brady (1933-49) and a young Neil T Blaney (1948-95) amongst others (Photograph courtesy of Donald Martin, Killybegs).

introduce a few unpopular measures, which I would say, led to their ultimate undoing. The reduction of the Old Age Pension in the budget of 1929 and the introduction of the Public Safety Act two years later, were enough to provide the final straw with which to break the camel's back. Fianna Fail's victory, therefore, in the General Election of 1932, came as no surprise. Paddy the Cope was with De Valera in that contest, and from that point he never looked back. Both men became life-long friends and the Cope founder always acted as Dev's host, whenever the Fianna Fail leader crossed the Gweebarra to enter the Rosses..."[6]

---

6 *Packie Bonner writing in The Cope's 75th Anniversary 1981 Booklet*

RELIGION

Paddy's religion was very important to him: there are many instances of his devotion to his faith in his autobiography and also in Sally's stories. He is uncharacteristically silent, however, on what was the biggest religious event in Ireland in his lifetime: the 31st Eucharistic Congress in Dublin in 1932 between 22nd and 26th June. This was a hugely popular event, not matched until the visit of the late Pope John Paul II to Ireland in 1979. A quarter of the population attended the final Mass in Phoenix Park and half a million people gathered round (or as near they could get to) O'Connell St Bridge for the blessing from the Papal Legate

The reason for Paddy's silence is clear from his story – he was very seriously ill in that year and was laid up in bed from March onwards. Otherwise, he would surely have been at the momentous events in Dublin and included his memories in his book.

Having missed, through no fault of his own, the 1932 celebrations, he was determined not to miss out on the next major event, the Patrician year in 1961, when his saint's name and the patron saint of Ireland would be commemorated.

The 'Patrician Year': celebrating Mass at the Mass Rock in Cleendra

1961 was celebrated as a 'Patrician Year' – St Patrick was traditionally supposed to have died in AD 461, which would have made 1961 the 1500th anniversary. More recent assessments have his death taking place in AD 493. However, at the time, the accepted wisdom was AD 461.

In Penal times, the Mass Rock at Cleendra would have had a sheet placed on it to let them know when a priest was in the area. It could be seen for miles around, including the islands which were then densely populated; people would travel great distances to hear Mass.

Paddy had suggested that it would be a good idea to hold a 'Patrician Year' service at the 'Ard an Aifrinn', the Cleendra Mass Rock; it would have been the first there since penal times. Paddy had asked His Lordship the Most Rev Dr MacNeely Bishop of Raphoe for the necessary permission for the Mass. The date of the mass was 19th July 1961 and mass was held at 5pm. Denis Tynan, the Glenties photographer, was on hand to take the photos which appeared in the Derry Journal.

The mass was celebrated by Paddy's godson the Rev Gerard Gardiner who was the son of an old friend of Paddy's from the very early days, Dr Gardiner of Dungloe. In the course of a short address, Fr Gerard said that he had climbed Cleendra Hill as a boy but had never visualised that he would climb it as a priest to celebrate Holy Mass there.

Apart from the visit by the late Pope John Paul I in 1979, the biggest religious occasion of the last century was the 31st Eucharistic Congress in Dublin in 1932. Paddy the Cope had little to say about this – he was confined to bed in March of that year with very serious knee trouble. He relates in 'My Story': "...When I was ill in 1932, and not much hopes of my recovery, when the crisis was over, Sally said, 'Paddy, you could not die, sure the factory girls were in the chapel every night praying and lighting candles for your recovery...". 1932 was also a momentous year for the election of Fianna Fail and Paddy's hero, Eamon de Valera ('My Story'; a letter in the IAOS records comments on Paddy's illness)

Ards Monastery, originally built in 1708 by the Wray family, was bought by the Stewart family in 1780. At the Bishop of Raphoe, Dr William McNeely's, initiative it was taken over by the Franciscan Capuchin order in 1930 and the name changed to Ard Mhuire (which translates, less poetically, as 'Mary's Hill'). In 1931, it became the Novitiate and Theological Seminary for the Capuchins; it was also available for retreats and was used by the Cope for this purpose. It became very popular, necessitating a major expansion, completed in 1966. Today, it is a peaceful and beautiful retreat and conference centre that people travel to from all over the world (Contemporary postcard, PB Collection; detail from 'The Heritage Magazine' 1956, article by John Gurdon, Josephine Davis Collection).

Cope Staff on a weekend retreat at Ards in 1950: (Back) Packie Gallagher (James), Packie Gallagher (Madgie), Jim Green, James Breslin Coll, John McCole, Owenie Boyle, Francie Houston, Neily Sweeney, Charlie Gallagher and Leo Brennan; (Front) Eugene Doherty, Owenie Sweeney, Paddy Gallagher, Dinnie Doherty, Connie Boyle, Jimmy O'Donnell, Dermot Logue and Paddy O'Donnell (Cope Archive).

Members of Dungloe Choir who sang at the Cleendra Mass Rock.

Back: Breid O'Donnell (McPaul), Evelyn O'Donnell (Chemist), Catherine Campbell, Bridget Ann Gallagher, Mena Melly, Kitty Bonner NT, Mary Sweeney, Margaret Ward (Reilly) Cha Sweeney (Gallagher), Ann McElwee, Ann Hanlon, Patricia McLoughlin, La Sweeney (Hotel), Mary O'Donnell, Mary Rose McLoughlin, Una Brennan, Ida Kennedy, Mary Joyce

Front: Agnes McCauley, Sally Duffy, Ita Brunnick, Ester McBride, Noreen Sharkey (McGlynn),
Breid McFadden, Kathleen O'Donnell, Kathleen Brunnick, Mary Ward (McGee)

Right Top: At the Mass Rock at Cleendra, Paddy the Cope is sitting with his sisters Hannah (Johnnie Cannon) on the left, Bridget O'Donnell, Marameelan, on the right. Above him is Canon Molloy, Father Gardiner (son of Paddy's friend Dr Gardner), and Paddy's son Jim. Among the crowds are: left, John Glackin, Maghery, between Fr Gardner and Jim, Dinny Houston, Maghery, and partially obscured by the cross, Charlie McShea (Loughsalt) (Cope Archive, Derry Journal Photograph by Denis Tynan, National Photographic Archive)

Right Bottom: Paddy at the Cleendra Mass with his godson Rev Gerard Gardner and a number of unidentified nuns (Derry Journal photo by Denis Tynan, National Photographic Archive).

The celebrants at the Cleendra Mass Rock were Dungloe born Rev Gerard Gardiner, O.P., of the Dominican Priory Sligo and the Very Rev Canon Molloy, D.Ph., P.P., as master of ceremonies. The Mass-servers were Jim and Pat Gallagher, grandsons of Paddy the Cope. The choir was under the direction of Kitty Bonner NT Dungloe (Derry Journal Photo, Denis Tynan; Cope Archive)

Paddy's cousin, the Rev Father Flavin O'Donnell, a US Major Chaplain stayed with him in Dungloe in June 1946. Fr Flavin had been in Italy for 3 years with the American forces fighting to liberate Europe. Paddy used his connections and called up Kathleen O'Connell, De Valera's secretary, to arrange for his cousin to meet the Taoiseach in Dublin (Cope Family Archive)

Right: Paddy the Cope, here photographed in a fine study in 1949, coming up to his eightieth year. He had lost his wife Sally the year before and was gradually picking up the pieces. From this period on, Paddy was a regular subject for Irish and international journalists, keen to meet and record the great man's story (Capuchin Annual, 1949 – the annual, which is a very useful source, was published by the Franciscans)

Paddy refers to the Mass Rock in his autobiography:

> "...The signal was the same as was used during the Penal Laws when there was a price of five pounds on the head of every priest. During all that time there was Mass celebrated in Cleendra in a place called 'Ard-an-Affreann' (Height of the Mass). The people would not know what day Mass would be said until two hours before the time, for fear the priest-hunters would be near. There was and is a large white marble stone on the brae face, which can be seen for miles round. When the priest would arrive the Cleendra people would cover it with a black cloth and the people of Upper and Lower Templecrone would rush to Mass. Those who had far to come, came on horseback, with their wives sitting sideways behind them and a youngster in front. The islanders from Arranmore, Rutland, Innisfree, and Innishall came out in their boats, and it is said that at each Mass the side of the hill was covered with people..."[7]

---

7   *'My Story' Paddy the Cope, 1939, Jonathan Cape.*

MR. PATRICK GALLAGHER
The Templecrone Co-operative Society Co. Donegal

Above: On the night of 9th November 1935, twenty islanders, returning from working in Scotland, foundered on a rock. Nineteen were killed in what became known as the Arranmore Disaster. The tragedy was deeply felt locally. Paddy the Cope knew all about seasonal migration and he had family connections himself in Arranmore. In this photo, one of very many fine photographs taken by Irish Press and Irish Independent photographers, Paddy, on the right, is standing next to Jimmy Frank O'Donnell, Burtonport. Senator Joseph Connolly, who was also Minister for Lands and Fisheries, represented the State, in recognition of the national dimension of the tragedy. The military representative has not been identified (Irish Independent, National Photographic Archive).

Right: During its 100 year history, the Cope has, thankfully, had only one fatal accident. Jimmy O'Brien, Upper Main Street, Dungloe died on 17th October 1946 as the result of a tragic accident that occurred while cutting trees in Fintown. While working alongside other employees of the Cope, one of the trees fell and struck Jimmy and another workman Jimmy Doherty who had a miraculous escape. Jimmy O'Brien died almost immediately as a result of his injuries. Jimmy was a brilliant forward on the Dungloe G.A.A. Team. On the day of his funeral he was to have played against great rivals Gweedore. Players and officials from both clubs walked alongside the large cortege to the family plot in Dungloe. Jimmy Doherty was father of John Anthony Doherty, Quay Road, who retired from t h e C o p e i n 1 9 7 0 . Jimmy O'Brien was an uncle of Mary Joyce, Upper Main Street, Dungloe (Cope and O'Brien family archive)

MARCHING BANDS

The marching band tradition in the Rosses is still very strong today and it goes back a long way. Paddy the Cope, while he did not play an instrument himself it would seem (he and others would have surely mentioned it), was very fond of marching bands himself and whenever there was a Cope event he would make sure that a band or bands were present.

Left Top: The 'Wee Maghery' Band marched in the same band competition as the Meenacross Band overleaf, in 1961. Leading is Columba McPaul, from the left, the flag carrier is unidentified, the first fife player is Charlie McPaul, and in the same row are Hughie Gallagher, Thomas Sweeney and Hugh Houston. Behind Hughie Gallagher is Oliver Huston and Edward O'Donnell. Looking towards the camera in suit and tie is Seamus 'Toy' McGuire, son of Paddy McGuire; in light coloured jacket on the right is Dermot 'Blondie' Bonner. Paddy the Cope can be seen, seated on a chair on the pavement (National Photographic Archive, Denis Tynan Collection, many thanks to Breda (Langan) Sweeney and Veronica Bonner for help with identification in both of the 1961 band photos).

Left Bottom: This is the Derrydruel Pipe Band in the 1940s - very possibly 1946: the Derrydruel Band along with the Meenacross Pipe and Maghery Flute bands played at the April 1946 celebrations for the Cope's Dungloe Main Store reopening after the devastating fire in January 1945. Included are (Back): Danny Quinn (in cap, not in uniform), Anthony O'Donnell, Alex Carr, Paddy the Cope, Michael Boyle Logue, Con Carr, Davey O'Donnell, Mia O'Donnell (partially hidden) and Neilly Carr; (Front): John Carr, John O'Donnell, James 'Red' Carr (bass drum), Paddy Campbell, James O'Donnell and Danny Carr (Local Collection and Cope Archive).

Next Page: The Meenacross Band is here marching past the Cope in Dungloe in competition in 1961. Leading the band are Veronica (Bonner) Boyle – holding the letter 'C' – and Mary Ellen (Boyle) Bonner; Mary Ellen later married Owen Bonner who worked 44 years in the Cope. Behind, holding the 'Brigid Naofa' (St Bridget) banner, are Sean Brennan and Charlie McCarron, then Madge O'Donnell and (obscured) Evelyn Sweeney Glackin. Following at a distance are the boy members of the band: Paddy Devenney (band leader), James Sweeney, Tony Glackin (Cosgrave), Peter Brennan, Denis O'Donnell, Gerald (Roddy) Gallagher, Anthony Brennan, Roger Solan, Charles John Solan, Michael Sweeney, Jimmy Brennan, Jimmy Sweeney, Dan O'Donnell, Joe O'Donnell, John Solan and on the big drum, Kevin Bonner. Paddy the Cope can be seen seated on a chair on the pavement, in overcoat and cap. Paddy enjoyed marching bands and band competitions and was a big supporter of the tradition. The photograph gives a fine view of the main store frontage with the petrol pump outside and a picket gate across the door; upstairs are a number of people (not identified) hanging out the window to see the bands (National Photographic Archive, Denis Tynan Collection)

Packie the Cope was a keen footballer; in this 1929 photograph of the Combined Gweedore and Dungloe team, he is standing at the left end. At this time there were no separate Dungloe and Gweedore teams. Back: Packie the Cope Gallagher, John Doney Sweeney (Kincasslagh), Patrick Johnny Sally O'Donnell (Saltpans), Paddy McPaul (Saltpans), Bernie Sharkey, Hughie Hanlon (Tubberkeen) and Pat Doney Sweeney (brother of John, Kincasslagh). Front: Tom Diver (Gweedore, Tom was a tailor with Charlie Campbell in Dungloe), Owenie McFadden (Gweedore), John Hughie O'Donnell (captain, Dungloe, from the Shamrock Bar), two unidentified Gweedore players, and John Gorman (Quay Road, Dungloe). The photograph is courtesy of Rosaline O'Donnell, granddaughter of Patrick Johnny Sally and the identification is by Packie Boyle (Ferry).

SPORT

Sport, whether GAA or football, was and is very popular across Ireland and the Rosses is no exception. The Cope people formed their own teams and participated fully in the local teams. Paddy's son Packie was a player himself and was a great enthusiast for the local teams:

> "...The achievements of the great Dungloe team of the 'Twenties and 'Thirties has been chronicled elsewhere down the years, and, at any rate, I think it is a subject that should call for a special publication of its own. Is it any wonder then that the all-time greats of those years are still talked about around the Rosses fires and wherever men gather together to discuss the victories and defeats of yesterday. Great credit was due in no small measure to the untiring efforts of their Secretary-

This is the victorious 1930 Dungloe team, which defeated Letterkenny 3-2 to 2-3 on the Mental Hospital (St Conal's) grounds in Letterkenny. This photo was taken in Belfast when they travelled to play the Antrim champions. Packie the Cope Gallagher, standing on the left in the leather coat, would no doubt have provided transport via Cope lorry. Under Packie as team manager, Dungloe appeared in five successive finals between 1930 and 1934, winning three of them. It was a glorious decade: Dungloe won four championships in the Thirties and also won in 1940. The winning team, not all identified uniquely here, here, were: J. Boyle, Kevin Sweeney (first left seated), Dessie Sweeney (second left, seated), John Sweeney, Patrick Sweeney, Paddy McPaul (middle row, second from the right), Hughie Hanlon, Bernard Sharkey, Owenie McFadden (Gweedore), Michael O'Donnell (Gweedore), Tom Diver (Gweedore), M O'Donnell, S Sweeney, C Coyle and J Ward (Photograph from the Packie Bonner Collection; details from the excellent 'The Story of the Donegal Senior Championship 1919-2001' by An tAth. Seán Ó Gallchóir SP, Gortahork)

Manager, the late Packie Gallagher (Packie the Cope), because without his contribution, things would not have been the same. Like Carnot of Revolution days, he deserved the title of Architect of Victory. He it was, who organised their training each week and, something that may not be generally known, he placed the Co-Op. lorries at the team's disposal in order that they might get to venues all over the county. This was necessary at that time because there were no cars as there are now..."[8]

---

8   Ibid. Packie Bonner 1981

Above: Cope employees played their part in the many successful Dungloe GAA teams of the 1930s and 1940s onwards. This team photo is from 1948 (back row): Daniel Doherty, Frank White (Guard), Nonnie Gallagher, Jimmy Boyle, Owenie Boyle (Cope), Charlie Campbell, Gerry Begley, Paddy Clark, Gerry O'Riordan (Guard), Bernie O'Donnell; (front row): Jimmy O'Donnell, Paddy Kennedy (Guard), Jimmy O'Brien (Cope), Paddy Prendergast (Guard), Dom Bonner (NT, current Cope Committee and ex-Chairman), John Gallagher (Cope), Hughie O'Donnell, Patsy Sweeney (Solicitor), Pa Ward (Cope) (Photo and names/information courtesy of Packie Walsh, Burtonport).

GAA has always been a passionate affair in West Donegal, in both the Rosses and Gweedore. The competition between the two teams was fierce and, occasionally, not just on the pitch. Over the years, many Cope employees played their part in Dungloe's successes from the Twenties onwards. This memorial card, however, commemorates a particular competitive Senior Championship final in 1961 which was won by Gweedore 2-5 to Dungloe's 0-6. The individuals named are the Gweedore team and the Gweedore team colours are green and white. (PB Collection, card designed and printed by Jimmy Coll, Gweedore).

Left: The last time that Dungloe won the Donegal Senior Championship was over 40 years ago, when they won back to back championships in 1957 and 1958. This is the 1956 team, including a number of Cope people, which won the Donegal League Championship: (back): Frank White (Guard, Dungloe), John Doherty (Jimmy Tom), Packie (Neil) Gallagher (Dooey), Paddy Sweeney (Guard, Dungloe), Jim 'Cookie' (Jimmy Pheadair) Boyle (Bunaman, Dungloe), Conal Boyle (Dooey), Hughie O'Donnell (Biddie Hughie), Dungloe, Dom Murray (Guard, Doochary) and Seamus Rodgers (Annagry, Kincasslagh & Burtonport Copes); (middle) Fergal 'Fred' Sweeney (Dungloe, the Cope), Paddy O'Donnell (Biddie Hughie), Dungloe, Patsy McCole (Meenmore), Ben O'Donnell (Kincasslagh - Ben later wrote 'The Story of the Rosses'), Donal Boyle (Dungloe), Owenie Boyle (Dungloe), Rory O'Reilly (originally from Cavan, Rory worked in the Northern Bank, Dungloe) and Patrick Roarty (Meenmore); (front) Packie Boyle (Ferry) and Hughie McGee, both Cope employees (Local Photo Collection, information from Packie Ferry and Hughie McGee)

The Cope Football Team in 1959: (Back) Seamus Rodgers, Packie Boyle, Cathal McCole, Pa Ward, Patrick Ward, Fred Sweeney, John McCole and Jimmy O'Donnell; (Front) Hughie Boyle, Neilly Sweeney, Liam McDevitt, Paddy O'Donnell, Andy Logue, Eugene Doherty and Hugh McGee (Cope Archive).

LAST YEARS OF THE COPEMAN

Paddy the Cope lived on a further eighteen years after his wife Sally died. In this period, he remained active, chairing the Cope Committee, but progressively leaving day to day operations to his son Packie, until he predeceased Paddy in 1958, Dan Deery, Leo Brennan and others. Paddy was in demand with researchers, journalists and official bodies although he was never gifted a major State position, for example Senator, which his achievements would have warranted

Presentation to "Paddy the Cope'

"...The National Co-operative Council last night presented "Paddy the Cope" (Mr. Patrick Gallagher) with a Waterford glass decanter and drinking set, to mark his 50 years' work in the co-operative movement at a function in the Country Shop, St. Stephen's Green. Dublin.

The presentation, one of the events of the third national cooperative week, was made by Mr. Brendan O'Carroll, Chairman of the Council, who said that it was an inspiration to them that Mr. Gallagher, whose struggle to set up a co-operative movement began 50 years ago, still had a keen interest in the movement.

In this studio portrait taken on a trip to Dublin, Paddy the Cope is in the centre with his granddaughter Annie; Packie and Mary (Campbell), or Mary Packie as she was known, are either side of him. Annie, born on 13th June 1939, was named for Paddy and Sally's lost daughter who was taken from them just before her third birthday. The photo probably dates from 1948 or 1949. Sally had died in March 1948 and would otherwise have been in the photograph. Packie managed the Cope from 1951 to his untimely death in 1958 (J.D. Stanley photographer, Dublin; Cope Family Collection; Paddy the Cope's 'My Story')

Mr. Gallagher's book would make an ideal textbook in national and secondary schools, and it would help to inspire the youth of the present day to do things for their country.

Mr. Gallagher. when he returned thanks for the presentation said that the credit for launching the cooperative in Donegal really belonged to his late wife.

Mr. Gallagher's "My Story", it was mentioned last night, is to be filmed in Donegal next year..."[9]

---

9   *Irish Times 11th October 1956*

Paddy featured regularly in newspaper articles in his last twenty years:

People of Ireland

PATRICK GALLAGHER of Dungloe

"...The grand old man of the Rosses is in his 93rd year. Age has slowed his step and dimmed his sight somewhat, but the spirit which propelled this fiery petrel from Cleendra is still very much that of the Paddy Pat Bawn of old. Though Mr. Patrick Gallagher—he would resent that formality –was a legend long before many of us were born, he is to the present day as much a key figure in Dungloe and in all Donegal as he was when this century was young and the impact of his movement, the Templecrone Co-operative Society, was fresh.

Paddy the Cope still holds the chair in that organisation and one can easily gather when speaking to the man that he is something more than a mere figurehead. He watches its many activities with the eagle eye which steered it successfully and spectacularly, on its rugged course from the hillside of Cleendra through the towns and villages of the Rosses to a fame that can reasonably be described as worldwide.

An Individualist

The years have brought no mellowing in Patrick Gallagher. He still has all the old fire left; the spirit which has earned him some enemies but also won him countless friends. He is a rugged individualist of the brand which nature seems to adorn better with the years and one cannot help but admire him.

His life's work, of course, is history. The leaders of the international co-operative movement have long feted him on both sides of the Atlantic. This may well he because he succeeded in breathing into the system an air of romance which they could not engender in the huge enterprises of a similar nature in their own lands.

But the intriguing thing about Paddy Gallagher today is his amazing memory. At the age of 93, he recalls without difficulty even minor incidents in the building of his enterprise and the names and character of people who but briefly flashed into its course..."[10]

Paddy was always very friendly with visitors and welcomed the opportunity in his last few years of talking to people and taking them around the area. Mickey Dawson (Lower Keadue) is originally from Belfast – his mother Margaret recalls the first time that the family, herself, Mickey's father – also Mickey – and their son Ciaran first visited Donegal in 1961.

---

10   *Irish Times 2nd May 1963*

Above: Paddy the Cope is here showing Cleendra to Michael Dawson and his son Ciaran from Belfast. It was Michael, his wife Margaret and Ciaran's first trip to the Rosses (Sally the Cope Gallagher Collection)

Next Page: Paddy the Cope was a member of the County Donegal Historical Society and, although we do not know whether he took a keen interest in their activities, he did attend the 1957 AGM.
Back row: Rev. E. J. Mullen; Very Rev. Canon Molloy; D. F. Ward; Dr Nancy Mc Glinchey; Eamon McGlinchey, next is *possibly* Dermot McMahon;
Middle Row: Rev. J. Mcloughlin; Paddy McGill (Ardara); to his left on Paddy's left shoulder is Sean McMenamin; Francis Cleary (Headmaster of the Four Masters School Donegal Town), C. King, C O'Doherty, and Rev. A McElwee (Glenties)
Front row: Liam MacMenamin (teacher from Falcarragh); Paddy the Cope Gallagher; the Franciscan in the middle front row is Fr Terence O'Donnell, from Kincasslagh, a local historian; then Fr Paddy Gallagher (Fr P O Gallachair, Bundoran); and J.C.T. 'Chris' MacDonagh. (Photo courtesy of Donegal County Archives, Lifford: ref P17/111)

Paddy gave an address at Frosses on 2nd April 1952 at poet Ethna Carbery's 50th anniversary; Ethna set up the Shan Van Vocht magazine in 1896 and later married celebrated Donegal writer Seamus McManus. Paddy called Ethna 'the greatest woman of her generation'. On Paddy's left is Charles J O'Boyle, local teacher and later Chairman of the Donegal Association; on his right in the fur coat Mrs Charlie Sullivan, a teacher in Mountcharles; she was originally from

Meenbanad and born a Cannon. Fr Tommy Gallagher, the curate at Mountcharles can be seen next to Seamus Gildea a local teacher, wearing the fáinne (a circular lapel pin signifying one could speak Irish) (Jim (Packie) the Cope Collection, likely a Denis Tynan photograph from the Derry Journal; many thanks to Helen Meehan for her help identifying the people and the occasion).

'Daddy Trout', again in the late 1940s, is sitting outside the Dungloe store with grandson John on his knee and granddaughter Sally behind in the doorway (Cope Family archive).

Right Top: Paddy the Cope outside the Cope House, Dungloe in August 1949 with his grandchildren from his son Packie's family. Sitting on his knee is a 1 year old Pat the Cope Gallagher (born March 1948), future TD and Minister; from left to right, Annie, Mary, John and Sally (a note on the back says 'Jim, baby, 1 month'). The grandchildren called their grandfather 'Daddy Trout': he was always bringing back fish from the lakes, the rivers or the sea – fishing had always been a passion of his. Paddy lived with them in the Cope House until he passed on in 1966. Sally had insisted that Packie and Mary came to live with them after they wed in September 1938 and when Sally died they and his son Jim's family in the Quay Road were a great comfort to him (Cope and Gallagher Family Archives; photo taken by Mr Oliver Ryan, Dublin)

Right Bottom: As well as fishing, Paddy enjoyed a spot of grouse shooting. He refers in 'My Story' to an incident in 1917 when he and his friend Joe O'Donnell were invited by a Mrs Logue of Doocharry to shoot 'on her mountain'. The shoot on the adjacent land was owned by the Lord Mayor of Londonderry - and watched over by his bailiff. After the bailiff shot at Joe's dog for going after birds on the Lord Mayor's land, Paddy chased him down the Corkscrew into Doocharry Barracks looking to shoot him – he said he 'might have been hanged for murder only I met with two men with much more sense than I' {Joe and the bailiff]. Paddy is on the right in this photo, no airs and graces - a piece of string tying his jacket together, socks rolled down and a pen in his top pocket. His two companions have not been identified at the time of writing (Cope Family Archive, 'My Story' Chapter 17, 2006 edition).

Immaculate Heart of Mary
pray for him.

Pray for the repose of the soul of

Paddy Gallagher

**Co-op. House, Dungloe,
Co. Donegal.**

who died

24th day of June 1966

Aged 94 years

R.I.P.

Eternal rest, grant unto him, O Lord.
And let perpetual light shine upon
him. May his soul and the souls of all the
faithful departed through the mercy of
Christ rest in peace. Amen.

Paddy passed away in 1966. Tributes were paid across Ireland and his passing was commented upon internationally in newspaper articles (Cope Family archive).

Left: Paddy the Cope visited Mary Sweeney (Mary Phaidi Bhrian) of Bunawillen on her 100th birthday; Mary lived on to be 104. Paddy himself was in his nineties at this stage. Mary's daughter Gracie Johnny Phaidi was an outworker for the Cope's knitting business and had a knitting machine at home; she was one of the Cope's best knitting workers (Sweeney and Gallagher family photograph)

A Cope Staff Management Training group in 1976. One of General Manager Cyril Winder's management innovations in the 1970s was an up to date staff development programme. There were 17 young Cope employees at the event: (Back) Thomas Donaghy, Fred Sweeney, John Moore, Gerald Glackin, Packie Gallagher, Packie McHugh, Kevin Bonner, Seamus Sheerin, John A. Gallagher; (Centre) Rose McGettigan, Sally McGettigan, Breid O'Donnell, Alice Hamilton, Kathleen A. Doherty, Angela Devenney, Sheila McGettigan, Mary Gallagher; (Front) Eugene Doherty, two course lecturers (not named), Cyril Winder and Charlie Boyle (Cope Archive)

Another of Cyril Winder's innovations was the big Christmas party, including bringing Santa to Dungloe for the first time, it is said. This is a group photograph of the Main Store Staff in 1981. At the back are: Mary Gallagher, John Gallagher, John O'Donnell, Joseph Sharpe, Denis Ward, John Boyle, Connie Boyle, John Walshe, Hugh McGee, Anthony Glackin, Gerald Glackin, Fred Sweeney, Jerry Hanlon, Brian Sweeney, Charles Solan, Margaret O'Donnell. In front are: Breid O'Donnell, Nancy Shovelin, Rosemary Gorman, Santa (Pa Ward), Ann Shovelin, Mary Coll, Sheila McGettigan

Working in the Cope was and still is like being in one big, extended family; workers from across the shops and Bakery and Builders' Providers' and elsewhere would socialise together, play football and feel a sense of shared purpose and belonging, inspired by Paddy the Cope and the cooperative ideal. Back: John Friel (electrician), Owen Sweeney (Dobell), John Gallagher (Fluke), Connie Boyle, unknown, Big Cathal McCole, Neily Sweeney and Owenie Boyle. Front: Jim McPaul, Owenie Sweeney (Teto), Pa Ward, James Breslin, John McCole, Dinny Doherty (Bakery and then a Cope driver), Paddy Gallagher (Mor) and Jimmy Ward (Sticks), At very front: John Gallagher (Gaga) and Patrick Coll (Acres). (Cope Photo Archive)

"...We arrived into Dungloe, it felt very different to what we were used to. The Cope had a small window, planks on the floor, with knots in the planks, and a big wide counter. There was a cup on a wire which shot up to the office – money would go in it, change and a receipt would come back. Mickey spied a book "Paddy the Cope" and went in and bought it. A man – it must have been Jim the Cope – said "Would you like the author to sign it?" He got Paddy out; he was wearing a black ganzie, not a soft woollen jumper. He was on the stick, Mickey put his hand out. Paddy asked "Where are you from?" he signed the book and they were talking. "Have you a car?" Paddy asked, "Would you like to see where I was born?" Paddy directed Mickey to Maghery. He pointed across the bay, pointed to where he was born, "And that's where we saw the fairies". He scowled and said some people didn't believe in them. He mentioned the story of someone who couldn't stop dancing..."[11]

Mickey, Margaret and family came back to Donegal year after year after that first time. They stayed at Maggie Neil's near Burtonport; Margaret Maggie Neil, Maggie's daughter, used to run it. Maggie had a shop and a wee guest house. Maggie had a wee kitchen, it was the hub of the house. Paddy the Cope had said

---

11 *This is a personal memoir by Margaret Dawson to the editor. Paddy tells the story about the fairies in his book.*

Cope Committee 1930s The Cope Committee in the 1930s: Denis O'Donnell, Dan McGinley, Jimmie Bonar, Dominick Bonar, John O'Donnell, Dan Sweeney (Secretary), Paddy Gallagher (President and Manager), John Gillespie, Dan Deery and Johnnie Brown (from 'My Story' 1946 edition)

The Cope Committee in 1979: Johnnie Doherty, John McHugh, Connie Devenney, John Gorman, John Joe Brennan; (seated) Hugh McGee, John O'Donnell, Dannie Breslin, Dom Bonner (Cope Photo Archive)

The Cope Committee 1975: Back: Eugene Doherty, Connie Devenney, Hugh McGee, John McHugh, John Joe Brennan, Charlie Boyle. Front: John Gorman, John O'Donnell, Dom Bonner, Dolly O'Donnell, Willie Durnin.

to Maggie "What do you need?" The Cope gave Maggie beds and bedclothes and when she started to make a few bob, she paid it all back.

COMMITTEE – the 'Twelve Apostles'

Committee Members 1920

From its very beginning, the Cope could not have been managed not by just the one man, not even by the exceptional man that was Paddy the Cope. The Cope has been blessed by being steered by gifted local people who have the community's interests at heart. In this 1920 Committee, the range of representation across Templecrone is very apparent:

Patrick Gallagher	Chairman
Daniel Sweeney	Secretary
James Bonner	Keadue
John Browne	Loughsalt
John Devenney	Maghery
John O'Donnell	Craghyboyle
Denis O'Donnell	Derrydruel
Dan Deery	Meenmore
Charlie Boyle	Meenbanad
James Durnin	Croveigh
Dom McGinley	Mullaghderg
James Doherty	Belcruit
John Gillespie	Saltpans

Committee Members: 1945 to date

*member before 1945, **current members are in bold**

Dominick Bonner*	Meenbanad	1945 – 1950
Charles Boyle*	Meenbanad	1945 – 1956
Charles Browne*	Loughsalt, Dungloe	1945 – 1958
Phil McCauley*	Dungloe	1945 – 1960
James Bonner*	Falmore, Dungloe	1945 – 1964
John O Donnell*	Cragheyboyle, Dungloe	1945 – 1965
Willie Durnin*	Croveigh, Dungloe	1945 – 1988
Dan Deery	Dungloe	1952 – 1972
John O Donnell	Annagry	1956 – 1996
Dessie Cannon	Lettermacaward	1957 – 1960
Paddy O Donnell	Belcruit, Kincasslagh	1957 – 1969
Dominick Bonner	Dungloe	1960 –
Conal Boyle	Dooey, Lettermacaward	1967 – 1995
Danny Breslin	Dungloe Rd, Burtonport	1967 – 1974
Fr. O`Callaghan P.P.	Dungloe	1968 – 1969
Dolly O`Donnell	Dungloe	1969 – 1993

Mary Logue (Gallagher)	Dungloe	1969 – 1972 and 1996 – 2001
Connie Devenney	Mill Rd, Dungloe	1969 –
John Gorman	Calhame, Annagry	1969 – 1988
John Mc Hugh	Narin	1972 – 1994
John Doherty	Termon, Dungloe	1972 –
Eugene Doherty	Meenbanad	1973 –
Charles Boyle	Dungloe	1973 – 1996
Hugh Mc Gee	Dungloe	1973 –
John Joe Brennan,	Fair Hill, Dungloe	1973 – 1999
Owen Bonner		1989 – 1992
Anne T Sweeney		1993 – 2002
Tony Cannon		1993 –
Jimmy Durnin		1995 –
Vincie O'Donnell		1996 – 2001
Pat Forker		1998 – 2005
Denis Ward		1999 –
Patrick Dunleavy		2000 –
Gerard McElwee		2000 – 2002
John A Bonner		2001 – 2003
Breda Langan Sweeney		2002 –
Marguerite McGee		2003 –
Kevin Bonner		2005 –
Pat Bonner		2005 – 2008

Chairman:

Patrick Gallagher, Paddy the Cope	1906 – 1966
Dan Deery	1966 – 1972
John Doherty	1972 – 1977
Dominick Bonner	1977 – 1986
John Joe Brennan	1986 – 1990
Eugene Doherty	1990 – 1997
John Doherty	1997 – 2009
Pat Dunleavy	2009 –

Secretary

John O'Donnell	1906-1908
Daniel Sweeney	1908-1937
Leo Brennan	1937-1970
Dominick Bonner	1970-1977
Charlie Boyle	1977-1987
Dolly O'Donnell	1987-1993
Anne Teresa Sweeney	1993-2002
Breda Langan Sweeney	2002-

Memories of the Cope

To help commemorate the Centenary, Cope people were invited to contribute their personal memoirs. Some of these were written before the actual date of the Centenary, some as early as 2005, and refer to anticipated developments, such as the Builders' Providers and the Dungloe Supermarket, that have since come to fruition.

DOM BONNER
Co-opted on to Cope Committee 1960
Vice Chairman 1966 - 1970
Secretary 1970 - 1977
Chairman 1977 - 1985
Committee Member 1985 - date

"…The Cope was about eighteen years in existence when I was born. My mother was a first cousin of Sally – Paddy the Cope's wife. Sally's sister Madgie Óg was married and living next door to us so that our family were always familiar with everything that was happening in the Cope.

Dom Bonner with some of his family at the Centenary dinner on 14th January 2006. Standing: Éimear Gillane, Aideen Gillane, Enda Bonner, Donegal County Councillor; and seated: Fr Neil Boyle, Phyllis Bonner and Dom Bonner (Cope Photo).

A few years before I was born, a branch of the Cope was opened at Meenbanad, about a hundred yards from our house. Meenbanad National School, which I attended from the age of three, was situated right beside the Cope branch. We, the scholars, spent all our playtime playing around the Cope and when Jimmy Mhanuis – the storeman - was elsewhere engaged we played in the Cope store around and on top of the sacks of flour, oats and meal but when Jimmy returned and reached for a whip which he kept on a shelf we all disappeared like rats. He never used it but found it more effective than wasting his breath scolding. He was a quiet, kind character. In the evening, we often had to run to the Cope for messages and were always given a few sweets to munch on the way home.

The Cope had many fascinations for us. After his lunch every day the teacher took a stroll over to chat with the Manager and Storeman and often took a few minutes extra to finish whatever topic they were discussing. That meant that we had an extended playtime most days.

The Cope had many other attractions for us young people, not least, the little two ton lorry which came with merchandise a few times a week. It was driven by a friendly character, wee Owen Sweeney who never was in a hurry and the lorry was one of the few vehicles to be seen regularly on the roads of the Rosses at the time.

My parents became members of the Cope very early on. They never shopped anywhere else and were very appreciative of the dividend paid to members at the end of every year.

The Cope gave quite a lot of employment in the area. A ship came regularly from Sligo and sometimes from Glasgow into Burtonport with cargoes of flour and meal. When the unloading of the ship was due to start there would be scores of men looking for work. Of course only a small number could be employed on every shift as there were only one or two gangways between the ship and the pier. It was hard work as each sack contained ten stone of flour and was carried on the backs of the workers – out of the hold, down the gangway and across the pier to the store. Sometimes if the tide was high the ship would stand far above the pier and the gangway could be quite steep. At the end of the shift the workers would look like snowmen and they had to walk or cycle home – most of them a distance of a few miles. Their wages were about ten shillings a shift – not much you might say but there was very little employment in those days and no dole or unemployment benefit. My oldest brother often worked on the flour boat and was delighted to get the work.

At certain times there was work available for casual workers cutting and saving the Cope turf, draining and fencing the Cope fields, cutting and

The Story of the Cope

saving the Cope hay and sealing the leaks in the Mill Race. I might point out that the Mill Race was used to conduct the water from the bridge on the Gweedore Road past the Garda Barracks down to the Generator at the Mill to provide electricity for the Cope premises and the homes of the town. The ESB didn't come to Dungloe until the early 1950s.

Another thing that stands out in my memory was the number of young women that were employed in the Hosiery factory in those early years. They worked in the factory on machines knitting gloves and socks. The fingering had to be done by hand and this was done in the workers' homes at night. Some had bicycles and cycled to work every day but others who lived miles from the town and had no bicycles rented sleeping accommodation during the week from friends and relatives in the town. The working hours in those days were from nine o' clock in the morning until seven in the evening with one hour for lunch six days a week. At that time there was no free day or half day as there is now. Some of these factory workers would leave the factory in the summertime and go off to the Isle of Man, Grimsby and Lowestoft in England or to Peterhead, Frazerborough, Stornaway and Lerwick in Scotland to work with fish. "Gutting" was the word used to describe this activity. There was more money at this work and it gave workers, with a flair for travel, an opportunity to see other parts. Indeed sometimes the Cope itself employed fish workers to cure herring in Burtonport and Kincasslagh. My sister worked in the Cope Factory for a number of years – the happiest years of her life she claimed.

From its foundation the Cope was the principal employer in the Rosses. As well as the Cope Staff scores of handknitters were employed making Aran Sweaters for the British and American markets. The wool was given out to the knitters who worked at home and turned out some beautiful garments. Some knitters could make two or three sweaters in a week. They worked into the early hours with the aid of poorly lit paraffin oil lamps – there was no electric lighting in country areas in those days.

When the Cope began, one or two members in each branch area were elected to the Committee. My Uncle Dominick and my father's cousin and next door neighbour, Jimmy Bonner were chosen to represent the Meenbanid branch. The monthly meetings were held on the second Saturday of the month at 3 p.m. For years these two gentlemen could be seen setting off walking to Dungloe to attend these meetings. I understand their reward was ten shillings per meeting. They kept this up until shortly before they died in the early fifties.

In 1960, one of the Dungloe members – Phil McCauley, who was also the local Post Master, died and I was co-opted on to the Committee to replace him. Paddy the Cope who was approaching ninety years of age at that time and was becoming very feeble never missed a meeting and was quite alert in the Chair. I served on the Committee for the last six years of Paddy's Chairmanship and during that time, I got to know him very well. He was a simple, modest, just honest and considerate man. He never took even a box of matches without paying for it. He never wanted to put pressure on poor people who ran into debt. He treated everybody equally. He was always on the lookout for schemes and projects that would improve the lives of the people of the Rosses. He never asked for or got help from the Government although he was a staunch De Valera man. I remember well the summer of 1937 when De Valera visited Dungloe. The Cope Lorry was used as a platform and Paddy chaired the meeting. When the meeting was over he took De Valera in to visit Sally and to enjoy a cuppa. The Main Street was crowded and I felt that Paddy must have been a proud man.

Taoiseach Eamon de Valera is seated in the Cope House, Paddy and Sally's home in Dungloe right by the Main Street Store. From left to right are: Donegal TDs Brian Brady (TD from 1932-49), Cormac Breslin (TD, 1937-77), Paddy the Cope and Canon Molloy. Paddy recalls in his book that Dev '...again visited Dungloe on 11th June 1943 and I presided at his meeting. Aye! Damn but he paid Sally and me a great honour by drinking a cup of tea with us in the Cope house...' The photo possibly dates from de Valera's earlier electioneering visit on 29th June 1937. On the wall behind are family photos still in the Gallagher family (Cope Archive, Derry Journal photograph)

I will never forget Paddy's delight and joy when at the AGM of 1964 the Auditor, PJ McCarthy announced that sales for that year had exceeded a quarter of a million pounds.

When Sally passed away it was left to Paddy's daughter in law Mrs Packie, as she was affectionately known, and her family to look after Paddy. This they did lovingly until he passed away on the 24th June 1966 at the ripe old age of 94. Not alone that but when the revised edition of "My Story" was published in 1946 it was Mrs Packie who corrected the script – no easy task, and rewrote long sections of it with her green pen. It was then typed by the two typists in the office, namely Mary Ellen Brennan (Paddy's niece) and Ann T. Sweeney Aboligan. Thanks to these three ladies we have a full account of the history of the Cope and its famous founder. Paddy always hoped for the day when his story would be made into a film but who knows – it might happen yet.

From time to time exams were held to recruit young apprentices and on many occasions tests were held to award Cope Scholarships to Rosses students to attend St. Eunan's and Loreto in Letterkenny and The McDevitt Institute, Glenties and I was given the task of setting the exam papers, superintending the exams and marking the answer books. I was privileged to be honoured with this task.

At this stage, I would like to pay tribute to Committee members and the Staff who brought the Cope to where it is today. I am privileged and honoured to have worked with them down the years. Many names come to mind but if I were to jot my memories of them all, I would end up with a bigger volume than "My Story" but I couldn't let this opportunity pass without mentioning a few.

Leo Brennan joined the Cope after leaving school at the age of fourteen. He never had any special training but he worked his way up until he became General Secretary, Financial Controller and Paddy the Cope's right hand man. At a very young age he became the anchor man who steered the Cope on an even keel through good times and bad until he died on the 6th December 1970. I am happy to say that I succeeded him as Secretary to the Committee.

Dan Deery succeeded Paddy the Cope as Chairman of the Society. He spent his early days in charge of the Corn Mill like his father before him. He was a sound man, conscientious and hardworking and always had the interests of the Cope at heart. On his death bed, I visited him on several occasions and during one of my last visits we talked about the Cope and he asked me to stay on the Committee as long as I could. He died on 23th October 1972.

Cyril Winder, a Dublin man was General Manager from 1969 until he died in November 1994. I was privileged to be on the interview board which appointed him. He was an energetic young man who carried out his duties with great sincerity. He had few hobbies but spent almost all his nights in his office, planning and organising and promoting the interests of the Cope. During his twenty five years in the Cope, he transformed the place completely. He streamlined the administration, extended the premises, gave the Society a new image and provided training courses for every section of the staff.

The senior management team in 1969, left to right, Dan Deery, Leo Brennan and Cyril Winder, the newly appointed General Manager. Within 3 years, Dan Deery (51 years service) and Leo Brennan (50 years service) had passed on having given the Cope great stability, continuity and strength (Cope Archive)

This Cope Committee is from 1981, when Dom Bonner was Chairman: (Standing) Conal Boyle, John O'Donnell, Connie Devenney, John McHugh, Hugh McGee, Johnnie Doherty; (Seated, going round the table from the left) Willie Durnin, Dolly O'Donnell, Cyril Winder (General Manager), Charlie Boyle, Dom Bonner, John J. Brennan, John Gorman, Eugene Doherty (Cope Archive).

I would also like to pay tribute to Eugene Doherty who was Chairman of the Society for a number of years. He brought about many changes for the improvement of the Society.

Last but not least, I would like to compliment the present Chairman John J. Doherty who is serving his second term as Chairman. Like Eugene, he was in the Chair during a period when Managers were coming and going and there were spells when we had no Manager at all but with the help of staff members of the Committee namely Tony Cannon, Denis Ward, Hugh Mc Gee and Ann T. Sweeney, he overcame every obstacle. He is now with the assistance of the present Manager Jimmy Nangle, engaged in providing new premises for the Builders Providers which has just been completed and re-furbishing the Main Street Premises and the replacement of the Supermarket which was destroyed by fire recently. It is a marathon development and I wish all concerned the best of luck.

I had hopes that some day one of Paddy the Cope's grandsons would take over as Manager of the business. At one stage Jim the Cope (Junior) who was Manager of the Supermarket and a talented and popular business man was a promising candidate but his young life was tragically ended by a freak accident. May he rest in peace.

I am very pleased to state that my son Enda's firm, Bonner and O' Donnell have been Auditors to the Society since P.J. McCarthy passed to his reward years ago.

I congratulate the Cope on reaching the centenary of its foundation and I hope that it will continue and prosper for another century.

Guim gach rath agus sonas agus adh ar Chomharchumann Theampall Chroine ins na blianta amach romhainn…"

HUGH M^CGEE
Cope Employee 1952-2001
Committee Member 1973 to date

Hughie McGee in 2006

"…I went to work in the Cope in 1952 and retired in 2001. Paddy the Cope was still Manager and Chairman of the Society when I started; he was over 80 by then. Emigration was widespread; there was a huge effort being made to bring some investment to the area. This prompted the late Dan Paddy Anna (Gallagher) to declare that the only investment that would survive would be a suitcase factory.

My first job was in the Agricultural Department where Josie McCole and Jimmy Doherty were the senior staff. I was later sent to Burtonport Cope where Joe Brennan was manager. After some time, I was taken back to Dungloe and sent out on the Tea Van (travelling shop) where Connie Boyle was the driver.

My next assignment was in the Grocery on the Main Street in Dungloe where Packie Bonner and Francie Houston were the senior people. Eventually in 1957, I was transferred to the Hardware Department where Timmy Doherty and Pa Ward were in charge. In 1958, I was appointed Manager of the Hardware Department and remained in that position until I retired in 2001.

In 1973, I was elected to the Management Committee or The Twelve Apostles as they were affectionately known. I was immediately impressed by the dedication and commitment of this group of people who gave of their time voluntarily. They would have at least twenty meetings per year. One of the items on the agenda at my first meeting was staff appointments. I am delighted that this item still appears on the Cope Committee Agenda. It confirmed for me that one of the main reasons that Paddy the Cope set up the Society in the first instance was to create employment for the area. Paddy's view was that a new job created meant that another family, a new home and a new Cope customer was in his area.

When Packie the Cope died suddenly in 1958, there was a gap where the Committee endeavoured to find a suitable replacement. But, as the staff have done on many occasions since, they took on responsibilities for the day to day running of the Society and under the watchful eyes of people like Leo Brennan, Dan Deery, Charlie Boyle, Pa Ward and Eddie McCullagh and of course from 1969, Cyril Winder, the Cope was in safe hands. It has been said that a good start is half the work.

While the Cope has had a very successful century, the Cope certainly has a bright future under the present management team and our excellent staff. With the opening of our €6m Builders' Providers, Agriculture and DIY complex in Sheskinarone, the modernising of our Main Street Shopping Centre and plans being well advanced for the opening of our state of the art Supermarket in July 2007. The €2m investment in our Annagry Branch has just opened. Further, there are exciting new development planned for our old bakery and factory site on the Quay Road.

I remember Paddy very well. There was a story about Paddy meeting a returned Yank who had accumulated a fair bit of wealth and property and was well known in America. Paddy and he got into an argument about who was more famous. To settle it, Paddy went into the Cope and brought out two envelopes and addressed one 'Paddy the Cope Ireland', the other man addressed his too, with the address Ireland. Paddy said 'When you go back to America post those two letters and we will see which arrives first'. Paddy's arrived in due course; the other is yet to come.

When I started working in the Cope in 1952 Paddy the Cope was still the boss. Two years previously his son Jim who was Manager had to retire with ill health. His other son Packie who was Regional Manager with ESSO was recalled by the Cope Committee to assist his father in the running of the business and although his sons were in charge of the day to day running of the Cope they always addressed their father as the "Boss". Paddy remained active and was involved in the running of the Cope until his death in 1966 aged 95 years.

In 1994 tragedy again came to the Cope family when Jim the Cope, Paddy's grandson died. Jim, at the time of his death, was Manager of the Supermarket and would have had a big future in the Cope.

One day, Paddy was supervising the unloading of a 10 ton consignment of flour into the store. This task was done manually, bag by bag. As was the custom at the time, when the old Angelus bell rang at the old church at the top of the town, all work stopped for prayer. After what seemed to Paddy to be an eternity he shouted "Hey boys is it the Rosary you are saying".

The big events in Dungloe at the time were Connie's Marquee, the Summer Fair Day, the Fancy Dress competition, football matches between Dungloe and Gweedore, the Cope's Winter Sale, St Patrick's Day and Sunday night dancing in Patrick Johnny Sally's hall.

'...The oldest and longest serving member of the Templecrone Cope Committee, Mr Willie Durnin, was given the task to gather all his puff and blow out all the 75 candles on the cake which was specially baked to mark the Cope's 75th anniversary...' (Cope's 75th Anniversary booklet in 1981)

THE WINDER YEARS (1969-1993)

Cyril Winder, General Manager 1969-93

The following appreciation of Cope General Manager was written by Hugh McGee, Cope Committee member since 1973. The building programme and business achievements of the Cope during Mr Winder's stewardship are described in the appropriate sections of this book. This appreciation focuses on the management innovations introduced by him in this period (1969-93) and on Cyril Winder, the man.

"...In 1969, the Cope Management made a bold decision and advertised in the National Press for a General Manager, resulting in the appointment of Dublin man Cyril Winder as General Manager of the Cope. In the late winter of 1969, Mr Winder bravely brought his wife and three children up to Dungloe to take up the reins at the Cope. His family had no prior connection to the locality. He wanted wide, open spaces for his children to grow up in, majestic scenery for his wife to enjoy and a business to nurture.

His passion for business had been forged in top retail establishments in Dublin and London. The names of the shops he worked in trip off the tongue: Switzers and Simpsons, Harrods and Roches Stores. He studied hard in night school and learned skills that he applied to his stewardship of the Cope: in sales, book-keeping, carpentry, electricity. He earned qualifications in work study, shop display and retail management.

He believed that a 'co-operative' should not be seen as a noun, but as an active verb and he was proud of being a jack of all trades. He spent hours on the front line working with his men and was an accomplished joiner and electrician as well as a business manager.

He always believed passionately in his staff. He organised training workshops in Ostan na Rosann, wrote a staff guide and many staff bulletins and introduced modern standards of employment. By 1975, four staff members had joined the management committee, one of his and the Cope Committee's many innovations during his time at the helm.

He introduced a staff Christmas party to celebrate the Cope's achievements across the year as well as to thank the staff. He was especially proud of being the first person in Dungloe to invite no less a celebrity as Santa to come to the Cope. The 1970s onwards saw a period of exceptional growth and the by-then 100 plus staff shared in the Cope's success, receiving national pay awards, qualifying for comprehensive pensions as well as having trade union recognition.

A lot of the developments that Mr Winder inspired, organised or oversaw might be taken for granted today. Under him, the Cope became a winning team, with him as captain. Consolidation, improvement in the appearance and efficiency of the store and merchandising of goods took up much of the remaining years of his stewardship of the Cope. Under his leadership, the "big shop in the main street" came of age.

He created a marketing image around the Cope that is still with us. The Cope logo is actually a sample of his handwriting. He launched the Cope stamp in 1973, modelled on the Green Shield stamp of the day. He organised advertising campaigns in the Democrat and Highland Radio, booklets to celebrate milestones in the Cope's exponential growth, a classy design for the Cope lorries and enjoyed laying out the front windows to an inviting design.

To a significant degree, Cyril Winder saw the Cope as a community centre. His design for the main building was all about inviting people in. Often he was seen dancing a welcome tap to the local characters that swarmed around the building. He encouraged people to meet and chat in the foyer, and invited people to browse while their families shopped.

He was always available from his home when people called: they might need provisions for a wake, or instruments for a plumbing disaster; Cyril Winder would be up with them to the shop to get them at all hours. His wife, Eithne, used to joke that he should take his bed up in the Cope. He worked there night and day.

He was a leader in that he took a group of people to a place that they would not have gone to without him. In the contemporary words of a Committee member, he was 'dynamic, untiring, energetic … he has already made the Cope what it is and I can say we appreciate very much what he is doing. He does a great deal more than we expect him to.'

He was relentless in his pursuit of growth. He had a sense of urgency. He was never content with his achievements but always wanted to push himself and the business that extra mile to achieve more because he believed that a business cannot stand still otherwise it will stagnate. His work was his heart and soul. He lived and died for the Cope.

He was very commercially driven and each step he took in building up the Cope was planned to achieve the desired result. He understood the product. He understood what the people of the Rosses wanted and built up the Cope where you could buy everything under a comfortable well laid out department store.

Although they'd never met, Cyril Winder was Paddy the Cope's disciple and I am sure that the Copeman would be proud to walk into the store today. The evidence of each man's success is in what he leaves behind. No doubt they're both looking down on the Cope and us all today. Indeed, when Cyril quoted Homer in honour of Paddy, it applied to himself too: 'He raised a monument more enduring than brass - if you seek his monument, look around you'.

Finally, If Cyril were alive today, what would he ask of the present and future management of the Cope? His words would ring out: 'Take it to the next step. Do not stand still. Do not rest on your laurels. Grow the business by capturing market share and developing the business's most important asset - our people'. The Cope people were the part of the Cope that he loved the best.

Hopefully, 30 years on from Cyril's departure photographs will again be taken that will dwarf the Cope that Cyril Winder left behind. Then how he and Paddy will smile…"

MARGARET FOLEY[1]

Cleendra's Paddy Pat Bawn

"…Paddy got the Co-op and dividend idea when he and Sally left Scotland to settle in his birth place Cleendra. He discussed it with a Cleendra neighbour – John "Charlie Shot" O'Donnell who became his first Secretary. In an old single building – an old kitchen below his old home – he filled this single room or kitchen with some groceries.

Their wee shop was only open for business at night. Their day hours were filled doing work in the fields or in the turf bog. John did the writing, including correspondence. There were two John O'Donnells in Cleendra, John "Charlie Shot" and Johnnie Hughdie. One day the postman arrived with a "John O'Donnell" letter and showed it to Sheila (mother of the Secretary). She remarked: "If it were for my John, it would have "Esquire" on it". John left Paddy and bought Hegarty's Hotel in Letterkenny. He also built a three storey house in Fairhill, lately owned by the late dentist Montgomery.

---

1   Margaret Foley wrote to Hughie McGee in April 1977 and provided further information again in 1992.

Paddy's second Secretary, Dan Sweeney,[2] taught in Roshine School nearly a hundred years ago. He taught James O'Donnell of Roshine, who became a teacher in Kilmacrenan, and he taught my mother Anna (Rodgie) Dougan, Cleendra. I once asked the late Eddie McCullagh "Why was Paddy such a success?" He answered: "Paddy was like a Queen Bee having help from good Secretaries. They included Master Dan Sweeney, Leo Brennan, Mr Deery and Charlie Boyle"

When Paddy collected the 14 half crowns that started him off, he laughed. My grandfather Rodger Dougan paid the first half crown but Paddy made him number two and his own mother Maggie Gallagher. The nickname of the people (his mother's people) may have been "the Tullys". At a meeting in Roshine School he called the names of these who had joined: - saying "Rodgie" Dougan, number two, and adding, "Nay forcing needed there". One of the Dungloe gombeen men called him "old Moses from Cleendra".

In February 1968, on R.T.E. radio, the late Liam Conaghan Letterkenny ("Fear Feasa") interviewed Paddy on a Radio talk show named "The Miracle of Templecrone".[3] I was visiting a Glasgow house of a Cleendra aunt where my uncle Andy Dougan also was. I was District Nurse in the locality but wanted to be with these two to hear what apparition or miracle happened in Termon, when who comes on the radio but Paddy. He was talking about the Cope. We enjoyed it so much I wrote a letter in the Derry Journal, signing it with a nom-de-plume (or pen name). Paddy found out who wrote it and the first time he met me (later) he took me into his house and into a front room and said "You are now in the room that De Valera stood in". Sally brought in a nice tea with bacon and eggs. Paddy gave me a gift of a copy of a first edition (hard back) of his book. I asked him to autograph it. He answered: "What does that mean?" When I explained, he wrote his name and mine (then) "Mgt. McCullagh". I have the book still (in 1992) and it was the first he autographed (if he autographed anymore).

Paddy was a very humble man. He would make visits to St. Peter's, minus socks and in old slippers. On one occasion he met me in Main Street calling me "Anna Rodgie's daughter". Embracing me in Yankee style, he presented me with a flounder – he was returning from a day's fishing (and maybe that was the only one "that didn't get away").

Paddy's grandfather left his native Aran and went to work for a landlord, Johnson, whose home was the present Crohey hostel. A landlord named Philpott left his big house in Termon to live in the house that is now Cassidy's Tubberkeen holiday

---

2   Daniel Sweeney, Dungloe, was Cope Secretary from 1908-9.

3   The interview cannot have taken place in 1968 as Paddy had been dead for two years by then – it was probably 1958. Liam Conaghan wrote as 'Fear Feasa' for the Derry Journal.

house. Philpott is buried in the Mill Road cemetery. Innisfree Duffy's was home of landlord Grant. The American President Ulysses S. Grant is descended from him and descended on his mother's side from Tyrone Simpsons..."

SEAMUS RODGERS

Seamus Rodgers

"Comharchumann Teampall Cróine

Céad Blian ag Fás

Is cúis bhróid agus áthais domh, mar iar-oibrí, an píosa seo a chur le chéile agus muid ag ceiliúradh 100 blian ó bunadh Comharchumann Teampall Cróine. Tá an comharchumann seo a chur "Paddy The Cope" an síol do i gcró beag faoí scáth an chnoic i gClaon Doire, ag soilsiú mar bheadh reált ann agus ina chrann taca do fhostaíocht agus feabhas eacnamaíochta na Rosa ó shoin.

Is íomaí athrú a tháinig ar chursaí trádála agus siopadóireachta ó 1906, ach níor sheasaigh an Comharchumann gan athrú, agus bhí said abalta aghaidh a thabhairt ar gach dushlán amuigh ansin roimpú go dtí an lá atá inniú ann.

Tá seo mar leac chuimhneachán do Phaidí agus do na daoine eile a bhí i gceannais atá anois ar shlua na marbh. Bhí said fad chionnach agus leag siad amach an bothair síos fríd na mblianta. Go fada a mairfídh siad ag tabhairt fostaíocht, seirbhís, cliú agus onóir do na Rosa agus iarthar Dhun na nGall.

It is my privilege as a former employee of the Cope to pen a few words on the centenary of the founding of the Templecrone Co-op by the late Paddy the Cope.

The dream born on a rocky hillside in Cleendra one hundred years ago has and is making a major contribution to the economy of the area it serves. Despite barriers being raised and early teething problems, the Cooperative spirit survived. This was manifested in later years when fire destroyed its Dungloe stores and Headquarters. Such was the resilience of its founder members and staff that it arose again Phoenix like from the ashes.

My first official employment was in the Annagry Branch of the Cope under the baton of the late Dermot Logue. While Dermot was a tough task master, we remained good friends until he passed on. I can still recall Dermot, who was an accomplished musician, taking out the accordion at times to entertain the customers. An elderly customer the late Peadar Sheáin O'Donnell from Loughnanoran would drop in and Peadar would complete the duet on the whistle. With a wink Peadar would state that one could make money from music, truly a prophet before his time.

In later years I entered calmer managerial waters being posted to the Cope in Kincasslagh under the stewardship of Eugene Doherty. I can always state that this was "The village I loved so well". The Cope in Kincasslagh was like an Open University where mountainy men and women, islanders and school teachers mixed, all characters in their own right, wonderful people who enriched my young life. Good natured banter and laughter would fill the shop and would spill out into the street. You were always sure to have a mix of topics such as farming, fishing, dancing, football, boxing, currach racing, education and politics on the curriculum or the menu.

I served under three general managers here all who sadly passed away at a comparatively early age: Packie Gallagher (The Cope), Edmund Carr and Cyril Winder.

The highlight of the season was the visit of Santa at Christmas. He was led into the village by noted horseman, the late Neily Gildea, accompanied by Pat Gallagher on accordion, Josie Janey Gallagher on fiddle and self styled majorette Nora Dan O'Donnell. Following distribution of presents to the children Santa and his team would join the customers on the floor for a dance, and all would then adjourn for refreshments in Logue's Bar.

Among the part time workers in the Kincasslagh store was one Daniel O'Donnell, who went on to another stage in later life.

I ended my career with the Cope in Burtonport, where again I can recall the characters. The Port was then a hive of activity with the fishing industry at its peak. I subsequently took up a full time post with The Irish Transport and General Worker's Union.

It was not a case of all work and no play in the Cope. They fielded a football team on occasions. I can recall a game played at Boyoughter, near the former Butcher's Shop of Paddy Gill's. The Cope played Lettermacaward, the Gweebarra side included players at the veteran stage Dan Bonner, Hughie McCready and Conal Boyle. The Cope side included Neily Sweeney and big Cathal McCole. Among several players guesting for the Cope was John Bosco O'Donnell, who boasts to this day that he blotted out big Dan Bonner.

My days in the Cope have left me the proud possessor of a piece of history that I cherish in memory of the wonderful people which were an integral part of our community.

I wish the Cope, its staff and customers the best of luck and good fortune as they cross the 100 mark line…"

DENIS WARD'S MEMORIES OF THE COPE

This memoir was written by Catherine Ward, Rosses Community School, Dungloe.

"…In 1968, Denis Ward, aged sixteen, was attending Loughanure Vocational School. Like most young boys of his age he wondered where he would find work when he finished school. As he had a strong involvement with the local GAA, he hoped he would not have to emigrate like his seven brothers and sisters. Fortunately for him, he heard there was a vacancy in the Menswear department in the Cope.

Denis Ward with the Sheskinarone soccer team in the early to mid 1970s, other Cope employees are underlined: (back): Danny Gallagher, Hugh McCole, Michael McGonagle, Hugh Sweeney, Packie McHugh, Michael Gillespie and Packie Gillespie Front: (front): Brian Quinn, Packie Boyle, Michael M. Ferry, Denis Ward, John Glackin, John Solan

in the old National School on the Quay Road, Dungloe. He was interviewed by Leo Brennan, who was acting manager at that time. As well as the interview he had to do a maths test. A number of candidates had applied for the position and he was delighted to hear from Leo Brennan that he had been selected for the job

On his first day at work, full of anticipation, he set out on a bright June morning on his bike. Little did he know that morning that he would be making the same journey for the next thirty seven years to date. There was no General Manager at that time, so Denis reported to Mr. Eddie McCullagh who was manager of the menswear department. Eddie was a very honourable man and taught him everything he knew about the business. Two other people worked in the department along with Denis and Eddie, which shows us how busy it was even then. Strangely, not only did they sell men's clothes and shoes, they also sold floor covering, the one part of the job he didn't like.

Edward (Eddie) McCullagh, 39 years with the Cope and Manager, Menswear

The arrival in 1969 of a new general manager, Mr. Cyril Winder, brought a lot of progressive change to the Cope. He had previously worked in. Roches Stores in Dublin and brought with him the experience he had gained there. He built a new supermarket and under his management the old Lough Swilly Bus depot was purchased. It was rebuilt to a new two storey structure with modernised departments. Life was getting easier for Denis; he now got a lift to work with Mr. Hugh McGee who was then manager of the Hardware department. A brand new flooring department opened; no more cutting lino! The wages weren't very high but he found the work interesting and rewarding.

During the early 1970s, Eddie McCullagh retired and Denis was offered the position of buyer/manager of the menswear department. He accepted the offer and put his heart and soul into improving an already well-established business .This entailed leaving Dungloe to go to trade shows to see what goods were on offer. The first trade show he went to was Levi jeans. It was held in Galway and, as there was no direct bus route from Donegal to Galway, he had to get a bus to Dublin and a train from Dublin to Galway. He returned home, full of excitement: for the first time Levi jeans were going to be available in Dungloe. This was the first of many trade shows he attended in Ireland, and international Menswear shows in England.

The Story of the Cope

A lot of changes have been made to the Cope over the years. When Denis first started work there were no cash registers. The system of payment was overhead lines going to the central office from each department, with a cashier accounting for all the money. The system was replaced in the early 1970s by cash registers in each department.

In 1981 the Cope celebrated seventy-five years in business and the Staff were treated to a party in Ostan na Rosann. In 1990 people had more time for leisure and Denis saw this as an opportunity to open a sports department. The only space available was a corner in the furniture department on the second floor. As the business flourished, further renovations in 1994 enabled it to be moved to a larger area on the ground floor. Mr Winder was the biggest influence on Denis's career and gave him great encouragement and support. There was great sadness when he died in 1994. Earlier that year a friend and colleague, Jim "The Cope" Gallagher, also died, leaving a huge void.

As a member of the Committee, Denis reflects on all the big changes that have occurred recently: a new hardware department and a brand new furniture and carpet store. There are also plans in the future to build a new Builders' Providers; work will start on this construction, hopefully later this year.

In 2006 the Cope celebrated 100 years in business. This is a great achievement but it would not have been possible without the loyalty of the people of the Rosses and Gweedore and the many visitors who come to Dungloe each year. Denis's story is only one of over one hundred people employed in the Cope. It reflects how one man, the founder, Paddy the Cope helped to influence the lives of others in such a positive way..."

JIMMIE NANGLE

General Manager of the Cope (2002-2008).

"...In the commemorative souvenir booklet, published in 1975 to mark the Cope having achieved the one million pound sales figure for the first time, Cyril Winder recording his thoughts on the occasion, reflected that Paddy the Cope not only left us buildings, but left us something far more valuable and lasting, and that is an indefinable spirit.

There can hardly be a more appropriate time to salute the spirit of all of those people who have brought us to where we are, than on this occasion, our centenary. I believe that Paddy the Cope would indeed be proud of where we are, and would caution us to be brave and be spirited in planning where it is we are going. Paddy the Cope would be very proud of our annual turnover, due to exceed €14 million in the present year.

The late Jimmie Nangle in a typical pose taken at the Cope Centenary Ball January 14th 2006.

He would applaud the Committee which was bold enough to recognize that our Builders' Providers business deserved 'state of the art' facilities and then brave enough to finance that belief, with the capital carefully and properly minded under their stewardship, and the stewardship of their predecessors. This investment in our future has cost many millions of the Society's wealth. Such figures would frighten men of lesser spirit. Paddy the Cope would have wanted nothing but the very best for the people of the Rosses, for our customers and our staff. All of our various departments are changing, improving and preparing for the future, and all of this is a fitting monument to our founders, our forebears and our present staff.

The importance of our responsibility to our community and our staff is an obligation which continues to be the bedrock of everything the Templecrone Society stands for. The co-operative ethos flows through every decision taken. Over the last ten years alone, the society can take pride in having contributed in excess of €16 million into the local economy in wages, whilst dispersing dividends of €1.4 million, in Cope stamps, to our customers in the same period. Credit facilities provided by the Cope were often a crucial ingredient in being able to manage a home improvement or house building, a facility not often talked about and easily forgotten. The history of the Cope has many examples of service to Community without the possibility of profit, to honour the ideals and principles upon which the Society was founded. This social conscience will continue to surround the decision making process as we embrace the need for change.

On this great occasion it is appropriate that we stand tall. Take a deep breath. Be proud of where we are. Be content with the growth of our fourteen half crowns and be resolute in the belief that together we can plan a course for the future. The loyalty of previous generations cannot be relied upon in the future. With renewed vigour we must set about earning the loyalty of the future…"

PACKIE BONNER

Recalls Paddy the Cope

Packie's writings from 1981 for the 75th Cope Anniversary have also been included in various chapters of this book. Here he gives his personal reminiscences of Paddy the Cope.

"…As I have commented at length on life in the Rosses as it was in Paddy the Cope's day, it behooves me now to say something about the man himself. For instance, did I know him well? Yes, I would say I did, notwithstanding the fact that there was a generation gap between us both. Paddy's fame, greatness and success, were talked about around the fires when we were growing up, and it only remained for me to meet the man himself and to see for myself how much of the myth about him was true or false. Whenever a person of any importance visited Paddy in Dungloe he was always sure to bring his guest or visitor out to Arranmore and we were always sure to meet. I remember in particular he once called to the island in the company of the late Brendan Behan. I remember it was a beautiful summer day, June 6th, 1960. Brendan and his wife, Beatrice, were holidaying at Maas and they called down to Dungloe to visit Paddy. I remember well that Brendan wasn't drinking then, but I recall that Paddy and I had a few drinks in the Glen Hotel, and later again in Phil Bawn's. After being some time together, I remember Paddy excused himself, adding that he had to go around to look up some friends and relations he had throughout the Island, while Brendan sat there singing for us "The Old Triangle" or reciting for us such compositions as his own English translation of Brian Merriman's "Midnight Court" — "Cúirt an Mhéanoíche".

It was late that evening when Paddy and his friends left the Island and I remember well their hair-raising experience in Phil Bawn's boat on their way out to the mainland. Paddy Joe Gill happened to be on the island that same day, buying cattle, and Beatrice and Brendan and the two Paddies, all travelled in the same boat on their way out to Burtonport. I think it was four head of cattle that Paddy Joe had bought that day, and, of course, he brought his purchases with him when he was going. The sea wasn't at all calm, and to make matters worse, didn't one of the four cattle break its tying when passing the Red Perch, and then started fighting with the beast that was tied beside it! Things looked really serious then as there was a danger that the other cattle would break loose as well and maybe upset the boat. Again, if cattle start fighting at a fair or mart, one can always step aside out of their way, but to think of it, where could one go when such a fight takes place on a small boat? However, Paddy Joe and Phil Bawn managed to have the offending animal re-tied, so that peace was again restored. Paddy Joe tried calming their nerves by singing for them the entire sixteen verses of Peadar Walsh's song, "Chuaigh mé seal tamaill ar cuairt". Phil Bawn's telling or description of it all was very much to the point. "By the time Paddy Joe had delivered his sixteen verses of sedative, my bould Brendan gave us the "Old

Triangle" and we jingled-jangled until we were at the Slip in Burtonport".
Paddy the Cope, being well up in years at that time, was visibly shaken over
it all. As he said to me afterwards, "It was God and His Blessed Mother that
saved us all. We nearly had another Arranmore disaster"...!"

RAYMOND CARTHY

Templecrone Co-op revisited

"...My first visit to Dungloe was in March 1969; I was a bright eyed 24
year-old with a full head of black hair, loads of ambition and a company
car, a Beige Ford Escort (VZO 60). I had been appointed as a company
rep for Berger paints. Donegal was my first journey and Templecrone
Co-op my very first call.

Coming from a small island (Coney Island) off the coast of Sligo and
having gone to work in the large town of Sligo I had expected Dungloe to
be bigger. It was a cold and wet morning, not unusual for west Donegal,
when I parked the new company car outside the Cope and proceeded
to do my first call. There was no problem then in finding parking space;
the car park at the back was only a dream.

I was aware of Paddy the Cope through my family, who had extensive
connections with the Gallagher family, so I approached the door with
a reverence of a pilgrim going to Mecca or Knock for the first time. It
was no pilgrimage. I met Hugh McGee who shook my hand and said
he wanted something, not a lot but at least it would mark my book. He
proceeded to order at a fast rate and, as I was not used to his Donegal
accent, I also lacked the confidence to tell him to slow down. I muddled
through the order put it in my folder thanked him and asked "Where
do I collect the cheque?" I was directed to a Mr. Brennan.

Leo Brennan was a big kindly man with glasses whose office was at the
end of the shop as you look down from the main door. It was a half glass
door having seen better days; you had to push it hard to gain entrance
- this made a noise which I always felt disturbed him. He always took
the statement and with a ruler darkened with the passage of time drew
a line in red biro. That was what he would pay-- and you knew not to
discuss it any further. The cheque was hand written and given to you
on the spot to deal with that night and posted with the order to Dublin
for delivery next week (no next day delivery then).
Many years have passed and a lot of water has gone under many bridges
but Templecrone Co-op is still there bigger and brighter. It has the
continuity of a great family business. Its foundations are firmly rooted in
the soil of the Rosses. The McGees are still represented as well as many
others. The Cope still holds for me the warm and friendly atmosphere

I got all those years ago and, guess what, the black haired 24 year old with the new Ford Escort still calls - only he is a little greyer, balder, older and perhaps wiser and very happy he made the journey…"

FR MICHAEL McCULLAGH

Part of Fr Michael's memoir has been included in Chapter 12, where he writes about the help Paddy had to edit his book. Fr Michael and the late Canon Michael McCullagh retraced Paddy the Cope's footsteps in Uphall, Broxburn, Pumperstown and Bathgate in 2002.

"…Paddy worked in open cast mining. You will find the places in his book. He also sent money home each week from a little post office.

I remember seeing that open cast mine and the little post office. The place where Paddy worked was near Bathgate and the little post office from which he sent home his money was Uphall (I have the name Uphall station, in my mind).

A modern day photo of the Buchan Arms, Broxburn, where Paddy the Cope and his friends would meet when they were working in the oil shale mines in Uphall and Broxburn, in the West Lothians, Scotland. This photo was taken by Fr Michael McCullagh when he and Canon Michael McCullagh retraced Paddy's steps.

The late Canon Michael McCullagh, whose mother was a Duggan from Cleendra and who met her husband while working in Tyrone, had a keen interest in Paddy the Cope. He took a priest, Fr. Fergus Kelly and I on a tour on places associated with Paddy on the outskirts of Edinburgh.

Canon Michael McCullagh who died in 2003 was a frequent visitor to the Rosses and to his home in Cleendra. He was a cousin of the late Andy, John Ned, Packie and the late John Aboligan. Kathleen Anne of Aboligan is a remaining cousin. His uncle was one of the shareholders. He had the share in a framed picture in his house in Cleendra.

Surprisingly, Paddy himself was never a shareholder. Breda Langan in the Cope has some copies of the shares or, Kathleen Anne of Aboligan may have access to the one the Canon possessed in his uncle's name in Cleendra.

Paddy had a sense of humour also. As young boys, nine and ten or so (and I do remember Paddy so well from those days. I often saw him on cold days out at the furnace in the back wrapping up old cardboard cartons for recycling in Dublin) Peter McCauley said to him: "I am only pulling your leg". Paddy replied to him: 'Pull the other one, it has bells on it'...!"

Humorous Memories of the Cope

These stories were recalled by the individuals named and pulled together by Jack Brereton for the Cope Centenary. Many thanks.

Every Cloud Has a Silver Lining

"…The West of Ireland is noted for the great diversity of weather that can occur within a few hours and the northwest is especially noted for these vagaries. The employees of the Cope know only too well of these conditions.

Leaving home in the morning to cycle to work in the Cope office, Sheila Brown (Devenney) looked out of her window over Lough Salt and decided not to bother with a coat… such a lovely June day. However, come 7 o'clock that evening it seemed that time had jumped forward by five months.

Huddled together at the corner of the main Street and Quay Road, the cold wind howling and rain pelting down, a merry band of Cope cyclists debated whether to brave the elements and make the five-mile journey out to Maghery and Falmore. They included Jimmy Brown, Lough Salt: Annie Hunter, Falmore: Michael Wallace, Maghery and, of course, Sheila.

But, all was not lost. Prayers said hastily were answered almost at once, a miracle! The Cope, founded to serve the community now came to the aid of its workers. Connie "Cook" Boyle to the rescue! A Cope van was commandeered.

Bikes, messages, workers, prayers and all piled into the back of the van and Connie delivered his special cargo safely out to the farthest reaches of the Rosses, content in the knowledge that all would be "dried-out" and ready for the cycle back into Dungloe next morning..."

A Difficult Choice

"...Sheila Devenney always enjoyed her work in the Cope office as wages and credit control clerk. The requirements for these jobs nowhere mentioned that at some stage during the year skills such as 'mind reading' and 'extra sensory perception' would be needed. These skills were very much in demand come Christmas when Sheila found herself helping out in the ladies and drapery departments.

"I'm looking for something for my Mum" said the young man slightly embarrassed.

With all her skill and tact Sheila ascertained what Mum was like and what Mum liked. With as little fuss as possible Sheila made the decision as to what to buy Mum for Christmas. The young man left the shop very happy that he had made a wise choice in the present he had selected. Sheila was happy that she had been of great personal assistance to a valued customer.

But, was Mum happy??? The question is absurd. Had anything been wrong we should certainly have heard..."

Easy Riders

"...Time was when you walked, rowed, cycled or travelled on horseback to work. In Dungloe in the early 1950s there were few cars to be seen.

One enterprising Cope worker came up with a novel way to travel from her home in Falmore to Dungloe. Annie Bonner (later to marry Paddy Hunter from Maghery) cycled the seven mile journey to her office twice daily until one day she hit on an idea with a colleague as to how to make the trip easier and quicker.

Dinny Mickey O'Donnell from Tearmon, who worked in the Cope's timber-yard, had just got a new motorbike. Dinny would wait at "The Strand View Bar" in Maghery for Annie to freewheel down the hill from

Falmore. Annie would then "hitch" herself to Dinny by holding onto his shoulder and off they would go – Dinny pulling Annie along on her push bike as he, motored serenely along, and them chatting away – what a sight!!

Annie arrived into the Cope as fresh as a daisy and was never late for work with her new "mechanised" mode of travel.

The Cope certainly spawned staff with ingenuity..."

Midnight in Moscow

"...Long distance driving is always a difficult undertaking. But, when the journey begins in West Donegal, then it becomes an ordeal not to mention an adventure.

When Michael Wallace started out from the Cope car park in Dungloe at 6.30 every Sunday morning with his precious cargo of fish, he knew that it would be in the early hours of the next day that he would finally reach his destination at Conon Bridge, northern Scotland.

But it came as a surprise to many of the Cope's managers that en route Michael would stop for a meal in Moscow.

The Cope's financial manager might have sleepless nights worrying about one of the employees cavorting around Red Square or rubbing shoulders with Tsars and laying out thousands of roubles on caviar and vodka.

No need to concern ourselves. Go three miles north of Kilmarnock and just off the A77 is the sleepy village of Moscow.

Caviar and vodka says Michael laughing... a bag of chips and a coke more as like...!"

Hitler over the Cope

"...The early 1940s saw terrible daily destruction and mayhem all over Europe as nations became locked in what we know as World War II.

But not every place in Europe saw the ravages of war.

On a pleasant spring day, in the quiet and peaceful village of Maghery in County Donegal, Kate Doogan was busy as usual looking after customers at the Cope's shop at the edge of Maghery strand. There

Paddy Hunter, in a photo taken at Connie Devenney's wedding.

were several people in the shop at the time among them Annie Doney Gallagher. A young local boy, Paddy Hunter, was waiting to be served when suddenly there was an almighty roar.

Kate blessed herself as Annie nodded towards the sky. "There's Litany again," she said "does he never sleep – he is on the go night noon and morning". Paddy ran to the door and looked up at the sky over Arranmore Island. He could see them. Three German bomber planes swooping low, making their way north west towards the open Atlantic.

Kate and Annie had now joined Paddy in the doorway. "Litany" Annie said again. Paddy knew exactly to whom Annie was referring. He smiled but felt sad when he thought of all the death and destruction being wreaked throughout Europe.

As the sound of the aircraft faded away the two women stepped back into the Cope. Paddy remained standing in the doorway. Damn Hitler he said…"

Wriggle Out Of This

"…Almost since its inception, the Cope has been transporting and delivering all sorts of goods around the Rosses and further afield. This service has always been the backbone of the Cope's strength and a major part of the social interweaving between the co-operative and the community. All kinds of goods and merchandise have been carried over the past 100 years - from apples to zucchinis from axles to zinc.

However, as Michael Wallace will tell you, one of the strangest cargos ever carried by a Cope lorry was a consignment of worms – yes, millions of the critters and, wait for it, tons of breadcrumbs, all being delivered to a company in Cootehill, Co. Cavan.

The story was that the worms were destined to become live bait to be used by fishermen. But the breadcrumbs…were they fed to the worms or… That remains a Cope mystery.
No stuffing for me thanks…"

Gracie Glackin (Boyle) in Maghery in 1949 with nephew Patrick and niece Nuala, children of Dolly (Bridget) Delaney (photo courtesy of their brother Noel Delaney's Archive, New York).

Hearth to Hearth!

"...When Gracie Glackin (Boyle) began working in The Cope, Nylon had just been discovered, the inventor Thomas Edison died, and in New York the Empire State Building opened. The year was 1931. Gracie Glackin's day started very early indeed — 6.30 a.m. to be exact.

As on all small farms, there were many chores that required attention, both in and out of doors. One of Gracie's first jobs each morning was to clean the grate and re-kindle the fire from coals embedded in the ash-pit the night before. A basket of turf would then be filled by Gracie and left beside the hob.

With the early morning tasks completed, the family would breakfast together then Gracie would set out on her seven mile walk to her office in the Cope, Dungloe.

Working conditions in the 1930s were a far cry from what we have come to expect in the twenty first century. Even simple creature comforts often had to be created by the workers themselves.

One cold January morning, Gracie's colleague and friend Nan Ward was arriving at the office just as Gracie landed.

"Good morning Gracie" Nan said cheerily on seeing her friend.

But the smile soon vanished when Nan walked into the office — the room was freezing.

"Look! No fire and no fuel in" Nan sighed,

Before she removed her coat Gracie walked out to the back of the Cope yard and gathered a basket of turf, some coal and chopped some sticks.

Setting a few sticks and paper around the turf it was no time before there was a healthy blaze in the small stove.

As the grey dawn started to brighten some other members of staff were just arriving. They were relieved to see that the stove was alight.

And so, twice that morning Gracie's hands were black.

Disappearing into the cloakroom to freshen-up she realised she had lost all track of time since leaving home. As she walked to her desk the clock struck nine — time for work..."

Chapter 12

'MY STORY'

Paddy's celebrated autobiography, *My Story,* was first published by Jonathan Cape, London in both England and Ireland in 1939, when Paddy was aged 69. A very successful American edition was later published by the Devin-Adair Company, New York in 1942. Revised and updated with photographs, a further edition was published in 1946 and reprinted a number of times. It was a steady seller for decades and remains so to this day and provided Paddy with a regular income from royalties. Later, options taken on the book by film producers meant a much welcomed addition to his income in retirement. Paddy always maintained he had never made anything other than a wage from the Cope.

Paddy, as he was often to remark, never got to the end of his 'third book', i.e. he was not at school past the age of nine. His work at home on the farm and the six months a year he was hired out in the Lagan put paid to his schooling. Writing a book then was something of a challenge for him. He had been urged by AE (George Russell), a man he had immense respect for and to whom he owed a great deal for his support in the early days, to write his story: 'I hope Paddy the Cope will leave his story behind him before he passes away.' AE himself passed on in 1935 and it was after this that Paddy began his autobiography in earnest. He'd had a stab at it earlier but had given up; there was always something better he could be doing with the Cope:

> "...Well, before I closed the Cope that evening, I stuck a copy book in my pocket, and when I went home I commenced to write. I did not stop until I had finished the copy book. Sally did not get saying the Rosary that night until it was very late. Every now and again when I was on my knees, I could only think of the grand story I had written. Sally said, 'Paddy, you are working too hard, why not get Jim [Paddy and Sally's son] or Leo [Brennan, Cope Secretary] to do the writing for you. You will kill yourself. You went through the two decades of the Rosary tonight. I never remember you missing a word before.'
>
> I did not sleep much that night. After breakfast next morning, I handed Sally the old copy and said, 'Read that, O won't it make a grand story?' At dinner time when I sat at the end of the table, Sally stood at the other end, her hand behind her back. She began laughing; she laughed and laughed. I got afraid she would break her sides. I said, 'Stop! What are you laughing at?' She then took around her hand with the copy in it and said, 'Paddy, this is surely a grand story! For goodness sake burn it. Do not let the boys see it. There is neither head nor tail to it. I can hardly make out a word of it.' I snapped it from her and put it in my pocket. That evening when the store was closed, I came into the house

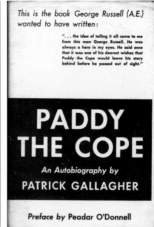

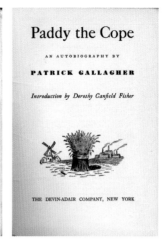

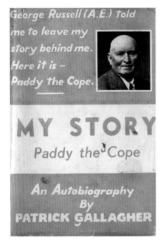

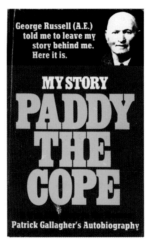

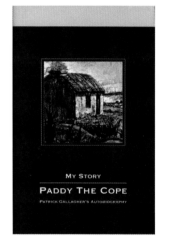

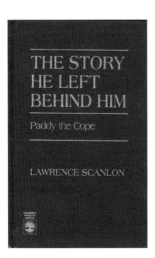

"...*My Story* was first published in 1939 by Jonathan Cape of London and then in 1942 in an American edition by the Devin Adair Company, New York. Subsequent New York editions and the London editions had a foreword by Peadar O'Donnell. An Irish edition was published by *The Kerryman* in 1946, 1971 and 1979, with a foreword by Canon Eugene McDermott. There are substantial differences between the texts of the New York and London editions, and smaller differences between the London and Irish editions..." (Kevin Bonner, Cope Committee member, writing in the introduction to the newly published My Story in 2006) Lawrence Scanlon's academic assessment of My Story, which was very complimentary both about Paddy's style and the importance of his book, was published by the University Press of America in 1994 as 'The Story He left Behind Him'. (Book cover scans from various sources, collections)

They all like *Paddy the Cope:*

"It brought back to me the flavor of the days when I was in Ireland in the summer of 1912, my various visits with A.E., and the days when my grandfather used to have me read aloud to him from the *Irish Homestead*. This background enables me to see that the book is definitely authentic. Sir Horace Plunkett, Russell, Arnold and Father Finlay indeed did a real job when they breathed life into the Irish Cooperative Movement and gave spirit to a man like Paddy the Cope."—HENRY A. WALLACE.

"It is a warm book in every way; and in its direct, singing quality it recalls a whole host of literary Irishmen, from Synge to Peader O'Donnell and Liam O'Flaherty. . . . The whole story is a saga of the little man's triumph over the devastating economic tides that have swept the world in our times."
—JOHN CHAMBERLAIN in *New York Times*

"It is the first human book on cooperatives."—*The Boston Herald.*

"It is a 'must' for the economist, the historian, and should be read by every person in whose veins there flows a drop of Irish blood."
—I. A. FLUHARTY in *Columbus (Ohio) Dispatch*

". . . . here is a book of 'social significance' that happens to be unusually well written. It is all of that, but it is also a colorful and compelling life story which will hold you if you care not two pins for cooperatives."
—MARSHALL BRAGDON in *The Springfield Republican*

"PADDY THE COPE is a book that every Irish man and woman should read for it again demonstrates the old truth that 'where there's a will there's a way.' Neither scoffer nor cynic, nor threats of imprisonment, nor the skullduggery of the Black and Tan, kept this excellent specimen of Irish manhood from achieving his object."—SHANE CONWAY in *The Irish Echo.*

"Ireland has had so many of the same problems as our own South that it might be given to us as a sort of textbook."
—PRISCILLA ROBERTSON in *Louisville Courier-Journal*

"Any review of this book should have but one purpose—to induce the reader to read the book itself."—HARRY LORIN BINSSE in *Free America.*

"It is the book for all of us today who still believe in democracy but who vaguely fear that the principles of democracy must be diluted by the methods of dictatorship. What is to keep the rest of us from doing on a large scale what one little group, moneyless, uneducated, was able to do in this one little desolate countryside?"—JOHN P. DELANEY in *America.*

". . . The story told in PADDY THE COPE is extremely encouraging to all who believe in the ability of the common man to do things for himself. Of course, a considerable merit of PADDY THE COPE is the style in which the story is told by Patrick Gallagher; that is unique."—The late MONSIGNOR JOHN A. RYAN, of the National Catholic Welfare Conference.

Paddy's book received very positive reviews in Ireland, Britain and the United States and was reprinted many times. These are just a few of the reviews received in the States (from the dustcover of the fifth US Printing of 'My Story', published by Devin Adair 1942, Pat Dunleavy Collection).

and opened the copy. I got the first line all right and damn but, I could not make head or tail of any of the rest. I threw the bloody old copy in the fire. Sally seemed to enjoy the scene and this annoyed me..."[1]

Paddy's method of writing was to jot things down in copy books, scrap books, on the back of bits of paper – on anything that came to hand. It was then the task of others to try and make some sense of it all while keeping the spirit of Paddy's narrative and his unique and 'real' style of writing. The 'others' included his daughter in law, Mary Packie (Campbell), his son Packie's wife, of whom he was very fond; Mary Ellen (Brennan) Walsh, his sister Sarah's daughter, who typed up the most of the first manuscript, Anne T Sweeney (Aboligan), Mary Boyle (Yankee) and his wife Sally who was a great sounding board for his stories.

Fr Michael McCullagh recalls:

> "...As for Paddy's quite wonderful book, people often said, wrongly, that it was Dr. McDermott who was the ghost writer. However, Mary Ellen, the late wife of Packie Walsh of the Port said to me during her last illness in the hospital that she herself typed out the manuscript. He would come in with chapters and pages written on the backs of old paper bags at the end of the day just as she was planning on a night out at a dance somewhere! I understand Mary Boyle, sister of Patsy the Yank on the Main Street, also typed some of the manuscript.
>
> Delia O Donnell, née Cannon, living near the Bistro, is the oldest living niece of Paddy's, which would make Jamesie Cannon a grandnephew. Mary Clarke, who now lives near Navan, is another niece. I remember her telling me once that all of Paddy's sisters bought as many copies of the book as possible with the purpose of the depriving the public of reading them. They were so ashamed of Paddy telling it warts and all... especially the poverty of his childhood. Neither then nor now is poverty a virtue and not many wish to remember those days. I suppose Paddy was only rejoicing in the fact that he had been liberated from them..."[2]

Mary Ellen (Brennan) Walsh worked in the Cope from 1938 to 1950. She married Packie Walsh in July 1950 and was then taken in November with a very bad case of TB (there were never any 'good' cases of this terrible affliction: Mary Ellen lost two sisters to TB: Peggy and Annabella). She eventually spent four years in the Mater, Dublin; one of the first to be given Streptomycin, she responded well to the new drug and left the hospital in 1954.

She and Anne T Sweeney worked in the Cope office; money would fly up in little wooden cups with a docket. There was one wire to the drapery, one to the grocery. Next the cash would all be taken in the office and change given and

---

1   *Paddy the Cope, 'My Story', 1939*

2   *Extract from an appreciation by Fr Michael McCullagh, 2006*

Paddy had help from a number of local 'editors' in pulling together his stories from the many notebooks and scraps of paper it was his way to write in or on. Here are two of his helpers on a bench outside the Cope House on the Main Street Dungloe in the mid 1940s – Mary (Campbell) Gallagher, wife of Paddy's son Packie and Paddy's wife and his inspiration Sally the Cope, with her granddaughter Sally, Mary's daughter (Photograph courtesy of Sally the Cope Gallagher, the baby in the picture).

Paddy also had help in pulling together his stories from Mary Ellen (Brennan) Walsh and Anne Theresa (Sweeney) Bonner, seen here (on the right) in Dublin outside the General Post Office in the 1940s with Mary Ellen's sister Peggy. Anne Theresa Sweeney was married to Dom Bonner NT, Chairman of the Cope Committee from 1977 to 1985; Dom is still an active member of the Committee in 2009 (Packie Walsh Collection, Burtonport).

Mary Ellen (Brennan) Walsh, who typed up most of Packie's first efforts before publication in 1939, always said that Packie would write on anything that came to hand – paper bags, notepads, backs of envelopes as well as exercise books, copy books he would buy. While Paddy had a wonderful sense of narrative and a distinctive and vivid use of language, his spelling reflected his early removal from school to work away in the Lagan. He wrote many words phonetically and it could take some interpretation to work out what he meant (Photograph and memories from Packie Walsh, Burtonport; Packie and Mary Ellen married in 1950)

then have to be balanced every night. Credit was handled by note and paid up after the October fair.[3]

Paddy's wife Sally, who died in March 1948 aged 77, herself left behind 16 stories, some covering very similar territory to Paddy's ones in 'My Story', others entirely new. These stories, more than 130 pages in total, were written as late as October 1947 when Sally had been unwell for a long time. They have lain in Limerick City Museum for over 50 years and have only recently come to light in the course of researching this book. They are written to her grandchildren and have a marvellous humanity and humour:

> "...Children dear, I would like to leave this wee story with you before I go. Since your grandfather and I got married, now nearly fifty years ago, I never had one minute of unhappiness..."[4]

---

3 *Packie Walsh, Burtonport, interviewed in 2006 and 2007, about his wife Mary Ellen's working in the Cope and helping Paddy with his book.*

4 *Sally The Cope Gallagher Stories, Archive in Limerick City Museum.*

Although her style is very different, the quality of her writing and storytelling may well have been an influence on Paddy's own writings.

A number of extracts have been included in this book, courtesy of Limerick City Museum and the Gallagher family. Quite how they ended up in Limerick is a bit of a mystery. The typescript has very characteristic lettering and it appears to have been done directly from Sally's manuscript (now lost) by the Limerick Museum archivist in the 1950s. The Gallagher family, for whom these stories had been written, were not aware of them until their rediscovery in 2006.

In fact Paddy himself was very aware of these stories. In the course of an interview with Fr Richard McKeon SJ, he said the following, very moving words in tribute to her:

> "...As soon as I was introduced to Paddy he went down on his knees for my blessing. Then began one of the most interesting conversations I have been privileged to share in.
>
> "So you are impressed by our humble work, Father?"
>
> "Yes, Mr. Gallagher. Your book, Paddy the Cope, is one of the finest expositions of the need of the cooperative movement. Now I have witnessed some of the fruits of your efforts."
>
> "Please call me Paddy, Father. Everybody does. As for the book, it was really a tribute to the people with whom I worked. Without their wonderful loyalty, failure would have crushed us at the start. And now may tell you a secret I have discovered among my dear wife's belongings, something I never dreamt existed. It seems that while I was keeping notes on the progress of the co-operatives she also was writing down impressions of the struggles we faced together. It is now my hope that her notes be edited."
>
> Tears came to Paddy's eyes, for Sally had been his devoted wife for fifty years. Then he continued: "Please God, Father, I shall be seventy-eight years old this Christmas Eve (1950): How I miss my dear wife. Long ago when skies were darkest and even the clergy were discouraging our efforts, I told Sally I was quitting and going to Scotland. She said 'Paddy you are a coward' and she walked out of the house. That stung me out of my worries and I have fought the good fight ever since..."[5]

Paddy was interviewed, in his ninetieth year, for the Irish Times. He describes the help he got from Sally and refers to Sally's own stories and an idea (which was never realised) for combining his and her stories:

---

5   The Irish Digest, from an article 'America' published in The Irish Digest in 1950

"...His opponents gave Paddy Gallagher the name 'Paddy the Cope" as a jeer, but when he came to set down his story years afterwards, he chose the jeering nickname as its title. "That was just before the war. I wrote the story at night in a copybook. My wife Sally (God called her since) was in the sixth book, ye see, and she helped in the mornings after I had made the letters plain. Peadar O'Donnell sent the book to Jonathan Cape in London, but they ran out of copies because of the war. Then it was published in America and Sweden [Paddy meant Iceland]. I've written another called 'Paddy the Cope and Sally the Cope's Story.' It will be published in a week or two..."[6]

Paddy received great encouragement and praise from Peadar O'Donnell, novelist, editor of 'The Bell', socialist and Republican who was born in Meenmore across Dungloe Bay from Cleendra. Peadar wrote to Paddy in 1937

> 176 Upper Drumcondra Rd,
> Dublin,
> 21/1/1937

Dear Paddy,

You may be assured that in giving an opinion on your work, I am just saying what I believe, an opinion which must later stand up to other people's opinions. So that you are to believe that I am just saying what I sincerely mean.

Your story is, as I wired, not merely good. It is tremendous. And its merit does not rest on the material alone. The style of writing is excellent; bare, hard, live. In its context the book will be the most valuable document that has come out of Ireland since Connolly wrote "Labour in Irish History". It will be a sensational piece of writing if you keep up to this level.

Now for a few hints; you are writing a story as it was lived so take care that the eager boy that went to the Lagan sees that face of those days and tells us his story, later the grown up man sees the face of other days and reveals them to us. And finally Paddy

---

6   Irish Times 2nd April 1960. Paddy's reference to his wife Sally's stories leads us to think he was engaged at combining his own book and Sally's 130+ pages into a new book to be published – quite an ambition for man who was about to turn 90. It still doesn't explain how Sally's stories ended up in Limerick - it is possible, but this is sheer speculation, that he had given them to someone who had offered to help edit them together.

Gallagher of today will close the story. To make it clearer; when Paddy Gallagher the boy, was in the Lagan he did not say to himself "I was sold for £3". This is a much later Paddy pushing a word in on the boy and it is a false coin in the setting. Be terribly careful of that. Let none of the wisdom of a later year - or bitterness of later days- seep into a part of the story to which it does not belong. You will see the importance of this. The freshness of your story- and my God man it reminds me of the green brightness of a field after a nice warm shower at the opening days of the new grass; live, clear, healthy. I hope you keep it as you begin.

And to show you that way right, with confidence let me quote an example; you close a scene with a sentence: "I must have shut the door just then for I didn't remember any more'. That is a land of sheer artistry. One touch of smartness would have ruined it. And it rings like a phrase of music.

Do the rest of the typing in quarto paper, double spacing. Could you have it ready by June to get it out next Autumn? Don't rush but don't delay.

I tell you I have never been as excited over a manuscript in my life. I always suspected you had a story to tell, but did not glimpse the quality to be so breath-taking. If you go through with this, with complete sincerity, resist every impulse to smart talk, all will be well. You have lived with sharp ears and eyes. The very roots of great writing are in you. And now I'll make a prophesy; this book of yours will be read when the works of the rest of us are as forgotten as withered leaves. So please don't delay.

I'll be down soon. Oh! Be damn there is one thing you talk of the Cleendra people gathering urine. The only bit of politeness I ever heard used was "piddle", though I think I did hear urine in Cruit. If the right word in Cleendra is "pish" then don't renege Cleendra. Write it. Urine, piddle, pish, it's all from the same taypot anyhow. Use the right word or by the living God. I'll make Sally scald you; urine is no word, but if it's Cleendra English then use it.

Give my love to Sally, Jack and Jim, and believe me I

```
rejoice in the book so much that I'll never forgive you
if you neglect your work on it. After all you shook the
souls in lads of my age and I want you to do the same
to others. See how much better the world would be if
all men were like me.

Again all the best of luck,

Yours

Peadar O'Donnell⁷
```

Paddy wrote to the IAOS letting them know that he had written his life story and requesting help in tracking down the many different visitors to the Cope over the years (and drum up sales no doubt):

> "...The story is naturally on the Co-operative Movement. We had many distinguished visitors who called here, some from India, some from Egypt, and a deputation from America, but my business methods are so bad that I have kept no note of these, nor their addresses. I am just wanting to know if you would have any records in your office of the people who visited us. If so, the publishers would probably send a circular to them, especially the Indian people as they were very interested in the Co-operative Movement.

> There was a Marie Harrison, an American lady, who wrote a very glowing report of the Irish people, in the "World's Work" and she spoke specially about us. The article was headed 'The Dawn of Ireland'. Unfortunately I have not a copy of it. I have been searching for it but cannot get it. I understand the "World's Work" has ceased publication.⁸

The reaction to Paddy's autobiography was very positive with his style and way with narrative and expression being much praised. The Irish Times reviewed the book on publication:

Story of a Great Irish Achievement

"Paddy the Cope's" Vivid Narrative

My Story, by "Paddy the Cope", London: *Jonathan Cape, 7/6d net*

> "...It is something of a pity that the struggle between cooperation and "gombeenism" becomes so vivid in this remarkable book. The author throws such a fierce light upon the development of the Co-operative

---

7   *Letter copy is included courtesy of Pat Dunleavy, Cope Chairman, and Chairman of the County Donegal Historical Society.*

8   *IAOS records, National Archives: 1088/871/5, letter to Dr Kennedy, IAOS*

PADDY THE COPE

My Story

'*Paddy the Cope* is one of the freshest, liveliest, warmest and most entrancing autobiographies imaginable. Paddy is a gorgeous, unaffected, pre-industrial human being . .   He founded a Co-operative Society in Donegal: . . Under him the book takes on the easy ripeness of a picaresque novel.'

V. S. PRITCHETT in the BYSTANDER

10s. 6d.

JONATHAN CAPE

A Revised Edition

My Story.   By Patrick Gallagher (" Paddy the Cope "). With Foreword by Rev. E. P. McDermott, D.D.   (Dungloe: Templecrone Co-operative Society. 12/6.)

The fact that the theme of this remarkable book, the autobiography of a gritty Donegal man, is soon to be filmed should quicken interest in its reappearance.   But apart from the prospect of seeing the story on the films, those who read it when first published some years ago may well hanker to read it in the revised and expanded form of the present edition.

This is more than an exciting autobiography: it is an important social document, a record of the triumph of an idea against seemingly impossible odds.   With a capital of fourteen half-crowns, the author, a migratory toiler, and a few neighbours got together to buy manure on a co-operative basis. Out of that small beginning grew the great Templecrone   Co-operative Society, with a sales turnover of more than £150,000 a year.   The story of this struggle and success is woven through the life-story of its moving spirit—Paddy the Cope.

M. H.

Society and the difficulties it had to face on its way to success that the reader is inclined to follow the narrative as a rather usual story of how the penniless boy achieved his fortune, or as the clash of different social conceptions, on a miniature stage. Viewed in either of these lights, the book is a successful one, but it has other qualities that set it in a class quite apart from books dealing with Irish Life.

The personal story of Pat the Cope is told with such gusto and naïveté – such self-revealing frankness – that it is only towards the end that the reader realises that its craftsmanship is masterly and unique. It is the story of a man who was inflexible in the pursuit of ideals without mistaking this inflexibility for courage, and, in his own way, obstinate without applauding himself for the resoluteness of his will. His faith in the co-operative movement was deep, but his appreciation of the things and people around him saved him from fanaticism, and the president of the £100,000 a year concern is the same man as he who founded it on fourteen half crowns a quarter of a century ago.

PATRICK GALLAGHER:

Þeir hjálpuðu
sér sjálfir

SJÁLFSÆVISAGA FRÁ ÍRLANDI

PATRICK GALLAGHER

ÞEIR HJÁLPUÐU
SÉR SJÁLFIR

SJÁLFSÆVISAGA FRÁ ÍRLANDI

GÍSLI GUÐMUNDSSON
ÍSLENZKAÐI

*Presented to Pat
& Cpe Gallagh → ?
during a visit to
Iceland aug. 1983.*

BÓKAÚTGÁFAN NORÐRI

FYRSTI KAFLI

Bernskuár mín heima á Írlandi.

Cleendra er sveitaþorp, sem stendur við fjallsrætur á vestur-
strönd Donegal-héraðs. Þegar ég fæddist, bjuggu þar tuttugu
og þrjár fjölskyldur. Mýrlendið við fjallsræturnar hafði verið
ræst fram og skiptist milli býlanna. Faðir minn átti tuttugu
ekrur lands, átján af þeim voru óræktað fjalllendi. Landsnytj-
ar annarra býla í þorpinu voru álíka miklar.

Faðir minn hét Patrick eins og ég. Og af því að hann var
ljóshærður, kölluðu nágrannarnir hann Pat Bawn. Þegar ég kom
til sögunnar, kölluðu þeir mig Paddy Pat Bawn, og var ég
þannig sæmilega ættfærður. Ég var elztur af níu systkinum,
átti einn bróður og sjö systur, og fæddist á jóladaginn 1873.

Húsið okkar var svipað öðrum húsum í í Cleendra, ein vist-
arvera með stráþaki og litlum glugga með einni rúðu í. Jafnvel
þeir, sem höfðu efni á að bæta húsakynni sín, veigruðu sér við
að gera það, því að þeir óttuðust, að jarðarleigan yrði hækkuð,
ef slíkar umbætur væru gerðar.

Við áttum eina kú gamla. Þegar hún eignaðist kvígu, létum
við hana lifa og seldum hana tvævetra. En nautkálfum slátr-
uðum við, átum fjórðapart af skrokknum sjálf, en hinu var skipt
milli nágrannanna. Kýrin var geld þrjá mánuði á ári, en ekki
minnist ég þess, að við þyrftum nokkurntíma að drekka teið
mjólkurlaust, því að nágrannarnir færðu okkur mjólk á hverj-
um morgni. Hið sama gerðum við, þegar okkar kýr var mjólk-
andi en eitthvert annað heimili mjólkurlaust. Nokkur heimili
áttu tvær kýr, og þau létu stöðugt eitthvað af mörkum til ann-

9

Paddy's book was published in Iceland
in 1949; the title page and first page of
Chapter 1 are shown here. The translator,
Gísli Guðmundsson, and his wife Margrét
Árnadóttir, stayed in Paddy's son, Jim the
Cope's house on the Quay Road for the best
part of a year around 1947 or possibly 1948.
The photographs show them in the Quay
Road house – both Mary Jo and Jim (Bimbo),
daughter and son of Jim the Cope remember
them staying (Photograph courtesy Mary Jo
(Jim the Cope) collection)

Gisli Guðmundsson

Margrét Árnadóttir

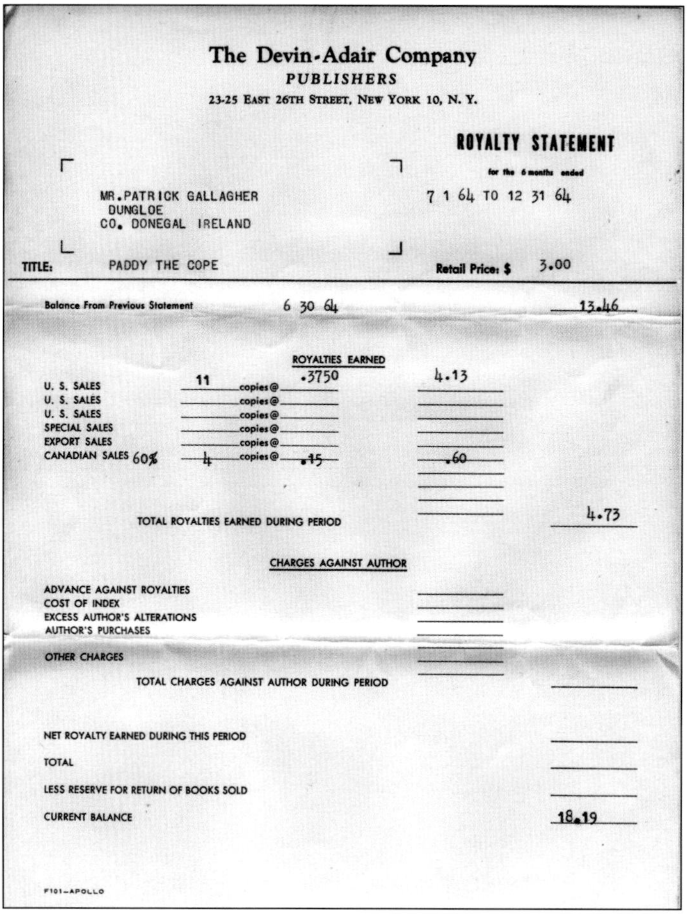

The Devin-Adair Company
PUBLISHERS
23-25 East 26th Street, New York 10, N.Y.

ROYALTY STATEMENT
for the 6 months ended

MR. PATRICK GALLAGHER
DUNGLOE
CO. DONEGAL IRELAND

7 1 64 TO 12 31 64

TITLE: PADDY THE COPE   Retail Price: $ 3.00

Balance From Previous Statement	6 30 64		13.46

ROYALTIES EARNED

U. S. SALES	11	copies @ .3750	4.13
U. S. SALES		copies @	
U. S. SALES		copies @	
SPECIAL SALES		copies @	
EXPORT SALES		copies @	
CANADIAN SALES 60%	4	copies @ .15	.60

TOTAL ROYALTIES EARNED DURING PERIOD   4.73

CHARGES AGAINST AUTHOR

ADVANCE AGAINST ROYALTIES
COST OF INDEX
EXCESS AUTHOR'S ALTERATIONS
AUTHOR'S PURCHASES

OTHER CHARGES

TOTAL CHARGES AGAINST AUTHOR DURING PERIOD

NET ROYALTY EARNED DURING THIS PERIOD

TOTAL

LESS RESERVE FOR RETURN OF BOOKS SOLD

CURRENT BALANCE   18.19

F101—APOLLO

'My Story' sold steadily from its first publication in 1939, providing Paddy with an income stream from royalties in the USA, Britain, Ireland and other countries. This is a Devin Adair (Paddy's USA publisher) statement for the second half of 1964, covering his US (four) and Canada (eleven) sales – sales and royalties there had tailed off somewhat at this point (Mary Jo 'Jim the Cope' collection).

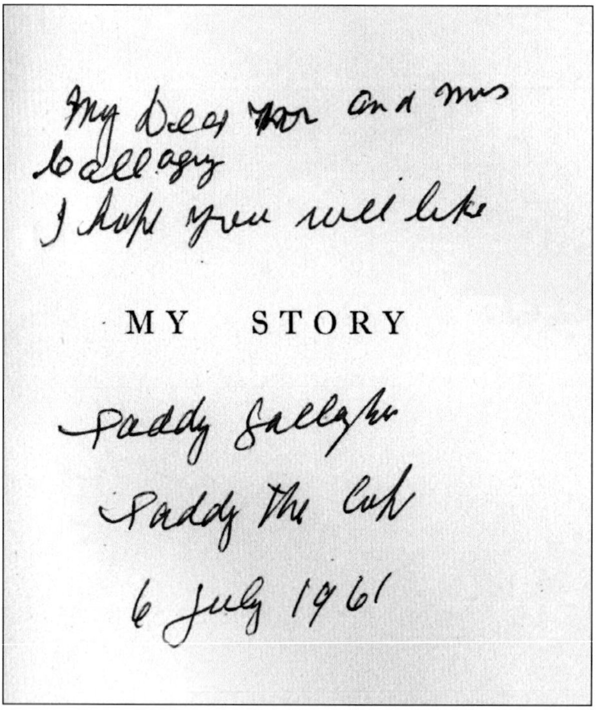

Paddy was always happy to sign his book in his own witty and distinctive way – he would write 'I hope you enjoy' immediately above the title 'My Story' and below, his signature. Over the 27 year period from publication in 1939 to his death at the age of 95, he signed many hundreds if not thousands of copies of his autobiography ('My Story' by Paddy the Cope, title page; PB Collection).

Paddy kept active until he was well into in his 90s; he lived on until 24th June 1966 when he was 95. Packie Bonner and Professor Scanlon's reckoned that his birth date was Christmas Day 1870 but on his Memorial Card, his age is given as 94. Pinning down Paddy's exact date of birth (for passports, insurance purposes etc) proved to be quite difficult over the years (Photograph courtesy of The Gallagher Family).

When Paddy travelled to the States in 1947, his third trip, his fame preceded him and he was greeted everywhere as a celebrity. His book was a major seller and the story of his struggle and eventual success made him sought after for newspaper articles and as a guest on radio shows. On 5th September 1947, he appeared on Mary Margaret McBride's daily radio program and inscribed this message on a copy of his book that he gave her. Mary Margaret, something of a celebrity herself, interviewed over 1,200 people ranging from President Truman to Bob Hope, Joe DiMaggio and Eleanor Roosevelt so Paddy was in good company (Pat Dunleavy Collection)

This photo dating from the mid 1940s is one of the last photos of Paddy and his wife Sally, who passed away on the 1st March 1948. She would have been 71 on the 17th March. Sally had been writing her own version of her and Paddy's life together and the story of the Cope ('Her Story' as it were) right up until she died – one tale tells about Paddy's trip to the States in mid 1947, indicating that she kept up her writing near to the end of her life. Paddy only found out about her stories after she had died when he was going through her papers (Cope Family Collection)

That personal story is etched upon a screen where the manners and customs, the hopes and fears of rural Ireland are depicted in broad outlines, and if the gaiety in it seems sometime the bitter salt of misfortune, its tenderness and its pathos are delicate and sincere. The story is told in an English that owes much of its charm to its purely Irish idiom, and has an evocative power that is sometimes almost disturbing. The local schoolmaster who taught his pupils athletics and boxing rather than the rudiments of an education comes to life in a few sentences just as in the later stages of the book George Russell and the "Cope's" fellow directors take vivid personal attributes.

The chapter dealing with the experience of the two Irish farm lads in Scotland, where the beautiful Scottish wife escapes from the cold conjugal hearth of a "made" marriage to sing in the barn with her protégées, or with a child's wonder and a child's love, listens to stories of Ireland, is wonderfully sweet.

This simple and touching poem appeared in the Derry Journal soon after Sally the Cope's death; it would have had Paddy's approval in that it ends on the pivotal role that his wife had in the Cope enterprise: *Verily she was the woman behind the man behind the Cope.* (Rose Johnnie Bonner Collection, Burtonport).

There are chapters dealing with emigrant life in Scotland – stories of poverty without degradation, of hardship without despair. When life at home is described – the life that begins to bourgeon to success – and death "waylays" the "Cope's" daughter, the telling is masterly in its sudden silences. The author applies his philosophy of life to the many things and movements he has seen, and when he calls something "lousy" or introduces a swear word the emphasis is obvious and generally well placed.

There are some additions to the narrative proper which were better omitted – an election address, newspaper cuttings, and the like – for they obscure the validity of the achievement in a cloud of words, and seem but empty flourishes of a strong man who does something for the mere sake of doing it. Shorn of its accretions, it would rank with a Cobbet or Jeffries in its hold on realities..."[9]

---

9   *Irish Times, 3rd July 1939.*

Above: A group of Cope workers in Dungloe, Main Street: James McGee, Charlie Greene, Ann Teresa (Sweeney) Bonner, Andy (Eggs) O'Donnell, Paddy the Cope, Neilly Sweeney, Josie McCole, John 'Big Dan' O'Donnell, Johnnie Hanlon, Hughie Boyle, *not known*, Connie Boyle, Owenie Sweeney ('Dobell'), Jimmy Doherty, Pa Ward, Owenie Frank Boyle, *not known*, Joe McLaughlin, Phil McCauley, *not known* (This is believed to be a photograph taken in February 1946, possibly by Michael Powell, the film director who had travelled to Dungloe to meet Paddy the Cope – Paddy is in the same hat and clothes as in the 1946 photograph with Michael Powell and his wife).

Left: Film director Michael Powell and his wife Frankie (Frances) Reidy are photographed here with Paddy the Cope outside his house on the Main Street in Dungloe in February 1946. Michael Powell loved to wear a kilt and sporran on his many trips to his beloved west of Scotland – he may well have assumed that the people of Donegal, with their strong Scottish connections would be dressed in a similar fashion. However, no-one locally then, or in living memory, would ever have dressed like this. The Powells' epic journey on horseback from Dublin to Donegal was covered in the Derry Journal and followed with great interest locally. In Glenties and in Dungloe, in two separate incidents, two men pretended to be the film director and his wife and rode down the Main Street on horseback – annoying Paddy greatly when he realised he was welcoming not the distinguished director but two lads making a joke. The photo is courtesy of Thelma Schoonmaker, the late Michael Powell's wife, who is an Oscar winning film editor with a long and successful professional partnership with Martin Scorsese. The photo is likely to have been taken by the Irish Times journalist who accompanied the Powells from Dublin to Donegal – it appeared alongside one of the newspaper articles on the trip.

Most curiously of all, an *Icelandic* translation of 'My Story' was published in 1949. The translator was Gísli Guðmundsson (1903-1973). He and his wife Margrét Árnadóttir (1904 -1988) stayed in Dungloe at Jim the Cope's house on the Quay Road. The family, in particular Paddy and Mary Jo remember them staying for 'almost a year' with them. Gísli was a teacher at the Icelandic Commercial School in Reykjavík and was also a member of parliament for the Progressive Party from 1934-45 and 1949–59. When the Copeman's grandson, Minister Pat the Cope Gallagher, was on an official Irish Government visit to Iceland in 1983, he was pleasantly surprised and a little taken aback at how well his grandfather and his struggle was known in Iceland – and amazed to be presented with a copy of the Icelandic translation!

Paddy's autobiography has stayed in print for over 60 years and has recently been reprinted in a fine edition by the Cope in 2006. It is not just a very entertaining read – the language and style are unique - it is a marvellous social document of its times, capturing what life was like in the Rosses from the late nineteenth century through to the middle of the twentieth century.

HOW 'PADDY THE COPE' - THE MOVIE - ALMOST GOT MADE

Critical and popular acclaim on both sides of the Atlantic and the book's subject matter attracted Britain's finest film director Michael Powell (1905-90) who made an epic journey to Dungloe to meet Paddy in early 1946. At this time, the Main Street store was being rebuilt after the devastating fire the year before.

John Betjeman, then with the British Council in Dublin, later a much loved Poet Laureate, gave Michael Powell a copy of Paddy's 'My Story' in January 1946. Powell immediately decided he had to go to meet the 'King of Dungloe'.

The story of Michael Powell's epic journey by horseback to meet the 'King of Dungloe' is told in two Derry Journal articles:

IN SEARCH OF DONEGAL

By Horseback from Dublin

Film Star and Wife on Way

To Land of "Paddy the Cope"

"...Like the prelude to another "Man of Arran" was the romantic spectacle - which paraded almost unnoticed before the eyes of Dubliners on Saturday morning when Michael Powell, the British film star, and his Dublin-born wife[10] set out on horse-back on a two hundred miles journey across Ireland in search of Donegal - the Donegal which "Paddy the Cope" pictured in his book of that name.

---

10 *Frankie Reidy - in Michael Powell's autobiography, he says she was born in Whitechapel London.*

What exactly the film star's intention is in adopting this strange means of coming to grips with the fancies which his reading of Mr. Gallagher's book has conjured up in his mind is not clear - at least he has not stated it clearly - but there is a suggestion that it is the beginning of a project to produce a film based on Mr: Gallagher's simple yet graphic narration of life's vicissitudes as he watched his enterprises growing amidst the barrenness of the Rosses.

All Mr. Powell has revealed - he stated it to the Pressmen just as he swung himself into the saddle of a borrowed blood chestnut mare at Finglass - is that ever since he read "Paddy the Cope" he has been anxious to answer the call of Donegal and explore its possibilities.

Mr. and Mrs. Powell plan to spend the next seven or eight days on horseback, travelling in easy stages of about 30 miles per day. They are due to arrive back in Dublin on February 11 and will make the return journey by train.

With them went Mr Mattie Gaul, a groom who will escort them on the journey driving a pony and gig, carrying luggage and equipment, and who will act as groom, guide, and general advance agent.

On Monday next the couple's six-months old baby Kevin, will be taken by his nurse to Donegal, there to await the arrival of his parents. Mr. Powell's film editor and chief scout for exterior films, Mr. John Seaburne, and his secretary, Miss Elspeth Day, a Glasgow girl, will also travel to Donegal by train.

Mr. Seaburne told Press representatives on Saturday that, he and Mr. Powell had become very interested in Donegal, especially the North West of the county, and felt it would make a fine background for a film story. They intended to meet the people, 'study their ways of life

Next Page: In February 1946, Paddy travelled down to Drumbeg Hotel, Inver, where Michael Powell, the film director, and his party were staying. With him – dressed impeccably and possibly hoping they might pick up some work as extras - were, left to right, Charlie Campbell, brothers Danny and Jackie Brennan and Daniel Doherty, all from Dungloe. The car (IH 4674, IH signified a Donegal registered car) was a 1938 Ford Fordor Saloon Fastback; one of 1,200 made in Dagenham for the British market, it had a 3622cc V8 sidevalve engine – a big, thirsty beast of an engine for such a relatively small car. It is likely to have been either Jackie or Danny Brennan's car- Jackie Brennan had a garage in Glenties and later a well known garage at the Barracks end of Dungloe. On the right, Paddy is standing with John Seabourne, who worked with Michael Powell as a film editor, most recently on 1945's 'I Know Where I'm Going', and location scout. It is tempting to imagine that the photographer was Michael Powell himself – it is a well composed shot and Powell would have taken many, many location shots and he is not in the picture - but there is no evidence for this (Photograph courtesy of Mary Jo (Jim the Cope) collection).

and customs and visit some of the islands. If they felt there was good material available they would make a film in due course.

Mr. Powell, who is aged 37 and a native of Kent is director and producer for Archer Films, Ltd., and also makes pictures for independent producers in the Rank group. Films he has made include "49th Parallel," Colonel Blimp," "Canterbury Tales", "A Matter of 'Life and Death", and "I Know Where I'm Going"..."[11]

Film Producer and Wife in Donegal

MEETING WITH PADDY THE COPE
A DAY OF INTERESTING VISITS

From our Special Representative

"...Michael Powell, ace producer of the "49th Parallel" and other British films achieved the object of his 200 miles trek on horseback across Ireland when yesterday he reached Dungloe, the capital of the Rosses, and was cordially welcomed by Paddy the Cope.

It was, however, by motor car that he entered Dungloe and I was the first to be introduced to the noted visitor and his party by Mr. Gallagher himself '*phones*' *our Special Representative.*

A message in the morning stated that Mr Powell might be expected at 11.30 am and as Mr Gallagher and myself sat in the comfortable sitting-room of his home awaiting him, he told me of the great success that had attended the publication of his life-story, under the title of "Paddy the Cope," in America. The appeal of the story had been phenomenal, several editions having been sold out.

Telling me that a further revised edition, with copious illustrations, was on the way, Mr. Gallagher showed me the typescript of extra chapters which bring the volume much closer to the present day and are of very special interest. The possibility of an American company making a film based on the book was he said at present under consideration.

It was 1.15 pm when the party drove up and, meeting them at the door, Mr. Gallagher accorded them a hearty cead mile failte. It was his great regret that his wife, Sally, who lives through the adventures of his book with him and whose help and encouragement in many difficulties he never ceases to praise, was not there also. She is at the moment indisposed, but will meet the party probably today.

---

11 *Derry Journal January 1946.*

The Story of the Cope

Mr. Powell, thirty-seven, slightly built and balding, looked a picturesque figure in a pleated tartan kilt and choker jersey. With him were his Dublin-born wife, secretary Elspeth Day and film editor John Seaburne.

LEFT HORSES AT INVER

To my question as to what happened to the horses, Mr. Powell said they felt obliged to leave them behind in Inver, where they had spent the weekend. His wife and himself had spent seven days in the saddle and averaged thirty miles a day across country. When I suggested that the weather had been rather unkind, he did not agree. "One can see and enjoy the beauty of the countryside in any kind of weather," he said. "We feel better now than when we set out. We got plenty of fresh air and lots of warm-hearted hospitality all along the way and everybody seemed greatly interested in our horses and turn-out."

Maureen O'Hara (b. 1920) was in the frame to play Sally, Paddy's wife in the film of 'My Story' – she would have been as marvellous alongside Cyril Cusack as she would be later be in 1952 starring in 'The Quiet Man' with John Wayne. What a shame the movie was never made! Later in the 1950s, Siobhan McKenna, another distinguished actress, was being talked about to play Sally (Photo courtesy of Delia O'Donnell, Dungloe, Irish Press or Irish Independent photo).

He added that on Monday they bade farewell to their horses after a pleasant ride out to Killybegs and Fintra.

WILL THERE BE A FILM?

The main question of the interview - "Was a film of the growth of the co-operative movement in contemplation?" - elicited a non-committal reply. He had he told me read the book, "Paddy the Cope", with great interest and much pleasure. It was a most romantic and appealing story, full of fine film material. He thought it should prove an ideal vehicle for a picture background by the scenic grandeur in which West Donegal seemed to abound. He was particularly taken by the part played by the late George Russell ("AE") in the founding of the co-operative movement in the Rosses. He seemed to have been the inspiration and intellectual guide of the starting of this many-sided enterprise, he said, and that was, one of the beautiful and appealing phases of the story that could be exploited. There were fine possibilities for a film here and it was his purpose to travel over the ground meet the people in their natural environment and see the beautiful and rugged scenery.

CAMERAS BUSY

After tea Paddy hurriedly assembled all available co-op workers and, with himself in the middle of them. Several cameras clicked to record a most unusual scene. Paddy was also photographed shaking hands with Mr Powell on the doorstep and also posed standing between the lady visitors. The day was beautifully fine and no time was lost in getting under way to visit some of the spots intimately associated with the co-op development.

I was the only other person to travel with them over the rugged, twisting roads that lead to remote, rock-strewn Cleendra, where both Paddy and the co-op first saw the light. With pride he pointed out the old homestead and the little deserted cottage where the idea of the movement first took shape.

On we went to Maghery, where Mr Powell photographed the gathering of sea-rods and their transport as a fertiliser by donkey and pony to the little fields on the hillside. The Atlantic, on which the sun's rays were reflected in soft hues, looked its most majestic and over the landscape a rainbow arched its lovely colours to give some grand material for Mr. Powell's camera. He took many pictures of islands, Mass Rocks and objects of historical interest.

Left: Cyril Cusack (1910-93) was lined up to play Paddy in the film; here he is with Paddy and John Seabourne, Michael Powell's editor on four of his films in the 1940s. Cyril Cusack was a very distinguished actor on stage, in Dublin and in the Royal Shakespeare Company, and screen, appearing in more than 90 films. He would have been an admirable Copeman (Photo courtesy of Mary Jo, grandson of Paddy the Cope, and Jim the Cope's daughter)

On to Croghey Head the cars laboured their way and there we saw the soapstone deposits which proved a profitable undertaking when revived during the Emergency years. Then back to Dungloe, where the party had an excellent appetite for lunch.

A FAMOUS PHOTOGRAPH

One of the objects of special interest to the visitors in Paddy's home was an enlarged picture of himself and his wife taken in Scotland nearly fifty years ago. It was shortly afterwards, on their return to the homeland, that the co-op was launched.

Later in the evening the party motored to Burtonport, and saw the herring kippering station.

Today it is hoped to cross to Arranmore.

The party have planned to return to Dublin to-morrow. Mr, Powell, who has just completed the filming of "A Matter of Life and Death," was delighted with everything he saw: indeed his highest expectations seem to have been exceeded. The other members of the party also were charmed by the scenery and the friendly attitude of the people everywhere they went..."[12]

"...It was during Michael's horseback ride across Ireland to research the film he hoped to make about Paddy the Cope that he and Frankie had to take shelter from a storm in Classybaun castle, the summer home of the Mountbatten family..."[13]

The Film That Never Was

The party stayed at Drumbeg Hotel, Inver near Killybegs, owned then by the Hemmersbach family. Why they stopped in Inver, some 40 miles away from Dungloe, may only be speculated on. It was a fine hotel and location, on Donegal Bay with a marvellous beach. It would have had good stables. The intervening miles to Dungloe would have been, as they still are today, much harder – less good roads – and by then they may have been strapped for time. It could also have been that something else had come up, either with the most recent film, 'A Matter of Life and Death', or another project, requiring them to cut short their trip.

---

12 *Derry Journal 6ᵗʰ February 1946.*

13 *'Million Dollar Movie' Michael Powell, 1995 American Edition, edited by Thelma Schoonmaker, Michael Powell's wife, a celebrated Oscar winning film editor in her own right..*

On his trip to Dungloe, Michael Powell was taken to Cleendra to see the 'wee shop' (and no doubt Paddy showed him the glen where the fairies were) on his way out to Maghery. Powell took lots of photos on his trip and was fascinated by the way of life in the Rosses. The newspaper article of the time records that in Maghery he "...photographed the gathering of sea-rods and their transport as a fertiliser by donkey and pony to the little fields on the hillside..." This is a more recent 1970s photo of sea rods on the wall outside Connie Devenney's house in Maghery (Devenney Collection)

Michael Powell and his party travelled by horseback to Drumbeg Hotel, in Inver, South Donegal. The hotel was then owned by the Hemmersbach family. William Hemmersbach, who was born in Cologne, Germany and married Emily Johnson of Tullybrook House near Donegal, bought Drumbeg in the mid 1930s. The hotel, as Helen Meehan writes in her fine book on Inver Parish, 'attracted a very exclusive type of clientele from home and abroad' (Contemporary postcard, by McGill, Ardara, courtesy Donegal County Museum, Letterkenny)

216. DRUMBEG HOTEL AND GOLF LINKS.

Paddy's story would have attracted Michael Powell on a number of levels. He would have seen the dramatic possibilities with the story of early struggle, working at the age of nine in the Lagan, seasonal migration at 16 in Scotland and then returning to Donegal to take up the fight against a system which kept his people in debt and poverty or doomed to leave for America or Scotland. He would also have loved the parts of the story which focused on the community: the evening airneál of music, storytelling, etc. He would have fallen in love with the landscape – he had a lifelong love affair with the West and Highlands of Scotland which has very similar scenery. His earlier works 'The Edge of the World' (1937) and 'I Know Where I'm Going' (1945), both set in Scotland, give some idea as to how he would have treated Paddy's autobiography. Cyril Cusack and Maureen O'Hara (and later Siobhan McKenna) were both talked about to play Paddy and Sally; they'd have made a marvellous pairing.

Michael Powell was keen to have Paddy act as an adviser – and Paddy was only too happy to help; he was very interested in the casting, and particularly who was to play Sally and himself. Paddy could hardly believe that Powell was proposing to pay him for this and in addition for an option to film his story:

> "...I said I would pay him £500 for a ten-year option and he danced with delight..."[14]

When the cheque came from London, Paddy went all round Dungloe showing everyone before banking it.[15] Paddy's excitement was real enough; he was 75 at the time and the old age pension in 1946 was a maximum of 10/- a week or £26 a year (in all likelihood, the State would have reduced his pension by a shilling because of other income). To receive 20 times that figure as well as his buoyant royalties from 'My Story' book sales would have made Paddy substantially better off.[16]

It must have been very disappointing for Paddy that after so much interest - and more than one reassurance of an imminent start to filming – that it was never made. He hoped to the end of his days that a start would be made and experienced many a false dawn with it with other film producers as well.

---

14 'A Life In Movies' Michael Powell, Heinemann,1986; extracts and information courtesy of Thelma Schoonmaker, Michael Powell's wife. This first volume of his autobiography contains seven highly entertaining pages about the film maker's trip to Donegal to meet Paddy the Cope.

15 Ibid.

16 'Wages in Ireland 1946-1962, ESRI. The average Irish national annual wage in 1946 was £176; agricultural £111; manufacturing £176; and construction £201.

"Paddy the Cope" Film

"...Michael Powell, British film producer and director, has signed a contract for the film rights of "My Story," by Mr. Patrick Gallagher of Donegal ("Paddy the Cope"), and work on the film has started.

Between £100,000 and £150,000 (approximately a half million dollars or more) will be spent on filming Mr. Gallagher's story, which portrays the founding and early struggle of the cooperative undertaking established by "Paddy the Cope" in Donegal.

The scenes of the film will be "shot" in the vicinity of Donegal, where Paddy established his first store..."[17]

———————————

"...His autobiography, "My Story" is now in its sixth edition in the States, and next Spring Michael Powell will begin shooting it locally in Technicolor with Cyril Cusack in the title role..."[18]

"...I hear that your book, Paddy the Cope, is to be produced in moving pictures. Is that so?

Yes. I have released the rights to Michael Powell, the British producer.

Did you lay down any conditions?

Only one: Positively there must be no stage Irish.

That answer pleased me exceedingly. I thought of all the stupid screen and stage atrocities depicting Irish life which have been inflicted on the American people. And the crudities presented by Irish-Americans on St. Patrick's Day.

Thanks to the inspiration, courage and genius of Paddy the Cope there is new hope in the hearts and a more abundant life in the homes of many Irishmen. Where once there was want there is now security. The spirit of true freedom has supplanted that of serfdom. If the New Ireland continues to produce leaders like Paddy the Cope, its future is well assured..."[19]

---

17 *'Consumers Cooperation', an American monthly magazine, May 1946.*

18 *Irish Times Profile 1949.*

19 *Irish Digest July 1951, Richard McKeon S.J.*

Delia (Cannon) O'Donnell and Annabella ('Bella') Brennan outside the Bridge End Bar, Dungloe. Delia has a fund of stories about her uncle Paddy the Cope and the various visits of cameramen and scriptwriters in connection with the proposed filming of 'My Story' (Photo dating from the 1930s, courtesy of Packie Walsh, Burtonport).

Far Right: In 2006, Delia O'Donnell, niece of Paddy the Cope, opened the Cope's Centenary Exhibition on the back stairs of the Main Street store, with Minister Pat the Cope holding the ribbon. At the time, Delia was a wonderful 96 and full of stories about her legendary uncle. In the photograph are also Paddy (Jim) the Cope, Mary (Packie) Logue – cousins, both grandchildren of Paddy and Sally – in Mary's arms, her granddaughter Aoibhe Boyle, then Patricia Harney and Shane Coyne. The two young girls in foreground are Liane Greene and Aileen Bonner, both granddaughters of Paddy (Jim) the Cope (Cope Photo Archive)

Paddy was still hoping in February 1951 that the film would be made; he wrote to Margaret Foley:

> "...My Dear Mrs Foley,
>
> I cannot find words to enable me to express my thanks for your lovely letter of the 11th inst. I hope and pray when the film will be produced in Cleendra that you and all the descendants of Rotchie Nabla will be there. Rotchie was our second member.
>
> The producers will be three months in Cleendra. They are giving me £20 per week for a minimum of three months. They paid me £500 when I signed the contract, but unfortunately, I overlooked (in the excitement) a clause giving them an option of ten years. I am however hopeful that it will be produced next year or the following year at the latest. It will I think, put Cleendra on the map, but there will be a big want – no Sally, but I am sure (I am crying now) that she will be watching down from Heaven.
>
> The film is going to be shown first in New York instead of London.

The Story of the Cope

I had a great welcome in America. I did three broadcasts. I was guest of honour of Lord Mayor O'Dwyer of New York City. I was guest of honour at a big party in Philadelphia. The Lord Mayor (he is not Irish) put the key of the city in my hand.

I was there for two months in the autumn of 1947. I could not attend more than half the parties I was invited to.

Give my kindest regards to your good husband and all your friends.

Sincerely yours

Paddy..."[20]

Delia (Cannon) O'Donnell is a niece of Paddy's, a daughter of Hannah and Johnny Cannon who had the shop at the bridge in Dungloe. Delia who was in 2006 a very young 96 years remembers Paddy very well. She recalls the

20 *Letter from Margaret Foley to Paddy the Cope, 22nd February 1951; Hugh McGee Collection.*

The Coll Family house, also called the 'Cran' because there was a stone quarry over the road and the *crane* used to be right opposite the house. Paddy the Cope, accompanied by his niece Delia (Cannon) O'Donnell, took two film cameramen here to meet his good friend Ciss Coll in the late 1940s and a party ensued, much to the delight of the two cameramen (This photo, courtesy of Mary Coll O'Donnell, Sheskinarone, was taken on September 20th 1958)

time that two cameramen came to Dungloe to do some preparatory filming, to suggest ideas for the main film:

> "...We all went with Paddy in a van to visit one of Paddy's friends, Ciss Coll, up at the Cran Brae. There was a big slab of butter, a 'masceán ime', on the table – it was shaped and patterned in the old way with wooden pats – the cameramen had never seen anything like it ('What's that?' they said). Both were spell bound by the house.

> The table was set, scrubbed white and with the masceán on it; there was a roaring fire with a kettle boiling on the crook. The floor was spotless. There was a patchwork quilt in the room. A scone of bread with a cross marked on it. Instead of cups we had bowls for the tea. Ciss Coll held the loaf under her arm buttered it and cut slices for everyone.

> Paddy had on a big knitted cape [or overcoat]; he got up and danced with Ciss - a Highland Scottish dance. The two of them were going at it, she was very tall and Paddy was very small, they looked quite a pair!

Ciss Coll is pictured here, in her younger days, when she lived in Scotland. Ciss was a great dancer in her time and a good friend of Paddy the Cope's. When Paddy the Cope visited her house with a film crew, the cameramen were taken aback at the dancing that Paddy and Ciss started and the traditional look and feel of the cottage (Photo courtesy of Mary Coll O'Donnell, Sheskinarone)

The cameramen kept filming, they couldn't believe their luck. The company went bust, a shame; the film must still be around somewhere..."[21]

In 2009, Ciss's daughter Mary Coll provided the following information on her mother and Paddy the Cope.

"...Ciss and Paddy were great friends alright; Paddy was always on at Ciss to bake bread so he could sell it in the shop. Ciss had enough on her hands so she never did. She was a great dancer in her youth: Scottish dancing.

She was called Ciss because her sister Mary used to say "...where's my sis'er..?" (i.e. sister), and the name stuck. Her real name was Sarah Kathleen née Alexander; she met and married Paddy Coll in Scotland, they both worked at the mines there. Paddy was from Sheskinarone; she became known as Ciss Coll.

---

21 *Personal reminiscence by Delia O'Donnell to the editor, November 2006.*

They moved back here, travelled by train to Strabane and got a horse and cart from there. Her bridesmaid bought her a 12 piece tea set as a wedding present, which was used at every wake and Station house (the priest would come to a different house each time in Lent and in October to say Mass and the Stations of the Cross) in Sheskinarone and Crickamore for years after. Mary Coll still has it; albeit with a few pieces gone and the cream jug broken. Ciss was a great one for wearing black. Mary remembers that the floor had a board on it which was used when they made brúitín (mashed potatoes butter and salt) – when the potatoes were cooked they would be tipped into the pot and mashed with a bog oak masher. You'd need a wooden base as the mashing would break the pot if on a stone or concrete floor. The wooden base is still in the cottage floor next door under lino. The house, the one Paddy and Delia went to with the film men, still has a thatched roof..."[22]

Delia O'Donnell also remembers the many visitors from all over the world that Paddy and the Cope attracted. In particular, one group of visitors from Africa, whom Delia recalls caused quite a stir in 1950s Dungloe:

A Donegal Lesson In Cooperation

"...Students of Loughborough College, Leicestershire, have concluded a two day visit to Dungloe, Co Donegal, as the guests of Mr Patrick Gallagher (Paddy the Cope). Their object was to study the operations of Templecrone Co-Operative Society, which Mr Gallagher founded. They came from Tanganyika, Sudan, Trinidad, Mauritius and Canada, and were much impressed by what they saw..."[23]

The promised start to the filming dragged on through the fifties and sixties:

"Paddy the Cope" to be filmed

"...Shooting of scenes may soon start in West Donegal for the film version of "My Story" the autobiography of Patrick Gallagher ("Paddy the Cope) of Dungloe. Mr. Michael Powell the film producer has assured Mr. John Curran, a New Jersey business man now on holiday in his native Donegal that the film's outdoor scenes will be shot in West Donegal, and it is hoped that the main part will he played, by Cyril Cusack..."[24]

---

22 *(Mary Coll O'Donnell, Sheskinarone, talking in March 2009)*

23 *Irish Times 30th March 1951*

24 *Irish Times 13th July 1956*

Paddy was still hoping in his ninetieth year:

> "...a gentleman called Michael Powell and his wife came to Dublin from London. They hired a couple of horses in Dublin and rode up to the Rosses to see the co-operative society and me. They stayed a week, thinking of making a film, and they took a lot of photographs and went away. Then Seán Mór Rice from Antrim came over from Hollywood, and he wanted to make a film of the book, but Mr. Powell had a ten years' option on it. A month ago, I went down to see John Huston in Galway. He has a fine place there - a grand house. A girl came out and said he was busy. She gave me a half-one of whiskey, and then Huston came out and talked about the book. He's a hardy man and a very nice fellow. I think he might make a film of my book."

> Talking about hardy men Paddy Gallagher is 88, but thought little of dropping down from the Rosses to Galway to see his neighbour. Yesterday, in a bitter wind that belonged to March rather than April, he was rambling round Dublin without an overcoat. It's easy, even now, to see why this man's purpose in founding his co-operative society was indestructible..."[25]

Epilogue

Sadly the film was never made. Donegal's 'Ryan's Daughter' or 'The Quiet Man' was never to be. Production on Powell and Pressburger's next movie, the magnificent 'Black Narcissus', appears to have started in May 1946 and this would have been, of course, the complete focus of their attention.

As Powell said with some regret in his autobiography some 40 years later:

> "...The story of Paddy the Cope was another of those films which only I would want to make and which I certainly should have made..."[26]

A draft screenplay for 'My Story' (dating from 1947-48) exists in the British Film Institute in London – waiting for a modern day Michael Powell to shoot.

---

25 *Irish Times 2nd April 1960*

26 *'A Life in Movies' Michael Powell, Heinemann, 1986.*

Chapter 13

The Cope Centenary and the Cope Today

The hundred year success story of the Templecrone Cope was marked with the launch by An Post of a commemorative stamp at the Ostan na Rosann in Dungloe on Monday 16th January 2006, the anniversary of the Cope's incorporation. On the previous Saturday, hundreds of current and past Cope employees, as well as invited guests, enjoyed an evening of celebration, stories and recollections.

Paddy the Cope's grandson, Marine Minister Pat the Cope Gallagher, TD, unveiled the stamp saying

> "...The Co-operative movement was tremendously important to the people of Donegal and I am delighted that the first such movement in Donegal, founded by my grandfather, Paddy the Cope, is now being commemorated by the launch of this stamp.

> Established in 1906 by Patrick Gallagher, Templecrone Co-operative Agricultural Society Ltd., trading as the Cope, became the first recognised Co-operative in the Rosses area of Co. Donegal and was a founding force for the Irish Co-operative movement in Ireland.

> Having experienced first-hand the benefits that accrued from taking control of supply and demand mechanisms, Patrick Gallagher urged friends to pool resources and start a Co-op based on the ideal of self-sufficiency. The Cope soon became intrinsic to the town's development and was a key focal point in all community activities and employment. The Cope catered for almost every household and agricultural need of the time, including credit facilities at low rates.

> Based on the ideals of social justice, the Cope prospered through the exceptional vision and initiative of Patrick Gallagher. His involvement in wholesaling, fishing and bakery mills provided employment for hundreds during the early years of the last century.

> Today, the Cope continues to be a leading source of employment in Donegal and it plays an important role in the area's ongoing development..."

Seamus Rodgers, who worked at the Cope for 25 years, said Paddy the Cope had

> "...sowed the seeds of the industrial revolution in The Rosses. Undoubtedly, he was a man before his time. The Cope was like a university..."

An Post Chairperson Margaret McGinley added:

"...This stamp is a fitting way to mark the centenary of such an important local initiative. As these stamps travel all over the country and all over the world, particularly to the homes and businesses of Donegal people, they will give out a very strong and proud message to all who see them. They speak volumes about who we are at an international, national and local level, where we have come from and about the fortitude, integrity and hard work of generations of families past and present.

"We are delighted to share with Minister Pat the Cope Gallagher, grandson of Patrick Gallagher, in the Cope's centenary celebrations..."[1]

---

1 Press Releases 16th January 2006 by An Post and the Department of Marine, Communications and National Resources (DCMNR) - quoting Pat the Cope Gallagher and Margaret McGinley.

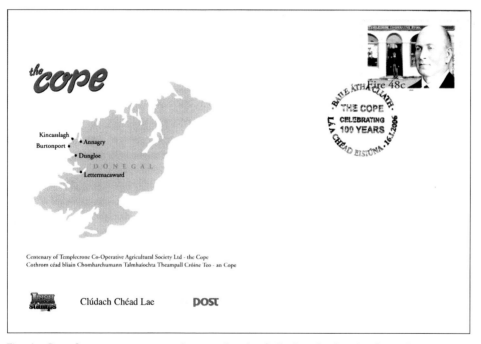

The An Post Cope stamp, a great honour for the Gallagher family, the Cope, Dungloe and Donegal, was designed by Steve Simpson. Mr Simpson used a studio photograph of Paddy the Cope from 1928 which had been taken as a passport photo for his trip to the USA (see Chapter 9 for further details). The shop scene on the stamp was taken from the 1912 photograph album compiled by IAWS Chairman Harold Barbour on his tour of Irish Co-Operatives. The two people standing with Paddy have been 'airbrushed' out, leaving Paddy standing alone. The Cope's shop sign has been extended by the artist to cover James Sweeney's shop name which was underneath the first Cope sign. The untouched photo is used as the cover of this book and also appears on page 72. (An Post 48c stamp and First day Cover, 16th January 2006)

The Cope held an art competition with local schools to commemorate the Centenary; the winners were as follows:

Centenary Presentation Schools Competition

Arranmore Secondary	1st €100	**Written**	**Frankie Costello**
Annagry National School	1st €100	**Written**	**Lorna McGinley**
Rosses (Dungloe) Secondary	1st €100	Written	Catherine Ward
	2nd€ 50	Written	Caitriona McGee
	1st €100	Pictorial	Grace Hindle
	1st €100	Pictorial	Christina Gallagher
	2nd € 50	Pictorial	Carmel O'Donnell
	3rd € 50	Pictorial	Anne Marie O'Donnell
Dungloe National School	1st €100	Written	Stephen Molloy
	(€25 each)		Peadar Sweeney
			Eimhin Bonner
			Meabh Sweeney
Rannafast National School	1st €100	Pictorial	Keevagh O'Donnell
	2nd€ 50	Pictorial	Cassie Ann Gillespie
	3rd € 50	Pictorial	Michaél Casey
	3rd € 50	Pictorial	Sorcha Doohin

LONG SERVICE AWARDS

The Cope has become part and parcel of the Rosses community and provided livelihoods for many families for over a hundred years. In return, the Cope has seen extraordinary loyalty from the people it has employed. Many people, indeed many families, have worked all their lives in one part or other of the Society as it is sometimes called.

On the Saturday before the An Post stamp launch, a celebration was held to commemorate the loyalty and commitment of so many people over the Cope's century. In the course of this very enjoyable evening, stories were told, people who had passed on were remembered and Long Service awards were presented to the following people or, for those no longer with us, collected their representatives:

Ann Shovlin (1979-2003) 28 years - Ladies Dept, Telephone Exchange
Anne T. Sweeney (1963-2003) 40 years - Head Office
Annie Hunter, née Bonner (1948-1963) 25 years - Knitting Factory
Breid (McCole) O'Donnell (1971-1995) 24 years - Grocery, Ladies Drapery, Manager, Household Dept
Bridget Bonner (1953-2002) 49 years - Head Office, in charge of supplier accounts
Bridget Byrne (1957 – 1983) 25 years - Knitting Factory

Cathal McCole (1953-1995) 42 years - Meenbanad Cope, Wholesale, Grocery

Cathal McCole, St Peter's Terrace (1939-1975) 36 Years - Lorry Driver

Charlie Boyle (1951-1987) 36 years - Head Office, Assistant to the General Manager

Charlie Doherty (1912-56) - Meenbanad Cope

Connie Boyle (1945-1994) 49 years - served in every department in the Cope, Tea Van, Delivery Van, Butcher, Supermarket, Hardware, Agriculture and Fuel, Burtonport, Lettermacaward, Drapery

Cyril Winder (1969-1993) 24 years - General Manager

Dan Deery Meenmore (1921-1972) 51 years - The Mill, Transport Manager, Chairman of Cope Committee, Assistant Manager

Dermot Logue (1931-1975) 44 years - Manager Annagry Cope

Dolly O'Donnell (1943-1980) 47 years - Head Office, Cope Secretary, Committee member

Eddie McCullagh (1936-1975) 39 years - Manager, Menswear

Eugene Doherty (1941-1989) 48 years - Meenbanad, Manager of Burtonport and Kincasslagh, Assistant General Manager, Committee Member, Chairman of Committee (1990-96),

Francie Houston (1932-1974) 42 years - Tea Van, Grocery Dept

Fred Sweeney (1953-2003) 50 years - Bakery in Confectionery Dept, Manager Carpet Dept

Hugh McGee (1952 -2001) 49 years - Agriculture and Fuel, Supermarket, Tea Van, Burtonport Cope, Manager Hardware Dept

James McGee (1932-1977) 45 years - Manager of Bakery

Jim Duffy (1962-2003) 41 years - Builders' Providers

Jim Ward (1953-1997) 44 years - Grocery Dept, Builders' Providers

Jimmy Doherty (1946-1970) 24 years - Agriculture and Fuel, Transport, Supervisor at Mill

Jimmy O'Donnell (1980-2005) 25 years - Builders' Providers, Transport Manager, Annagry Cope

Joe Brennan (1922-1965) 43 years - Main Shop, Dungloe, Manager, Burtonport Cope

John Gallagher (1940-1987) 47 years - Grocery, Tea Van, Men's, Manager, Furniture Dept

John Neil John Gallagher - Burtonport, Manager Leitir Cope

John McCole (1938-1972) 34 years - Maghery Cope, Head Office

Josie McCole (1935-1965) 30 years - Agriculture & Fuel

Josie O'Donnell (1968-1988), 20 years - Builders' Providers, involved in the reconstruction and extension of the main street premises, and building the new store in Burtonport

Leo Brennan (1920-1970) 50 years - Drapery, Cope Secretary, Financial Controller, Assistant Manager

Mary Gallagher (1944-1990) 46 years - Manager Ladies' Drapery

Michael Wallace (1955-1997) 42 years - Tea Van, Delivery, Bakery

Nancy Shovlin (1969-2003) 34 years - Grocery, Tea Van, first to go to Narin, Leitir, Manager, Ladies' Drapery

Neily Sweeney (1927=1974) 47 years - Transport, Lorry Driver, Bread Van Salesman
Owen Bonner (1957-2003) 44 years - Burtonport Cope, Manager, Narin Cope.
Owenie Boyle, Main Street (1946-1991) 45 years - Wholesale
Owenie Sweeney (1910-1938) 28 years - Transport, Lorry Driver
Owen Sweeney (1932-1980) 48 years - Bakery and Head Office
Pa Ward (1929-1976) 47 years - Overall Buyer, Bakery
Packie Boyle (1954-1994) 40 years - Bakery, Transport Manager
Packie Bonner, Fair Hill (1927-1975) 48 years - Kincasslagh Cope, Grocery
Packie Boyle (1972-2000) 28 years - Manager Burtonport, Annagry and Grocery
Packie Gallagher (1970-1993) 23 years - Manager Kincasslagh Cope
Packie Gallagher (James) (1934-1970) 36 years - Served in the Bakery
Packie McCahill (1972 – 1996) 24 years - Builders Providers, Transport
Packie McHugh (1977-1998) 21 years - in most departments, Manager Dungloe Supermarket, Manager Maghery
Pat Forker, (1961-2001) 40 years - Burtonport Cope, first to go to Narin with Nancy Shovlin, Manager Builders Providers
Patrick 'Panda' Ward (1951-2001) 50 years - Bread Van salesman, Delivery Van, Tea Van
Sally McGettigan (1974-2000) 26 years - Supermarket
Seamus Rodgers (1952-1975) 23 years - Annagry Cope, Manager Kincasslagh Cope
Sheila McGettigan (1974-2000) 26 years - Household Dept, Toys & Souvenirs Dept
Susan Doogan, Termon (1931-1980) 49 years - Manager, Maghery Branch and Toys and Souvenirs Dept, Dungloe
Timmy Doherty (1947-1993) 46 years - Meenbanad Cope, Manager Annagry Cope

The Cope Today

The Cope's Fun Day in July 2008, and again in 2009, continues a tradition of involvement in the 'Mary from Dungloe' festival, dating back to its beginning in 1968. The Cope has always tried to be at the heart of Dungloe and Templecrone cultural development through its people, the Committee and through its many different commercial activities over its first hundred years.

It continues to play a huge role in the area, both as an employer and as an investor in the local community, its recent major building works being a very visible example. Its commitment and energy are undimmed; the Cope is clearly determined to move with the times.

However, as its Committee and Chairman know only too well, it continually has to revisit its purpose, its raison d'être. The economic circumstances which existed when it was founded are long since gone – the days of the gombeen man are, thankfully, over for good. The Cope was the prime agent in the Rosses of this transformation and has reaped the rewards of this success, and the loyalty of local people, over the subsequent decades. The town of Dungloe and the

Rosses are more substantial places because of what the Cope has done over the years for employment and industry.

Its business model has nevertheless had to change significantly. While it was once a major manufacturer and exporter – its knitting factory being the most obviously successful example out of many – it is now essentially a retail operation, buying in goods and selling them on in its outlets, and a Builders' Providers, itself a retail outlet for local builders and domestic self-build customers. Both of these are very competitive markets and, as many have commented, the Cope is 'not the only show in town'. In one sense, the urgent need for the Cope that existed in 1906 is simply not there anymore and, while there have been many laurels earned over the years, resting on them now is just not an option.

These thoughts occupy the minds of the Committee and help it plan its next steps. There is always the thought 'What would Paddy have done?' and 'How would Dan Deery, Leo Brennan and Cyril Winder have managed today?' The answer always comes back the same now as it did then. The Cope has to look to the community it serves and see how it can help by investing in and developing businesses that bring benefits to local people, by creating employment and ensuring that real customer needs are met locally.

The Cope's introduction of an office and computing supplies business is the most recent example of this. The Cope identified a real market need, something its customers had been looking for, and saw a gap in the market. While still relatively small scale, it is now looking to develop this commercial opportunity which will hopefully benefit not just the Cope and its customers but the people of the wider area as well. Anything which allows people to shop locally and avoid having to drive out to Letterkenny or Derry has to be good news. The local shop will become more and more important as energy and fuel prices increase.

On the plus side, the good news is that the Cope has enormous reserves of goodwill and experience and thriving retail stores. It has assets and resources both in its people, who are always willing to help move things along as well as in its building footprint in Dungloe and elsewhere. The new supermarket was built with a top floor of 16,000 square feet – plenty of room for expansion or attracting other businesses into the area.

The Cope will also be looking to develop its core departments, like Grocery and Sports, which are both strong lines of business as well as developing in new areas. It can use its scale, expertise and buying power to bring the best of what is needed to its customers. Its commitment to excellence, its continued focus on the needs of the local community and relentless business development all help to position it well for its next hundred years. The Cope has thoroughly deserved its place in our local and national history and, going forward, it has the regard and warmth of its community to help propel it to even greater successes.

Above: At the 14th January 2006 Centenary Ball, six of Paddy and Sally the Cope's grandchildren enjoy the moment: Jimmy 'Bimbo' Gallagher; Mary Jo Murrin; Mary Logue; Pat the Cope Gallagher; Annie Sweeney; and Paddy the Cope Gallagher.

Left Top: Marine Minister Pat the Cope Gallagher TD and An Post Chairperson Margaret McGinley at the launch of the Paddy the Cope 48c stamp on Monday 16th January 2006. On the previous Saturday, the Cope hosted a Centenary Ball attended by Cope family, friends and people of all ages at which Long Service certificates were awarded. (Cope Photo Archive).

Left Bottom: Some of the Cope family photographed at the Centenary Ball on 14th January 2006: (back row): Mary Jo Murrin, Mary Logue, Helen Gallagher, James Gallagher, Teresa Dwyer, Pat the Cope Gallagher, Ann Gallagher, Conal Gallagher, Frances Gallagher, Patricia Harney, Vera Creavin, Cha Gallagher, Paddy Gallagher; (front) Nancy Mc Cready, Mary Clarke, Sinead Sweeney, Delia O' Donnell, Peggy Jameson and Annie Sweeney.

Above: (Back): Fred Sweeney, Conal Gallagher, Packie McHugh, Pauline McCole, Anne T. Sweeney, Francie Houston, Teresa Ward, Charles Solan and Neil Gallagher; Front: John A. Gallagher, Hugh McCole, Louise Boyle, Fidelma Logue, Nancy Shovlin and Dennis Brennan.

Left Top: Receiving long service awards at the Centenary celebrations are: (back row) Timmy Doherty, John A. Doherty, Roshine Kelly (née Brennan), Hugh McGee, Mary Ward (née Brennan), Bríd O'Donnell (née McCole), Nancy Shovlin and Teresa Ward; (front) Cathal McCole, Denis Brennan, Neil Gallagher, Michael Wallace, Noel Brennan and Sean Brennan (Cope photo).

Left Bottom: Michael Wallace, Anthony Ward, Frances Boyle, Jim Ward, Sheila Ward, Sheila Boyle, Joseph O'Donnell and Seamus Rodgers.

At the Cope's Centenary Ball, 14th January 2006: (left top) Cope Chairman Johnny Doherty and his wife Maureen; (left bottom) Cope General Manager, the late Jimmie Nangle and his wife Bernie; (above) Bishop Philip Boyce and Fr John Joe Duffy; and (below) Denis and Dolores Ward with their daughters Sarah-Anne, Denise and Catherine

Jimmy Durnin, Mary McGee, Vincie John O'Donnell and Hugh McGee celebrating the Centenary.

Sean McCool and Ben Colangelo are pictured here with the winners of the Cope Design Competition (the names are grouped with the schools and not as in the photograph): *Arranmore Secondary*: Frankie Costello; *Annagry National*: Lorna McGinley; *Rosses (Dungloe) Secondary* Catherine Ward, Catriona McGee, Grace Hindle, Christina Gallagher, Carmel O'Donnell, Anne Marie O'Donnell; *Dungloe National School* Stephen Molloy, Peadar Sweeney, Eimhin Bonner, Meabh Sweeney (absent from the photo); *Rannafast National School* Keevagh O'Donnell, Cassie Ann Gillespie, Michaél Casey, Sorcha Doohin (Cope Photo Archive)

At the unveiling of the statue of Paddy the Cope on the Cope's Fun Day, 26th July 2008: Jimmy Molloy (above) and John Wallace (below) of the Rosses Pipe Band, lead in Pat the Cope TD, Councillor David Alcorn and Fr Seamus Gallagher

On the Cope's Fun Day, 26th July 2008, Bobby Sweeney, David Conway and Anthony Glackin in a first for Dungloe – three Cope forklifts driving up Main Street from the new Builders' Providers. They formed part of the Fun Day parade, and are just turning in to Chapel Road on the way to the Cope car park (Cope Photo Archive).

On the Cope Fun Day, part of the large crowd in Cope Street present for the unveiling of the statue of Paddy the Cope.

The Burtonport Variety Group helping the Cope celebrate its 26th July 2008 Fun Day in the new Grocery Department: Carol Alcorn, Marie Gallagher, Margaret Bonner, Patsy Bonner, Mary Philomena Boyle, Kathleen Bonner, Thomas Boyd (partially obscured), Noreen McGarvey, Seamus McGarvey, Debbie McGarvey, Mary (Coll) O'Donnell, Eugene McGarvey, PJ Sweeney, Margaret Riley, Peter Boyle, Dom Sheila O'Donnell, Joe Rodgers on guitar and, the Man in Black: Connie Ellen John Boyle. Conducting operations: Mary McGee, Meenmore.

Paddy The Cope Gallagher
25th December 1871 - 24th June 1966
Founder of the Templecrone Co-operative Agricultural
Society Ltd in 1906

Erected in 2008 by The Management Committee on
behalf of all his Loyal Past, Present & Future Staff,
Customers & Family.

a thug dúinn é

Bridget 'Biddy' McGee, from Annagry, the Cope's oldest customer at 102, receives a bouquet from the new Cope Managing Director, Mark Sharkey at the unveiling of the Paddy the Cope statue (Cope Archive).

Left: For the centenary, the Cope Committee commissioned a bronze statue of founder Paddy the Cope. Paddy's grandson, Pat the Cope Gallagher, unveiled the statue on 26th July 2008. The statue, a permanent memorial to Paddy and the Cope, now welcomes shoppers and visitors to Dungloe in the newly created Cope Street, which links Dungloe's Main Street with the Cope car park. The inscription on the statue reads: "Paddy the Cope Gallagher, 25th December 1871 – 24th June 1966, Founder of the Templecrone Co-Operative Agricultural Society in 1906, Erected in 2008 by the Management Committee on behalf of all his Loyal Past, Present and Future Staff, Customers and Family, Dia a thug dúinn é, Dia a rug uainn é (Cope Photo Archive).

On the Cope's Fun Day, Anton Bán Sweeney leads the Keadue Fife and Drum Band up the Main Street in Dungloe. In the first row, from left to right, are Francie Ward, Joe Boyle and Ruaidhri Ward; in the second row, Matthew Smith, Packie Ward and John Bosco O'Donnell. Also playing that day were Laura Cusack, Anne O'Donnell, John Moy, Stephen Cowley, John Michael Bonner (on bass drum), Josie Gallagher, Joe Neily and Mickey Cusack (Cope Photo)

Right Top & Bottom: The Keadue Fife and Drum Band marching up Main Street, stopping to play outside the new Cope supermarket.

On the Cope Fun Day, in front of the new Cope Sports retail shop, fresh from marching up Dungloe's Main Street, are Gemma Davis, Aisling Sharkey, Andrea Ogilsby and Caoimhe Bonner of the Keadue Fife and Drum Band (Cope Photo).

The Paddy the Cope statue on the new Cope Street welcomes shoppers and visitors to Dungloe. In the background, crowds are enjoying the Fun day and the band on the trailer in the Cope car park.

Where it all started: the Cleendra shop as it is today, a ruin and overgrown with ivy, whins and bracken. The old shop still gets the occasional visit from 'pilgrims' marvelling at the humble beginnings of the Cope. The contrast between the small stone building and the Cope's fine new buildings in 2009 is a dramatic one (Cope Photo Archive, photograph by Brian Sweeney).

Appendix 1

'The Templecrone Co-operative Agricultural Society Story of Its Origins and Struggle'
Irish Homestead Pamphlet (published 1910)

The Irish Homestead weekly periodical was the public relations arm of the Co-Operative movement. It was founded in 1895 by the Irish Agricultural Organisation Society (IAOS) and designed to be an information vehicle for the movement and offer advice and support to individual Co-Operative Societies.

NOTICE.

The Subscription to the IRISH HOMESTEAD for Inland Postage is 6/9 per annum; 3/6 for the half-year, with the Christmas Number.

The Subscription for Foreign Countries is 8/11 per annum; 4/7 for the half-year, including the Christmas Number.

All Subscriptions should be addressed to the MANAGER, "The Irish Homestead," 28 Clare Street, Dublin.

The IRISH HOMESTEAD is now on Sale at the Railway Bookstalls, LONDON—Euston Station, Piccadilly Tube Station; Oxford Circus Tube Station and 6 & 7 Creed Lane, E.C.

The New Irish Direct Supply, Ltd., 94 Victoria Street, London, S.W.

LONDON OFFICE:—5 & 7 Long Lane, Smithfield, E.C.

Telep one:—1181 City.

MANCHESTER—Exchange Station.

FISHGUARD—G.W.R. Station; as well as Eason and Son's Bookstalls throughout Ireland.

Sir Horace Plunkett described the purpose of Irish Homestead:

> "...To complete the description of the propagandist activities of the central body, there is a ceaseless flow of leaflets and circulars containing advice and direction to bodies of farmers who, for the first time in their lives, have combined for business purposes; while a little weekly paper, the 'Irish Homestead', acts as the organ of the movement, promotes the exchange of ideas between societies scattered throughout the country, furnishes useful information upon all matters connected with their

George William Russell (1867-1935), also known by his pseudonym 'AE', had much to do with the success of Templecrone Cope. His first involvement came before the Cope even existed. He visited Dungloe in 1903 as an IAOS organiser, where he set up an Agricultural Bank. He ensured that a local farmer, who had subscribed £5, a significant sum then, was co-opted onto the Committee. This was Paddy the Cope's first official position – it gave him an insight into the economics of buying manures at wholesale rates, compared to what he and his friends were paying. Over the formative years of the Cope, AE was a regular visitor, supporter and a chronicler of the unlikely success of Cope. The serialisation of the Cope's story in 1910, complete with photographs, was entirely due to AE as was his encouragement to Paddy to write his story.

AE is a fascinating man: it is impossible to do justice to his achievements, influence and interests in a short profile. He was a poet, an artist, a mystic, a theosophist, a journalist in addition to his work in the co-operative movement, which is of most interest in this context. He joined the IAOS from 1897 as an organiser; his friend W.B. Yeats, concerned that he might leave for the USA and his talents would be lost to Ireland, arranged this role with Horace Plunkett. From 1898 he was appointed Assistant Secretary of the IAOS, under Robert Anderson. Plunkett, Anderson, AE and the Rev Tom Finlay, blessed with complementary skills, were of great assistance to the Cope. From 1905, AE edited the IAOS's weekly journal, the Irish Homestead. Many of his articles and publications were very influential, providing the Irish co-operative movement with both a rigorous and well thought through philosophy as well as a wealth of practical advice for farmers (Source: Dictionary of National Biography).

business operations, and keeps constantly before the associated farmers the economic principles which must be observed, and, above all, the spirit in which the work must be approached, if the movement is to fulfil its mission…"[1]

The Homestead's most famous editor was George Russell ("AE"), distinguished artist, poet and socialist who edited it from 1905 till its demise as a weekly in 1923 after the War of Independence and Civil War had torn apart the Irish Cooperative Movement. AE helped a 22 year old James Joyce (writing under the pseudonym Stephen Dedalus) in 1904 by helping him get published in the Homestead three of his short stories (at a fee of £1 each):'The Sisters', 'Eveline', and 'After the Race', later these were included in 'Dubliners' (1914). Joyce repaid this and other favours by including AE as a character in Ulysses (1922), referring to him with "A.E.I.O.U."

---

1   'Ireland in the New Century' Horace Plunkett, 1904, John Murray, London.

The Templecrone Cope was a particular favourite of the IAOS and of George Russell himself. The Cope had unequivocally demonstrated that co-operation could work wonders in the most unpromising of environments; its pluck and spectacular success against all odds earned it huge respect in Ireland and internationally.

AE remained a lifelong friend and campaigner for the Templecrone Cope. Writing to IAOS organiser Richmond Noble in 1907 he said "...I always thought these were splendid people, and I will try to do them all the justice I can in the "Homestead". Gallagher seems to be a very fine fellow..."[2]

The Irish Homestead serialised the Templecrone story over a number of issues in 1910 and published the story as a pamphlet, priced 3d, later that year. It was updated and re-issued in a smaller edition in December 1916 as 'Templecrone – A Record Of Cooperative Effort' and comprehensively revised, expanded and reissued in 1924 (extracts from the 1924 edition have been included at appropriate points in the main body of this book). Russell had a hand in all three, in particular the 1916 edition which he wrote entirely by himself.

The pamphlets had a very wide circulation; Paddy found that the Cope's story and his fame preceded him, e.g. in 1911 and 1912 when he went with Cope handknits to the Aonach in Westminster, London (Chapter 5). In America, the story was held up to rural farmers as an example of what co-operation could produce (the Templecrone success story was extensively syndicated in 1914 across America in both small towns and large cities). George Russell, Horace Plunkett, the Rev Tom Finlay and other leading figures in the Irish cooperative movement were fulsome in their praise of the Cope and sent visitors from all over the world up to see for themselves the miracles being worked in West Donegal.

AE was visited by American writer Ruth Russell in 1918 and she describes his working environment:

> "...One day I went to discuss Irish labour with AE. I climbed up to that most curious of all magazine offices – the "Irish Homestead" office up under the roof of Plunkett House. It is a semi-circular room whose walls are covered with the lavender and purple people of AE's brush. AE was ambushed behind piles of newspapers, and behind him in a grate filled with smouldering peat blocks sat the black tea kettle. As a reporter, one of the few things for which I am allowed to retain respect is the editorial deadline. So I assured AE that I would be glad to return when he had finished writing. But with a courtesy that is evidently founded on an inversion of the American rule that business should always come before people, he assured me that he could sit down at the fire with me at once..."[3]

---

2   *IAOS records, 1907, National Archives.*

3   *An extract from 'What Is Wrong With Ireland' (published in 1920) by Ruth Russell, an American journalist who travelled to Ireland in 1918-19; Eamon de Valera wrote the introduction to her book, de Valera was himself in the USA for 18 months from June 1919 to December 1920).*

... The ...

Templecrone Co=operative Agricultural Society,

CO. DONEGAL.

Story of its Origin and Struggles.

DUBLIN:
The Irish Homestead Limited, Clare Street.

PRICE THREEPENCE.

The cover of the 1910 Irish Homestead publication describing the Templecrone Co-operative Society. The booklet had a very wide distribution across Great Britain, the USA and Europe as well as, over time, the rest of the world.

THE TEMPLECRONE CO-OPERATIVE
AGRICULTURAL SOCIETY,
CO. DONEGAL

Story of its Origin and Struggles

The Manure Question

For many years back the farmers of the districts lying around Dungloe had been using a considerable quantity of artificial manures, and purchased from the local traders. With these manures no guarantee of quality was ever given or asked for; they passed under the very comprehensive names of guano, or slag, and both dealer and farmer seemed quite indifferent to any further particulars regarding quality. Some years ago Mr. Gallagher, the present manager of the Templecrone Co-operative Society, who had been reading something of the analysis of these manures, asked a local trader if he could give him any guarantee of their analysis, and was informed that they never got such a thing, and knew nothing about it. Mr. Gallagher, however, was not satisfied, and wrote to the Department to know if they could assist him in getting manures of a reliable quality. From the Department he was referred to the Irish Agricultural Wholesale Society, and the latter informed him that they could only deal with societies.

The question of forming a co-operative society with which he had been now brought face to face was not at all new to Mr. Gallagher; in fact, it had been talked over and over again by himself, Mr. O'Donnell (who afterwards became secretary), and a few friends, and many a night around the blazing peat was the possibility of such a society discussed. In the year 1905 the IAWS sent to the Agricultural Bank which had been established in Dungloe a price list of their manures, with guarantee of their analysis. Mr. Gallagher, who was then, and is still, a member of the Bank Committee, was struck with the difference between the prices quoted and those hitherto charged in the district, and he suggested to the Bank Committee that advantage should be taken of the Bank to purchase these manures for its members. But as the big men of the Committee were themselves dealers in these manures the suggestion was only laughed at. Mr. Gallagher was not, however, to be turned from his purpose ; he gathered together the farmers of his own district and pointed out to them the enormous advantages to he gained both in quality and price by purchasing direct from the IAWS The result was that a 20 ton lot was ordered through the Donegal Co-operative Society, and a saving thus effected of £40, besides securing superphosphate of 30 per cent instead of 22 per cent, and dissolved bone instead of a worthless compound.

Seeing the handsome saving they had made in this single purchase, there was no further question as to the advantages of a society of their own; it now became a question of how to set about it. With this object Mr. Gallagher wrote to the IAOS, and after some delay Mr. Shaw came down to address the farmers on the benefits of the movement and make the necessary preliminaries to forming a branch in the place.

Mr. Thomas Shaw

The long and tedious journey from Dublin to Dungloe is a rather trying one at all times, and for Mr. Shaw, who for the week previous had been journeying all over the country from one point of duty to another, it must have been particularly so. Such a journey, followed by a drive of six or seven miles, was enough to damp the ardour of the most enthusiastic. However, Mr. Shaw arrived at his destination in fine spirits, and evidently enjoyed the rugged wildness of his surroundings. But he could not help giving utterance to his surprise that human beings could eke out a subsistence in such a place. On one side of his route stretched a ragged coast, and on the other rugged and barren hills, showing here and there a cultivated patch that showed no bigger than a flower garden. Dotted along the dreary coast and up the bouldered hillside to their very summits could be seen the whitewashed cottages. But where were the farms? What was to support all those homes? No wonder he could not help admiring the energy that could force a subsistence out of such a soil, and no wonder he threw himself heart and soul into the struggle against poverty and oppression that he found going on there.

The meeting was a great success, but not so much from its size as from its enthusiasm and determination. Both old and young attended, and the former, if anything, were the more enthusiastic. It is a pleasing and inspiriting thing to find old men who have lived through a good many changes in the conditions of life almost flinging their hats to the roof with enthusiasm. Mr. Shaw's address, which was listened to with the keenest attention, was enough to kindle the spirit of co-operation in much less responsive hearts. He is a true propagandist, and he so endeared himself to the meeting during their few hours' acquaintance that they felt like carrying him on their shoulders. A provisional committee was appointed, with the following officials: Mr. Patrick Gallagher, President; Mr. Daniel Sweeney, Treasurer; and Mr. John O'Donnell, Secretary.

Farmers' Representatives on the Councils

There were, of course, at the meeting, as there are at all such gatherings, those who shook their wise heads and said that co-operation would end like all the other movements that had hitherto been started for their benefit in the locality. But these were only a few, and the great majority looked with greater hope on this new movement than on any that had gone before it. They saw it differed from all those in one important respect—that while they (the farmers) had hitherto entrusted their business to others they were now going to look after it themselves. Hitherto they had put forward business men to represent them on the Rural and County Councils, and these men, though perhaps with the very best intentions, could not afford to give to agricultural questions the attention they required, and too often they allowed their own business interests to sway their actions. The farmers' interests were of very secondary importance, and how could they be otherwise to a body of men who never perhaps gave an hour's consideration to the special needs of farmers from one Council meeting

The Story of the Cope

to the next. Occasionally a farmer was selected to sit on these Councils, but his voice was seldom heard and never heeded among a body of consequential business men.

The result has been that many of the projects for the benefit of the farming class have been either thrown aside or attended to in a very half-hearted manner. And all this time the rates had been growing to an alarming figure. There is no doubt that if the farmers throughout the county (and probably the same might be said of other counties), who form the vast majority of voters, should put forward representatives of their own class on these Councils, that much more good might he derived from the many schemes and facilities offered for the improvement of agriculture. Some of these, no doubt, have been availed of here and there, and there are many earnest workers on these Councils who have a direct interest in agriculture, but they are too few to guide the actions of the Councils, or to create an all-round enthusiasm among the farmers, and a desire to make the most of the advantages offered.

The Rosses Improvement Society

The farmers of Templecrone were becoming convinced that it was only by representatives from among their own class that their interests, here or elsewhere, would be attended to. But if they still retained a hope, like Micawber, that someone might "turn up" and do their work for them, that hope was finally dispelled by their experience of a society called "The Rosses Improvement Society", which started about this time in Dungloe. The objects of this society were to get up local industries, to improve the breed of cattle, fowl, and pigs, and to root up landlordism out of the Rosses. It was started by the young men of the village, chiefly shopkeepers and professional men. The farmers were invited to these weekly meetings to be lectured upon farming methods, and told what was being done for them from one meeting to another. All the great troubling questions of the day, from land nationalisation to microbes, also turned up for discussion, and a great many schemes and reforms suggested, but absolutely nothing achieved; nothing to mark its few years' existence but a long record of well-phrased resolutions, and the memory of a fine display of village eloquence, which impressed, as it was probably sometimes meant to do, the countryman with the superior eloquence of townsfolk.

After a time, however, the country audience began to thin away with a grim smile on their faces, and a deepening conviction in their minds that trusting one's own business to others is not the right way to set about it. It was in this mood they found themselves when the question of an Agricultural Co-operative Society came before them, and if there were some who pointed a warning finger to "The Rosses Improvement Society" there were far more who gathered their hopes from its very failure. They had up till now been watching and waiting for others to do their work for them; they were now going to do it for themselves. In this respect the new society was unlike any that had preceded it. The farmers, too, were proud of a society which, for once, they could call their own.

The Sturdy Little Band of Co-operators

But, after the first flush of enthusiasm, comes the cooler period of sober calculation and persistent labour. The circumstances of the locality and of the people presented many obstacles to the successful working of such a society. Indeed, it is doubtful whether in all Ireland a spot could be found presenting so many discouragements. The farms (if they could he called farms) were merely patches scattered here and there along the hillsides, or strips of low-lying and saturated bottoms. The people, as might be expected, were extremely poor, and though not quite so bad as a local shopkeeper put it who said that there were not half a dozen families in the parish they (the shopkeepers) could not leave on the roadside, yet a great many of them were tied to one business house or another. Again, the people looked to their earnings in Scotland or to herring fishing rather than to their little patches of land for support, with the inevitable result that their land was cultivated in a very indifferent manner, and little attention given to the question of procuring the most suitable kinds of seed, manures, etc.

But what seemed the greatest obstacle was want of capital; there was absolutely no money to begin with, and as yet the local banker knew them not. But this very dearth of capital was, if we might apply the word, providential; it was just what the brakes are to an engine at the top of an incline, which regulate the speed till the untutored hands have learned the mysteries of driving it. And over and above all these difficulties there was the certainty that the local traders—and they were the ruling power—would do their utmost to crush any movement that might interfere with their monopoly. As a matter of fact they at once formed a Traders' Association, pronounced the work of the Society "illegitimate trading" and forthwith began a fierce onslaught upon the little outlaw. To withstand such attacks and surmount all these difficulties the Society must have had some great asset that outweighed them all. Its members were a fine, loyal, sturdy, intelligent little band, with whom it was a pleasure to enter on any struggle—that was the one asset of the Society, and that was enough. Gather such a band again in any spot in Ireland and you have all that is necessary to start a flourishing society.

First Year – 1906

Towards the end of January there was a second meeting of members. Mr. Shaw was present and gave a very instructive lecture on manures. The appointment of the provisional Committee at the last meeting was confirmed, application forms were filled for 46 shares, and orders taken for manures. The Society was now launched under the name of the Templecrone Co-operative Agricultural Society, and handed over to the guidance of the Committee. Meetings of the Committee were held fortnightly. Orders for seeds and manures were received through the members, and the work of ordering, storing, and giving out to the members fell principally on Mr. Gallagher and Mr. O'Donnell, who gave their services free and ungrudgingly for upwards of six months. This was principally the work of the Society for the first half-year, and they probably would have never gone beyond serving these and other agricultural, needs had it not been for the vindictive action of many of the local traders.

Towards the end of autumn they got a small order of meal, flour, and bran at the request of some members. A small disused house of Mr. Gallagher's was used as store, and he, Mr. O'Donnell, and Mr. Glackin volunteered to keep the place open two nights each week. There was no credit, there could he none, and thus money was always on hand to meet bills as they became due. All was plain sailing for so far, and the work of the Committee and volunteer corps of storemen became almost monotonous from pure simplicity. There were, of course, a great many little difficulties connected with their first attempts at shopping, but these only gave zest to the work. Neither Mr. O'Donnell nor Mr. Gallagher had the smallest knowledge of shop work. They could read and write fairly, but were total strangers to day book or ledger, not to speak of such details as practical knowledge of the necessary weights and measures, of egg-packing, etc., which they dismissed as trifles.

The first attempt at egg-packing, which involved the greater part of the Committee, was, however, a dismal failure, but as there is nothing in their method worthy of imitation, perhaps it is better to follow the graceful example of the consignees and pass it over in silence. But it is due to Mr. Gallagher and Mr. O'Donnell to say that if their first attempts were such as might only excite ridicule, their business methods now, after an experience of three years, would, perhaps, compare favourably with any business house in the county. It should be welcome news to those districts about to start Co-operative Societies to find that it is not necessary to place at their head at once trained business men. On the other hand, we should consider it a fatal blunder to place at the helm a man trained in the enemy's camp. In our opinion, the most suitable person to guide the business of a society is a local man of intelligence and aptitude, who is moved by the true spirit of co-operation, and in whom the members have the utmost confidence. In this the Templecrone Society has been exceptionally fortunate, and it must be allowed that its phenomenal success is due in great part to the selection of Mr. Gallagher as Manager, and Mr. O'Donnell as Secretary and Accountant.

Hostilities

The meetings of the Committee were, after a few shuffles, fixed in the little store. This was a single apartment about 12 feet square and also served for shop and general store. A temporary counter and shelves were fitted in for the modest sum of ten shillings, and the remaining space was occupied with the little stock-in-trade of the Society. Neither could the sitting accommodation provided for meetings of the Committee be called sumptuous or luxurious. Two empty upturned boxes, one on each side of the fire, were all the premises afforded. The Chairman, it is true, occupied the woolsack on rare occasions, and just as that useful article of commerce offered itself, but he was much oftener found perched among his fellow-members on the surrounding piles. But whatever the accommodation, they were always pleasant gatherings, those meetings of the Committee, full of robust spirit and freedom and tolerance of opinion, and brightened by many an amusing episode and happy interchange of pleasantry.

The contents of the fortnightly letter bag were of a very miscellaneous character. There was here a letter from some wholesale house saying that the Traders' Association had threatened withdrawal of trade in case the Society was supplied, and then a curt refusal from some other firm without stating any reason. Those Derry wholesale houses - and so far as they had been then approached there were few exceptions - seem to have been coerced into a very rigid boycott of the Society. From a business point of view they could hardly he blamed – at least many of them afterwards tried to justify their refusal on this ground. This boycott was by no means confined to the Derry houses, but extended as far as the traders could force it, and if, for a time, the Society succeeded in stealing a march on some unsuspecting firm, and secured a first order, they were sure to he refused the second. It is a rather saddening fact in these times of industrial regeneration to find a Society, whose object it is to encourage home industry, and thus in the most practical way to stem the tide of emigration by making the lives of the farmers possible in their own country, that such a Society should be banned by Irishmen who call themselves patriots, and should have to pass its orders on to the stranger.

Driven thus from their own soil, they found a friend in the Scotch Co-operative Wholesale Society, where they got all they were refused at home. There was also the rumour of another strategy being resorted to by the Traders' Association that they had agreed to subsidise those of their members who traded in the district in which the Society was working. The rumoured plan of action was to subscribe amongst them a certain sum, by means of which those who traded in this district could undersell the Society. In their opinion, one of two things must happen – either the Society should sink itself in the struggle, or its members would he attracted away from it by better bargains in the neighbouring shops. It is possible that had the Society confined itself to this district such a plan of action might have succeeded in killing it, but a Society bred from oppression and nursed to warfare was not to be crushed out of existence so easily. If such a hostile cordon of shops could lay siege to it in a small district, they could not do so throughout a large area. There was nothing then left the Society to do but to enlarge its field of operations, and so the Committee without delay fitted out a goods van, which visited the different parts of the parish. This proved a fortunate step for the Society, for it not only considerably increased its business, but brought it into touch with outside districts, and added to it a host of new friends and members. There is nothing in the history of the Society more encouraging than the enthusiasm with which the "Cope" van was hailed in every district it visited.

Jonahs

But the Committee meetings, as already mentioned, were by no means taken up with dry deliberation and artful strategy. There was always something to amuse. Gossip had a free foot, and among its votaries is the inevitable prophet.

One of these distinguished himself by declaring that the Society was to die about Christmas (1906), that is to say, after a period of about twelve months' existence. At the end of this period the Society turned up, not out of its grave, but full of the flush and vigour of youth and with a handsome dividend on its finger-tips. The prophet again appeared and gave the Ninevites of Templecrone another year to change their ways and do penance, or at the end of which period the Society should meet disaster, and drag into destruction every person connected with it. Contrary to prophecy, the Society turned up again at the end of this period with a turn-over of sales ten times greater than that of the first year, and with a still more substantial dividend to its members. As a prophet this man has not been heard of since. The members themselves stood loyally by the Society throughout. They rightly looked and still look upon it as their own shop, of which they are shareholders and controllers, and neither slanderous tongues nor tempting bargains could turn them away from it. There were, at times, complaints against the Committee and employees, but these were not at all discouraged, and were always carefully investigated by the Committee. These little incidents of the struggle of the Society, snatched here and there from the minutes, are merely recorded here to give a glimpse of its inner life, and as human nature is everywhere the same, and other committees, like ours, shall have their critics and malcontents, it may be a kind of satisfaction to them to know that they are not specially cursed, and may hope, like our own, to outlive them all.

Eggs

As already mentioned, the Society only dealt in manures, seeds, and spraying material during the first nine months, and during this time payments were always in cash. When it became necessary to supply customers with general groceries, eggs had to be accepted in payment. It then became necessary that the packing and sorting should he done in the most up-to-date manner, and a good market secured. To secure the latter, shares were taken in the Irish Producers' Society, and then Mr. Gallagher was directed to apply to the Department for a course of training in the egg and poultry business. He was directed to Dunboe Society, and here he gained a thorough know ledge of packing of eggs and poultry, and also book-keeping and general business so far as they were followed by that society.

Up to this time Mr. Gallagher had given his services to the Society gratis, he was now employed at three shillings per day. Packing of the Society's eggs was now done according to the most approved method, and a good market found for them through the Irish Producers, so that the Society was able to compete on favourable ground with the local buyers. The result was that the price of eggs immediately rose throughout the entire district, the local buyers following, and even at times leading the Society's prices. All along the prices have stood at a figure much more favourable, perhaps, to the producer than to the buyer. It had been estimated that in this item alone the Society had effected a gain to the farmers of the district of something like £3,000 for the year 1906. But it has done much more than this for the egg trade; it has shown members and others what an important source of income it may be made. It has aroused in the district a much greater interest in the care and selection of fowl, and has had a poultry station established in the locality. Men, who had hitherto looked upon the hen as one of the pests of the farm, now began to look upon her with more favour, so much so that a local wag declared that if you met a good laying hen on the road at present you should "put your hand to your hat".

Herring nets were also supplied to members at cost prices, and a market was found, through the Irish Producers, for Carrageen moss, wool, and other local products. The total turn-over of the Society for this year, including, towards the end, a little groceries, was £490[4] but then the working expenses were very small, so that there was a dividend of 1s and 9½d on purchases and £3 set aside as the nucleus of a reserve fund. It was a very small beginning, but its growth was fast, as may be seen from the fact that the turn-over in goods for the second season was, roughly, £4,000, and for the third year £7,000. At the end of this year there were eighty members in the Society.

1907

The little store occupied was now becoming quite too small for the business of the Society, and as no other available place could be found in the neighbourhood the Committee decided on having one built. They made application to the Congested Districts Board for a grant in aid of building a store for their manures and other requirements. Mr. Walker, of the CDB, visited the place and made out an estimate of the cost, but for some reason or other the grant was afterwards refused. They next applied for a loan, but were also refused. After further consideration, they decided to take a place in Dungloe, which is about three miles distant, as the Society was rapidly extending itself in that direction. This little village would also be a more convenient centre for the Society's van, and was also more convenient to the railway station.

Here, after casting around for some time, they rented a little two-storied dwelling of about sixteen feet square. The upper floor was used as office and general goods store, while the lower flat served for packing store for eggs, for grocery department, hardware department, boot and shoe department, meat and fish store, etc. How such a business could be transacted in such a place was a puzzle. As the stock-in-trade gradually grew, the working space became reduced to a mere passage, while the space overhead was occupied to the last inch with boots, hams, brushes, etc. It might be amusing at times to see a visitor of slightly over the average stature with a pair of heavy-soled boots (and if you like an imaginary occupant) standing on the crown of his hat, or to watch him hobnobbing with a home-cured ham. It might afford a smile to the malicious to watch the struggle or the tactics of two corpulent customers in their endeavour to pass each other in the passage, but for those who had to work from morning till night they were anything but pleasant surroundings. But however unaccommodating the place may have been, the members still flocked to it, and a great many of the

---

4   *The audited turnover figure for the first year, published in the Irish Homestead, was actually £381.*

townspeople began to patronise it as well. New applications for membership continued to pour in, and the business grew steadily.

Pig Rearing

The Society has also done something to encourage pig rearing, which could hardly be said to have been followed at all in the district previously. Occasionally a young sucker was bought at a neighbouring fair and fattened for the Derry market. These the Society bought in at Derry prices, and thus saved the cost of carriage and the almost certain reduction in prices made by buyers for every imaginable flaw in the carcass. The local consumers also appreciated the constant supply of fresh and cured pork which they had at very reasonable prices. Anything done up to the present, however, was only by way of experiment, but the Committee hope to be able to further help in reviving an industry which was at one time a source of considerable income in the place.

Spraying and Threshing

Precaution was also taken to have a supply of spraying material on the ground in good time. This the Society gave out at cost price. They also purchased a few spraying machines which they hired out to members at 3d per day. Some time after the Society had moved in this matter the Department of Agriculture arranged to supply spraying material to farmers; the Donegal Agricultural Committee also sent a few spraying machines to each parish to be given out on hire. But by the time these arrangements had been carried out the blight had already made its appearance. Fortunately the Society had anticipated them in this good work otherwise the earlier fields of potatoes might have suffered. The incident affords us another example of a fact which cannot he too clearly impressed upon the farmer, that if his business is to be properly and punctually looked after he must not entrust the work to others. Later in the season the Committee purchased a small threshing machine which they hired out to members at 2s per day. The investment gave great satisfaction, and proved a great saving of labour compared with the flail.

Friends

Towards the end of the year Miss Reynolds, of the IAOS, visited the Society, and rendered great assistance in preparing the books for audit. Mr. Barbour, who had already honoured the Society by becoming a member, also sent Mr. Boyd, Manager of the Lisburn Co-operative Society, to visit the Society about this time. Mr. Boyd has a very thorough grasp of book-keeping and of business methods generally, and his hints and suggestions were of the greatest service to the Society. The deep interest which Mr. Barbour has taken in the Society, and his presence at all its general meetings, have probably given rise to the rumour that he has been financing it from the start. One of its critics declared that nothing less than £1,000 could float such a business, and that the subsidy hitherto given by the Department to the IAOS was thus disgracefully used; another has discovered that the profits of the Society are being used "to build

Orange Halls"! With the opinions of such persons we are not at all concerned; nobody now heeds them, and they may be safely left, like the above pair, to dispose of each other like the famous Kilkenny cats. We are only concerned with those who, like our own little community of farmers, are struggling to uplift their lives, and our greatest glory would be to find that our example and the success of our efforts should give them any encouragement to make a similar effort. For their information we may repeat

(1st) The Templecrone Society had no capital to begin with.

(2nd) The members paid for all purchases either in cash or in eggs which could be converted into cash within a fortnight.

(3rd) After a little time small deposits were received from members who could afford, and this enabled the Society to extend its dealings. It was encouraging to his fellow-members to find that the very first to offer a deposit was one of the members of the Committee.

(4th) Together with the above there were the few pounds of subscribed share capital, and the small beginning made on Reserve Fund. In the case of ordinary shop-keeping this floating capital is probably necessary, but in the case of a co-operative society like this the one thing necessary is that its members should be solvent, and to guard against any risk in this respect the Society needs only to deal in cash. The Templecrone Society allows its members no credit except where the special circumstances of individuals render it necessary, and where the Committee is unanimous that it is safe to do so.

A Reliable Market

A very important factor in the success of the Society—in fact, an essential one — was the finding a ready and reliable market for its eggs. This the Irish Producers secured, though, perhaps, leaving much to be desired in this respect. It is to be hoped that the IAWS, which has taken over this important branch of co-operative work, may still improve on their predecessors, and may have the support and patronage of all societies, if not for the sake of the ultimate gain it is bound to bring to all, at least for the sake of the younger and future societies whose existence so largely depends upon it. On the other hand, the IAWS will recognise that their responsibility is no ordinary one, and their efforts accordingly should be such as will entitle them to the confidence and patronage of all. The membership at the end of this year stood at 100. The turnover for the thirteen months ended 31st December was £4,692 16s. 9d, and the net profit £145 9s 9d. A dividend of 2s in the £ was paid on members' purchases, and £74 9s 9d. carried to the Reserve Fund.

1908

The prospects of the Society at the beginning of its third year were brighter than ever. Trade was rapidly increasing, and new members were flocking in. The very best proof of the moderate charges in the "Cope" is in the fact that a very large trade was done with non-members, who had no prospect whatever of a dividend! It was not quite satisfactory to members to find that the audit of previous year's accounts was delayed for some months, but from the monthly statements prepared for Committee meetings a rough estimate could be made of how the Society stood for the year. The actual state of affairs, however, as revealed by audit even surpassed their expectations. Acting on the very helpful suggestions of Miss Reynolds, of the IAOS, and of Mr. Boyd, of the Lisburn Co-operative Society, and benefiting by his own experience of the past year, Mr. O'Donnell set out with a much improved system of book-keeping, while Mr. Gallagher's efficiency as Manager was keeping pace with the rapid growth of the business. It would, indeed, be hard to find again two men who could have so quickly grasped the intricacies of their new duties, or who could have entered upon their work with the same spirit and enthusiasm.

District and County Councillors

Seeing that much might be done for the advancement of agriculture at District and County Councils, if properly manned, the Templecrone Committee, when the time arrived, nominated candidates who would look carefully after those interests. Mr. Gallagher, Manager of the Society, was returned, unopposed, for both District and County Council. Mr. K. J. Brennan, Secretary of the Agricultural Bank, and a staunch supporter of co-operative principles, headed the poll for the rural electoral division of Dungloe, and Mr. W. Gorman, a loyal adherent of the Society, was co-opted member by the Rural District Council. A few other members of the Society would have also contested other divisions had it not been for some flaws in the nomination papers. From this it may be seen that besides its economic value to the district the Templecrone Society has done its part towards securing for the farmers the representation at those Councils which their numbers entitle them to, and which they certainly have not got at present. The farmers, to a man, are in thorough sympathy with the Society, and through it are being taught to wield their power, while the more intelligent of the artisan and other classes, seeing that what adds to the farmers' prosperity makes for their own welfare, are also amongst its staunchest supporters.

Old Age Pension Sub-Committee

Later on, when the duty devolved upon the County Council of appointing sub-committees to administer the Old Age Pensions Act, the Committee of the Templecrone Society saw the desirability of having in their own district a committee who should deal impartially with the claims that came before them. Believing as they did that the shopkeeper does not make an ideal committee man, they instructed Mr. Gallagher to suggest to the Council only persons who had no connection with business as members of the Pension Sub-Committee for the district. Such an appointment was no easy matter, as the other County Councillor representing the Sub-Committee district (a shopkeeper) had a list of his own selection to propose, and which consisted largely of shopkeepers. There was nothing in two such lists that invited compromise, for, outside the clergy, whom both lists included, one was made up exclusively of farmers and the other of shopkeepers. However, whether from good luck or good pleading, Mr. Gallagher returned with his own selection practically adopted by the Council. Needless to add that this Committee have done their duty faithfully, impartially, and well.

Premises, Sales, and Membership

Towards the end of the year the Society was fortunate in securing from the landlord an unoccupied flat, to which it transferred the business. This relieved the congestion somewhat, and enabled it to turn the old premises into a grocery and egg store. The total sales for this year, including eggs, was £7,048 9s. 2d, an increase of £2,335 12s 5d on the previous thirteen months. The working expenses were reduced from 9.48 per cent of the total sales, of the previous year, to 8.64 per cent. for this year. The membership at the end of year was 140. The net profit on the year's working was £177 2s. 3d, out of which a dividend at the rate of 2s. in the pound was paid on members' purchases, and the balance carried to the Reserve Fund.

1909

The Society still continues to grow in favour and the business of the store bids fair to surpass its previous records. The store with its unobtrusive frontage attracts the passer-by as being the one busy mart of a usually quiet village. The Committee, who meet monthly, have always some new success to record, some new scheme or venture to take counsel upon, something to mark the onward progress, and there is never a meeting which has not its fresh applications for membership to deal with. A Shop Committee was formed to consider questions concerning the store and business generally, and an Agricultural Committee to attend to that particular branch of the business. The recommendations of both these Sub-Committees come before each monthly meeting of the Committee for adoption or otherwise.

Village Hall

Towards the beginning of the year the Society made application for, and was awarded, one of the six free grants offered from the Pembroke Irish Charities Fund to the six most deserving societies in Ireland for the erection of Village Halls. The grant amounted to £200 and being made purely on the ground of merit, is a gratifying proof that the efforts of the Society are appreciated outside as well as within the district in which it operates. The hall will be a great boon to the village and district which up till now has had no place where the young people could meet for recreation or improvement. A suitable site has been secured, and the hall is at present in course of erection.

The Eggs

The Committee, who had given frequent consideration to the question of buying eggs by weight, decided early in the year to give it a trial, being convinced that it is not only fair to those bringing in the larger eggs, but that it is the best, and in fact the only inducement to the rearing of an improved breed of fowl. Old customs die hard, and many of the members looked askance at the novel method of calculating the price of their goods. But on the whole it has found favour. There is already a marked improvement in the size of the eggs throughout the district, and with a poultry station in the neighbourhood and the inducement to avail of it which is offered by the new method of buying, there is every reason to hope that egg production in the district may become a much greater source of income in future. Mr. Gallagher has also supplied his poultry station with trap nests, so that during the coming season members will be able to procure the eggs of the best laying strains. As an instance of what might be achieved in this direction, the Society has received this year for one case of 18 lb eggs the record price of £1 per hundred, or 2s per dozen. This small case was, of course, picked from among a large quantity, and sold when prices were highest; still it is a very striking example of what may be gained by a careful selection of layers. The fact that the Templecrone eggs gained third place at the Sheffield Poultry Exhibition held this year, and second place at the Bristol Exhibition, shows that Mr. Gallagher is doing his part in building up a reputation for them.

Buying and Curing of Pigs

The buying and curing of pigs, at which a very successful start had been made already, only requires a proper curing store to make it a complete success, and now that this is about to be provided, the Society will soon be in a position to buy in all the pigs which its members can offer.

The New Societies

During the year three new societies Sprang up around the Templecrone—the Iniskeel Society at Fintown (this society came into existence earlier, but only got properly launched this year), the Lower Rosses Society at Iniscoe Island, and the Gweedore Society. These have, no doubt, gained their inspiration from the Templecrone, and in their earlier stages Mr. Gallagher gave them every possible assistance, cheering them on when enemies and difficulties loomed biggest, and guiding them when guidance was needed. Mr. Noble, of the IAOS, who must have sniffed co-operation on the western gales, was early on the scene to mould their ideas into shape and marshall them for the noble battle they were to engage in. Since then he has become a kind of stormy petrel to the hitherto undisturbed land captains of those sequestered seaboards.

Mr. Harold Barbour

The membership of the Society increased from 140 to 200. In its roll of membership the Society prides itself in the name of Mr. Harold Barbour. Mr. Barbour became a member of the Society in its very earliest stage, and at a time when there was very little to attract membership and very much to deter. He has been present at every one of our annual meetings to help, advise and encourage. His unfailing presence at all these meetings, as well as on several other occasions, is a noble example of the spirit of unselfishness and fellowship that pervades the whole co-operative movement, and an example that is not lost on his fellow-members of Templecrone.

A Justification

We believe we have shown in the foregoing little narrative that the Templecrone Society has justified its four years of existence; but this is not the object with which it was written, seeing that the only earthly masters before whom it has to stand in judgment are its own members. Its one object, as already stated, is that it may answer a question that hundreds of farmers and others are just now putting themselves, viz. : Is co-operation of any real value to struggling farmers, and if it is, have we of ourselves enough business capacity and cohesion to avail ourselves of it? The Society has done a great deal for its members and for the whole district over which it spreads itself. In the report of its first annual meeting it is stated that it has effected a gain to the farmers of the district of about £3,000, and if this is true of that year how much more has it done since? And besides, how much has it done to improve the character of its members? It has made them better farmers, better business men, better Irishmen. Co-operation, which frees the individual from local tyranny, cannot but fire him with a hatred of the serpent wherever it raises its head. By the manly spirit of freedom which it insists upon in his home life it inspires him with a yearning for the larger instalment of national freedom which is to come, and by the business habits and self-reliance which it inculcates it prepares him to take his place in the battle for pre-eminence which is at present agitating the nations. It is Sinn Fein in its policy without repudiating parliamentary methods, and parliamentary in its outlook without offending against Sinn Fein. And who knows but it may one day hold the flag of truce beneath which the sons of Ireland, worn with fight and weary of strife, may sit in conference and discover that they are all faithful sons of the same grand old nation and with but one cause to fight for – the uplifting of our native land.

The Cope had benefited greatly from its links with the IAOS, whether from advice, professional help or simply from helping them make business and selling connections. However, the close association with Templecrone and other retail concerns caused great problems for Horace Plunkett and the IAOS Their detractors did have a point - the IAOS was set up to help farmers and cooperatives not to assist a grocery store set up in direct competition with other traders.

The following correspondence between Sir Horace Plunkett and Paddy the Cope dates from the end of the conflict between IAOS and DATI regarding IAOS support to grocery co-operatives. From 1912, funding was restored to the IAOS. The letters show a mutual respect and warmth between the two men.

Sir Horace Curzon Plunkett (1854-1932) almost single-handedly created the Irish co-operative movement. Born into an Ascendancy family, his interest in agriculture and co-operation were formed on his family estate. In 1879, he established, in conjunction with the family's tenants, the Dunsany Co-operative Society. In the 1880s, for health reasons initially, he travelled to Wyoming where he learnt much about agriculture and cattle – and made a large fortune in the process. Returning to look after his family business, he set out to bring best practice, from Europe (in particular, Denmark, which had modernised its bacon and butter businesses), Britain and the United States. He was a founder member in 1891 of the Congested Districts Board and remained a member until 1918. He was instrumental in the setting up the Recess Committee in 1895, which led to the setting up of the first Department of Agriculture and Technical Instruction (DATI) in 1899, where he was the first vice president. In 1894, he founded the IAOS – his slogan for the co-operative movement was 'Better farming, better business, better living'. He was a Unionist MP from 1892-1900 but managed to isolate himself from his fellow Unionist MPS, who thought him too conciliatory to Home Rulers, as well as antagonise Nationalist leaders with his views on Home Rule being a subsidiary issue to transforming the economic position of Ireland, its agriculture and industries. He later converted to a Home Rule position, albeit one which advocated maintaining strong links with Britain. The various tensions meant that working relationships between IAOS and DATI, both his creations, became strained. Plunkett's support for co-operatives like Templecrone, which had expanded from being an agricultural concern to setting up general grocery stores, caused many problems and led to IAOS funding being withdrawn for a time. These stores were in direct competition with local merchants, who typically were important members of the Nationalist movement. Throughout, Plunkett retained an admiration for the Cope and Paddy himself, often visiting Dungloe and offering assistance whenever he could.

3rd October 1912

Confidential (manuscript addition by Plunkett)

Dear Mr Gallagher

    I wish to consult you, as one of my very best associates in Irish economic and social work, upon the situation which is likely to be created in the immediate future by the winning of our long fight for justice at the hands of the Development Commissioners.

You are aware, and, indeed, it has been publicly announced in the press, that the Development Commissioners have made the grant conditional on the IAOS ceasing to be connected with societies which do other than agricultural business after 1st January 1913. This decision is not one of principle but it is statutory, the words "organisation of co-operation" as a means of "aiding and developing agriculture" being undoubtedly intended by Parliament to exclude dealings in domestic requirements. Of course all your friends are perfectly aware that, in the circumstances of the community in which you live, there is no more important way of improving their economic and helping them towards a better social condition than enabling the people to obtain the necessaries and a modest degree of comforts for their homes of the best quality and at the lowest possible price. Yet, we of the IAOS have to recognise that this good work never has been part of our programme, that many traders who have supported us would not have done so if it had been, and that the Development Commission are bound by statute to enforce the above mentioned restrictions.

    I am in hope that we shall meet at the conference to be held at Strabane at 2pm on Monday October 14th, and it is probable that by then the grant will have become available. We are extremely desirous of maintaining the connection between the IAOS and the splendid co-operators of Dungloe and the other districts where the example of Dungloe has penetrated. In some cases it is probable the co-operation in domestic requirements will be the chief business of the society and affiliation with the IAOS, but I am in great hope that in the majority of cases there will be a sufficiently important agricultural business, including seeds, manures, implements, poultry and eggs to justify the affiliation of a purely agricultural society and the starting of a separate society to do the non-agricultural business, either independently, or in affiliation with the Irish section of the Co-operative Union.

    The day may come when all restrictions may be withdrawn and when the farmers of Ireland will be as free as the farmers of Denmark to do their own business in their own way, and will have the means, the intelligence and co-operative spirit to provide all the funds that are necessary for the educational and organisational purposes of their movement. But we must recognise that, taking Ireland as a whole, there is an urgent need for a very active campaign of education in co-operative principles and methods and that the only way of setting this in motion at the present time is to avail ourselves of the assistance provided by Parliament and given freely to the societies of England and Scotland. If we were to refuse the money on account of the conditions laid down, we should give a setback to the movement in every part of Ireland where the Dungloe spirit did not prevail which we might not live to see put right. I should be very glad to have your views and we count upon your help,

Yours very truly

Sir Horace Plunkett

Paddy the Cope replied on 10 October 1912, in manuscript, on 'Templecrone Co-Operative Society, Ltd., Dungloe' headed paper.

Dear Sir Horace,

Many thanks for your letter of the 3rd inst. I am sorry I was not able to reply sooner. I wish to congratulate you on your great success in gaining for the Irish farmers recognition of their rights. You have through your untiring efforts to assist them and the Irish people generally overcome the greatest campaign of mischievous and lying statements that could be directed against any movement, and I hope that with your great success that your health will improve and that you will be long left amongst the Irish people and see them enjoy the fruits of your long years of labour.

With reference to societies as ours, I know that they will be disappointed to be disconnected with the parent body, but the cause of dissolving partnership is such a good one that I am quite sure not one society such as ours will be dissatisfied. I think I can guarantee this, as far as the 6 societies here is concerned, of course we shall always expect a surprise visit from Tom [Rev Tom Finlay] and Harold [Harold Barbour]. I think we would not have enough trade here to start a separate agricultural society but I think anywhere there is a good agricultural trade it should be done.

I am quite sure what is now wanted is to get the Irish farmers organized in Agricultural Societies and that if one such society was established in every parish in Ireland it would show the farmers the advantage of cooperation. And if the traders or shopkeepers didn't give them fair play they would soon find out the remedy to apply. If I might take the liberty to offer a word of advice, I would say any new society should make a very firm rule "that no businessman or shopkeeper be eligible for membership".

I hope to have the pleasure of meeting you at Strabane on the 14th

Yours sincerely

P. Gallagher[5]

---

5   *Both of these letters have been made available by the Horace Plunkett Foundation, www.plunkett.co.uk*

Appendix 2

How It Is Done in Europe and
May Be Done in America to the
Profit of Both Farmer and Consumer

By Matthew S. Dudgeon
Copyright 1914 Western Newspaper Union

The Hen to the Rescue

Dunglow, County Donegal, Ireland. This is the story of how the Irish hen scratches a living for the people of Dunglow out of the desolate bogs and hillsides of County Donegal. The hen could not do it so long as the farmers failed to market profitably the eggs she laid. She could not do it in America where the men who market the eggs get more of the selling than does the farmer who owns the hens. The Donegal hen is a money maker for her Donegal owner because co-operative marketing has made eggs a profitable produce for the farmer.

Hens to the Rescue

Throughout the more fertile parts of Ireland the American party continually saw evidences that co-operation prayed an important part in making possible the prosperity that was everywhere apparent. It was several times mentioned to us, however, that if we wanted to see what co-operation would do under most adverse conditions we must go to Dunglow, in County Donegal. So to Dunglow we came. The adverse conditions are here, yet the people are neither ragged nor starved. The children are as happy as American children and the first little girl that we saw in the community had a store doll in her arms. That means money from some source, for toys wait for the necessities of life. Inquiry soon revealed that the first source of income which is depended upon is the sale of eggs through the co-operative society conducted by a native boy, Paddy Gallagher. It is true that the soil is so poor and so thin that a living can not be dug from it. But the industrious hens are busily scratching away where the soil is too thin for hoe or spade or plow. Formerly no farm product brought good prices and prior to the organization of the co-operative society the local price for eggs was four to six cents less than the price quoted upon the nearest market at Strabane or Derry. Generally, too, this price was paid in trade at the store and there was never any certainty that the merchandise delivered was worth the prices charged. Egg raising was not profitable and the few eggs produced were merely an incidental by-product.

When the co-operative organization, "The Templecrone Co-operative Agri-cultural society," as it is called, was formed, however, there was a change. The farmers soon learned that if they furnished good eggs they got good prices. They were told how to pick out good layers; how to keep the eggs fresh and clean; how often to gather them; how frequently to bring them to market. They were instructed as to testing eggs and breeding egg layers. They bring in the eggs. The association does the rest.

Good Business Methods.

This is how they do it: Each week the agricultural wholesale society at Dublin sends to the local manager a forecast giving the figures that will be obtainable for eggs, butter, and poultry, and stating where there is likely to be a demand for eggs. Each day, on the other hand, the manager writes to the wholesale outlet telling just what be has on hand and what the prospects are for the next few days. Sometimes they use the telegraph. Then every few days the wholesale society writes or telegraphs definite directions as to where and when the eggs must be sent. The eggs however, it should be noted, are not sent to Dublin, but are sent directly to the place where they are to be eaten. There is no complicated machinery, no red tape, no delay, no waste, no bad eggs and, best of all from the standpoint of the members the price of eggs, instead of being four to six cents below the figures quoted in the nearest city markets is now two to four cents higher than there. It is all simple and we see no reason why the entire plan cannot be introduced in any American village and the results duplicated,

Expert Knowledge Necessary

The association did not rush into the egg business without preparation. Patrick Gallagher, the manager of the society, after he had made a beginning with the society, felt the need of more expert knowledge. He went to the Dunboe Co-operative Society and here he gained a thorough knowledge of packing and dealing in eggs and poultry, and also learned co-operative book-keeping and the general business methods used by that society. Up to this time Mr Gallagher had given his services to the society gratis. He was now employed at 75c a day. The society's eggs were now handled according to the most improved method, and a good market found for them, so that the Society was able to compete on favourable terms with the local buyers. The result was that the price offered for eggs by the other buyers throughout the entire district immediately rose and all egg producers profited.

The association, after giving careful consideration of the question of buying eggs by weight, decided to give it a trial, being convinced that it is not only fair to those bringing in the larger eggs, but that it is the best, and in fact the only inducement to the rearing of an improved breed of fowl laying the larger eggs. Old customs die hard and many of the members looked askance at the novel method of calculating the price of their goods. But on the whole it has found favour. There is already a marked improvement in the size of the eggs throughout the district and there is every reason to expect that the production of larger eggs in the district may cause eggs to become a much greater source of

A VISIT TO PADDY GALLAGHER

Where the Co-Operative Concern Now Buys and Sells.

THE HEN TO THE RESCUE.

(Courtesy, Ill. Western Newspaper Union.)

1—Where the Members Bring Their Co-operative Eggs.
2—Guaranteed New Laid Irish Eggs Selected.

Co-Operative Farm Products Marketing

How It Is Done in Europe and May Be Done in America to the Profit of Both Farmer and Consumer

By MATTHEW S. DUDGEON.

THE "GOMBEEN MAN."

1—Where the Gombeen Man Flourishes Among the Rocks.
2—Paddy Gallagher Tells the American Visitors How the Gombeen Man Charged Him 166 Per Cent. Interest.

Left: Journalists from the United States visited Ireland in 1913 and 1914 to investigate the co-operative movement, to see what lessons could be learned for communities back home in America. In Ireland, they met Sir Horace Plunkett and other leading lights of the Irish Cooperative Movement who steered the journalists toward Dungloe and the Templecrone Cope.

RAA (Robert Anderson, IAOS Secretary) wrote to Paddy the Cope on 8th July 1913, requesting that a visit to Templecrone Cope be arranged for Mr John P Wallace Des Moines Iowa, Assistant Editor of "Wallace's Farmer" which had an enormous circulation in America and quoted the Irish Homestead regularly. The Cope story became known worldwide and a stream of visitors from all over came to see how it had been done.

Sir Horace was a great ally of Paddy's and championed his and the Cope's cause. Paddy's story and the success of the Cope was held up as an example of what could be achieved in difficult circumstances and offered as a model for American farming and smaller communities. They asked the question: if it could be done in Donegal, why not then in the United States?

The newspaper articles were syndicated very widely across the US in 1914 both to cities, smaller towns and farming communities, e.g. The Daily Herald in Chicago, The Cedar Rapids Republican and The Hamburg Reporter both in Iowa, The Stevens Point Daily Journal and The Benton Advocate, both in Wisconsin, The Deming Headlight, New Mexico, The Van Nuys News And The Van News Call, California, The Frederick Post, Maryland and a wide range of other cities and states.

This American newspaper interview with Paddy in 1914 (below) illustrates how the Templecrone Cope worked with and was given great assistance by the Irish Co-Operative movement. The success in Dungloe was celebrated in articles like this across the farming states of America (Extract from Western Newspaper Union 1914)

Connected With Central Society

"...Our little local society could not stand alone and do what we are trying to do. We are helped all the time by Sir Horace Plunkett's organization society and by the Cooperative Wholesale Society at Dublin. Each week the wholesale society sends us a forecast giving the figures that should be obtained for eggs, butter and chickens, and stating whether or not there is to be a demand for these products. Each day we write to the wholesale society, telling them what we have on hand and what we will likely have. Sometimes we telegraph. Then they may either write or telegraph back what they want as to send and when and where to send it. We send it, not to Dublin, but directly to the places selected by the wholesale society. In this way we save freight, we save commission, we save time, and we save the eggs themselves.

"You most not get the idea," Mr. Gallagher continued, "that this concern is a large mercantile establishment. We know enough to know that we can only do business to a modest way. We think we are doing it well and we hope it will continue to grow as it has in the past".

"I am more and more convinced" he adds, "by what I see every day, that if we want to have a happy and contented people here, co-operation is the way to bring it about".

And so they are making a fight that would put the ordinary American community to shame – a fight that is making this desolate region habitable and this hard-working people happy..."

The Cope's building of a professional egg exporting business which, as well as generating a respectable profit for the Cope and local farmers, won prizes for its quality across Britain, was an example of Paddy and his fellow co-operators genuinely creating a new business in the Rosses. The situation before the Cope initiative was dire, as W.L. Micks, Secretary of the Congested District Board, reported in 1892:

"...The poultry in "The Rosses" are good for laying, but the eggs are small. Poultry are not sold. Eggs, as a rule, are exchanged with shopkeepers for tea, tobacco, etc., and in most localities eggs are brought to the shops before they are a week old. Itinerant egg-dealers are now almost extinct in the district. On an average, I should say it tales about three weeks for the eggs to reach the consumers in Great Britain. The tendency exists to some extent among the exporting shopkeepers of keeping back eggs when the market is rising, and, similarly, of losing no time when a fall in prices is anticipated. From "The Rosses" eggs are generally sent by sea to Derry, and from Doochary and Lettermacaward they are sent by cart to Letterkenny and thence by rail to Derry. All the eggs of the district therefore have to bear the cost of the Derry merchants' commission, and harbour dues in Derry, as well as the profit of the local shopkeepers, before they reach Great Britain..." [1]

---

1   W. L. Micks 1892: Congested District Board, Union of Glenties, District of "The Rosses" – Baseline Report, Section (8).

income in the future. The association has also supplied its poultry station with trap nests, so that members will be able to procure the eggs of the best laying strains. As an instance of what might be achieved in this direction, the Society has received this year for 18-pound eggs the record price of 60 cents per dozen. Those eggs were, of course, picked from among a large quantity and sold when prices were highest; still it is a very striking example of what may be gained by a careful selection of layers. The fact that the Templecrone eggs gained third place at the Sheffield poultry exhibition held this year, and second place at the Bristol exhibition, shows that Mr. Gallagher is doing his part in building up a reputation for them.

Quality the Big Thing

The fact must not be ignored, however, that the results are obtained not altogether by good business management in the marketing. Higher prices prevail not only because the eggs are sent promptly to a good market, but because the eggs are actually the eggs of the highest possible grade, and are sorted in such a way as to form an attractive and profitable article of commerce for the retail dealer who purchases from the marketing association. In other words it has been demonstrated that good marketing can only succeed where the eggs themselves are good. Quality is a primary importance.

The first point to be considered is the outward appearance of the eggs. Dirty or cracked eggs are always rejected. Rough shells constitute more or less of a defect since roughness may raise the suspicion that the egg is a pickled egg. New laid eggs have what might be called a rough finished gloss upon them which cannot be duplicated or imitated in any way. The egg which has once been soiled is unmarketable. Any effort to remove the dirt removes also the glow and produces an appearance that is inconsistent with the general idea of freshness. Not only must the egg be of a good appearance but it must be good throughout. The testing is by the now well known system of 'candling' in a dark room. It is held up against a powerful light to reveal whether it is a fresh egg or one in which there has begun the process of deterioration. The co-operative associations, handling as they do so large a number here, generally test their eggs in large traps, the trays often holding 120 eggs at a time. Dirty eggs, bad eggs questionable eggs no longer appear. Because of care on the farmer's part they are no longer produced. Since the Society buys by weight, which is after all a far more just measure than the count, the average egg is gradually growing bigger. If small eggs are produced they do not reach the market.

Co-operation Helps the Consumer

It is of course conceded that if there is a big supply of good food, food will be cheaper than when it is scarce and more people will be able to get it. If co-operation not only sends better eggs to the city, but sends them in double or triple the quantity then eggs will in the end be plentiful and cheaper As a result, the consumer will profit This is particularly true if, under co-operation, the eggs are produced at less cost and with less waste.

It will be readily understood that, if the farmer finds that egg producing is a profitable enterprise, the quantity of eggs produced will vastly increase. Comprehensive figures for Ireland are difficult to obtain, but this has proved true in Denmark. In 1895, according to official figures, there was exported from Denmark something less than $2,000,000 worth of eggs. Fourteen years later, when co-operative marketing had demonstrated the profit that was in the business, there was exported in one year nearly $7,000,000 worth of eggs. Wolf states that while in 1892 the number of hens kept in Denmark was about 5,900,000, in 1911 the figure had reached the 12,000,000 mark. It is significant that while the number of hens had only a little more than doubled, the value of the yield had become nearly four-fold. This was largely the result of the fact that the improved conditions under which poultry was kept had greatly improved the laying ability of each hen. The same sort of thing is occurring everywhere in Continental Europe. In Germany, in France, in Belgium, in Italy, co-operative societies have undertaken the marketing of eggs with great profit to the farmer and with considerable satisfaction to the consumer.

Democratic Management

All the offices of the concern are in the hands of officers elected by the members. It is a most democratic organisation. Every man has one vote. No man has more. The member who markets eggs produced by a dozen hens has as many votes as he who owns a thousand layers. In Dunglow and elsewhere as well, they consider this "one man one vote" plan essential. "The man should vote," they say, "not his money."

They pay a good price in cash for the eggs. And when the annual settlement comes there is always a dividend to investors. But those who have invested their money, much or little, get only five per cent. No society under the supervision of the Irish Agricultural Organization society is permitted to pay dividends upon shares in excess of that percentage. What is left is distributed to the Members in proportion to the amount of eggs they have marketed through the co-operative society. It goes as an additional price paid for eggs. These two principles are considered fundamental and essential: first, one man one vote; second, all profits in excess of a small dividend to investors must go to those who contributed to the profits by furnishing the product.

Why Not in America?

Why hasn't this sort of thing been done in America? It isn't because the American farmer and his wife do not need the money. They do. It isn't because there is no demand for good eggs. Eggs were never so much in demand and buyers are more particular than ever about quality. The strictly fresh eggs find buyers every where. The fact is there is no good reason why American farmers should not do business as intelligently as Irishmen. Some of them do, but not many. It takes no capital and can be done on a small scale.

Interview with Dr. McCarthy

Dr. Charles McCarthy, who is looking over the Dunglow co-operative situation, has studied cooperation not only in Ireland, but in Italy, Germany, Belgium, Denmark and elsewhere. No one knows better than he, conditions abroad and at home. He understands American rural conditions as few understand them. In his opinion co-operative organizations that exist in Dunglow will do just as well in Massachusetts or Minnesota as they do in Ireland. One thing, however, the farmer must learn and must learn thoroughly. That is, that simple co-operation will not make over a bad business man into a good business man nor will it make egg packing or any other farm industry profitable. Along with co-operation must come good business methods, good book-keeping, good salesmanship, careful packing, and full knowledge of the market.

The Story of the Cope

History of Co-operatives in County Donegal

By Patrick Bolger
Donegal County Development Officer

Mr. Bolger was author of the excellent 'The Irish Co-operative Movement; Its History and Development' (1977). This article was written in 1975 and published in the Cope's commemorative souvenir for achieving £1,000,000 in sales and service in 1975. Mr Bolger, Paddy as he was known, gave a speech at the Cope staff dinner dance held on Monday 5th January 1976 at the Ostan na Rosann in Dungloe.

The Co-operative Movement in Co. Donegal is popularly identified with the Templecrone Society and the legendary figure of Paddy Gallagher (the Cope). Few people realise that the emergence of this spectacularly successful Co-operative (and its colourful leader) came not as a beginning but rather at the end of an intensive ten-year effort to establish the Movement in the County of Donegal - "a remote and difficult county to organise", from the viewpoint of a central organisation based in Dublin.

By the time Paddy established his embryonic co-op shop in his wife's kitchen in 1906 there had already been some 60 co-operatives of various kinds set up within the county. The first stirrings of interest arose in a milieu very different from the poor crofters of the Rosses - the Protestant gentry and substantial landowners of East Donegal. These were the people who had been following with interest the efforts in Munster of Horace Plunkett and the early founders of the Movement which in its earliest years drew practically all its leadership from the aristocracy and the landlord classes. With the establishment in 1894 of the Irish Agricultural Organisation Society (IAOS) Plunkett had given the Movement a much wider base. The first national committee of the IAOS carefully contrived to have representation well balanced between all shades of class, creed, political opinion and occupational pursuits - landlord and tenant, Unionist and Nationalist, farmer and businessman, clergy and laity.

Horace Plunkett was appointed to the Congested Districts Board (CDB) on its inception in 1891. He found that he had two notable colleagues on that Board who quickly became interested in his co-operative ideals and whose enthusiasm and hard work was largely responsible for the establishment of Plunkett's Co-operative Movement on a broad base throughout Donegal. They were Most Rev. Patrick O'Donnell, D.D., Lord Bishop of Raphoe, and Hugh A. Law, of Marble Hill. The careers of O'Donnell (1856-1927), youngest Bishop in Christendom, later Cardinal, and Law (1872-1943), landowner, writer, politician, subsequently MP and TD for Donegal, are too well known to need recounting here. Their efforts at Co-operative organisation were greatly enhanced in 1897 with the appointment of George William Russell (AE) as IAOS organiser. This trio worked so effectively that by the time that AE gave up his organising work in

Gweedore Co-Operative Society Store in Glasha c1911/12, a photograph taken by Harold Barbour, Chairman of the IAWS on his tour of cooperatives across Ireland. Gweedore was incorporated in 1909 and covered the area to the north of Templecrone. (Harold Barbour Photograph Collection, University College Dublin Archives (UCDA P168)

1906 to become full-time editor of the Co-operative Weekly newspaper, "The Irish Homestead", the Co-operative Movement in Donegal was established on a firm footing.

The first Co-op in Donegal was the Lagan Co-operative Creamery, established in 1896. Ramelton Creamery came a year later and between then and 1905 some 17 Co-op creameries were set up in various parts of the county. Of these only about half a dozen survived or flourished for any length of time. Donegal never became a dairying county (cf. Tyrone which at one time had over 40 co-operative creameries) and even to-day milk production is minimal, whereas in

Munster the term "Co-op" became almost synonymous with "Creamery". Co-operation in Donegal was destined for the most part to connote "general store". This was because of the establishment and persistence there of a great number of Co-operative Agricultural Societies. These Societies modelled on the Syndicats Agricoles of France and the Consorzio Agrario of Italy were designed originally to provide farmers with their agricultural requirements, the raw materials and equipment for their industry - seeds, manures, animal feedstuffs, building materials, machinery and equipment, etc. It was also intended that they should purchase and market the farmers' produce and concern themselves generally in agricultural development, the improvement of breeds of livestock, varieties of crops, and provide any service which their farmer members required. Many of the early Agricultural (store) Co-ops kept sire animals - bulls, boars, rams and even stallions. These same Societies can claim full credit for establishing the spraying of potatoes as a standard farm practice. By the turn of the century it was reported that "nearly every one of the 106 Co-operative Agricultural Societies in Ireland was the proud owner of an efficient horse-drawn sprayer". It was the Co-operative Movement also that really established and made effective the analysis of fertilisers and feeding stuffs for quality and the testing of seeds for purity and germination. Regulations had previously existed but were very much a dead letter until the Co-operative Wholesale Society, IAWS Ltd., (established 1897) set the headline in adherence to these standards which merchants were (often reluctantly) compelled to follow.

The first Co-operative Agricultural Society in Donegal was a small store set up at Copany outside Donegal town in 1901. This was the only Society of its type until Templecrone was founded five years later. Opposition to farmer trading (some creameries did a small store trade) was intense. The merchants and the gombeen men were all-powerful and many farmers and small holders were in debt to them. The majority of community influentials - clergy, doctors, professional men and local politicians had ties of kinship or friendship with the merchants. Nationalist politicians obsessed with the idea of political solutions to Ireland's problems, looked on the Co-operative Movement's efforts towards economic improvement as "a red herring dragged across the path of Home Rule". Many Unionists, on the other hand, felt that too much had already been conceded to the tenants and Plunkett's co-operative organisation would only train them for further mischief.

Before any real progress could be made in trading it was necessary to do something about the farmers' indebtedness to the gombeenman. Fr. Tom Finlay, S.J., was one of the prime movers in the establishment of the Agricultural Banks, the first of which was established in Doneraile, Co. Cork, in 1894. These Banks operated on the same Raiffeisen principles as the modern Credit Unions. In areas where the people were too poor to provide enough deposits to get the lending process started, the Congested Districts Board, and later the Department of Agriculture, gave small loans, usually £50 to £100. In Co. Donegal, Bishop O'Donnell, Hugh Law and AE spoke brilliantly and organised efficiently. Law and O'Donnell often subscribed generously of their own money to get a Bank

Inishkeel Co-operative Store in Glenties c1911/12; again a photo by Harold Barbour. Inishkeel was incorporated in 1908 and its coverage was south and to the west (in Fintown) of Templecrone. The Templecrone Cope was bounded by other local, friendly co-operatives which may have had the effect of constraining it within its Templecrone boundaries (apart from its first branch move to Lettermacaward in 1911 – outside Templecrone but still in the Rosses). (Harold Barbour Photograph Collection, University College Dublin Archives (UCDA P168)

The Story of the Cope

started and the Bishop often persuaded his clergy to back the Movement with their approval and some funds. £100 was a small sum but not inconsiderable in the days when a good milch cow could be bought for £15 and bonhams fetched from five shillings to ten shillings each.

Four Agricultural Banks were founded in 1898, Glenswilly, Inver, Killybegs and Kilmacrenan. By 1905 there were 24 such Banks spread fairly well throughout the county but not impinging very much on the "Lagan" area of east Donegal. The most famous (and I believe the longest lived) of these Banks was at Malin (established 1901). By 1908 the Malin Bank had some 300 members, deposits of nearly £1,500, of which over £1,000 was given out annually in loans. The Dungloe Co-operative Credit Bank founded by Hugh Law in 1903 had a profound influence on young Paddy the Cope, as recounted in his autobiography. These banks declined after 1912 when loans from the Department and CDB were discontinued, making it difficult to establish or expand in the most needy areas. The prosperity of the war years 1914-1918 also had its effect, as had the system whereby Creameries and other Co-ops often gave credit or advanced money to their members without going through the formalities of a loan through the Agricultural Bank.

The village banks proved to be tremendously popular. A widespread belief took hold that somehow they had a special charm - their money was "lucky money". Some put it down to the essential goodness of the neighbourly helping hand or the fact that the Bishop had given it his blessing. Materialistically much of the luck could be attributed to the practical way in which the business of the Bank was done, and especially there was something very "lucky" about the rate of interest charged - 5% or 6%, compared to the 50% to 100% per annum commonly charged by merchants. Paddy the Cope in his evidence before the Departmental Committee on Agricultural Credit (1914) recounted the following experience:

> "On 28th May 1906, my father and I bought seven stone of flour and one cwt. of Indian meal each. My father paid for his, 17shillings. I was not in a position to pay for mine until 11th July 1906, forty-four days later. The gombeenman then presented me with a bill for 21shillings and 3d. I disputed his right to charge me 4s 3d interest and pointed out that my father bought the same goods on the same date for 17s. The gombeen-man argued that my father paid him 18s and that he was only charging me 3s 3d extra or 144% per annum".

In their day the agricultural Banks provided a most necessary service and in the words of Horace Plunkett performed "the apparent miracle of giving solvency to a community composed almost entirely of insolvent individuals".

Around the turn of the century the Co-operative Movement was attaining considerable strength and there was a nationwide trend towards diversification. Co-operatives were set up for a wide variety of purposes - Farm and Garden

At the 1976 celebration of the Cope's achieving over £1,000,000 in sales, Patrick Bolger gave a speech about co-operation in Donegal and the role played by Paddy the Cope, the Templecrone Co-op and the people of the Rosses. He caused quite a stir by reminding his audience about how Paddy saw his fight against the 'gombeenmen' in Dungloe. His audience, many of whom were descended from the, some would say, unjustifiably vilified group were not impressed. A lesson to all to let sleeping dogs lie. The group here at the January 1976 dinner in the Ostan na Rosann are: Dom Bonner, Cope Secretary, Patrick Bolger, Patrick Kelly, Secretary of the IAOS, Cyril Winder, Cope General Manager and Michael Mellett, IAOS, Letterkenny. (Cope Photo Archive).

Societies (horticulture), Home Industries Societies (homecrafts), Poultry Societies for the marketing of eggs and poultry, Beekeeping Societies and Flax Societies. Attempts were also made to establish Fishing Co-ops and Livestock Insurance Societies, but without much success.

It was soon discovered that small single-purpose societies of this type were unable to stand on their own and it was recommended that they be incorporated with the stronger creamery or store societies to afford them better facilities and better management. Six Cooperative Poultry Societies were established in Donegal in 1899 - Clonmany, Milford, Glenvar, Tamney, Kincasslagh and Lettermacaward. Very little is known of their activities and except for Tamney which lasted until about 1909, they were all out of business by 1902. An attempt was made in 1900 to establish a large poultry enterprise (North West Poultry Society) at Strabane, with a poultry fattening station at Lifford and

The Story of the Cope

several egg collecting depots at various centres along the Donegal and Great Northern Railway systems, but this failed to materialise. More fortunate was the Sessiagh O'Neill Society (Ballybofey) founded in 1903 which flourished for a good number of years and was incorporated with the Co-operative Wholesale IAWS in 1915. In 1914 it is recorded as having a membership of 199 and an annual turnover of almost £3,000.

The formation of three Co-operative Beekeeping Societies - Inishowen, Glenties and Milford - in 1902 would have passed unnoticed by the general public as no elaborate structures were involved but merely the coming together of a number of local beekeepers to market their honey and buy their beekeeping requisites co-operatively. Another Beekeepers' Society was planned for Dunkineely following a visit there of the outstanding beekeeper and co-operator, Rev. J. G. Digges, who founded Ireland's first bee-keeping Society in South Leitrim. Incidentally, Mr. Digges is commemorated by a stained glass window in the little church at Farnaught, Co. Leitrim, depicting a Welsh saint tending his hives of bees. Unfortunately bad weather in three successive seasons following 1902 virtually destroyed all efforts at co-operative beekeeping not only in Donegal but throughout Ireland.

Co-operative Home Industries Societies mainly concerned with lace-making in the home (also crochet, knitwear etc.) were registered in Ballyshannon and Bundoran (1900) and in Ramelton (1902). The Ballyshannon Society with 85 members sold £600 worth of goods in 1902 but subsequently declined. Bundoran, after a weak start, flourished for a brief period. The Ramelton Society (59 members) concentrated most of its effort on teaching the crafts and had very little sales. All three Societies had ceased to function by 1909.

A number of the Flax Societies, mostly scutching flax in rented mills, were established in 1905 — Castlefin, Letterkenny, River Finn and Stranorlar. The Pluck Society and the Swilly Valley Society followed in 1907. The Castlefin Society was the most successful as it owned its own premises, including a corn mill, which kept some staff in employment all year round. All the flax Societies did a good volume of business during the years of World War I and the two new Societies were founded in 1918 — Raymochey and Convoy. The post war slump and decline in flax growing led to the winding up of most of these Societies but the Raymochey and Convoy Mills survived to do some business when flax growing boomed briefly again in the 1940s.

Co-operative Societies in Co. Donegal did not involve themselves very intensively in the Grow More Food Campaign in the years of World War I. Whilst Co-ops in the South were operating machinery and implement hire and engaging in such activities as bacon curing and milling the Donegal Societies (with the exception of multipurpose Templecrone) took remarkably little part and seemed content to leave these activities to private enterprise. The Lagan Creamery undertook corn milling in a small way and in Ardara a separate Co-operative Milling Society was set up in 1916. This was an occasion of some controversy.

CREAMERIES

The Lagan	1896
Ramelton	1897
Finn Valley	1898
Pettigo	1899
Drumholm	1900
Sessiaghoneill	1901
Termon	1901
Carndonagh	1902
Donegal	1902
Glenfin	1902
Gleneely	1903
Iniskeel	1903
Inver	1903
Kilbarron	1903
Kilteevogue	1903
Bruckless	1905
Taughboyne (1909)	1903
Letterkenny	1953

BANKS

Glenswilly	1898
Inver	1898
Killybegs	1898
Kilmacrennan	1898
Burtonport	1899
Clondahorkey	1899
Cloughaneely	1899
Termon	1899
Ballydevitt	1901
Clogher	1901
Killygarvan	1901
Knockalla	1901
Lough Eske	1901
Malin	1901
Townawilly	1901
Tullynaught	1901
Ardmalin	1903
Creeslough	1903
Dunaff	1903
Dungloe	1903
Innismacsaint	1903
Straid	1903
Kilbarron	1904
Bruckless	1905
Porteons	1913

AGRICULTURAL

Copany
Templecrone
Iniskeel
Gweedore
Lower Rosses
Downstrands
Ardara
Killybegs
Slieve League
Clondahorky
Ballyshannon
Meentiagh
Buncrana
Cloughaneely
Conwal
Doochary
Glassagh
Moville
Clondavaddog
Corkey
Deele Valley
Doe
Fanad North
Kerrykeel
Rathmullan & District
Traighena
Gartan & Kilmacrennan
Falcarragh
East Donegal
Clonleigh
Tirconaill
Errigal
Inishowen Farmers' Co-op.
Inisleigh

POULTRY

Clonmany	1899
Bunlin, Cratlagh & Milford	1899
Glenvar & Killygarvan	1899
Kincasslagh	1899
Lettermacaward	1899
Tamney	1899
Sessiaghoneill	1903

FISHING

Tory Sound Fisheries	1920
West Donegal Fisheries	1920
Comhar Chumann Iascaireachta Rosgoill	1955
Foyleside Co-op. Fisheries	1966
Greencastle Fishermen's Co-op.	1966
Donegal Co-op. Fisheries	1965
Burtonport Fishermen's Co-op.	1967
Porthall Fishermen's Co-op.	1968

BEEKEEPERS

Inishowen
Glenties
Milford

-op Data

AX		HOME INDUSTRIES SOCIETIES		MARTS	
lefin	1905	Ballyshannon	1900	Inishowen	1958
erkenny	1905	Bundoran	1900	East Donegal	1961
r Finn	1905	Ramelton	1902	Milford	1963
norlar	1905	Glencolumbkille		Donegal	1966
k	1907	Knitting Co-op.	1966		
ly Valley	1907	Glencolumbkille			
voy	1918	Cottage Knitting	1968		
mockey	1918	Glencolumbkille Metal			
		Craft Co-op.	1968		

-OP. TURF SOC. 3 - 1935	MISCELLANEOUS	
many	Ardara Milling	1916
logans	Rosses Productive Soc.	1943
hey Bar	Donegal Co-op.	
ydish	Fisheries	1963
nswilly	Glencolumbkille Co-op.	
ghmourne	Society	1965
ck	Glencolumbkille Farm	
	Services Co-op.	1968
	Glencolumbkille	
	Housing	1968

The Congested District Board had promised a site but subsequently withdrew the offer, allegedly because of local merchant influence.

The years of World War I were years of "great but spurious prosperity" for the Co-op. Stores and Creamery Societies. Farmers were getting good prices for their produce and money was plentiful. Euphoria grew as prosperity continued into the post war years. Co-ops gave credit freely (often interest free and without security) and in turn took almost unlimited credit from wholesalers - notably the IAWS

The Co-operative idea was taking hold, not merely because of easy credit (which was available also from private merchants) but because farmers were coming to realise the advantages of owning their own business and their consequent ability to start new enterprises and provide new services. Six new Store Societies were founded in 1919 and ten more in 1920.

Suddenly towards the end of 1920 the prosperity bubble burst. Widespread unemployment had reduced the purchasing power of the British workers and matters were aggravated by the flood of cheap food products flowing into Britain from America and the Colonies once shipping was restored. Co-op Societies which had purchased large supplies of erstwhile scarce and expensive goods found them devalued almost overnight to little more than one-third of their value. This hit all the Co-operative Societies in Donegal very hard, but especially the new Societies which were thus, one might say, crippled from birth. Nevertheless, a great many of them struggled on for a long period, but none of them ever really recovered, and to-day only two societies of the 16 survive - Buncrana and Moville, both founded in 1919. But indeed the old store co-ops did not fare much better and of the 12 established in the earlier period only Templecrone (1906) and Inniskeel (1908) are still with us.

Despite repeated attempts to bring Co-operation into the fishing industry the first Co-operative Fishing Society was not founded until 1915. This Society was based in the Aran Islands off Galway and enjoyed a fairly spectacular success during the war years. Donegal fishermen, however, were unable to emulate the fine achievement of the Aran men for the very good reason that all fishing off the Donegal coast was banned by the British Government because of the suspected presence of German submarines - and presumably the fear that disloyal Donegalmen might consort with the enemy.

Thus it was not until 1920 that two Co-op Fishing Societies were established in Donegal - the Tory Sound Fishing Society and the West Donegal Fishing Society. The motive force behind the latter Society (based in Kincasslagh) was Paddy the Cope. Both Societies were short-lived. The disastrous decline in the German and American markets and the enormous increase in freight rates left fishing with larger boats as used by these Societies quite unprofitable. Paddy the Cope and his Templecrone Society continued with some level of activity, both in fishing and shipping of goods, for many years. The Torymen never really got started. Their large boat, the "Ferry Bank", which they had purchased to bring their island catches to the mainland markets, was destroyed in circumstances described non-committally in the official IAOS report as "lost through burning in the war conditions then prevailing". No first-hand evidence was produced, but it was widely held that Crown forces were responsible for the burning.

During the 1920s and 1930s, Co-operative Societies of all kinds retreated into a very restricted shell - afraid to entertain any thoughts of expansionist policy. There was a general air of apathy. Co-op meetings were poorly attended and much of the members' sense of belonging was lost. In many cases the Co-op became little more than another trading post. Expansion during the years of World War II (1939-45) was seriously inhibited by shortage of supplies. It was not until the early 1950s that Societies could contemplate any worthwhile development.

The only Co-operatives of any kind formed in Donegal during the 1930s were seven small turf-cutting societies set up in the years 1933-35 - Clonmany, Shallogans, Laghey Barr, Tullydish, Glenswilly, Lough Mourne and Knock. These were very simple loose-knit groups on the pattern of some 300 Societies of this type organised by the IAOS at the behest of the Minister for Industry and Commerce. Their function was to arrange the production and marketing of turf in conjunction with the newly appointed Turf Development Board. The Board secured contracts which it passed on to the nearest Turf Cutting Co-operative to fulfil. Board contracts assured the turf producers of a basic minimum price. This provided many hard-pressed small farmers with some market for turf which in remote areas might otherwise prove unsaleable. The price, 10/- to 12/- per ton, often left very little net return when rail freight costs were deducted and difficulties arose when producers defaulted by disposing of some of their turf to more favourable local markets and were unable to put up the full tonnage they contracted for. The Co-operative organisation for the most part lapsed when other organised groups took over the large scale production of turf during the war.

The upsurge of Co-operation in Donegal in the post war era is self evident. We have seen the building of a number of strong Agricultural Societies, e.g. Clonleigh, Tirconaill (1952) and Inishowen (1963). The establishment of Letterkenny Creamery in 1953 led subsequently to the rationalisation embodied in Donegal Co-op Creameries Ltd. The 1960s saw the beginnings of the comprehensive Co-operative development in Glencolmcille and (in the face of much gombeen opposition) the foundation of the Co-op cattle mart system. From the mid-sixties onwards Fishermen's Co-ops at Killybegs, Greencastle and Burtonport performed a necessary and useful function in the auctioning of fish and the IAWS Ltd. acquired the fish meal factory in Killybegs. Further co-operative involvement in fish processing and marketing is anticipated. A number of Co-ops came together in 1968 to establish Inisleigh Farm Foods Ltd – the first serious venture into co-operative milling of feedstuffs. Other areas of co-operative development are being probed, e.g. co-operative fattening of pigs and lambs, and interest is awakening to possibilities in many fields.

In the year in which Templecrone Society attains its £1 million turnover Co-operatives in Donegal are doing a modest share of the county's business. Total Co-op. turnover is estimated at approximately £14 million and aggregate Co-op. membership is slightly over 10,000. Allowing for duplication it is estimated that no more than 5,000 of Donegal's 27,000 householders are as yet committed to any real participation. There is amongst the general public (town and country) a great amount of goodwill and sympathy with the Cooperative ideal. Something of the idealism, energy and courage of the early pioneers of the Movement applied in the modern context will most certainly earn rich dividends in "better farming, better business, better living" for the people of Donegal.

THE TEMPLECRONE
CO-OPERATIVE . .
AGRICULTURAL SOCIETY,
COUNTY DONEGAL.

An interesting Story of its origin and struggles. ❧

To be had from
The SECRETARY of the Society ; or from The MANAGER of the "Irish Homestead,"

Post Free, **3½d.**

Maghery Strand, Dungloe, Co. Donegal.

References:

General
My Story: Paddy the Cope, Patrick Gallagher (1939, 1942, 1946, 1979, 2006)
Sally the Cope Gallagher Personal Archives – Limerick City Museum.
IAOS records: 1088/871/1-8, National Archives, Bishop St Dublin
'The Templecrone Agricultural Society', Irish Homestead, 1910 and 1924
Templecrone: A Record of Co-operative Effort (by AE), 1916
The Cope 75th Anniversary 1981 Booklet (Packie Bonner et al)
'From One Million Pounds to Five Million Pounds' 1975-1985, Cyril Winder
'Commemorative Souvenir of Our First £1,000,000 in Sales and Service' – The Cope, 1976
The Cope 1924-25 Secretary's Letter Book (Jim 'Packie' the Cope Archive)
The Cope Minute Book – selected by Hugh McGee, Cope Committee Member
Derry Journal - various archived articles as cited
The Irish Times - ditto
The Manchester Guardian - ditto
The Times of London - ditto
The Donegal Democrat - ditto
Irish Parliamentary Papers and Hansard
Dail and Senate Papers: 1922 to date
Dail Historical Debates: http://historical-debates.oireachtas.ie/
Quest for Quality: 100 Years of the IAWS 1897-1997
Fruits of the Century: Irish Co-operative Organisation Society 1894-2004
Ireland Under Coercion, William Henry Hurlbert, 1888, Edinburgh, David Douglas
The Irish Homestead (weekly periodical): 1906 to 1923
The Story of the Rosses, Ben O'Donnell, Caorán Publications, Lifford, 1999
The Buildings of North West Ulster, Alistair Rowan, Penguin 1979
Pumpherston, Story of a Shale Oil Village, John McKay, Sybil Cavanagh et al., Luath Press, 2002
Rosses Annuals, 1st edition 1995-6 (and 1998 second volume)
Donegal Highlands, Guide Book, Ward Lock & Co, 1910, 1918 editions
'The Economic Development of Ireland in the Twentieth Century' by Kieran Anthony Kennedy, Thomas Giblin, Deirdre McHugh (Routledge, 1988)
Horace Plunkett: Co-operation and Politics, An Irish Biography, Trevor West, 1986 by Colin Smythe and Catholic University Press Washington D.C.

Chapter 1 – Cleendra
Census of Ireland – Province of Ulster, County of Donegal HMSO, 1841-1911
The Changing Distribution of Population of Donegal, with Special Reference to the Congested Areas, T. W. Freeman Trinity College Dublin 1940
Thorough Guide Series: Ireland (Part 1) Northern Counties 1902, Thomas Nelson and Sons
'Irish Passenger Steamship Services: Volume 1 North of Ireland' by DB McNeill (David & Charles, Newton Abbot, 1969)

'Clyde and Other Coastal Steamers, Duckworth and Langmuir, T Stephenson & Sons 1939, 1977 edition
Old Broxburn and Uphall, Peter Morton, Stenlake Publishing, 2000
Peak District Mines Historical Society - Linlithgow Mines
Donegal History and Society, Geography Publications 1995:
- Chapter 21, 'Seasonal Migration to the Lagan and Scotland' Anne O'Dowd
- Chapter 22 'The Congested Districts Board and the Co-ops in Donegal, Patrick Bolger
Harold Barbour Photograph Collection, University College Dublin Archives (UCDA P168)
Cassell's Pictorial Guide to The Clyde, 1900
The Irish Famine, A Documentary, Colm Tóibín and Diarmaid Ferriter, Profile Books 2001
'Irish Distress and Its Remedies: The Land Question: A Visit to Donegal and Connaught in the Spring of 1880', James H Tuke 1880
1911 Census of Ireland, online at www.census.nationalarchives.ie
National Photographic Archive, Meeting House Square, Dublin

Chapter 2 - Dungloe
Taylor and Skinner Roads of Ireland 1776
1824 population survey, Irish Parliamentary Papers
Rural Reconstruction in Ireland: A Record of Co-operative Organisation, L. Smith-Gordon and L. C. Staples, 1917, P.S. King & Son Ltd, London
'Agricultural Co-operation in Ireland: A Survey' Nov 1931 by 'The Plunkett Foundation'

Chapter 3 – The Branches
The Templecrone Agricultural Cooperative Society; the Story of Its Struggles', Irish Homestead 1924

Chapter 4 – Builders' Providers
'In Search of Islands': A Life of Conor O'Brien, by Judith Hill, 2009, The Collins Press.

Chapter 5 - Knitting
James H. Tuke's 'A Visit to Donegal and Connaught in The Spring of 1886'
'What is the Matter with Ireland' (1920) Ruth Russell, New York, Devin-Adair
Women in Ireland 1800-1918, Maria Luddy, Cork University Press, 1995
The United Irishwomen, Their Place, Work and Ideals, by Horace Plunkett, Ellice Pilkington and George Russell (AE), with a preface by Rev. T. A. Finlay, 1911, Maunsel & Co Ltd Dublin.
'And See Her Beauty Shining There' - The Story of the Irish Countrywomen, Pat Bolger, Editor, Irish Academic Press, 1986

Chapter 6 - Bakery

Chapter 7 The Mill and the Pier
The Templecrone Mill Book (1923-45), Donegal County Archives, Lifford
The Conyngham Papers, (MS 35,339 – 35,434) Manuscript Collection, National
Library (catalogued by Sarah Ward-Perkins in 2000)
The Quiet Revolution – The Electrification of Rural Ireland, 1946-1976, Michael
Shiel, O'Brien Press, 2003

Chapter 8 – The Sea – the Cope Boats
Killybegs Now and Then, Donald Martin, Anvil Books, 1998
The Zulu Fishermen, Pat Conaghan, Bygones Enterprise, 2003
Ireland's Sea Fisheries: A History, John de Courcy Ireland, Barnacle Books
1981
Are You Still Below? The Ford Marina Plant Cork 1917-1984, Miriam Nyhan,
The Collins Press 2007

Chapter 9 – By Road and Rail and Overseas
That Old Sinner, Frank Sweeney 2006, Irish History Press
The Lough Swilly Railway, Edward M Patterson 1964, David & Charles
Londonderry & Lough Swilly Railway, Steve Flanders, Midland Publishing
The Londonderry & Lough Swilly Railway: A Visitor's Guide, Dave Bell and
Steve Flanders, County Donegal Restoration Society

Chapter 10 – Granite and Soapstone
Account of a Mineralogical Excursion to the County of Donegal, Charles Lewis
Giesecke, 1826, Royal Dublin Society
Prospectus for Donegal Granite Quarries 1887
Geological Survey of Ireland, Dublin: various articles, file notes
Irish Press article 26 November 1946
'They All Made Me', Rex Herdman, 1970, S.D. Montgomery Ltd, Omagh

Chapter 11 – Cope People and Events
Capuchin Annual 1970
The Heritage Magazine, 1956, article by John Gurdon on Ards

Chapter 12 – 'My Story'
Inver Parish in History, Helen Meehan, 2005, published by the author
'The Story He Left Behind Him', Lawrence Scanlon, University Press of
America 1994
Million Dollar Movie, Michael Powell, 1992, William Heinemann
A Life In Movies: An Autobiography, Michael Powell, 1986, William
Heinemann

Chapter 13 – The Cope Centenary and the Cope Today

Appendix 1 – 1910 Irish Homestead Articles
The Templecrone Agricultural Society: The Irish Homestead 1910
The Irish Homestead (periodical): 1906 to 1923
Co-operation in Ireland, Lionel Smith-Gordon and Cruise O'Brien, 1921, Cooperative Union Limited, Manchester

Appendix 2 - The Cope's Egg Business
1914 newspaper article syndicated across America
History of the Congested Districts Board, 1891-1923, W.L. Micks, Eason & Son Ltd Dublin, 1925; in particular Appendix 3, the 1892 baseline report on the Rosses.

Appendix 3 – The Co-operative Movement in Donegal, 1975, Patrick Bolger
The Irish Co-Operative Movement (Patrick Bolger), Institute of Public Administration, Dublin, 1977